The Making of a Happy Old Man

This outstanding biography provides a multi-windowed view into the times and influences that shaped a gifted linguist and committed missionary to the Muslim world. I was enriched by my dear friend's theological reflections which permeate the story. A must read for those interested in and called to Christian missions.

John Mahaffey, former Lead Pastor, West Highland Baptist Church, Hamilton ON, Council Member of The Gospel Coalition, Canada

These memoirs read like a long pull of good espresso. Peter Pikkert, of a shrinking tribe of old school, career missionaries, leads readers across four decades during which the "old paths" were repeatedly challenged by missiological fads and bad ideas. Readers learn how to begin and end, to bungle and recover, to dare to trust God with the seeming impossible, with eyes always on Christ, resting in His faithfulness, and looking to Him for fruit. Especially recommended for those considering a career in missions. Invaluable.

Joost Nixon, VP of Mobilization & Ministry Advancement, Training Leaders International, USA

Pikkert was a courageous pioneer missionary at a pivotal point in the evangelical mission to the Middle East. He relates his story authentically and intricately weaves his biography within the larger dynamic of Middle East culture, politics and languages. This book is a great primer for anyone interested in the enterprise of the church in the Middle East. It also testifies to the work of God in a believer who has willingly surrendered to His purposes and plans. The interplay of God's salvation plan for Peter, the people of the Middle East and, in fact, for all people is a reminder to each reader that they too are part of a larger picture of God's purpose for the world He created.

Colin Meikle, Deputy Director, WEC International, Canada

Many have attempted to answer the question of how to find happiness and a fulfilled life. Pikkert offers a pragmatic approach through an engaging narrative based on his own life story, intertwined with the journeys of heroes of faith who came before him. Real happiness lies beyond the exciting tales and voyages; it is deeply rooted in a relationship, a conviction and an act of obedience.

Tiago Fonseca, Dean of Students, Cornerstone Bible College for Mission Training, The Netherlands

Pikkert's book is fascinating, informative, insightful, honest, and even appropriately romantic. But more than all that, it is a story of God's amazing grace as Peter, with the help of his wife Anna, reflects on a lifetime of walking with God and serving as Christian missionaries in the Middle East and in other places around the world. I have enjoyed Peter's friendship for many years, and yet, as I read this work, I realized that God has been at work in his life in ways I knew nothing about. This story is God-honouring, full of real-life wisdom that will strengthen and encourage the reader—highly recommended!

Kirk Wellum, Principal, Toronto Baptist Seminary, Canada

What began as a gift for the author's grandkids grew into a rich reflection on faith, history, and the joy of serving God. Set against the vibrant backdrop of the Middle East, this story traces Peter's pioneering work among the Kurds while weaving together moments of global history, Christian culture, and honest storytelling with styles reminiscent of Indiana Jones adventures, philosopher, evangelist, prophet and dreamer.

Ken Benson, Director, MissionPREP, Canada

This is an honestly written biography, pungent with vibrant quotes, dynamic imagery, exotic and challenging vistas, sparkling verbiage, varying ministry approaches, and thoughtful reflections on missiology and the changing environment the church is facing in the Middle East and Canada. Every student of missiology (or would-be missionaries, especially in Muslim-dominated areas), should read this book as it challenges to long-run ministry, depth and quality of communication, and discipleship. It shows a "how-to" for ministering in hard places. Read the hard lessons endured, interspersed with humorous anecdotes; follow the curiosity-led peripatetic ramblings to isolated and strange cities and villages. It's fun to read, just to enjoy the descriptions of people and customs! I enjoyed seeing how his missiology and theologies developed stage by stage; how they had to trust God and see His provisions on their behalf. Peter ends the book well: "Serving God has been a great and satisfying privilege, an adventure with eternal implications, animated by a flickering trust in the Trustworthy One's unfailing covenantal promises."

John Kayser, Lead Missionary Field Trainer, Bethany International, USA and WEC International

The Making of a Happy Old Man

P. Pikkert

ALEV Books
168 Cornwallis Road
Ancaster, ON
Canada L9C 4H3
www.alevbooks.com

ISBN: 978-1-7752353-5-4

Layout: ALEV Books
Cover photograph: Anna Pikkert

Keywords: Autobiography, Christian missions.

"Happiness cannot be pursued; it must ensue, and it only does so as the unintended side-effect of one's personal dedication to a cause greater than oneself or as the by-product of one's surrender to a person other than oneself... you have to let it happen by not caring about it."

Viktor Frankl

For grandkid(s)

"Let this be written for a future generation,
that a people not yet created may praise the Lord."

Psalm 102:18

With profound gratitude to the churches and
individuals who upheld us before the Throne of Grace
and supported us financially all these years.

You know who you are, we know who some of you are and,
most importantly, the Lord knows who all of you are.

This is also your story.

Contents

...

Preface

*"The most ordinary movement in the world, such as
sitting down at a table and pulling the inkstand towards
one, may agitate a thousand odd, disconnected fragments
(of memory), now bright, now dim, hanging and bobbing
and dipping and flaunting, like the underlinen of a family
of fourteen on a line in a gale of wind."*

Virginia Woolf

. . .

WE LIVE IN a pleasant apartment building of hopeful
immigrants, jaded divorcees and modestly living retirees. Anna
and I are "that friendly old couple" who still hold hands. Some
know that we are involved in our church, lived overseas for a
long time, and that I have cancer. We do not share much of our
story with them. A few friends know snippets.

Some time ago, however, our daughter urged me to write our
tale for the sake of grandchildren. Anna initially resisted the
notion; she entered the world a Northern Irish Presbyterian, a
genus which cringes in the face of self-aggrandisement. She need
not worry for this is a record of divine unmerited favor.

Stories matter. Many people suffer because they don't have
good stories to fall back on. I don't want that to be true of our
grandchildren for there is, I believe, an organic connection
between descendants and ancestors. This tale may help them
make sense of things later in life. Forgetting or erasing one's
story, even if it is not a heroic one, leads to rootlessness and a
lack of identity.

The paucity of good personal stories is compounded by a
shortage of relevant heroes. Even our Christian ones are
antiquated! How can pre-World War I missionary stories be
relevant today? Who cares about David Brainerd, William
Carey, Lottie Moon, Adoniram Judson, David Livingstone, the
Moffats, Mary Slessor, Hudson Taylor or C.T. Studd? Didn't

they serve under the secure aegis of that globe-spanning historic anomaly of Anglo-Saxon cultural pre-eminence, materialism and triumphant Victorian Protestantism known as the British Empire which, though flawed, produced previously unimaginable levels of freedom and prosperity?

That gilt-edged colonial era came to be reviled. Corrosive values, drawing not from without but from within, first from within the working classes, then from within the *volk*, and lastly from within the individual human psyche have dissolved like sugar cubes in hot water the fundamentals on which that Anglo-Saxon Protestant culture was built. Those who hold that truth exists independent of personal experiences and that it must be pursued through logic and science, or that it is granted through divine revelation, came to be seen as antiquated relics of a bygone era. They were relegated to the margins of the public sphere by the "progressives" of the age. Yet this happy relic believes that his grandchildren need to have some secular heroes reinstated as well as be given some updated Christian ones if they are to be saved from the prison which is the self. Although my heroes are flawed and reflect their own cultural biases, they did not look within as the standard by which to live. This enabled them to overcome great odds in order to accomplish great good.

In my lifetime world communism was defeated, apartheid dismantled, and the great expansion of the evangelical church in Asia, Africa and Latin America took place. While hordes of moral midgets broadcast their inanities across cyberspace, my Christian heroes have, by and large, kept a low profile. That, in itself, is heroic. Crossing paths with a number of these inconspicuous giants is one of the joys of my life for they were, by and large, infectiously happy people.

Ours was a life filled with transitions and learning curves as technology evolved from the mechanical to analog and then to digital. My early correspondence was written in longhand or banged out on a Remington typewriter. We went through the height of the Cold War, then saw the collapse of the USSR. We saw a younger generation destroy the Judeo-Christian heritage, then saw many turn to Christ, grow in their faith and respond as Christians have always done during periods of cultural decline and anarchy: by regrouping and gently but firmly standing for revealed truth.

Within evangelicalism we witnessed the concept of "gospel" shifting from "Christ died to set you free from divine righteousness and judgement" to "Christ wants to deliver you from your brokenness and heal your hurts", from "sacrificing for Christ" to "finding satisfaction in life" and from missions as "making disciples" and "church planting", to *missio Dei*, the idea that God invites everyone to get involved in any and every good and worthwhile activity. By the turn of the millennium I became so uncomfortable with the evangelical label that I started referring to myself as a "historic evangelical" or simply as a "Bible believing Christian". Then a trickle of young people rediscovered that "old-time Bible-embracing gospel", a trickle which became a steady stream. I have had the joy of teaching some of them in Bible colleges in North America and Europe. Now they too are preachers, teachers and missionaries proclaiming that truth is not innate to us, but must be sought like a treasure hidden in a field.

My wife and I spent much of our life in the Middle East, where we witnessed the shift from Arab, Turkish and Iranian nationalism to the rise of Islamic fundamentalism and the subsequent civil wars and strife. Yet we also saw evangelical churches led by former Muslims take root and bear fruit in places like Kurdistan, Turkey, and the Arab world.

I believe that future historians, both secular and Christian, will recognize the post World War II era which ended with the pandemic of 2020-22 as a golden age. I certainly experienced it as such. Yes, life often appeared yo-yo-like in the moment, but it was as if The One holding the loose end of the string was striding uphill, taking the unwitting object to a beautiful, happy place while testing its capabilities and limits. Eventually it found itself doing things it could not have imagined: around-the-worlds, elevators, sleepers, trapezes... Through all the ups and downs of life I have been carried like that yo-yo by One who, for reasons rooted in sovereign grace, chose me, cares deeply for me, and taught me things I could not have imagined possible. This conviction is the deepest source of my happiness.

Yes, we are a very thankful, happy old couple. This makes us quite unique as few people our age are happy. Some are bitter, some stoically resigned to their fate, some in denial, pretending to be 20 years younger than they are. But we are happy, for happiness is a byproduct of other, more fundamental things. Get those basics right, and you'll become happy. Happier, anyway. Hopefully my grandchildren—and you too—will discover what those life-changing things were for me, for us, as I tell our tale.

I realize that memory is not infallible. It filters and discards, represses, blocks and misattributes. Preconceived notions and attitudes bias it. My wife, children, extended family and former colleagues may remember particular incidents differently. Thankfully much of my personal correspondence has survived, as have the circular letters we wrote every two months to our supporters. The code PL in the footnotes stands for Prayer Letter. Those missives, along with boxes of old slides and photographs, have triggered manifold memories, the vast majority of which are happy.

Peter Pikkert
Hamilton, Ontario, 2025

Part 1: Rebirth

1959-1982

"Hyper-Calvinism is all house and no door;
Arminianism is all door and no house."

John "Rabbi" Duncan

1

Beginnings

*"If you don't know where you're going,
any road will take you there."*

George Harrison, quoting Lewis Carroll

. . .

ONE OF MY EARLIEST continuous memories is of the M.S. Parthenon of the KNSM shipping company. Upon successfully crossing the Atlantic—we hove-to during a storm—the old freighter docked for a day or two at a string of ports as it worked its way up the chain of islands from Grenada to St. Martin. That's where we disembarked, for that is where Dad had accepted a teaching position. I was six years old.

I was the only white kid at the Martin Luther King Jr. primary school. It was 1965, and outside the USA they were already naming schools after the famed civil rights leader. Three years later we returned to The Netherlands.

Two other memories stand out from that period: the Beatles and my paternal grandparents. Our dour Calvinist subculture didn't follow pop culture. I had, however, heard my mother declaim "beatles" for their negative effect on otherwise "gezonde hollandse meiden", that is, healthy Dutch girls. I could not imagine what beetle might negatively affect "gezonde hollandse meiden". I later developed a soft spot for 1960s music: The Beatles, of course, along with Elvis Presley, John Denver, Joan Baez, Simon and Garfunkel, Roy Orbison...

My mother's parents, stern and aloof, were equally certain of their unmatched religious superiority and unequaled sinfulness. They didn't figure in my life. My father's parents, on the other hand, were cheerful, low-class pagans completely outside the pale of Christianity. Opa Pikkert had been a bootlegger. While my unbending opa hid people from the

Germans during World War II, pagan Pikkert kept his stills trickling by stealing sugar from them. My parents didn't move merely for adventure's sake but because they wanted to escape each other's families—or so I have come to believe. And so, within the year, we left the Netherlands a second time. I was eleven.

I don't remember the flight to Canada but recall the journey from the airport. I was pressed against a car window looking at the new world we were to call home. It was raining. The other vehicles seemed massive. We moved into a large white house on the edge of Sarnia, Ontario. A huge wooden crate filled with oak furniture arrived a few weeks later. Some of those antiques now furnish our condominium apartment.

I sometimes wonder if those early travels sparked my sense of adventure. If so, that was undoubtedly nurtured by National Geographic, the entire collection of which had been left behind by the previous occupants. I spent hours looking at the pictures and plastered their maps on my bedroom walls, even hanging one of Africa from the ceiling so I could stare at it before I fell asleep. I dreamt of becoming an explorer, or a travel writer, or an international news reporter. We also possessed a dog-eared but marvellously illustrated *Golden Book Children's Encyclopedia*, volumes which stirred a thirst for knowledge, a curiosity about all things which I still nurture. I wanted to see with my own eyes the pyramids of Giza, the Great Wall of China, a proboscis monkey, the giant banana tree, an aardvark, a Hottentot, the cave paintings of Lascaux and other such wonders.

Or maybe it was Tintin, the intrepid journalist with the odd lock of hair who sparked that sense for adventure. I read and re-read my Tintin comics, first in Dutch, then in English and, much later in Arabic and Turkish as well. I self-identified with this young, resourceful reporter who, upright and incorruptible, travelled the world to fight evildoers of every description.

Or maybe it was my mother's fear that my brother and I would turn into sissies. Seesees as she would pronounce it in her strong Dutch accent: "I don't vant you to become seesees".

Her fear of us becoming seesees meant that our parents gave us a lot of leeway. I was 13 when dad enrolled me into the Army Cadets. I eventually became corps commander, and paid for my first years of college by teaching at Canadian Forces Base Ipperwash. When I turned sixteen a Dutch cousin and I back-packed from Ontario through Quebec and around Canada's Maritime provinces.

I hated school. On average I was sent to a different school every two years, and the change from Dutch to English between grades 5 and 6 didn't help. I also had a phobia, still there, with respect to all things numeric—to the despair of my father, the math teacher. I inevitably sat at the back of the classroom, near a window, envying the freedom of the sparrows and the gulls and the crows hopping and flitting outside, while the system pushed me from one grade to the next. I once overheard part of a conversation between my parents. "Denk je dat hij mischien een beetje achterlijk is?" my mom asked. That's Dutch for, "Do you think he might be a bit retarded?" I couldn't make out father's muffled response; they did not nurture high aspirations for me.

Books were the saving of me. After learning sufficient English I'd head for the library and borrow the next volume of the Hardy Boys or a Louis L'Amour, to spend pleasantly convivial hours escaping into fictional realities. When I was about 14 or 15 my reading ability took a quantum leap. I discovered Mark Twain and Jack London, John Steinbeck, Ernest Hemmingway and, a bit later, Graham Greene, Ayn Rand and other American icons. They inflamed my thirst for adventure even more.

My friends and I were once arrested for stealing a ceremonial cannon from the local armory and made it into the local newspaper: "Barrel of Fun for Youngsters". We re-enacted Richard Connell's "The Most Dangerous Game" by hunting each other with pellet guns. I lost my front teeth that way. I once shot my friend Andrew, responsible for the loss of my teeth, between the eyes. I had to pinch the pellet from the bridge of his nose. That scared us sufficiently to stop stalking each other.

Yet in spite of the books, my dreams, capers and army cadets, life was not particularly happy. My pseudo-adventures were not merely an escape from reality, but also a search for self-esteem, the aspiration that my life might amount to something, count, be worthwhile, even heroic... I wanted to BE someone—but had no idea how to achieve that.

There is, of course, nothing unique about this. The urge to achieve something great, to be regarded as heroic, is a common banality in male teenagers. I wasn't destined to be a hero who overcame overwhelming chaos, whether that be theological, like, say, Athanasius, or whether that be raw evil, like, say, Winston Churchill. It took a long time for me to appreciate the heroics of the simple: coming alongside a few hard-pressed Christians in the Middle East, raising a family cross-culturally, or scribbling away at some project in which no-one seemed to believe... But I'm running ahead of my story.

2

The World As It Was

"The past is a different country:
they do things differently there."

L. P. Hartley

. . .

SOON AFTER WE landed in Canada an event occurred which kindled in me a lasting interest in "the news". During the October Crisis of 1970 prime-minister Pierre Trudeau invoked the War Measures Act. Tanks rumbled through the streets of Montreal and the sense of crisis was so palpable it even filtered down to little me. I asked Dad, an avid newsreader, what was going on. He explained that a terrorist group fighting for an independent Quebec was kidnapping and murdering politicians, and that no one knew what would happen next.

I was fascinated. Dad's interest in these events suggested that we had come to stay. Canada would be home. Suddenly I wanted to know all about everything that was going on everywhere, and for a youngster to whom the world-at-large was opening up the '70s had a lot to offer.

Beside the October crisis there was the Oil Crisis of '73, Canada's hosting of the Olympics in '76 (the only time the host nation failed to win a gold medal), stagflation and sky-rocketing interest rates. I once expressed delight at the way my paper-route money was growing of its own accord. Dad looked bemused. "You're the only one here profiting from this," he said.

I started reading Canadian authors like Pierre Berton, Farley Mowat, and Grey Owl. I grew to love my English and history classes. Mowat's books *People of the Deer* and *The Desperate People* moved me deeply, though I wondered why the Indians and the Eskimos, as we called them then, couldn't compete with new immigrants like ourselves. On a whim I purchased a dog-eared copy of H.A.L. Fisher's 2 volume *History of Europe*. Though it only told the story up to 1937, I read and re-read it, thereby developing an abiding interest in the roots and rise of Western Civilization, in people like the Hebrew prophets, Plato, Aristotle, Jesus Christ, St. Paul, Augustine, Erasmus, Luther and numerous others, as well as in the movements—the Renaissance, the Reformation, the Enlightenment—which lifted Europe from its barbaric pre-history and set it on its uniquely rich trajectory.

In December of 1975, when I was 16 years old, I stood before a magistrate and, right after Dad had done so, pledged the oath of allegiance. I still have the Bible on which I did so. Though proud to be Canadian, I was fascinated by our big neighbour to the south, no doubt due to the American novelists I was reading, the music we played on our transistor radios, the dynamism of its history, its brashness, boldness, and its global presence culturally and politically. The distinctions between the Canadian and American experiences were not lost on me. We modestly accepted peace and order, celebrated diversity even back then, and were "nice." Once in college I found it easier to converse meaningfully with American students (there were a lot of them where I went) than with Canadian friends. Though I would not have been able to express it at the time, I sensed that Canada's "cultural mosaic" had no center. I was drawn to the American ideal of "life, liberty and the pursuit of happiness," to this aggressive and individualistic nation which, back then at least, perceived itself as a winner, which believed in meritocracy, which revelled in the rebel and assumed people can create a better world through the entrepreneurial spirit. At the same time the youth culture (Woodstock, the birth of Rock and Roll) and the mass demonstrations of '68 were not far back in time. Malcom X's autobiography fascinated me; the days of the irenic Martin Luther King Jr. had been overtaken by black militancy.

We feared "world communism" more than anything else. Solzhenitsyn had revealed the horrors of the Gulag, and the

Soviet Union's ocean-spanning navy, its submarines with nuclear warheads and its increasingly powerful ICBMs loomed menacingly over the free world. Mutually assured destruction, MAD, was the shadow under which we grew up.

Vietnam also featured prominently, and as an army cadet I followed the conflict with interest. How could a policy of constant escalation merely to contain be successful? Saigon fell in 1975. The image of a Huey helicopter perched on the roof of an apartment building crowded with desperate people trying to climb into it is etched onto my generation's retina. The Vietcong would incarcerate hundreds of thousands of those who had cooperated with the Americans. Nearly 800,000 more took to the high seas, facing storms, starvation and pirates in an effort to escape. In Cambodia Pol Pot exterminated a third of his population, anyone with any education at all. The Soviet invasion of Afghanistan in 1979 confirmed our worst fears. President Eisenhower's stark warning in 1954 of a domino effect in which the fall of one nation to the Reds would lead to the fall of the next in line seemed corroborated. I became—and still am—allergic to intimidation-and-power-grab neo-Marxist utopian political movements.

I became mildly interested in the Middle East because of the Yom Kippur war of 1973. The Dutch tended to be very pro-Israel and the Holocaust was still a living memory. Would the Israeli state which had emerged from the Nazi genocide survive? I remember the tension in our home as my parents followed events on the radio—we didn't have a television for according to the church it was the devil's conduit. And, of course, I recall the overthrow of the Shah of Iran. I thought his wife Farah was beautiful. She reminded me of the stunner Sophia Loren.

The '60s and '70s saw the decolonialization of many African countries. Undemocratic, corrupt elites incapable of governing their populations with a modicum of equity and social justice, yet remarkably adept at exploiting them, filled the vacuums left by the departing Europeans. Successive waves of immigrants and refugees—all who could vote with their feet—testified that some socio-political constructs are so degenerate that decent people will pay any price to leave them. Societies and cultures, I learned early in life, are not all of equal worth.

For a time Western civilization too seemed to unravel. Instead of controlling events the hapless Jimmy Carter seemed controlled by them. But the pendulum swung back during the '80s, the decade dominated by Ronald Reagan and Margaret Thatcher. But we are, once again, getting ahead of ourselves, for by then I was a missionary trekking around the Middle East.

3

Breakaway

"But at night, when all the world's asleep
The questions run so deep for such a simple man.
Won't you please (Won't you tell me)? Please tell me what
we've learned? (Can you hear me?) I know it sounds absurd.
(Won't you help me?) But please, tell me who I am."

Supertramp

...

AS ALREADY MENTIONED, I was not the happiest of
teenagers. First of all, our constant moving made long-term
friendships difficult. Secondly, life in our Dutch-Canadian
subculture can, for those who don't fit in, be brutal. Though not
highly endowed with such attributes as sensitivity and
gentleness, many of us are convinced of the superiority of our
little world: "If you're not Dutch you're not much." The fact that
Dad was a teacher in their alternative school system did not
help; kids he crossed took it out on me. Things became so bad
that he pulled me out of the private system and dispatched me
to a public school for grades eleven and twelve. This was a
courageous decision and, in retrospect, the right one. During
that time I caught a glimpse of a non-Dutch world which, in my
experience, was gentler, kinder.

Thirdly, my parents'—particularly my mother's—theological
convictions were a variant of hyper-Calvinism which
promulgated some gloomy notions. The church in which she
was raised, popularly known as "the black stockings church,"
taught that one first had to sense the depths of sinfulness
before one could approach God with the appropriate attitude.

No one, however, could explain what levels of misery were sufficient to satisfy God. This groveling "worm theology" led many in my extended family to wrestle perennially with doubt, ever wondering whether their experience of sinfulness was sufficiently acceptable. This uncertainty was compounded by an extreme take on the doctrine of election, the idea that God selects some people unto salvation and not others. As the reason for God's electing grace lay entirely within his inscrutable will, mere mortals could neither know nor question what he had decreed.

This amalgam of teachings led to the notion that God was a distant judge and that assurance of salvation from sin is the goal of the Christian life. This is very different from classic evangelicalism, which teaches that assurance of salvation is the basis, the starting point, of a healthy Christian life. Mum's search for certainty, inner peace and a more intimate relationship with God led her to the likes of such health and welfare preachers as Benny Hinn and Kathryn Kuhlman. Although she responded repeatedly to their altar calls, they did her no good.

Fourthly, my deophobic mother was a force of nature. She didn't contextualize to her surroundings, her surroundings adapted to her, and did so willingly. She was lady-like, yes, but with very strong ideas of right and wrong, of the way things should be. Much of my early adulthood was marked by resisting her strong but, in my mind, misguided ideas on how I should live my life.

All that to say that I wanted to escape, to break away, to travel far from Sarnia, Ontario, and start life over, away from everyone I knew. A fortuitous event in my last year of high school allowed me to do just that, an event which set me on the road to becoming a happy man.

The question arose as to what I would do after high school. Like Gray Owl or Robert Service I thought I might go up north, live a simple life and write the Great Canadian novel. By then I had added Kierkegaard, Sarte and Kafka to my list of favorites. As it is, I would not get to the Yukon until I was in my sixties, and few people purchased the novels I did eventually pen. Joining the army was also a possibility; I'd done well as a cadet. However, my high school grades were too low to be admitted into university, and joining the army as a private, a lowly grunt, had no appeal.

One evening Dad asked if I'd do him a favor: go to a Baptist clergyman friend of his and ask for advice. If only to humor him, I acquiesced. He made the appointment and I rode my bicycle to a largish brick building in a poorer part of town. In my wildest dreams I could not have imagined that one day I would be preaching from the pulpit of that self-same building, nor that the imposing man I was about to meet would one day serve with us on the mission field.

Pastor Lambert towered over me. I do not recall the conversation, but do remember his last lines. "Son," he said as he looked at the top of my head, "you should go to Bible school. Maybe they can straighten you out." He turned to a filing cabinet, pulled out some brochures, copied something onto a scrap of paper and handed that to me. "Write to these addresses and see what happens," he said and he ushered me out the door.

I'd never heard of Bible schools before, but wrote to all three addresses. One was an information bureau which forwarded my contact info to just about every evangelical college on the North American continent for in the course of the next six or seven weeks over 50 Bible school catalogues landed in our mail box. The first to arrive was from a place called Prairie Bible Institute.

As I perused the growing pile an idea took shape: if I applied myself for a year at one of these no-name schools I might get into university afterwards and study American literature. Prairie Bible Institute met my very relaxed criteria. It looked easy to get into, was in Canada—no US immigration issues—yet in Alberta, i.e., a looong way from home. It was the only place to which I applied. I knew enough Christianese to sound pious, lied my way through the Christian lifestyle statement, had two friends fill in the reference forms, and waited. In due course I received my letter of acceptance.

Thus it was that in late August 1977 I packed my army duffel bag, boarded a train, transferred in Toronto, and disembarked in Calgary several days later. I found the Greyhound station and boarded a bus bound for Three Hills.

Life was about to change for ever. For eternity.

4

Rebirth

"To be born again is, as it were, to enter upon a new existence, to have a new mind, a new heart, new views, new principles, new tastes, new affections, new likings, new dislikings, new fears, new joys, new sorrows, new love to things once hated, new hatred to things once loved, new thoughts of God, and ourselves, and the world, and the life to come, and salvation."

J.C. Ryle

• • •

THE GREYHOUND left me on Main Street. I extricated my duffel from the hold and watched the vehicle trundle off. Both ends of a perfectly straight street lined with one- and two-storey brick and clapboard buildings disappeared into the prairies. There was a general store, two banks, a florist, an eatery and a few other establishments. There was no one about. The place had a distinct Western feel: spacious, empty, big sky. No sign of a college.

I entered a store and asked if there was a Prairie Bible Institute nearby. She pointed down the road. I slung the duffel over my shoulder and started walking. It struck me then how little I knew about the place. I hadn't the foggiest idea what the school stood for, what, if any, denomination it belonged to, how large it was. The black and white photographs in the catalogue pictured a number of rectangular 4 or 5 storey structures and a large building with a curved roof called The Tab, for tabernacle. Tabernacle.... were they Mormons?

At the bottom of the street a simple brick and wood sign saying Prairie Bible Institute informed me that I'd arrived. There wasn't a soul about, and I wandered aimlessly around the deserted campus. Someone stepped from a building and beckoned. "Can I be of help?"

"I'm a new student, just arrived," I replied.

"Welcome! What's your name? Peter? Peter, you arrived early. We're not expecting folk to show up for another two days. Not a problem. Come with me." The friendly gentleman led me to an office, checked a list, grabbed my bag and led me across the quad to a largish rectangular wooden building. Up three flights of stairs, down a corridor and through a door.

"Here is your room. I'm afraid the dining room isn't functioning yet, but there is a kitchenette down the hall. Make yourself at home." The room was spartan but functional and clean. Small but not pokey. The window looked over the endless prairie. I claimed the bottom bunk, one of the closets and a desk, unpacked and lay down. The mattress was plasticky but firm. I got up and ambled back into town for some provisions. I clearly recall the details of my arrival on campus but don't remember much of my first weeks there. I clicked with my room mate, an imperturbable fellow who played the violin.

The four years I spent at PBI were the most formative of my life. Somehow, in God's mysterious economy of things, I ended up—without any effort on my part—in a genuinely Christian community. These people, students and staff alike, had something I knew I lacked: a cocktail of peace and joy, a sense of purpose, a relaxed affability... things which clearly stemmed from their version of the Christian faith, a version I had never before seen or experienced. I'd been raised a certain way, in a subculture certain of its own superiority. Yet the little world in which I had landed appeared vastly more attractive. I tried to fit in but that wasn't easy for I was not like them. I envied what they had, but how to get it? I came from a world which celebrated doubt. These people had no doubts. I wanted their certainty, but didn't know where to find it. I was in turmoil.

My next memory is very vivid, etched on my mind. That October the school invited one Stephen Olford to address the student body. One of his messages was based on Psalm 37:4-6: *"Delight thyself also in the LORD; and he shall give thee the desires of thine heart. Commit thy way unto the LORD; trust also in him; and he shall bring it to pass. He shall bring forth*

*thy righteousness as the light, and thy judgment as the
noonday sun"* (AV). For some inexplicable reason those verses
registered with me. I suddenly knew I had to "get right with
God." I didn't know all that entailed but did what I could. I
walked to the bank in town, withdrew a significant amount of
cash, stuffed it in envelopes and mailed these to the
establishments from which I'd shoplifted. I then wrote letters to
family members and others to whom I felt I owed apologies.

After a busy week of making amends I tucked my Bible
under my arm and walked out onto the prairies. It was a lovely
autumn day. The sun scintillated off the distant Rockies and
harvesters moved in tandem across the brown fields. I sat down
on the grass, re-read Psalm 37 and started praying. "Lord God,
I don't know what's true and what's not. Is the way I was raised
true? Have these people got the truth? I just don't know. But it
says right here that if I commit my way to you and trust in you,
you will bring it to pass. You will make me as righteous as light,
as the noonday sun. Lord, I'm drawing a line below my past. I
want to start over. I'm going to commit my way to you and trust
you to make me as righteous as the sun."

Even though I'd garbled the quotation it didn't matter. An
overwhelming joy flooded my being. I had no idea what had
taken place—but one thing I knew: in spite of my sin, in spite of
my past, things were good between God and me. I jumped up
and found myself dancing unselfconsciously over the prairies
singing the only bit of a hymn I could remember, the refrain of
"O Lord my God, when I in awesome wonder, consider all the
things thy hands have made."

*Then sings my soul, My Savior God, to Thee,
How great Thou art! How great Thou art!*

The grass appeared greener, the wheat fields turned from
brown to gold, the wispy clouds became whiter, and the sky
bluer. It was October 17, 1977, and Peter Pikkert, age 18, was
born again, regenerated—though I had, as yet, no idea what
those words meant. Still, nothing would ever be the same again.

The first component to my becoming a happy man was in place. It would be challenged and years later, during the first Gulf War, I came perilously close to turning my back on this God-of-the-Bible I was now lauding. But we are, once again, jumping far ahead in our story...

5

PBI As It Was

*"Every strong conviction ends by taking possession of us;
it overcomes and absorbs us, and tears us ruthlessly from
everything else. Has the Cross so seized upon your life?"*

L. E. Maxwell

. . .

MY YEARS AT Prairie Bible Institute were life-transforming. Its location, far from urban temptations and distractions, combined with the simple lifestyle and sacrificial spirit of staff and faculty, gave the place a monastic ambiance. It provided what I needed: a loving Christian community, discipline, and teachers I looked up to who taught subjects I grew to love. I arrived an unregenerate and, four years later, left an evangelical missionary. I've had a soft spot for monastic communities ever since.

By odd happenstance I witnessed the end of distinct eras in widely disparate parts of the world. My years at Prairie were the closing act of the so-called L.E. Maxwell era. Old L.E. as we knew him, had come up from Kansas to co-found the school in 1922. In his 80s when I arrived, he was still its moral centre, holding the school to its theologically and socially conservative roots, still "training disciplined soldiers for Jesus Christ".

This "Lion of the Prairies" could thunder against evolution, communism, secular humanism, and doctrinal drift, yet he was unlike the cantankerous fundamentalists which came to typify the era. He was no Carl McIntire, no John R. Rice, no Frank Norris, no T.T. Shields. He was wonderfully good-humoured, cheerful, optimistic, upbeat, big-hearted and on good terms with such early proponents of the neo-evangelical movement as Charles Fuller and Harold Ockenga. Under L.E. the school bridged the divide between the new evangelicalism and its fundamentalist heritage. Separation from worldliness and theological liberalism, yes, but a wide embrace of all who loved Christ. He was a premillennialist but did not trumpet dispensationalism. He refused to dismiss the charismatic movement yet did not get caught up in it. Instead, he warned against a cold, barren spirituality. The pillars of his faith rested on the verbal, plenary inspiration of the Bible, on the centrality of the cross, on the importance of holiness and personal revival, on living life in the expectation of the imminent return of Christ, and on the importance of the missionary enterprise. Jesus Christ might return at any moment and we should be "found ready" to "meet him in the air" on the day he "descends from heaven with a trumpet sound". Being "found ready" meant living in the light of eternity, living a life distinct from, separate from, the world. We were to "march to a different drummer". We were to be holy as Christ is holy. We were to draw close to the Saviour and be his disciples. We were not to engage in any activity of which we would be ashamed if Christ suddenly showed up.

One of his many aphorisms, Maxwell 1:1, was "the hardest thing in the world is to keep balanced". It has stood me in good stead (another one was, "Cheer up, the worst is yet to come!"). That striving for balance kept him from deductively reasoning any theological truths beyond the boundaries of the inductive Bible study method for which the school was famous.

The school's spiritual DNA was most evident during its two annual conferences. The Fall Conference sought to nurture "deeper life," i.e., spiritual revival among students and staff. Justification by faith in Christ's substitutionary atonement was a wonderful thing but it had to be experienced in daily life to prove its reality. Conversion was to be followed by sanctification and service. The point of penal substitutionary atonement was to produce fruit that was joyful, missional, suspicious of secular and liberal academia yet without rancor. Following a rigorous academic curriculum was less important than being marinated in the Bible and cultivating a life of faith, prayer and grass-roots service. The heart mattered more than the intellect. A personal walk with God mattered more than Greek or Hebrew.

Not that theology didn't matter! We drank deeply from theological wells dug by D.L. Moody, A.J. Gordon, A.T. Pierson, R.A. Torrey, James Orr, James Gray, Arno Gabelein, H.C.G. Moule, Charles G. Trumbull and G. Campbell Morgan. People like Horatius Bonar, Oswald Chambers, Madame Guyon, Watchman Nee, Griffith Thomas and Major Ian Thomas were inspirations of Christian spirituality, of the idea that a genuine Christian life flowed from identification with Christ in his death and resurrection. Maxwell referred to it as "the crucified life", the theme of his most famous book, *Born Crucified*. Identification with Christ in his death and resurrection as an ongoing, post-conversion reality was to be the source of an effective, fruitful, transforming, rewarding Christian life. It was the key to deliverance from the power of indwelling sin.

I didn't understand what this was all about until much later, long after graduation. I did, however, comprehend that all which once held our affections, like material things, social standing, pleasure-seeking and professional success were to be subservient to the most exalted of pursuits, namely to know and serve Christ. To drive that home life at PBI was strictly regulated. Dancing and rock-and roll were out, as were cards, smoking and alcohol. Our social interaction with the opposite sex was carefully controlled lest we be distracted from our high calling. We adhered to very specific dress codes: women couldn't wear jewelry and had to dress conservatively so as not to excite the baser instincts of us guys, while we couldn't sport long hair and had to wear neckties to class (I slung a bolo tie around my neck). Those who had "presented their bodies as living sacrifices to God" did not flaunt them.

The lineup for the fall conferences was a Who's Who of deeper-life speakers. Harold Wildish, Roy Hession and Alan Redpath featured regularly. We were to "surrender ourselves to God", "have dealings with Him", and "crucify" aspects of our life that had not been submitted to Christ. Throughout the year missionaries spoke in chapel, and weekly Friday-night missionary meetings enabled us to meet agency representatives. Periodic Biography Nights featured missionary heroes such as Hudson Taylor, Adoniram Judson, David Livingstone, Jonathan Goforth, Mary Slessor, Amy Carmichael, Eric Liddell, John and Betty Stam. There were required courses on evangelism and missions, and when we sensed the Lord leading us towards a specific ethnic group, ministry or organization we were urged to share this publicly.

Every spring, towards the end of the school year, the school organized the annual Missions Conference. We would be challenged to follow Christ "anywhere, at any time and at any cost." Former students spoke, such as Elizabeth Elliot of *Through Gates of Splendor* fame, Ralph Winter, the founder of the World Center for Missions and Don Richardson, author of *Peace Child.* Together with other missionaries like George Verwer, the founder of Operation Mobilization, and Helen Roseveare, they would urge us to preach "repentance and remission of sins in the name of Christ to all nations." We were challenged to go to those languishing in spiritual darkness, particularly those overseas. After all, people who had surrendered their wills, crucified their selves and surrendered all to Christ would inevitably take his last command, the great commission, seriously. Becoming a missionary was the highest possible calling, the apex of spiritual service for God. The school measured success by the percentage of graduates who "went overseas." Emblazoned across the stage in gothic letters was the challenge:

> Is there a soul who died, who died because of me,
> Forever shut away, from heaven and from Thee?
> Because I tightly clutched my little earthly store,
> Nor sent Thy messenger to some distant shore?

Staying within a theologically conservative, strong Bible-based framework, a Keswick style spirituality and an emphasis on cross-cultural, overseas missions, turned the school into a boot camp for several generations of missionaries. People from a range of theologically conservative backgrounds trained there, absorbed the passion for foreign missions, and became the backbone of organizations such as the China Inland Mission (Overseas Missionary Fellowship today), Sudan Interior Mission (SIM International today), The Evangelical Alliance Mission, The Regions Beyond Missionary Union (WorldTeam today) and the agency I ended up with, the Worldwide Evangelization Crusade (WEC International today).

Were we brainwashed? Well, I recognized that my brain, at least, stood in need of a good washing. I recognized that life at PBI was not the normal Christian life. It was a boot camp designed to mould and shape me so I could be set free to serve Christ in the world-at-large. The only regulations I evaded were the rigid social guidelines—a bit of rebellion which kept me from becoming a legalistic twit. Yet Prairie Bible Institute was exactly what I needed. The values it held may appear quaint today. They may be considered old-fashioned by contemporary, post-evangelicals. I still embrace many of them.

L.E. Maxwell—one of my heroes—died three years after I graduated. It was the end of an era. His son, and then his grandson, took over the helm and changed course. The Lord has since raised up other schools in that old PBI spirit. I would teach at one later in life.

6

Early Influencers

*"Remember those who led you, who spoke the word of God to
you; and consider the result of their way of life,
imitate their faith."*

Hebrews 13:7 (NASB)

• • •

A NUMBER OF others also influenced me deeply during those
spiritually formative years. An erudite Scot named Ted Rendall,
a graduate of London Bible College, came to Prairie in the
1950s. A wonderful expositor, Mr. Rendall would walk us
through some Bible passage, give its context, present various
interpretations or problematic issues, then take us back to the
text and apply its implications to current realities. His course
on Isaiah made the ancient prophet come alive and relevant.
The big theological debate back then was the so-called Battle
for the Bible. Mr. Rendall unequivocally defended the inerrancy
and verbal and plenary inspiration of the Scriptures, along with
a categorical call to demonstrate one's high view of it through
the personal application of its teachings, holiness of life, and
involvement in missions. He was the kind of teacher I later
sought to emulate.

Ruth Dearing, who joined the staff in the 1940s, also left her
mark. When I arrived in '77 the aging spinster taught a range of
courses, including New Testament Greek. The one that affected
me most, however, was her second-year Theology course. For
the first time I was exposed to a synthesis of what the Bible-as-
a-whole taught, along with the classic proofs for the existence of
God.

Alban Douglas was a dynamic former missionary to China
who painted cross-cultural missions as a great adventure for

God while John Kayser, a loose-limbed, gregarious young teacher, strode across campus as if he owned the place. He challenged me to read a chapter from Proverbs every day. I did so for nine months, until its instructions were baked into me: avoid intoxicants, be diligent, play the long game, don't talk overmuch, flee flirtatious women but marry a godly, capable one, lovingly discipline the kids and save money. Proverbs allowed me to categorize those who don't follow this advice as fools and maintain a strictly platonic relationship with suchlike. The book has contributed greatly to my happiness.

John would have faded from memory had he not showed up on our doorstep years later. After that we stayed in touch. One day he invited me to participate in a training venture in the Far East. More later; John would become one of the unsung heroes of the modern missionary movement.

Two people not on staff also left their mark on my impressionable soul. The first was the aforementioned George Verwer of OM. Their two ships, the Doulos and the Logos, took the gospel from one exotic port to another, and the stories of students who'd served on them fired my imagination. George had a way of connecting with young people. He showed up on campus once to speak about sex: "There is nothing so uncomfortable as sleeping in the arms of a woman," he asserted. I found that hard to believe back then, but it's true. Years later I came to know various other OM missionaries, and they all seemed to share George's "laugh of faith", his radical, and wonderfully liberating ability to believe great things of God and attempt great things for God. He referred to himself as "God's bungler," a salute to "God's smuggler." George is, without doubt, one of the heroes of the post W.W.II missionary movement.

God's Smuggler was Anne van der Bijl, a Dutchman better know as Brother Andrew. In the 1950s Brother Andrew started smuggling Bibles into Communist Eastern Europe, praying that God would make seeing eyes blind when he crossed borders. His book *God's Smuggler* stirred my adventurous streak. This was the kind of divinely-sanctioned daredevilry I wanted to get involved in. He is another one of the heroes of the modern missionary movement. After the fall of Communism his organization, Open Doors, embraced the Muslim world, where I ran into him a couple of times. He even wrote a nice back-cover blurb for one of my poorly selling novels.

7

Early Experiences

*"Good judgment comes from experience,
and experience - well, that comes from poor judgment."*

A.A. Milne

■ ■ ■

ONE EVENING a week was set aside for a testimony meeting when everyone, staff and students alike, assembled in the cavernous tabernacle for spontaneous attestations to the work of God in their lives. The week of my conversion I walked up to the mic, shared that I'd committed my life to Christ and now wanted to live for him. Afterwards several staff members shook my hand and said how pleased they were as they'd been praying for my conversion. I was flabbergasted. How could they have known that I hadn't been a genuine Christian?

"Because of your language," one said. "You swear."

Of course! I'd spent the summer training army cadets and, as one of the youngest NCOs, had felt the need to prove myself. Army cadets swear. Casually. All the time. And so my first major struggle as a "born again" Christian was to clean up my speech. It didn't come easy. Swearing came so naturally that I feared opening my mouth in public. I even inked the words "kop dicht," Dutch for "shut up," on the palm of my hand. Thankfully, over time and with setbacks my speech became less colourful. I relaxed. One day I slipped on an ice patch and my tongue went into action, leaving me downcast. I wondered if I'd ever change. During my sophomore year I slipped and fell again. I got back on my feet, dusted myself off and looked around sheepishly. Suddenly it struck me. I hadn't sworn! I was exhilarated. I could change! People can be transformed! They can become better than they were!

■

In the winter of 1977 revival broke out on campus. A sudden, spontaneous sense of our sinfulness and God's holiness enveloped the place. There was no emotionalism, no fiery speakers nor any other kind of manipulation. Classes were suspended and for several days students lined up behind a microphone to confess their sins and make things right with God. As I had just recently been saved, in the process of which I had made amends with those I felt I had wronged, I didn't feel the need hang out my dirty laundry. I was still revelling in the imputed righteousness of Christ. But the event drove home the fact that God's Spirit convicts of sin, of righteousness, and of judgement to come and that he wants us to live Christ-like. I still hold those convictions.

.

Because I'd repaid those I'd stolen from, I was short of money. The dean called me into his office and said that if I didn't pay my bills soon I'd have to leave at Christmas. I determined to leave the matter with God. Had he not led me to Prairie? Had he not drawn me to himself? If these things were true then he'd finish the job he'd begun. November rolled into December. One evening an envelop appeared under my door. It contained money, which I promptly deposited into my account. Not long afterwards it happened again. I yanked the door open, but the individual was gone. Maybe it was an angel... This happened several more times. Then I received a letter from the Canadian army. It contained a substantial cheque, a back-payment I was not expecting. It was more than enough to cover the rest of the school year. The envelopes stopped coming but I had learned that the "life of faith" I'd heard and read about actually works. Years later it would be severely tested.

.

I discovered that death had lost its sting. This idea, when firmly grasped, makes a person very happy indeed! Students had to be involved in Christian service and I signed up for the Drumheller Prison Ministry. Once a week we drove 70 kilometers to this penitentiary to hold a worship service, provide refreshments and chat with inmates. One icy evening our car slid into a ditch. I was the one scheduled to preach so I decided to hitch-hike the rest of the way.

The individual who picked me up was not heading for Drumheller and, albeit reluctantly, dropped me off at the intersection of Hwys 21 and 575. It was dark and very cold. There was no wind. I wasn't dressed for that kind of chill. Several cars passed but did not stop. I felt the cold penetrating my body. There was no house, no light, nothing, and I thought I would die. Instead of freezing to death along the side of the road I decided to lie down in the snow in the adjoining field. I stared up at the brilliant night-sky, the myriad of stars, the milky way—and great joy filled my soul. I knew I was right with God. I knew he had led me to Prairie, drawn me to himself, and that I was ready to meet him face to face. I was ready to go. Hallelujah, Lord, here I come!

A truck ground to a halt. I got to my feet and stumbled towards it. The driver reached across the cab and flung open the door. "What the hell are you doing out there," he demanded. I explained, my teeth chattering, not as nearly as close to death as I'd supposed. He looked at me as if I was nuts, but dropped me off at the prison gates. I was late, but they let me preach anyway. I never preached like I did that evening.

.

Every so often my friend Pete and I would go for an evening stroll to talk and pray. One blustery evening as we walked along the train tracks we decided to pray, and knelt beside each other on one of the railway ties. Caught up in our prayers, the wind in our faces, we were oblivious to the world around us. Suddenly I felt a light vibration followed by a train whistle coming from behind.

"Pete, a train!" I shouted. We leaped off the tracks just in time. With pounding hearts and grinning stupidly we watched a long convoy of freight cars rumble past. Pete became my first supporter when I went into missions. He kept the numerous letters I wrote him during my early years overseas, graciously returning them decades later.

■

Pecking letters home on my Remington was part of my Christian witness. Though my parents were dubious about the evangelical subculture into which their oldest son had been absorbed, the weekly missives suggested that positive things were afoot. Hoping the same would be said of my younger brother they decided to send him to the high school associated with the college. They put him on a bus and three days later he disembarked at the Calgary Greyhound terminal. He looked tired and stressed as he pushed through the turnstile but lit up like Broadway when he saw me awaiting him. I had the privilege of leading him to the foot of the cross a few weeks later. He has since had a remarkable career as a Bible translator and literacy worker, first in the jungles of Papua and then globally. He too is one of my heroes.

■

As mentioned, the one realm in which I bucked Prairie's legalism pertained to its strict social regulations. I found a loop-hole: the handbook said nothing about students dating staff!

I wanted to study New Testament Greek even though the idea was terrifying, for high school French had defeated me. Although I'd scraped through Prairie's required course on English grammar I decided to retake it during the Spring session, hoping to master the subject. This time it all fell into place, and grammar never fazed me again. In time I even wrote descriptive grammars for both Kurdish and Turkish, the former becoming one of my better selling books.

The grammar teacher—let's call her Ashley—was a freshly minted graduate, cheerful, smart, vivacious, attractive. As I'd aced her course, I became a grader for the English department—and was assigned to the beautiful Ashley. We clicked.

One day she confessed that she'd fallen in love with me. I was flattered. This led to a semi-clandestine relationship;

nothing untoward—I was a good boy—but we were in a gray zone in terms of school regulations. We went public on the last day of school. Jaws dropped.

While I completed my Junior and Senior years Ashley went on a missionary stint to the African Sahel. That kept me from undue distractions. However, during that time I also received my "call to the Kurds," a complicating event duly reported in our extensive correspondence.

8

The Call to the Kurds

*"If a commission by an earthly king is considered an honor,
how can a commission by a Heavenly King
be considered a sacrifice?"*

David Livingstone

. . .

FROM THE CREATION of the state of Israel in 1948 to the Iranian revolution of 1979 the Middle East did not feature prominently in the Western media. There were, of course, spikes like the Suez Crisis of 1956, the Six Day War of 1967, the Yom Kippur War of 1973, the subsequent oil price shocks and the occasional outrage in Palestine or Lebanon. For most of those three decades, however, the focus was on the Cold War, Vietnam, free love, and Watergate. On the other hand, feverish apocalyptic writers of the '60 and '70s—think Hal Lindsey, Jack Van Impe and Salem Kirban—perceived the creation of the State of Israel, the H-bomb, world Communism abroad and secular humanism at home as auguries of the end times in which the Middle East was destined to play a prominent role.

Salem Kirban's daughter Diane, a very skinny girl, was a classmate. Once, when Mr. Kirban visited the campus, a fellow student nudged me. "That's Diane's father," he said, pointing across the dining room to a dapper Semitic-looking gentleman. "He's a famous writer on the end times. He's sold hundreds of thousands of books." Curious, I went to the library and pulled one off the shelf. It was hokey, far-fetched stuff. In addition to an imminent Armageddon and other dire predictions, the man also promoted the restorative power of fruit juice. All that to say that, back then, the Middle East was not within my conceptual horizons.

After daily chapel we were expected to attend a prayer group. There were a lot of them, each one focusing on a different region of the world. The leader would read missionary prayer letters and then we'd commit its contents to the Lord. If no letters were forthcoming the leader would cull for information from books like *Hidden People*, a forerunner of the popular *Operation World* series. I floated from one group to the next, trying to figure out God's plan for my life. My friend Pete, part of the Middle East group, invited me to join them. We were the smallest group on campus. That changed in the tumultuous year of 1979 when a series of events reshaped the region's social and political dynamic and created the context in which I would operate for years after my arrival there a mere three years later.

The first of these pivotal events took place on January 16 when the Shah of Iran fled his country. Shiite fundamentalists hijacked a popular uprising and their hero, Ayatollah Ruhullah Khomeini, returned from exile, led down the plane's boarding stairs by an Air France pilot. He turned the country into an Islamic Republic.

The second event took place on March 26, when Anwar Sadat, president of Egypt, and Menachim Begin, prime minister of Israel, signed a peace treaty. The normalization of relationships between the Arab world's most populous nation and Israel was deeply unpopular with Arabs. Egypt was expelled from the Arab League and Sadat would be assassinated during a parade two years later. But the agreement held.

The third event took place on July 22, when Saddam Hussein convened an emergency meeting of Iraq's ruling Ba'ath (Arab Socialist) party. Six days earlier he had forced the resignation of the country's president and appointed himself to the post. His purge of 1979 took place on live TV. Smoking a cigar on the stage of a conference room packed with senior party members, he consolidated his power Stalin-style. Then, seeking to profit from the chaos in Iran, invaded it the following year. The Iran-Iraq war dominated events in the Middle East during the 1980s.

The fourth event began on the morning of November 20 in the Grand Mosque in Mecca. It was the last day of the hajj. Tens of thousands of worshippers had gathered for prayer. Suddenly some 500 Sunni fundamentalists, emboldened by Iran's Islamic revolution, pulled weapons from under their dishdashas, chained shut the mosque gates and started broadcasting their demands over the minarets' loudspeakers: the overthrow of the kingdom's ruling dynasty, an end to oil exports to the USA, and the expulsion of all non-Muslims from the kingdom. It took the military until early December to regain control. Hundreds were killed, hundreds more injured. Surviving rebels were shipped across the country to be decapitated in public as warnings to those unhappy with the status quo.

The shock waves these events generated reverberated around the world, even to little Three Hills, Alberta. The Middle East became a focus of attention for chapel speakers, and we were sitting cheek-by-jowl in our once cozy little prayer group. Lindsey, Van Impe and Kirban appeared vindicated.

Early in my senior year the leader of our group had us pray for the Kurds. I'd never heard of Kurds but a Lebanese classmate knew all about them. He told us they were a fanatical Muslim mountain people who had killed friends of his in Beirut. "Guys," he concluded, "this may sound strange to you, but I don't have the faith to believe that a Kurd could be saved..."

That statement surged through me like an electric shock. Not possible for a Kurd to be saved? What a challenge! My breath came quickly and I clutched my chair to keep my excitement to myself. Was God calling me to be a missionary to the Kurds?

I headed for the library to find everything available on this people. There wasn't much: an essay in the *Encyclopedia Britannica*, a couple of National Geographic articles and a few references in other works. They were a hard-pressed ethnic group, possibly the descendants of the Medes, eking out an existence in the mountains of northern Iraq, south-eastern Turkey and north-western Iran, nations which sought to eradicate their distinct language and cultural identity. Their only friends, they claimed, were the mountains.

Unlike other notions I'd entertained, the idea of becoming a missionary to the Kurds refused to die. I kept on the look-out for anything pertaining to them and, in time, the conviction grew that God was leading me to serve him among this people.

Getting a call to the Kurds and getting to Kurdistan were two different things. I unsuccessfully approached 27 mission agencies. For some I was too young, for others too inexperienced, or I didn't have secular skills that would warrant a visa to otherwise closed countries. Others were not opening new fields, or just not interested in the Kurds.

One day two old gentlemen, representatives of an agency I'd never heard of, arrived on campus. Undaunted I made my appointment. One of them, a man with friendly eyes and a substantial forehead, offered me a chair and asked what they could do for me.

"Sir," I said, "I believe the Lord has called me to be a missionary to the Kurds."

"We've been praying for the Kurds since 1977," the man replied.

"That, sir, is the year I became a Christian," I responded.

"Well," said he leaning forward with his eyes agleam and a bony index finger pointing at my chest, "You must be our man."

And that is how I ended up with the Worldwide Evangelization Crusade. The man with the friendly eyes and the high forehead was Ken Getty. I would come to know him well; the more I did, the more my respect for him increased. He too became one of my missionary heroes.

9

Joe and Bill

"Every Christian should be a theologian... we all need to work it out. I want all Christians who can read, to read their Bibles and to read beyond the Bible - to read history and theology."

D.A. Carson

. . .

DURING MY SOPHOMORE at PBI year the family moved to a farm near the gritty city of Hamilton, Ontario. Instead of teaching army cadets that summer I lived at home and worked as a bricklayers' helper. George was cheerful and hard-living, with an explosive laugh. Henk, quiet, solid, steady and with a ready grin, was the artist stone-mason. We called the third man Ome Joop, Dutch for Uncle Joe. He wasn't a blood relative but his wife hailed from the same town in the olde country as my mother.

Joe was otherworldly; in another place and time he could have been a contemplative Trappist. Whenever he drifted into his inner world instead of, say, finishing a chimney, George would shout up the scaffolding, order him to stop thinking about his sins and get on with the job. But Joe wouldn't be thinking about his sins so much as about the wonderful gift of salvation from sin in Jesus Christ. Joe was unique in our Dutch circles because he had assurance of salvation.

It took guts to leave our small, church-centered, hyper-calvinistic Dutch-Canadian immigrant sub-culture. It was our security. It looked after its own. Yet Joe had left it, basing his choice on deeply thought-through theological convictions. He had discovered "the doctrines of grace" and joined a small Baptist church where he was "re-baptised". Getting re-baptised amounted to rejecting your cultural and theological heritage. This, as I would also discover, evoked deeply emotional responses from those closest to you.

Joe was remarkably well-read. For an immigrant with little formal education his grasp of theological issues I wouldn't get my head around until years later—like the nuances of various Puritan streams of thought and the differences between covenant and new covenant theology—was amazing.

One day I told him I was looking for a church.

"Well," he said slowly, "you'd better come with me". And that is how I was introduced to Bill Payne, pastor of a little group meeting in a small red-brick country church. They called themselves Reformed Baptists.

The Reformed label came as a shock. Had I not turned my back on the spiritual paralysis that comes from wondering if God had actually elected you before you were even born? How can you choose for Christ when you don't have the power to choose? If God's election of one person over another is an utterly random act how can you know whether or not you belong to that select group? And didn't those elect live super-holy lives? Wasn't assurance of salvation the culmination of a life of deep and abiding sorrow for sin, heightened spiritual awareness, and an exalted emotional state? What if you had not been blessed with these subjective experiences? These were questions my mother struggled with for the duration of her life. I came to see it as a dreadful teaching and wanted nothing more to do with it.

> "The Calvinism with which I was familiar left me with a bitter taste. It tends to sow doubt and spiritual frustration (and) tends to keep people from embracing the cross in all simplicity and joy. The other variety of Reformed teaching with which I was familiar simply assumed one was right with God from the time one was baptized. It did completely away with repentance and faith. Because of these two unbalanced extremes I tended to be drawn into the Arminian camp as it does not prevent anyone from coming to the cross."[1]

---

[1] Letter to Joop Brokking, June 8, 1982.

And now Joe, who'd come from that doubt-inducing hyper-Calvinist background, who'd struggled for years with exactly those issues, took me to a church which gloried in its Reformed, Calvinistic heritage! Yet these Baptist Calvinists were different. For them, as for the folks at Prairie, assurance was not the culmination of the Christian life but its starting point. Instead of leading to spiritual paralysis, the sense of being objects of unalloyed grace produced joy, along with an evangelistic and missionary zeal.

Pastor Bill couldn't get enough of these doctrines of grace! Sinful mankind was under the judgment of an utterly just God. But God had satisfied his own demand for perfect righteousness in the life and death of the impeccable second person of the Trinity, Jesus Christ, whose righteousness was now available to all who laid claim to it. Sadly, people were blind to these wonderfully liberating realities but when God's Spirit opened their eyes to them nothing else was of greater significance...

> "Am really feeling how inadequate Prairie has been. I thank God for my years there but it was but an introduction, a skeleton on which to hang the rest of what we are learning... Am leaning more and more towards the old Calvinistic, reformed doctrines of grace."[2]

As I read the books and brochures Joe and Bill pushed my way I came to appreciate much of what I had formerly rejected.

> "I have serious questions about the whole concept of the carnal Christian... There is no such thing... All Christians have areas in their lives that are carnal, but if there is no spiritual life then that person is not a Christian. Every Christian sometimes strays from the Lord. Some more than others. But no Christian can continually live in a state of carnality. Think of the old Reformed statement,

---

[2] Letter to Peter Vermeer, Nov. 29, 1981.

the fifth point in TULIP, the Perseverance of the Saints, backwards: the saints will persevere."[3]

Bill's enthusiasm for Reformed teaching was infectious. If, according to him, certain things were difficult to harmonize, well, that was due to the darkness of human understanding not to any inherent inconsistency on God's part. His job was to preach "the whole counsel of God" and so in the same sermon— he was a great preacher—he could preach full-throated five-point Calvinism yet end with a moving plea that "today is the day of salvation" and "sure is salvation for those who repent and believe". He stressed that God doesn't act against your will but graciously enables you to make choices you could never otherwise make.

Bill urged us to worship God with reverence and godly fear. God was majestic, holy and glorious, the one before whom the angels of heaven never stop crying "holy, holy, holy". Christian joy, Bill taught, was not based on feelings but arose from a mixture of assurance that one was a child of God along with reverence for and obedience to our creator and savior. He introduced us to rich veins of Christian teaching of which I'd only been marginally aware: the Puritans and Charles Haddon Spurgeon, A.W. Pink, Iain Murray, Martin Lloyd Jones, J.I. Packer, R.C. Sproul, Cornelius van Til...

"Balanced Reformed teaching actually inculcates great joy, is a great drawing power, and the doctrines of predestination and foreknowledge are not meant to keep anyone from coming to the cross but are, rather, a great comfort to the believer. They are also a great missionary force... because God has a people whom He has chosen before the foundation of the world unto good works. To those individuals God's word will have an effect—it will not return void but will accomplish that which it was intended to do, i.e., the salvation of sinners and the establishment of the church of Jesus Christ. I am reminded of the words of the Lord to the apostle Paul as

---

[3] Letter to Peter Vermeer, June 5, 1982.

he entered the wicked city of Corinth, 'Do not be afraid, keep on speaking, do not be silent. For I am with you and no one is going to attack and harm you, because I have many people in this city."[4]

Like the equally cheerful and positive L.E. Maxwell, Bill had a fundamentalist streak most evident in his love for the old King James version of the Bible. He once invited me over for dinner. While wife Hetty was fussing in the kitchen he took me down to his study. Feeling impish I lifted his oversized King James tome from the desk and held it to my chest.

"Good news for 17th century man", I declaimed.

Bill opened his mouth, closed it, then burst out laughing. Soon afterwards the church switched to the New King James version.

In 2009 Time magazine listed the New Calvinism as one of the ten ideas changing the world. Canadian church historians will recognize Bill Payne as one of the pioneers of that movement. He was preaching it and organizing pastors' and family conferences around the theme and in 1983 founded the Sovereign Grace Fellowship of Baptist Churches, long before Keller, Wilson and Dever emerged to champion the cause south of the border, and well before Grudem wrote his *Systematic Theology*.

---

[4] Letter to Joop Brokking, June 8, 1982.

10

Initial Hurdles

"By perseverance the snail reached the ark."

Charles Spurgeon

. . .

I WAS – AND REMAIN — comfortable with my Dutch-Canadian heritage. I speak unaccented Dutch, enjoy salty licorice and strong coffee with *stroopwafels* (two thin wafers stuck together with coagulated syrup). I appreciate the virtues of hard work and straight talking. I'd turned my back on particular religious aspects of a subculture within that subculture, not on the subculture as such. That distinction was lost on my parents. Things at home were tense during the weeks prior to my "rebaptism." However on December 13, 1981, Bill Payne did the deed. Although interpreted by the family as a rejection of my heritage most of the tribe showed up. Yes, they disapproved, but clan cohesion won out. It was a beautiful day.

Girlfriend Ashley timed her return from Africa with my return home after graduation and we were engaged. She would rejoin Prairie faculty and the school had offered me the position of high school dean. But... I began to have doubts. Ashley had visions of a ministry to North American women—a needy demographic, no doubt, but not one to which I was drawn. One afternoon we found ourselves in the local library looking at house plans. She dreamt of building a house near Prairie and serving the Lord from there. I felt my chest constricting. Had my call to the Kurds been delusional?

A day or two later the phone rang. Ken Getty, the old man with the high forehead, invited me to the mission headquarters for supper. Yes, of course I could bring my fiancée. We pulled up to a mansion on a hill, ascended a long stairway, knocked on a heavy oak door and were ushered in. There was some small talk, then we gathered around a large table. Someone said,

"Peter, there are two kinds of people in WEC: the quick and the dead. Reach across the table and help yourself". I do not remember anything else from that visit—except that something felt right. As Ashley and I descended to street level afterwards she turned to me. "I don't think I could work with these people," she said.

"I think I could," I responded slowly.

Several days later I drove her to the airport. She was in high spirits for she had led my little sister to the Lord. I returned home deep in thought: The good is the enemy of the best... the best comes at a high price... One evening Ken Getty called again. Was I still serious about the Kurds?

"Yes", I said. I pulled my Remington to the edge of the desk and pecked out a difficult letter. I would have broken our engagement in person but didn't have the money to fly across the continent for that purpose.

> "I really cared for her, and she was willing to come with me to the Middle East—for my sake, not for the sake of the Lord. Well, though it about broke my heart at the time, that wasn't good enough. May God spare us from ever accepting less than the best. 2nd best can appear so good and desirable but it is not good enough. Just like Jesus explained in the parables about people who sold everything they had for the best—a pearl or a treasure in a field or whatever... was it worth it? A dumb question! Of course. Well, I'm more determined than ever to never settle for anything but God's best, no matter how costly. Only then can we be shining lights in the universe."[5]

The idea of me becoming a missionary to the Kurds seemed preposterous to my parents. They held that my assurance of salvation was delusional, misguided, something of my own imagination. Didn't real Christians read their Bibles all the time, weep over their sin, and have a great burden for the lost?

---

[5] Letter to Peter and Grace Vermeer, Nov. 11, 1983.

I read my Bible but I wasn't weeping over my sins overmuch as I considered them covered by the blood of Christ. It was also true that I didn't have a great burden for the lost. However, I really did want to see Christ's church take root in places where it had not yet penetrated and to disciple new believers in the faith. That still ranks near the top of my priorities.

My parents' resistance wasn't solely rooted in religious considerations. Like all immigrants, they had crossed an ocean hoping to create a better life for themselves and their children. They had worked hard to succeed and the suggestion that their oldest son should beg for money in order to chat with Muslims in some Middle Eastern tea garden, well, that was simply disgraceful. Time softened them.

> "Here at home things were pretty rough for a while. At one point dad asked me to leave but we are slowly getting reconciled. They had great difficulty with some of the doctrines we take for granted (assurance, acting on faith, etc.) and I was being a bad influence on my sister since I left the church, got baptized, joined WEC and other things. Well, things between dad and I are not good but mom actually promised to support me $25.- a month. You cannot possibly appreciate the full significance of that! She said that through me coming home as often as I could, seeing me at work around the house, etc., she is beginning to believe that what I'm embarking on is from God."[6]

---

[6] Letter to Peter Vermeer, May 10, 1982.

11

Becoming a Crusader

*"If Jesus Christ be God and died for me,
no sacrifice can be too great for me to make for him."*

C.T. Studd

• • •

"After some last-minute scrambles, I now find myself at
the WEC candidates school... I just love it here... Even
though, at times, it is costly to be obedient, afterwards
you berate yourself for having been such a fool to have
almost stepped out of God's will to satisfy your own
desires. How precious is the presence of the Lord, and
how wonderful to rest in Him as He moves in His
indefinable ways."[7]

An energetic missionary in charge of us eight hopefuls walked
us through the fine print of *WEC's Principles and Practice*, a
challenging document which enjoined us to walk in holiness,
and to please God by living a Spirit-filled life in "union with
Christ in his death and resurrection". Under the motto coined
by the agency's eccentric founder, "If Jesus Christ be God and
died for me no sacrifice can be too great for me to make for
Him", we were "to see Christ known, loved and worshipped by
the unreached peoples of the world". We were to preach the
gospel and gather new believers around Christ and his word,
the Bible, so that, empowered by God's Spirit, these people
would, in turn, make disciples in their communities and
beyond. This was to be done with a sense of urgency,
commitment to each other, in dependence upon the Holy Spirit,
and in fellowship with the Church.

We were to walk by faith. Among other things this meant
living in total dependence on God as the supplier of our needs.

---

[7] Letter to Peter Vermeer, Oct. 20, 1981.

We were to look to him not only to bless our evangelistic, discipling and church planting ministries but also at the practical level, meaning we were not allowed to make direct appeals for finances. WEC does not pay a salary; each of us has to "raise support", i.e., get individuals and churches to sponsor us without actually appealing for funds. This is one of the aspects about WEC that I still appreciate.

We were to live sacrificially by placing God's will before personal goals, comforts or desires. We were to embrace being despised for the sake of the gospel, to identify with the people among whom we ministered, to willingly embrace every kind of hardship, including loneliness, separation from family and Christian fellowship, persecution, and imprisonment. The cross of Christ was to be our defining symbol. We were to walk in fellowship with Christians from various theological backgrounds as our oneness in Christ would enable us to serve together as brothers and sisters. Our fellowship was to be shaped by the Spirit's transforming work in us; we were to recognise only one head, the Lord Jesus Christ, only one church, those who love our Lord Jesus Christ in sincerity and truth, and only one nationality, fellow citizens of the heavenly kingdom. We were to reject all national, ethnic, denominational or other prejudices. Instead, we were to accept, love, mutually support and humbly submit to one another. We were signing up for something so meaningful that we should be prepared to lay down our lives for it. And rightly so: how can something be profoundly meaningful if you're not ready to die for it? The Kurds; lost souls; building up the church, the "body of Christ"; becoming part of that crowd of saints which had gone before us in taking the gospel to the ends of the earth—what could be more meaningful than that?

I have fallen far short of the expectations, demands and ideals. In fact I nearly turned my back on Christianity altogether during a period of great difficulty. But, by the grace of God, I didn't. I still love the lofty ideals. Yes, the organization has at times drifted from its roots. It has had to remove leaders who sought to take it in unorthodox, even heretical directions.

Yet, like a Magna Carta, the *Principles and Practice* forced it to re-evaluate itself against the fundamentals on which it was founded.

Fellow candidate David and I were often assigned jobs together. While the women cooked and cleaned we raked leaves or painted. In spite of its grand mansion WEC didn't have much money. We emptied cans of left-over paints from bygone eras— latexes, oils, the lot—into a large pail, stirred, and daubed the battleship gray goop onto the basement walls. Whether painting or raking, we worked in slow motion—not from laziness but because we had much to talk about.

One of the recurring joys of my life is having unexamined presuppositions challenged by bold, intelligent individuals. Hyper-Calvinism had to give way to Prairie pietism which had to integrate the reformed baptistic teachings of Bill Payne. David introduced me to such systematic theologians as Louis Berkhof, B.B. Warfield and Herman Bavinck. I'd read sections of Berkhof at night and we'd discuss it the next day. I also read through Kenneth Scott Latourette's magisterial *A History of Christianity*. Later other bold, intelligent men—Muslims, liberals and others—would challenge me. I'd read the books they'd feed me and come to grips with their claims and arguments. However nothing and no one ever shook the bedrock conviction that Jesus Christ was who he claimed to be: the Son of God and the Saviour of sinners like myself.

The four months of mission orientation ended in December of 1981. One after another we were called into a room full of people and questioned. Nothing was off limits. After the interrogation they asked us to wait in the dining room while they discussed our destiny. To my utter astonishment the couple before me was rejected. I re-entered that room convinced I would share their fate. I was wrong. Ken Getty gave me "the right hand of fellowship" and I signed a declaration stating that I would endure inconvenience, hardship, sickness, death and imprisonment in order to fulfill the Great Commission, and that I would be a loving, loyal, prayerful and unselfish Crusader.

"How challenged I have been and how humbled at the thought that I am allowed to go out... How I praise Him for that. When I look at what He has done in the past, how He has led, then I am thrilled with expectancy to see how He will work in the future. And the future is not clear. There are many hurdles yet to go over, or through... But the Lord is faithful! He will see us through!"[8]

I was now expected to "raise support". As mentioned, WEC—like most evangelical mission organizations—does not pay a salary; your church and other personal connections were expected to finance you. I had few connections.

"You asked about my finances. My minimum support figure is $400 a month. That's what I need to live on. Currently I have about $3000 on hand in cash, and $35 a month promised support. My church will support me for about $150-200 I believe."[9]

I went back to work as a bricklayers' helper. George and Henk had recently come to faith; we were now an all-Christian crew singing hymns from chimney tops. Bill Payne and his wife Hetty had dreamed of becoming missionaries to Tunisia, but for health reasons that did not happen. Now they did everything they could to help me on my way. The church pledged $300 a month. Bill then introduced me to some like-minded churches and their pledges, along with friend Pete's support, suddenly made the enterprise feasible.

WEC sent me to Amman, Jordan, to study Arabic at Kelsey's Language School, run by the eponymous George Kelsey. First, however, I had to take a month-long intensive course at the Toronto Institute of Linguistics. I groused about that for it was jolly expensive. However, I did as told, incapable of imagining the fabulous consequences which would emerge from that introduction to applied linguistics. Decades later I would co-develop a successor program for numerous missionary candidates from across the denominational spectrum.

---

[8] Letter to Peter Vermeer, Feb. 10, 1982.
[9] Letter to Peter Vermeer, June 5, 1982.

12

The Collapse of Missionary Preparation

"Don't be so open-minded that your brains fall out."

G.K. Chesterton

. . .

BACK THEN MISSION agencies took pre-field training seriously. Today it is much easier to become a missionary; anyone who "loves Jesus" is a potential candidate. As a result the western missionary enterprise is in disarray both theologically and methodologically. The reason agencies went down this short-sighted, self-destructive road is as follows:

I am a Baby Boomer, i.e., of the generation born in the wake of W.W. II. Between 1946 and 1964 an average 250 women out of every 1,000 had babies annually, as compared to 150 in 1988[10] and a mere 59 in 2018[11]. In other words, there were a lot of us, though we are now dying in droves—my own is not far off.

We Boomers are an aviary filled with birds of many feathers. However the particular Boomer-bird with which I self-identify does not fit the typical labels and stereotypes attached to us, though we made a significant impact on the Anglo-Saxon world's socio-political agenda. We are the conservative evangelical Boomers. We shared the same historic setting and social context as our peers. We were also raised on Dr. Spock and entertained by the half-Vulkan of the same name.

---

[10] Finzel H. 1989. *Help! I'm a Baby Boomer: battles for the Christian values inside America's largest generation.* Wheaton, Illinois: Victor Books. p. 15.

[11] https://www.vox.com/science-and-health/2018/5/22/17376536/fertility-rate-united-states-births-women. Accessed Nov. 12, 2020.

We vaguely recall the Kennedy assassinations and vividly remember the chilling shadow of the cold war, the Patty Hearst kidnapping, the moon landing, the threat of nuclear holocaust and the Vietnam debacle. 58,000 of our American counterparts lost their lives there and 300,000 came home wounded or permanently disabled. After the collapse of Communism we learned that my hometown of Hamilton, Ontario, famous for its steel plants, was slated to be on the receiving end of the first wave of Soviet ICBMs.

However, my stripe of Boomer was not into free love, LSD, eastern religions, occultism, campus protests, Carl Jung, Aldous Huxley, Alan Watts or Jack Kerouac. We do share an appreciation for Simon and Garfunkle, John Denver and Bob Dylan, as well as the cynicism wrought by Watergate, and—and this is important—a certain disdain for our pre-boomer parents' values. Haunted by the Great Depression and the World War, they were risk-averse. They were, by and large, still religious— being associated with a religious institution was socially acceptable in their day—but the idea of launching new ventures in unstable regions of the globe was not on their conceptual horizon. Many of us conservative evangelical Boomers spurned their need for security rooted in material things. We'd read G.K. Chesterton, C.S. Lewis and J.R.R. Tolkien and were primed for adventure! We formed the back-bone of the post-war missionary enterprise, an undertaking which would take evangelicalism to the ends of the earth in ways never seen before. As a result of Boomer missionary activity there is scarcely a nation on earth today without a national Christian presence, however small.

We gravitated towards interdenominational evangelical agencies, and in the wake of the Iranian Revolution headed for the Middle East in significant numbers. In 1978—the year before the revolution—there were some 1300 of us in the region[12], a number which grew exponentially after Khomeini's arrival. We could not resist a challenge! So many of us applied

---

[12] Johnstone, Patrick. *Operation World*. STL Books and WEC Publications. Bromley England & Waynesboro Georgia. 1978:134.

that mission agencies could keep standards relatively high. An organization like WEC required a 3 or 4-year diploma or a degree in theology from a residential seminary or Bible school plus pre-field linguistics training plus three to four months of pre-field candidate orientation. Even then there was no guarantee that you would be accepted.

As noted, the generations after us were much smaller numerically. Aside from other considerations this led to a scarcity of missionary recruits. Most mission agencies (though not WEC) take a certain percentage of their on-field missionaries' support to pay for home-end expenses so, in order to keep finances up and ministries going, standards plummeted, then dropped even further. By 2003 "1 year of Bible or its equivalent" to be obtained during one's first 5 years overseas was deemed sufficient for acceptance into my own agency.

As a result of this dumbing down, naïve people got on planes "to minister cross-culturally" without having a basic understanding of Christian doctrine, nor of the principles of contextualization, nor of the history of missions in their region, nor of basic language learning techniques. As a result a very high percentage do not learn their target lingua-culture well enough to develop meaningful relationships with locals, let alone preach or teach in those Boomer founded churches. Those few who do learn the language are often so theologically fuzzy, and have absorbed such levels of post-modern "woke" tolerance, that they are suspicious of claims about objective truths. They have little to share in terms of the "old fashioned gospel" which saves and transforms[13]. Many of today's cross-cultural workers provide social services, minister to other expatriates, or return home defeated. The drop-out rate of career missionaries in the first 5 years is so high that agencies do not publish that disheartening statistic.

---

[13] See Pikkert, 2017. *The Essence and Implications of Missio Dei*. Alev Books, Ancaster.

Thankfully, the pendulum has oscillated to its highest extremity and is swinging back. Towards the end of my career I taught numerous missionary candidates the basics of applied linguistics, classic evangelical theology and traditional evangelical missiological practices. This too contributed to making me happy.

Part 2

Exploring: 1982-1986

"The world is a book;
those who do not travel read only one page."
Saint Augustine

13

The Middle East, Back Then

"I shall see the hatred in the eyes of my son and your sons... If they do not know how to take revenge, I shall teach them. And if they agree to a truce or peace, I shall fight against them... I want them to be callous, to be ruthless, to take revenge. I want them to wash away the disaster of 1948 with blood... We'll enter their lairs in Tel Aviv. We'll smash with axes, guns, hands, fingernails and teeth."

Nasir al-Din al-Nashashibi, from "Return Ticket" (1962)

• • •

ON THE LAST SUNDAY of August 1982 I knelt beside the pulpit of Trinity Baptist Church while pastor Payne and the elders laid hands on me and commissioned me for missionary service. The following Thursday, Sept. 2, the folks at WEC also prayed for me and then someone — I don't remember who — drove me to Toronto airport. It was evening. I walked down the chute onto a Royal Jordanian airplane. To my delight I was bumped up to business class.

We flew to Amsterdam, then on to Cairo. There we sat on the tarmac while some passengers disembarked and others got on. Then we were airborne again. Arab airlines could not overfly Israel or the Sinai, so we headed south, down the Gulf of Suez. I photographed *Ras Muhammed* (Muhammed's Head), the tip of the desolate Sinai Peninsula jutting into the azure waters of the Red Sea, as the plane wheeled around. We flew up the length of the Gulf of Aqaba and entered Jordanian airspace. More desert. At 5:45 PM on Friday, Sept. 3, we touched down at the old Marka airport. I walked across the tarmac and entered a small sandstone building. My duffel bag followed soon afterwards. No trouble at customs. A mousy man with an artificial smile was waiting for me. George Kelsey. Greetings and handshakes. He drove me to my new home, a couple of rooms built around a little courtyard. It had a higgledy-piggledy sheet metal roof, and mud walls two feet thick. "Very primitive but sufficient"[14]. There were some basic provisions in the kitchenette: powdered milk, bread, jam... I would be sharing the place with another guy.

We lived between a mosque and the railroad station. The noise emitted by the crackly speakers wired to the top of the minaret was so loud it nearly blew me out of bed an hour before sunrise on my first morning. I discovered that Friday afternoons were also raucous for that was when they preached sermons and read whole Surahs for the benefit of the entire district. The station was no trouble as only a couple of trains departed per week, an ancient steam-engine pulling a string of passenger and box cars along the narrow-gauge track to Damascus.

Back then the region's ruling ideology was Arab nationalism. It had been the galvanizing force behind the struggles for independence which, in some cases, had been long and bloody. As one Arab state after another gained self-government, however, there was a euphoria, a sense of optimism and a fresh resurgence of racial and cultural consciousness, "a great new sense of release and élan"[15]. The Arab League, feeding nationalist hopes, aspired to see the Arab world united, strong in wealth, power and influence.

Since independence the region had been run by former freedom fighters or army officers—"strong men" like Hafez al-Assad of Syria, Saddam Hussein of Iraq, Gamal Abdul Nasser, Anwar Sadat and Hosni Mubarak of Egypt, Boumedienne and Bouteflika of Algeria, Habib Bourghiba and Zine Al Abidine Ben Ali of Tunisia, Muammar Kaddafi of Libya, along with a few monarchs in Jordan, Saudi Arabia and Morocco. While paying lip-service to the Arab nationalist cause or, in the case of Syria and Iraq, to Ba'athism, a form of secular Arab socialism, they enacted draconian measures to hold their artificial constructs of states together; with the exception of Egypt and

---

[14] Letter to Peter and Grace Vermeer, Sept. 5, 1982.
[15] Cragg, Kenneth. *Sandals at the Mosque*. Oxford University Press. New York 1959:62.

Morocco, borders between Arab nations had been drawn by the colonial powers with little reference to ethnic realities on the ground.

One ever-festering issue was the "Palestine Problem." Its roots go back to Theodore Herzl's vision of a Jewish state and the Balfour Declaration, which promised the same land to both Jews and Arabs, and to the Nazi Holocaust, which convinced many of the world's Jews of the need for a homeland to call their own.

In 1948 Britain, exhausted by World War II, returned its Palestine Mandate to the United Nations. The UN partitioned the region into three entities: a Jewish state, an Arab state, and Jerusalem under international jurisdiction. The Arab League opposed the plan; Jewish leadership accepted it. On May 14, the last day of the British mandate, David Ben-Gurion announced the establishment of the state of Israel within the territory granted by the UN. Syrian, Jordanian and Egyptian armies, reinforced by Palestinian *fedayeen*, immediately attacked. Israel withstood the assault, then expanded its territory. Between 750,000 and 900,000 Palestinians fled or were forcibly driven from their homes and scattered into refugee camps in Jordan, Lebanon, Syria, Gaza and Egypt. Only Jordan granted them citizenship.

I was eight years old when the next defining conflict, the Six Day War of 1967, erupted. I vaguely remember my parents following events breathlessly for that generation of Dutch Calvinists were fervent supporters of Israel. Israel routed the Egyptian, Jordanian, Syrian and Iraqi expeditionary forces, took the West Bank and Jerusalem from Jordan, the Golan Heights from Syria, and the Gaza Strip and the Sinai Peninsula from Egypt. Many devout Christians saw that war as a fulfillment of biblical prophecies.

One of the ramifications of that war was that now, instead of having four enemies – Egypt, Jordan, Syria and Israel – the Palestinians only had Israel to contend with. With his scruffy beard and rakish kaffiyeh Yassir Arafat, founder of the

Palestine Liberation Organization, became their symbol, and his organization their *de facto* government.

The PLO first operated from Jordan. When it threatened the balance of power there, King Hussein drove them from the country in September (Black September) of 1970. They moved to southern Lebanon where civil war and a weak central government allowed it to establish a virtual state-within-a-state. In 1974 the Arab world recognized it as the legitimate representative of the Palestinian people and paid it to fight Israel on their behalf. In 1982, the year I landed in Jordan, Israel, tired of PLO raids launched from southern Lebanon, invaded and, with their Lebanese Maronite allies, expelled the organization. Arafat set up shop in Tunisia, far from Israel, safely out of the way. The Lebanese, though renowned businessmen since the Phoenicians plied their wares across the Mediterranean, are a tribal society. Brutal militias organized along sectarian lines (Christian, Druze, Sunni, Shia) proceeded to tear each other, and their country—once the jewel of the Levant—apart.

All this took place against the backdrop of the cold war. The USSR supported Egypt, Syria and Southern Yemen by providing diplomatic support against Israel, selling them sophisticated military hardware and providing advanced technical and logistical support. This, in turn, led the United States to deepen its relationship with Israel, becoming its principal diplomatic and financial supporter. As far as the Arabs were concerned, America had become the enemy's friend.

Oil wealth enabled formerly underdeveloped nations such as Oman, Kuwait, the United Arab Emirates, Bahrain and Saudi Arabia to develop modern social services and integrate into the world economic system. Foreign labor, initially highly specialized Westerners, were brought in to develop the infrastructure. This led to a missionary phenomenon known as the "Tentmaker Movement," so named because, according to the Book of Acts, the apostle Paul sewed tents to provide for himself while engaging in missionary activities. Christians with specific skills moved into regions that were hostile to traditional missionary worked as guest laborers and started "living evangelistically." As the standard of living in the oil-rich nations rose, domestic and other help from South East Asia also arrived. Not a few of these were active Christians as well.

The nationalistic hopes and aspirations of the 1960s had soured by the 1970s. The regional "strong men" did their brutal best to keep a lid on such Islamic fundamentalist movements as the Muslim Brotherhood and, later, Al-Qaeda and its affiliates and factions. The first nation to overthrow its "strong man" was Iran, in that fateful year of 1979. The subsequent Iran-Iraq war threw its long shadow well into the 21st century.

Today many secular-minded Arabs think of the period between independence and the so-called "Arab Spring" of the 2010s, i.e., the era of the "strong men," as a golden age.

This was the world I stepped into.

14

Early Ups and Downs

*"From the first I loved the Arab world. I loved
the haggle of the market place, the cacophony of
the traffic, my little dirt-walled house, the
putrid and aromatic smells, the call of the
muezzin and hawker."*[16]

• • •

"The East is a different world... The busyness, the dust (it
hasn't rained since March), the pace of life... I spent the
first couple of days learning how to buy food, learning
how to haggle, learning how to use the bus system...
Before I buy anything I first have them tell me what it is
in Arabic, as well as a couple of other things on display.
Went to an Arabic church this morning, a tiny group
meeting in a little building. I didn't understand a word...
Have to do my own cooking, which till now has been a
disaster. I had the most horrible tasting rice for supper
yesterday and for breakfast this morning. But it filled me
up. Lots of fresh fruits (grapes, tomatoes, plums and
melons) available in the market, the sook."[17]

LIFE FELL INTO a routine of school, private study, hanging
out with Arabs and chilling with my housemate. Gerhard was a
gentle German and linguistic genius. I wanted to be like him:
courageous and free, living a simple, unencumbered Pauline
lifestyle travelling around the region with a knapsack of
Christian literature, sharing the gospel with anyone who had
ears to hear.

---

[16] Pikkert, P. 1992. *Letter from Kurdistan*. Gerrards Cross: WEC
Publications. p.15.
[17] Letter to Peter Vermeer, September 5, 1982.

I've always enjoyed exploring. At fifteen I travelled around The Netherlands and at sixteen I hitchhiked around Canada's maritime provinces. The Middle East let me take that passion to new levels. Sometimes alone, sometimes with a friend, I climbed ancient citadels and Crusader castles, camped in Wadi Rum using camel dung as fuel and meandered around Jerash's magnificent ruins. Sometimes I'd take a random bus and see where it took me. Once when hiking in the hills along the shores of the Dead Sea we found a large cache of stone arrowheads, hand-axes and other artifacts, photographs of which we sent to the Ministry of Antiquities. On the way to school I looked up at the walls of ancient Rabbat Amman, where Uriah the Hittite was killed. The Zarqa River is the old Biblical Jabbok and Mount Nebo the place from which Moses gazed over the Promised Land. The Kings Way of Exodus fame still runs north to south.

> "Sometimes I feel like I'm walking back into history... You can visualize the Biblical accounts... this is where Jacob wrestled with God, this is where the Jews were refused travel through Edom, and that is the route they took afterwards. This is where the Lord walked, and that is where some of the great battles of the crusades were fought."[18]

I returned repeatedly to Petra, "the rose-red city hewn in stone". Back then it wasn't touristy. Bedouins still lived in its caves. You took a bus to Ma'an, the nearest town, hitched a ride to the *ghour*, shouldered your backpack and started walking. The *ghour* is a kilometer long crack in the mountains. Then, as if by magic, the magnificent *Khazneh*, the treasury, appears, carved into the face of a mountain—just as in TinTin in Arabia!

I'd hike around the amphitheater, along various architectural marvels, past the obelisks showing how high the mountain had been before the ancients leveled the pinnacle to build the Throne of God and the sacrificial high place. Then up

---

[18] Letter to parents, Jan. 22, 1983.

850 steps to the monastery, where I'd scoot up the side of the hollowed-out mountain into which it was carved and stand above the world on the rim of its roof. From there you can see Mount Hor—Jebel Harun—where Aaron, Moses' brother and Israel's first high priest, is said to be buried. I climbed it too. For a dinar you could spend the night in a cave with a Bedouin family. Either that, or I'd find my own cave, spread my sleeping bag on the soft sand, cook a meal on my camping stove and sleep soundly. "I've probably seen more of Jordan than others who have lived here for much longer."[19]

Canadians were given a one-month visa upon entry. After that we had to test our luck at the Ministry of the Interior—a tiresome business. In December 1982 I received a delightful Christmas present. I dressed in my Sunday suit and boldly requested three months. "It took some time, but who can describe my amazement when they returned my passport with a three month visa in it! I was so grateful to the Lord."[20]

Whenever I had to leave and re-enter the country I'd take the train—the old Hejaz line which Lawrence of Arabia had harried—or a shared taxi to Damascus. I'd spend a couple of days exploring its great souk, visit Ananias' house, where the apostle Paul received his call to missions, and play a game of chess under the stern portraits of Yuri Andropov or Konstantin Chernenko on the fourth floor of the Soviet cultural center. I might sip a glass of tea at the al-Nawforaa café and relax in the great Ummayad mosque, once the Cathedral of St. John the Baptist. When the Muslim conquerors absorbed the basilica into their great structure they sought to erase all hints of its Christian origins. They failed. I'd read in George Adam Smith's *The Historical Geography of the Holy Land* that there was a lintel over the south portal which preserves this prayer and prophecy: *"Thy kingdom Oh Christ is an everlasting kingdom, and thy dominion endureth forever."* It took me a long time, but I finally found it. The doorway is bricked-up; you can only see the lintel with its Greek inscription by climbing to the

---

[19] Letter to Peter and Grace Vermeer, March 27, 1983.
[20] Letter to WEC, Dec. 24, 1982.

second floor of the building across the alleyway. I justified all this exploring because I wanted to know everything there was to know about the Middle East: its languages, people, geography, history... I have trays of slides of every place I visited.

Obtaining visas became increasingly problematic. "I received another month's visa. Will have to leave again at the end of the month. This situation cannot go on indefinitely."[21]

"We are hanging on by the skin of our teeth, yet the day before yesterday my room mate and I had supper at the king's palace. This English girl, a music tutor there, had invited us over. She lives there. The contrast was striking. Nothing in this world is what it is in reality. Someday both the church will be shown for what it really is—the bride of the lamb, and the world be shown for what it is— wood, hay, stubble, passing away like a wisp of smoke."[22]

I was driven to master Arabic. I sought fluency not merely to communicate my needs but because I wanted to share the truths entrusted to me with clarity, with power and with conviction. I'd gauge my progress from week to week based on how much I understood of Sunday's sermon. George Kelsey, who pastored a small church, was much easier to follow than native Arabs. As my knowledge of the language, the culture and the region developed, that which initially seemed strange and odd morphed into the familiar. "I am learning to love living in the East more and more. It kind of grows on you after you've gotten over the initial shock."[23]

Then winter hit. There was no escaping the chill in our mud-brick shack. The snow fell almost a foot deep and refused to go away. That was followed by fog and rain. Then Gerhard fell ill, getting sicker and sicker, until he was bedridden and finding it increasingly difficult to swallow. Next his eyes turned almost as

---

[21] Letter to Pete and Grace Vermeer, May 26, 1983.
[22] Letter to WEC Canada, June 22, 1983.
[23] Letter to Peter and Grace Vermeer, Oct. 17, 1982.

yellow as egg yolks; he had hepatitis, but bad. We talked it over and he decided to go home, to Germany.

I missed him. Two new guys moved in, but they weren't of the same caliber; the Dane in particular was a trial. How do you help a burly Viking who misses his mother?

The others had been invited out that Christmas Eve, 1982, but not me. "I'm by myself in this cold shack. However, the Lord was in a cold shack as well on this night."[24]

Christmas Day. It was well after dark. I was watching large snowflakes whirling and glistening in the light of a street lamp. My roommates were huddled homesick and mopey around the kerosene stove. "Guys," I suddenly declared, "I'm gonna find us a Christmas dinner". They watched me grab my coat and leave with the pensive melancholy only the lonely can emote. "Lord," I prayed, "we could use some cheer. Christmas dinner, PLEASE!"

I walked up the dim street. Stores were closed. I saw a light burning down a side street and turned in that direction. It was a tiny store I'd not noticed before. Cigarettes, toilet paper, bread, goat cheese... I glanced up and my eye lit on a large tin of Danish ham. How that pig meat ended up in that Muslim's store I do not know, but I returned home in triumph. The Dane's hollow eyes lit up. We cooked it together, served it with fresh pita bread and olives, and ate by candle light. It was a wonderful feast! But the cold wouldn't let up.

> "The reason there are so many spelling mistakes is because my fingers are literally stiff from the cold. You will be amazed at how cold it gets here. I don't have any heating other than a space heater. I walk around all day in my coat, even wear my woolen hat to bed... Had three eggs for dinner."[25]

The wonky roof leaked in numerous places and we'd walk through the house dodging drips of water. I woke up one night with a steady trickle dropping onto my chest. February became

---

[24] Letter to WEC Canada, Christmas Eve, 1982.
[25] Letter to Peter and Grace Vermeer, Jan. 3, 1983.

March, and the weather did not improve. Fresh snow, numbing cold. Roads were closed, snowplows non-existent. The homesick Dane returned to his mama. Life in the Palestinian refugee camp down the road was pure misery. Old men couldn't remember a winter that severe. Tempers flared.

> "This is a violent world. I've seen people get beaten by the police so badly it wasn't funny anymore. One night after dark we were downtown, and three or four policemen were whaling on this guy. Don't know what he did to deserve that. Then someone from church shot his daughter with a Kalashnikov... She'd married a Muslim, brought shame on the family and the score had to be settled. The only way to do that is to kill the erring family member."[26]

As I stepped out of bed one morning a large portion of the water-logged mud roof fell where my head had been; the top half of the bed was covered in a thick layer of slimy red muck and I thanked God my guardian angel hadn't been asleep at the switch.

I got a bad cold, followed by severe headaches combined with pressure on my teeth and eyeballs. While shivering in bed with a sinus infection and missing school I wondered what the Lord was trying to teach me. It eventually dawned to me.

> "I spent virtually all my time studying or in other language-learning related activities. My spiritual life and my devotional life suffered... Well, with those headaches I couldn't do any language study but did have time to think and get my priorities straightened out...
>
> There is nothing more important than our personal relationship with the Lord, as it is the source of the rest of ministry and relationships. However, don't think I've given up on studying! It is my no. 2 priority!"[27]

---

[26] Letter to Pete and Grace Vermeer, Feb. 8, 1983.
[27] Letter to family, Feb. 9, 1983.

"The Lord has been doing good things in my life... showing how selfish I can be in the realization of good and worthy goals. When the Lord shows us a little more of what lives in our hearts—that is not easy. But it does crowd us to the Lord Jesus... Nothing matters more than knowing Him and walking closer with Him. The existential aspect of Christianity is very real. I pray that I may be one who is able to break the bread of life to many with love and tears."[28]

By April things started to improve. Late one evening Gerhard re-appeared looking hale and hearty. He'd travelled overland from Germany; Gerhard always traveled overland, no matter how far or distant. In the meantime I'd started to connect with some locals. Sitting on a sack of rice, one elbow resting on the counter, I spent long periods of time listening while Ali, the owner of the tiny grocery shop, conducted his business. When things were slack we just shot the breeze or listened to the radio. "Language learning can be really humbling at times but I don't mind making a fool of myself if the reward is fluency."[29]

I fell in with two friends, Basil and Akram, who played chess in a tea house on El-Saada street. We'd sit on a small balcony on the second floor, play a game or two, sip glasses of *chai u na'na'* (tea with mint) and talk politics and religion. In time Basil invited me into his family. With me clinging to the back of his gasping Kawasaki 125 we visited clan members all over Amman and the neighbouring city of al-Salt. He became my entry into the Arab world. Years later I dedicated one of my poorly selling novels to him.

"I simply would not want to be any place else. Many times when walking the streets of Amman, or during devotion times... my heart just wells up with praise to the Lord for the privilege of being here, learning this language and, with every word learned, being one step closer to that

---

[28] Letter to Peter and Grace Vermeer, Jan. 16, 1983.
[29] Letter to family, January 22, 1983.

distant, faraway yet very sharply defined goal of a church composed of Kurds!"[30]

"Oh, there is no greater privilege than to be a missionary... even if your audience is hard and unwilling. May God's Holy Spirit continue His faithful work in the hearts of men, drawing them unto Himself... Reality outside of Christ is the worst of self-delusions. A worldview wrapped around Christ makes sense but outside of Him, well, what a terrible shock people will get on the judgement day. We should almost not be able to think about it without weeping. May God soften our hearts and toughen our skins."[31]

---

[30] Letter to WEC Canada, June 22, 1983.
[31] Letter to Peter and Grace Vermeer, Jan. 24, 1983.

15

Lingua-Cultural Rebirth

"Words do not fade.
What starts as a sound ends up as a deed."
Abraham Heschel

● ● ●

I WOULD BECOME something of an expert on second language acquisition. Much of what I taught later was rooted in the experiences I racked up during my years in Jordan and honed afterwards in Turkey.

Allowing one's self to be reborn lingua-culturally is not easy. It involves more than learning to haggle with vendors in the souq; it is about developing the ability to feel and express one's self in another dimension. This takes years. It is, in fact, a life-long process. It never ends. Not many missionaries manage it, and those who don't—the majority—end up frustrated and with credibility problems. Why should anyone listen to someone who is uncomfortable with their language and culture? And few things are as harmful as missionaries perceived as immature for they undermine the idea that the gospel is powerful and life-changing.

Being reborn lingua-culturally means maturing once again until you are accepted as someone who can speak into the locals' lives with insight and understanding. "It is not enough to just be able to manage. No, but to be able to truly express ourselves and the truths entrusted to us clearly and with power and conviction. That is the goal."[32]

Kelsey's school provided a framework for my day. Every morning his teachers—housewives he'd trained in his method—drilled simple sentence structures into us.

---

[32] Letter to family, February 9, 1983.

Once a week was Show & Tell; we were to take something to class and talk about it. I inevitably forgot so would ad-lib about an item of clothing and, after exhausting that, a body part. On Thursdays Kelsey explained some aspect of the grammar. "You asked if Arabic is difficult. Yes, it is... There are not many westerners who are really fluent. Most stumble along"[33]; "I do a lot of listening. Very helpful."[34]

Arabic is normally written without vowels; you have to know grammar well to insert them correctly. Long before we were ready Kelsey had us adding vowels and reading sections from *Al Ayam* by Taha Hussein, the "dean of Arabic literature". That, I felt, was ridiculous; all this cerebral grammar stuff and rote memorization wasn't me. I wanted to understand what people were saying, not learn where to place jots and tittles. That could come later. If I was to learn the language, I realized, I'd have to do my own thing in the afternoons.

I adopted a child-like approach by finding places in which I could listen to massive amounts of stuff that wasn't over my head—otherwise it was just noise, gobbledygook. If I could understand the essence of what was going on I was learning.

> "Different neighbours have taken it upon themselves to help me... The grocery man downstairs will not let me go until I can name the different items on the shelf. Another guy makes me say the parts of the body every time I meet him."[35]

I went to six different church meetings a week. "Am starting to understand the sermon illustrations pretty well. As soon as they get to the application I get lost."[36] I played a lot of chess with Basil and Akram, all the while listening, listening, listening. Then I started asking simple questions for which I already knew the answers—that way the responses were intelligible.

---

33 Letter to Peter and Grace Vermeer, October 16, 1982.
34 Letter to Peter and Grace Vermeer, January 24, 1983.
35 Letter to Peter and Grace Vermeer, Sept. 19, 1982.
36 Letter to WEC Canada, Jan. 30, 1983.

The vastness of the vocabulary was my biggest challenge. My unfailing companion Hans Wehr, the Arabic-English dictionary, gave multiple Arab words for every one in English. The trick was knowing in what context to use which word. By putting all my energy into understanding I learned to respond intelligently without having to say much. I could nod sapiently and say *na'am, na'am* (yes, yes) in the right places and so keep the other person talking. Concentrated listening also developed my ear, which helped reduce my accent for if you can't hear a sound properly you won't say it right—you revert to the nearest equivalent in your mother tongue. All that listening also helped develop a feel for the grammar.

> "It is almost like a compulsive hobby. When I have nothing to do I enjoy nothing more than... memorizing a new word or two, or put on an Arabic Bible reading tape and follow along in my English Bible."[37]

I bought a small black and white television and watched children's programs and cartoons. I purchased simple children's books and comics. Comics were great because it was all spoken language; there were no difficult descriptive passages. I eventually graduated from TinTin to Agatha Christie. Years later I found myself reading Taha Hussein's *Al Ayam* for pleasure.

Those thousands of hours spent listening and reading paid huge dividends. My vocabulary grew faster because I grasped meanings from context. Now I didn't need to fake it as frequently, pretending to understand when I didn't. I felt shut out less often. When I eventually opened my mouth I could put more mental resources into putting sentences together.

I remember when I started talking in simple sentences in public. One of the mid-week meetings I attended was a young adults' group. One evening they organized a general knowledge quiz on Jordanian history, with each question increasing in difficulty. No one knew the answer to the last question, an arcane bit of info about King Abdullah, Jordan's first monarch.

---

[37] Letter to family, Jan. 30, 1983.

I raised my hand. The emcee looked at me sitting where I always sat, in the back row. He hesitated but when no one else raised their hand, pointed at me and nodded. I answered the question easily in clearly understood Arabic. People turned to look as if they'd witnessed a miracle: the mute had spoken!

Every time someone corrected me I was the winner. I also started hearing my own mistakes, which allowed me to restate what I should have said. Of course I hit plateaus, times when I lost my sense of progress. Each plateau was longer than the previous one. Knowing 500 words only made a big difference at the start. I soon found myself able to greet people, purchase basic necessities and find the right hymn in church. Instead of being perceived as a tourist, I was now accepted as a resident foreign fool. I thought I was condemned to live forever as such, but persevered and eventually experienced a breakthrough. A few tense forms fell into place and my vocabulary grew enough so that I could function reasonably well. That's when people in church—mostly "experienced missionaries"—started asking me to do stuff for them. I readily agreed at first because it made me feel useful. I had reached the level of milk cow, that is, someone to be exploited. To my consternation, however, I discovered that most of the "experienced missionaries" whose language I had admired upon arrival had plateaued permanently at milk cow. I started turning down those ministry opportunities to refocus on language and culture acquisition.

Escaping from the milk cow plateau was difficult. Not only is it easy to coast along at this level, I also faced the problem of decreasing returns. Now, instead of 500 new words, I needed 5000 new words to reach the next level. I didn't think I'd ever break through milk cow. One day I took my Arabic Bible, dictionary and grammar, stacked them on the floor, stood on the pile and cried out to God in frustration, claiming God's promise to Joshua, "every place on which the sole of your foot treads shall be yours!" I persevered because I wanted to earn people's respect. One day I found myself using relative clauses. I also learned to distinguish between formal and casual speech. I had left the milk cow stage behind.

Initially language learning and developing an appreciation of the culture were separate foci. In time the two fused. My growth in linguistic ability had cultural overtones, and I couldn't delve deeper into the culture without expanding my language ability. I learned to differentiate between the central and peripheral meanings of words and discovered how the numerous low-frequency words helped create nuance. I learned to watch people's reactions: what were their facial expressions, gestures and posture communicating? Did I inadvertently offend or say something funny? I started memorizing proverbs; busting one out at the right time always went down well. I grew to appreciate the cuisine, the film, some of the music. Every so often I still listen to Feyruz, Farid al Atrash, Majida ir-Rumi and Marcel Khalifa.

Spending large amounts of time with Basil and Akram and the church's other young adults allowed me to absorb something of their beliefs and assumptions. I repeatedly caught myself saying, "Oh, that's how they feel about that" or "Oh, that's how they say that!" I had graduated to the level of "active member of the young adults' group."

> "I think I have a little bit of a feel for this language... Am having virtually all of my devotions in Arabic now. Just finished memorizing 1 Cor. 13. Am now working on the book of Philippians... In spite of everything I love it here. I relish the challenges. I sometimes sense myself changing character-wise... and any interest in material things is totally eclipsed by a desire for knowledge and character."[38]

"I sometimes sense myself changing character-wise..." Cross-cultural missions is, to a large degree, a cultural and linguistic battle, not just a religious one. How could I model godliness before my new Arab friends if I didn't grasp their values and approach to life? My job, at this stage, was not helping them become like me, but allowing myself to become like them. This was not easy. I'm an introvert and my Arab

---

[38] Letter to Peter and Grace Vermeer, July 11, 1983.

friends loved to, needed to have people around them. They delighted in ribald humour, slapstick fun and laughter late into the night, and had their own unique, and to me, aggressive speech patterns, especially when arguing a point. They happily talked over each other and could track several conversations at a time. Initially I found them loud and chaotic and rude; I couldn't get a word in edgewise. I'd feel excluded because, initially, I could not bring myself to interrupt someone in midsentence. I learned.

My Arab friends had strong opinions about politics, soccer and religion, and loved to argue about these things, marshaling every argument—good, weak and ridiculous—to bolster their position. They'd spend all their ammunition in a single, extended, aggressive verbal attack. This, I discovered, could work in my favour because once they'd expended their ammo I could pipe up and say, "Hey, have you thought of this?" My friends were neither circular nor linear thinkers, but dogmatic and romantic, "feeling deeply" thinkers. They felt strongly about certain things which, I believe, explains honor killings and why the region produces so many suicide bombers.[39]

The unstable economic environment led my friends to different ideas about money and budgeting. If the money was there to meet an immediate need, then use it! It'll all work out in the end! There were things which were not verbalized, things which one needed to sense, things related to sexual matters, or anything likely to incur loss of face. This was tricky to navigate for one not nurtured in it. My friends respected power and the powerful. Without meaning to, they taught me that democratic forms of government could not resolve the chaotic, unstable nature of their world. Open discussions and slowly forming a consensus was not how things were done. Social structures, including the church, cohere around strong leaders and are strongly hierarchical. It's the business of the big man, whether in the family, politics or religion, to set the agenda and he expects "his people" to follow. He won't entrust anything to

---

[39] See Meral, Z. Towards a relevant theology for the Middle East. *Evangelical Missions Quarterly*. April, 2000, p. 210-215.

anyone, no matter how gifted, if they don't embrace his agenda. The straying individual is marginalized or worse. The big man only steps aside at death or if there is a *coup d'etat*.

My Arab friends found it difficult to trust others. I, a naïve Westerner, typically trusted people until they proved themselves to be untrustworthy. My Arab friends would not trust anyone until they had proven themselves to be trustworthy—and then still reserved judgment. For my part, I learned that I could not trust my Arab friends and, later, my Turkish and Kurdish friends, not to use Middle Eastern cultural means to pursue their agendas. That's why cross-cultural missions is, in large part, a cultural battle, not simply a religious one.

> "Making an impact on the thinking of people here is not through well thought out apologetics and argumentation, nor through relief work or hospital work, etc. No, the way is to live and work among them for extended periods of time, eating with them, visiting, listening much more than speaking, learning from them. Oh for a spirit of humbleness and humility. And oh, may that 'aroma', that spirit of the peace of the Lord, rest on us here. There is so little rest and quietness of spirit. The entire culture militates against that spirit of rest, as does the political instability."[40]

Happiness is, at least in part, related to the depth of the relationships we enjoy. The ability to relate meaningfully with those outside the narrow, constricting confines in which we are raised is particularly satisfying. I learned to enjoy being my Middle Eastern self, even if the Dutch-Canadian me always lurked below the surface. However, contextualization at this level is also dangerous. "The other" became a concrete reality: "the Palestinian" is now enfleshed forever as my friend Akram. You also start seeing neighbouring nations and ethnic groups the way your friend does—and you can be certain that is not how Jesus Christ sees them.

---

[40] Letter to Peter and Grace Vermeer, Jan. 4, 1983.

16

Dutch, American, Bangladeshi, Deportation

"We might think that God wanted simply obedience to a set of rules: whereas He really wants people of a particular sort."

C.S. Lewis

. . .

I FIRST MET Frieda Muller at the Sunday evening services held in Kelsey's living room. Miss Muller, as she was universally known, was born in 1911 in The Netherlands. In the 1940s she responded to an advertisement for a "companion for a lady". As the interview wrapped up she was told that in the event she got the job her majesty's secretary would contact her. That was the first indication that she was dealing with royalty. She was hired and became the companion to Her Majesty Zein as Sharaf Talal, King Hussein's mother. I'm not sure when, exactly, this took place, but she appears in a number of photographs taken in 1950 by the Dutch photographer Willem van de Poll. She already seemed very much at home in Raghadan Palace, the king's residence at that time.

Some thirty years later Miss Muller still enjoyed speaking her native Dutch, so she and I often drifted towards each other while helping ourselves to Martha Kelsey's post-meeting refreshments. One day she asked if my roommate and I would accompany her on a picnic. She enjoyed picnicking, she explained, but her position would neither let her go alone—which was, in any case, boring—nor could she go with another man. Taking two youngsters like us, however, would not be frowned upon.

That Saturday my new housemate and I made our way to the palace gates. Miss Muller's blue Volvo, a gift from the king of Sweden to King Hussein, was waved through and we hopped in. She drove with cheerful, reckless abandon to a forest outside the city and popped the trunk. I hauled out a large wicker basket filled with salads, dainty sandwiches and cold drinks prepared by the royal cook, spread out a ground cloth, and we had a jolly time.

Picnicking with Miss Muller became a monthly event. We would stand at the palace gate like Mordecai of old until the azure Volve hove into view. She then chauffeured us at speed to some of Jordan's most beautiful locales where, in the shade of a gnarled olive or an ancient ruin we'd consume food from the king's table and talk.

Miss Muller shared about the fear gripping her and the royal family as they hid in a bomb shelter while Israeli aircraft destroyed the Royal Air Force on the tarmac at the nearby Marka airport. She described the shared angst during the Fedayeen uprising of 1970, and what a close run it had been. She told of looking for a toilet in the lengthy halls of Istanbul's magnificent Dolmabahçe Palace during a royal visit.

I invited her to my birthday party. One of the girls had baked a lovely cake. When someone started slicing into it Miss Muller stepped forward. "Let me take that knife my dear," she insisted. "I cannot bear seeing you butchering that beautiful cake. One of my responsibilities in the palace is cake-cutting." She approved of the girl who butchered the cake and whom I eventually married. After Anna and I moved to Istanbul she became one of our supporters. For years our prayer letters went to *Miss Muller, Raghadan Palace, Amman, Jordan.*

One day the support stopped. Frieda Muller died on Feb. 4th, 2002. She lies buried in the Christian graveyard of Umm al Hiran. Etched on her modest gravestone are the words of Jesus: "I am the resurrection and the life. He who believes in me will live, even though he dies."

■

The Evangelical church in Jordan started in 1926 due to a quarrel among the Orthodox *Al Fawakhri* clan of the town of as-Salt. The dissenters left the old church and asked the Assemblies of God in Jerusalem to send them a cleric. One Roy Whitman, a young missionary recently arrived from the United States, rose to the challenge. His move to as-Salt would be described later as "a major milestone of the evangelical work in Jordan."[41]

Roy married Dora, and in 1941 they established the Evangelical Free Church. Five years later, in 1946, the British established The Hashemite Kingdom of Trans-Jordan and installed King Abdullah as its head. The freshly appointed king made a dusty crossroads with a magnificent Roman amphitheatre his capital.

Bob Blincoe, former US director of Frontiers, tells of Roy's visit to the newly installed monarch during *Eid al-Fitr*, the celebration at the end of Ramadan. When he offered the king his best wishes the monarch's response was jarring.

> "The Christian here before you lied to me," he said. "I asked him to explain the difference between Christianity and Islam, but he said, 'Your majesty, Muhammad and Jesus were like brothers.' Now, Reverend Whitman, I want you to tell me the truth."
>
> Whitman gathered his thoughts and preached the gospel to Abdullah that day. Whitman preached Jesus Christ, the Son of God, the only sufficient Savior, the lamb of God who takes away the sins of the world. He preached the crucifixion, the resurrection, the Great Commission and Christ's glorious ascension to the right hand of God. It was a day Whitman recalled for the rest of his life.[42]

---

[41] Dalleh, Geryis. *The Revival*. Mansouriat Al-Meten, Lebanon: Baptist Publishing House, 1987, p. 145.
[42] https://bobblincoe.wordpress.com/2011/08/12/whitman-a-lesson-in-honesty Retreaved Jan. 3, 2022

This must have taken place in the late 1940s for the king was assassinated in 1951. When I eventually met the Whitmans in the early 1980s they were icons of Jordan's evangelical church. The Arabs referred to him politely as "Mr. Whitman", even if they didn't know another word of English. According to my friend Basil he spoke unaccented, fluent Arabic.

Mr. Whitman's judgement was not, however, flawless. When a Bangladeshi claiming to be a convert from Islam showed up at his door asking for help Roy was hoodwinked. He asked if I'd be willing to house this poor brother-in-the-Lord until they could make alternative arrangements. I wasn't keen, but who was I to say "no" to the great Mr. Whitman? I was living alone for a brief spell so had no excuse. The next day he and Kelsey dropped off a short, skinny nut-brown man boasting a mop of black, oily hair and clutching a large yellow suitcase. I cannot remember his name; he claimed to be a medical doctor. I could not put my finger on it, but I didn't trust the chap. I voiced my concerns to both Kelsey and Mr. Whitman, but was told not to worry. They had checked him out and he was legitimate.

As the weeks rolled by I grew tired of feeding the man and keeping him comfortable. Then he commandeered my typewriter, pecking away late into the nights. One afternoon while he was typing furiously I barged into his room. He tried to shield what he was writing and shouted angrily for me to leave. I left the room but as soon as the typing resumed, stormed back in and yanked the paper from the machine. He grabbed hold of one end of it and in the tussle we tore it in half.

"Are you happy now," he shouted, and began ripping his half of the paper into little pieces. I took a firm hold of his scrawny Bangladeshi arm, yanked him towards the front door, tossed him onto the street and bolted the door behind him.

"Wait till I pack your stuff!" I threw his belongings into the big yellow suitcase and pushed it through the door.

"You'll pay for this," he shouted.

"*Ma' salaami!* (go in peace)", I shouted back, drew the bolt, took a couple of deep breaths and brewed a restorative mug of Arabica. Then I collected the bits of paper strewn about and pieced them together using Scotch tape. It was a report on Christian activities addressed to some police chief. Next I made my way to the Kelsey/Whitman house. They lived in the same building. George opened the door.

"Something wrong?" I handed him the report and told him what had happened.

"Where is he now?"

"I threw him out."

"Hmmm. Yes, we'd become aware that he wasn't who he claimed to be..."

"I nearly lost my sanity over that guy... Unreal. He was such a deceiving wretch! He stayed with me for about a month. Horrible that man. A deceiver... He left the day before yesterday for Syria. He made off with about $1200,- from the church. But the whole affair gave me some real insights into how everything works here, both the foreign work and the national church. I was NOT impressed."[43]

Mr. Whitman had the grace to apologize. After that he'd invite me over for coffee and listen to my stories whenever I returned from an expedition to Kurdistan. "I see you also have the manners of a Kurd," he once groused when I extracted marmalade from the pot using a breadknife. Dora quickly handed me a dainty spoon.

Roy died on Christmas Day, 1992. They had no children but were spiritual parents to many Jordanians. "Three generations of Christians knew him as a man of God. I never heard anyone in my whole life say one negative thing about him. They (i.e. the Arabs) all had great respect for him."[44]

Dora died two years later. A Christian school in Amman is named after them.

They too are missionary heroes.

■

---

43 Letter to Peter and Grace Vermeer, December 1, 1982.
44 Email from Basil Qaqish, December 23, 2020.

One Saturday in March 1983 I went to extend my visa and was told to leave the country within 24 hours. After some arguing that was extended to 48. I was given a police escort, a short, stout fellow carrying a large rifle. He couldn't keep up as I strode from the building and down the street so they replaced him with a slim, long-legged fellow with a pistol strapped to his hip.

I wasn't the first to be deported; during the previous weeks three other students had been given the boot. It looked like the authorities were trying to phase out Kelsey's school.

> "I know they did not kick me out because of anything I've done so much as what we represent—I've been very careful. The others didn't even have a chance to get into trouble as they'd only just arrived from the States and didn't speak any Arabic."[45]

The authorities wanted to put me on a plane to Canada. I protested, so was escorted to the Syrian border instead. There they returned my passport and driver's licence and watched me disappear into no-man's land. The Syrians accepted anyone the Jordanians didn't want.

In Damascus I shaved off my beard, then headed back to the border where I managed to get a fresh entry visa for Jordan. My deportation stamp, buried among a lot of other entry and exit stamps, went unnoticed. Safely back in Amman, I spent the next week or two going from one random embassy to the next filling my passport with visas for countries I had no intention of visiting. Then I applied for a new passport. "My, you travel a lot," the lady at the Canadian embassy commented. "We'll give you a businessman's passport; it's got twice the number of pages".

"Please don't," I pleaded. But she insisted.

---

[45] Letter to WEC, Sunday, March 27, 1983.

That wasn't the end of the story. Miss Muller, indignant about my unwarranted deportation, arranged a meeting with Prince Ra'ad Bin Zeid, chamberlain to King Hussein and who, in the unlikely event Syria or Iraq reembraced the monarchy, was heir to both those thrones. Bin Zeid's investigation revealed some junior officials with Islamist tendencies throwing their weight around. Kelsey received a hand written letter from the prince to help his students get visas, and I had my deportation revoked.

> "The appointment with the prince included myself, George Kelsey and miss Muller, the old lady. It's amazing how the Lord works, isn't it? When I think how down I was when I was expelled—and then this as a result!"[46]

In the midst of all this drama I plodded on with the hard slog of language study.

---

[46] Letter to Peter and Grace Vermeer dated April 22, 1983.

17

First Foray into Kurdistan

"Travelling will leave you speechless,
then turn you into a storyteller."

Ibn Batuta

. . .

Dominated by Mount Ararat, divided by the Tigris and Euphrates rivers, painted ochre by the sands of the Anatolian and Mesopotamian plateaus, dotted by a thousand unexcavated tells, Kurdistan is majestic. It is, however, politically dismembered, linguistically divided, socially fragmented and suffocating under the onerous weight of Islam. For all its majesty, Kurdistan was never more than a pawn in endless tournaments between various combinations of Eastern and Western despots. The Great Powers finally quartered it after the First World War. Kurdistan became a forgotten country, her twenty million souls a forgotten people left to the tender mercies of the Persian, the Arab and the Turk. The very word "Kurd" was wiped from the Turkish vocabulary... But Kurdistan would not be forgotten. Like the mythical Phoenix, first one then another part of Kurdistan rose from the funeral pyre and boldly, briefly, spread its wings before being crushed once again.[47]

I SPENT THE SUMMER of 1983 exploring Kurdistan.[48] A shared taxi took me to Damascus which by then I knew fairly well. This time I kept moving northward to Homs, then to Hama. From there I made my way to Aleppo.

---

[47] Pikkert, P. *Letter from Kurdistan*. WEC Publications. n.d. p. 17.
[48] The highlights of this trip are preserved in the transcription of a cassette recording I sent to WEC in September, 1983,

I spent several days in each city. Hama shocked me. The previous year Hafez Al-Assad's forces had crushed an uprising of the Muslim Brotherhood by bombing the city's heart to smithereens. I wandered through the rubble, awestruck by the scope of the devastation, reminded of photographs of Berlin in the aftermath of World War II. Some haggard women in faded chador haggled for vegetables at a stand between two razed buildings and a motorcyclist zig-zagged down a partially cleared street. An enormous wooden waterwheel in the Orontes river moaned languidly.

I loved Aleppo and would return to it many times. It still retained traces of the vitality and cosmopolitanism which Cairo and Beirut had also shared in their glamour days, before narrow nationalism and militant Islam browbeat them into submission. Located on the trade route between India, Mesopotamia, Asia Minor and the Mediterranean, it had since time immemorial been the main entrepot for savvy middle men trading the exotic carpets, spices, pearls and silks of the east for the wines, woolens, olive oils, perfumes and jewelry of the West. I made my way from the great citadel, where Crusaders like Balwin II, king of Jerusalem, had been incarcerated, to the stone- and brick-vaulted warren of stall-lined alleys and cul-de-sacs of the main souq. I wove my way past stacks of dried fruits, nuts, mounds of new and used clothing, keffiyehs, galabiyas, endless rolls of textiles, stacks of cheap plasticware, racks of copper goods, inlaid boxes and backgammon boards. Old men bent double under grossly overweight loads plodded hither and yon, teenagers navigated heavily laden dollies with reckless abandon, languorous young men sucking cigarettes and ogling girls wandered aimlessly. The aggressive vibrancy of cheerful, clamorous vendors in face-to-face trading hadn't changed in three millennia. I sat on a stool, sipped a rejuvenating glass of sweet tea and enjoyed the hubbub. Then I made my way to the Antioch Gate through which camels loaded with merchandise once entered with heads held high.

From the murky souk to the Baron Hotel, that silent witness to modern Levantine history, is a ten minute walk. I sauntered up Bab Al-Faraj street, where clap-trap Soviet trucks and belching Turkish Fiats vied for space, passed the old clock tower and turned left onto Yarmouk. Four or five minutes later I entered Baron Street and came to its eponymous hotel; the street was named after the hotel, not the other way around.

The Baron encapsulated everything that appealed to my romantic reconstruction of that bygone, glamourous era of late 19th and early 20th century Levantine life. Founded in 1911 by Anatolian Armenians escaping Turkish pogroms, it has seen the rise and fall of every empire—Ottoman, French, British—that had sought hegemony over the region in the 20th century. She survived the roilings of the modern Syrian state until the brutal civil war which, like a gargantuan over-ripe boil, burst and scattered its puss across the region in the wake of the Arab Spring of 2011.

I could not afford to stay at the Baron even back in the '80s, long past her famed glory days, but could still order a drink from the same bar and sit in the same leather armchair on the same arabesque tiles under the same lampshade where Atatürk, the founder of modern Turkey, sipped his beloved raki and where the British double agent Kim Philby drank from dawn to dusk to still his troubled soul. I could savour coffee and nibble baklava where Gertrude Bell, Lawrence of Arabia, Theodore Roosevelt, David Rockefeller, Gamal Abdul Nasser, Winston Churchill, Charles de Gaul, the Shah of Persia and Yuri Gagarin had eaten. Agatha Christie drafted *Murder on the Orient Express* on its terrace and in 1947 King Faisal announced Syrian independence from there.

In the wake of independence the free-flowing stream of adventurers and spies arriving on the Berlin to Baghdad railway slowed to a trickle. Foreigners who called Aleppo home left or were pushed out. A glamourous era faded, though traces of the original vibrancy still stirred. The city still boasted both Islamic and *fin-de-siecle* European architecture, an energetic night life, numerous art galleries and a great museum of antiquities. It was still famous for its cuisine and musicians and large Armenian and Syriac populations; towns and cities with significant Christian communities had a much more easy-going ambiance. As Islamic fundamentalism's stifling grip tightened, the colours faded. By the spring of 2013 all was black.

I crossed the border to Gaziantep, Turkey, then travelled eastward to Urfa, ancient Edessa, the first Middle Eastern city to embrace Christianity. I climbed its castle, wandered through its ancient souq and fed the sacred fish in the pools around the Halil urRahman mosque. I swung south to Haran, of Abrahamic fame. Other than some adobe beehive houses inhabited by the very poor, there was nothing there. I bussed across Anatolia to Elazığ, or Harput in Kurdish. This was my first city with a majority Kurdish population. It had been the center of an uprising, the famed Sheikh Said Rebellion of 1925. From there on to Tunceli, or Dersim in Kurdish. In 1937-38 the Turkish army massacred thousands of civilians in retaliation for a rebellion by Alawite Kurds. Then over the Pontic Ranges to Trabzon on the Black Sea, ancient Trebizond, now a dour, nationalist/Islamic stronghold. I hiked up to the famed 13th century Sumela monastery clinging to the ledge of a cliff outside the city. It was in bad disrepair. Years later extremists from Trabzon would cut the throat of a friend as if slaughtering a sheep for their feast of sacrifice. I was forcibly struck by the morose, heavy, non-progressive ambiance hanging over towns like Trabzon, Dersim, Harput and Elazığ which had had major Christian populations prior to the Armenian genocide of 1915.

I traveled eastward along the Black Sea coast to Hopa, then south, down twisty, minor roads along the Soviet border to Mt. Ararat. I climbed the minaret of a deserted castle overlooking the famed mount and took some photographs. From there I made my way across the Armenian Highlands to Van, on Lake Van, Turkey's largest inland body of water, sallied south along the Iranian border, through some of the most desolate, yet spectacularly beautiful country imaginable. Westward from there over the Zagros mountains along the Iraqi border, and across the Mesopotamian plain to the city Diyarbakir, the unofficial capital of Kurdistan. I'll describe it later, as I returned to it frequently. I then took a bus to Nusaybin, where the

Nestorians once had a famous university, and walked across the border to Syrian Qamishli. From there I made my way to Hasake, then to Raqqa on the Euphrates, a dusty backwater sunk in the natural apathy of desert heat and *kismet,* punctuated by periodic bouts of joyless religious extremism. It gained momentary notoriety as ISIS's capital city. Then to Deir ezZor, Auschwitz for Armenians, and the famous ruins of Tadmor, Palmyra of Solomonic and Queen Zenobia fame. I finally turned homeward, back to Jordan, via Damascus.

It was with trepidation that I embarked on that first trek as back then only eccentrics ventured to these places. I wondered what I would face when I stepped off the bus: where would I sleep, would people be friendly, would I be in danger? Initially I imagined all sorts of unsavory scenarios but after a week or so my fears evaporated. Things always worked out, sometimes in the strangest ways. The Lord took care of logistics and I always found a place to sleep, usually in some inn charging between $1 and $3 a night. For $3 you got a swept room and a decent bed—though I did wake once in a $3.- hotel to find a big rat sharing my mattress. In the evenings I'd hang out in a local tea house. One after another small-time traders and country yokels wearing flat caps, dusty waistcoats and baggy shalwars dribbled in. They'd step through the door, nod amiably in all directions, greet acquaintances and, with a grunt, lower themselves onto a stool. When the glass of tea arrived they inserted a piece of rock sugar between lower lip and teeth and sip the strong brew through that filter. Through the acrid haze of Samsun Oriental or Lattakia we'd watch a pint-sized general sporting an oversized cap with double braids on the bill harangue us on the flickering black-and-white T.V. I couldn't understand the man who'd led the 1980 *coup d'etat* any more than a suckling child, but sensed the tension around me. Every so often the place would burst into angry expostulations.

Those six weeks on the road gave me a feel for both eastern Turkey and north-eastern Syria. Each town had its own ambience. Van was different from Hopa, from Diyarbakir, from Urfa. To my surprise few of the larger cities were solidly

Kurdish. Though there were millions of Kurds in the region, certain districts contained large minorities of Arabs and Turks. The lingua-franca everywhere, however, was Kurdish, still an illegal language. I learned that the dialects spoken in Syria and Turkey were very similar.

I made two contacts whom I followed up later. Hassan worked for the PKK, the Kurdish Freedom Fighters, in Van. One of his jobs was to contact any foreigners who strayed that far east, find out what they were up to and excite them about the Kurdish cause. I spent a lot of time with him. Hassan was adventurous. He had taught himself English from cassettes and books and was keen to practise it. I spent several days with him climbing around Van's castle, hiking, and talking late into the night about all things Kurdish, as well as about my beliefs and his. He wasn't sure about Islam because, as a Kurd, he felt deserted by the rest of the Islamic world. I sensed a hunger. He introduced me to his family and gave me other contacts to follow up. For some time he reappeared repeatedly in my life.

My other contact was in the Syrian border town of Al-Qamishli. As soon as I walked across no-man's land into the city I sensed there was something different about the place. The streets were orderly—the French had laid it out—and the majority of women wore western clothes. Also, I could communicate again. I felt at ease, safe, and wondered if there might be a large Christian minority there. I heard bells pealing in the distance, followed the sound to a Syrian Orthodox church and asked the janitor if there was an evangelical church as well. Voila, he lived beside it! I walked home with him and he introduced me to pastor Butrus. Pastor Butrus was a big-hearted young man so interested in the work I was contemplating that he offered to find me a place to live when I was ready to tackle Kurdish.

Exhilarating as it was, the trip took an emotional toll. A case of food poisoning in Hakkari had left me weak. Seeing terrible poverty up close was emotionally draining: filthy villages; people with no legs dragging themselves along dirty streets; lepers with stubs for hands and half-eaten faces begging for pennies... and the sense that this had gone on year in year out, for centuries, without let-up, without progress, life just rolling over in an endless cycle of birth, cruelty and death. I felt powerless; was I really expected to introduce change to this? I questioned divine love. "God, how can I, supposedly your representative, claim that you love the world? I am here today and gone tomorrow while these people continue to eke out their miserable existences until they die, only to perish eternally after that! Something doesn't compute, God... And if you don't love them, how can you expect me to...?"

It is a dangerous train of thought, one which would haunt me years later. I snapped out of it this time by reading Isaiah and by focusing on the positive: cliff climbing with Hassan, earning his approval; travelling through country so desolate yet so beautiful that the Kurd in the seat next to me exclaimed in Arabic, "Oh, that I could die and be buried here"; eating rice and beans high in the mountains, up in the clouds, barely able to contain my joy: I had made it to Kurdistan yet, instead of feeling lonely, I was filled with that marvellous sense of destiny you get when you sense that you are in the stream of God's will. I found an old Kurdish *Injil*, the four gospels, in a used bookstore and came to believe that I could learn the language in spite of the Turkish government's efforts to eradicate it. I hung on to the vision that, in the long run, the church of Jesus Christ would be established and shed its light in these gloomy crevasses of the kingdom of darkness.

I arrived back in Amman lean and exhausted both physically and emotionally, but with a stronger sense than ever that these were the people to whom the Lord had called me. For the next three months I threw myself into my Arabic studies. I planned to return to Kurdistan at the first opportunity.

18

Longings

"Only the lonely (know the way I feel)."

Roy Orbison

• • •

December 23, 1982

"Some day the Lord will bring the right girl into my life. Right now there are no prospects... How I shudder when I think how close I got side-tracked through Ashley. I have really mixed feelings about that romance. Sometimes when I think back it about breaks the heart, and sometimes I leap for joy when I think that God gave the character to break up that relationship, because I really did love her very much."[49]

February 27, 1983

"There are some nice girls in the language school, but they don't stir me in the slightest. You remember how easily I used to get infatuated? Well, no more. Ever since breaking up with Ashley, nothing has stirred those dead embers. I can think of her now with detachment."[50]

March 27, 1983

"It is important to be married if you want to have a viable ministry here... If you are not married, you don't really count... Your ministry is restricted to other single guys...

---

[49] Letter to Peter and Grace Vermeer, December 23, 1982.
[50] Letter to Peter and Grace Vermeer, February 27, 1983.

I'm convinced that it is most important to reach the heads of households. You've got to be married to be able to do that... As a single you have an advantage in language learning. I travel very easily... I hope I can lay a firm foundation in this first term into which I can bring a wife with a clear conscience, something I could not do now because of the nature in which I'm operating, i.e., running the risk of being expelled any moment. How can you raise a family under that kind of pressure?"[51]

June 7, 1983

"I had braced myself about having to wrestle my emotions under control on a regular basis but, praise the Lord, that has been one of the least of my problems, in spite of the fact that the language school is a veritable bachelors' paradise, with all these single girls running around."[52]

September 13, 1983

"There are two new single WEC girls here, one from the States and one from Germany... a refreshing setup."[53]

October 13, 1983

"Sometimes, to be quite honest, I wish I were married."[54]

November 11, 1983

"I was most interested to read that Grace has taken it upon herself to pray for a wife for me. I admit I have been praying almost daily myself in that

[51] Letter to Peter and Grace Vermeer, March 27, 1983.
[52] Letter to WEC Canada, June 7, 1983.
[53] Letter to WEC Canada, September 13, 1983.
[54] Letter to Peter and Grace Vermeer, October 13, 1983.

direction—that the Lord will work in both her heart—whoever she may be—and mine, that we may serve Him well together. I suppose the characteristic that I'm really looking for is that she really backs me up, spurs me on in reaching the Kurds for the Lord whatever the price involved on ourselves. How I would love a girl that has the same goals and aspirations as I have."[55]

March 16, 1984

"If I'm sure of one thing it's that He truly wants His best for me, that He loves me and gives me the grace to grow and live as a single at this point in time. However, the desire to share intimately and deeply with someone is sometimes very strong. But He will bring the right girl at the right time; I fear manipulating anything in that area!"[56]

---

[55] Letter to Peter and Grace Vermeer, November 11, 1983.
[56] Letter to Peter and Grace Vermeer, March 16, 1984.

19

Second Foray into Kurdistan

"I am not free and independent;
I am a traveler with duties."

Said Nursi

• • •

IN NOVEMBER 1983, less than three months after my first foray, I returned to Kurdistan. After picking up a new passport at the Canadian embassy in Ankara to stem the flow of increasingly difficult questions from Jordanian border guards I boarded an overnight bus to Van. I'd hoped to reconnect with Hassan but he was nowhere to be found. I wandered the drab winter streets of that bleak frontier town wondering what to do next when I heard a British accent behind me saying, "Oh, yes?" I turned, saw a foreign gentleman speaking English to a Turk, and butted into the conversation. I learned that the Englishman worked for the World Bank, was supervising the vaccination of cows in eastern Turkey, had been living in a dreary hotel for months, was behind in his work and was lonely and depressed. For the next couple of days he took me to outlying villages during the day while I typed up his reports in the evenings.

I eventually connected with Hassan; he'd been on a smuggling expedition to Iran. When asked how he got across the mine fields he explained that donkeys were cheap; just push one or two in front to clear the way. I said goodbye to the World Bank man to begin two weeks of Kurdish language study in the backs of carpet shops and tea houses. Learning Kurdish was illegal, so we had to be careful. Although my association with the World Bank fellow had kept the police from inquiring too closely, learning Kurdish in secret was difficult to pull off. I wondered about staying in a Kurdish village, away from prying eyes and eavesdropping ears. Hassan, about to embark on another clandestine trip to Iran, said he would leave me with relatives in the village from which he launched his border crossings and pick me up on his return two weeks later.

We traveled to said village where I was introduced to the elders, enjoyed a communal meal and, late that night, bedded down with the Pesh Merga, the Kurdish guerilla army. It was still dark when Hassan and a relative shook me awake. They were visibly tense. Leave as fast as possible, they whispered. Informers had seen us and knew Hassan was going to Iran. They assumed he was to fetch drugs for me and had sent someone to Van to inform the police.

Informers get a bounty for every smuggler they turn in, and drug offenses have grave consequences. Police and judges are corrupt, the notion of innocent until proven guilty blatantly disregarded, prisons awful, and the Kurdish east considered a suitable place to make someone disappear from mankind's sight. The book *Midnight Express* is most eloquent on some of these matters. I ran to the road as fast as my legs allowed, flagged down a vehicle and returned to Van—an ignominious retreat for one who'd arrived the previous day wondering if this was the first of many villages to respond to the gospel. In Van I headed straight for the bus terminal and boarded the first vehicle leaving town.

Before we parted Hassan had penned a short, introductory letter for me to give to the elders of his home village. It took three fear-filled days to reach Beytüşşebap, the nearest town. Once we were stopped at a road block where a military policeman pulled me aside and led me into one of those squalid but scrubbed buildings common to armies the world over. There they started interrogating me. It was like being in a Grade B movie: a little room with the single bulb dangling over a rickety wooden chair while a beefy, Arabic speaking officer threatened and blustered. I told him I would truthfully tell him anything he wanted to know about me personally but wouldn't say anything about anyone else under any circumstance.

"Why not?"

"Because, sir, I don't want them to end up in this chair." He looked at me for a while, left me alone, then returned and told

me to leave. When I finally reached Beytüşşebap I headed
straight for the military police station. They found an Arabic
speaker. I informed them I was a Canadian doing research on
eastern Turkey and would appreciate all the help they could
give. That was a good move. I was shuttled from office to office,
with the interpreter in tow. The offices got nicer and nicer until
I left the building with a written and stamped police permit
letting me visit not only the village of my intentions but several
others as well. They even provided me with a guide! I wasn't
happy about that, knowing he'd be an informer. However, they
could not find the chap they wanted so they collared an old man
from Hassan's village and ordered him to look after me.

I would visit Bezal a number of times during the next several
years. Bezal was its Kurdish name[57]. Note the past tense. In the
late 1980s the Turkish army razed it, along with hundreds of
other villages, forcibly ending thousands of years of pastoral,
migratory Kurdish tribal society. Hoping to dilute the Kurdish
nationalist movement they'd hoped to "catch the fish by
draining the swamp", i.e., by driving the villagers into the cities
where they thought they would be easier to control. This was a
terrible miscalculation for instead of controlling the problem
they exported it all over the country. The rapidly expanding
gecekondos (shantytowns) on the outskirts of Diyarbakir,
Istanbul, Ankara, Izmir and elsewhere became hotbeds of
embittered young Kurds planning and executing revenge.

Bezal was located high in the mountains, nestled in a
beautiful *yayla* (highland plateau). From Beytüşşebap it was a
stiff, three hour climb over narrow mountain paths through
some of the most spectacularly beautiful, wild country I have
ever seen. My guide turned out to be an uncle of Hassan and
upon me producing Hassan's letter his attitude changed from
worried aloofness to a bear hug. "Hassan's friend is my friend;
Hassan's enemy is my enemy!" he exclaimed in Arabic. Upon
arrival he introduced me to the rest of the family. Because of its

---

[57] It was called *Orah Köy* in Turkish, meaning "Over There Village".

proximity to Iraq a number of the villagers spoke Arabic, allowing me to communicate with them.

I had several scary moments, the worst occurring during my first evening. Bezal was controlled by the Pesh Merga. Because of my two weeks of Kurdish studies with Hassan, and because certain words in the conversation swirling around me were similar to Arabic (notably the word *jasus*, "spy") I knew they were trying to decide whether or not I was sent by the government. Hassan's family thought I was OK, the neighbours wondered. Thankfully, the decision fell in my favour.

I entered into village life drinking endless glasses of tea, chopping firewood, being introduced to everyone including the village head, sleeping with the men in a communal sleeping room, Kalashnikov guns separating us, eating what they ate, freezing when they froze. I learned many things, including stripping and assembling various firearms.

I was reading the Acts of the Apostles at the time and was not just struck by the miraculous power that accompanied the establishment of the Jerusalem church (healings, movements of the Spirit, powerful and convicting preaching), but also by my own impotence. One night I cried to God, asking what good my being there actually was, barely able to communicate, and with half the inhabitants viewing me with suspicion.

While eating breakfast with a neighbouring family I noticed a dumb looking boy of about 4 or 5 years of age. The father communicated that the child was deaf by standing behind him and yelling at the top of his voice. The kid was completely oblivious to the father's clamor. The mother's dumb cow-eyes gazed at me hopefully. My heart sank. Who do these people think I am, I thought.

This was not the first time someone had approached me for healing. Earlier an Arab had accosted me, asking if I was a disciple of Jesus. When I answered affirmatively he challenged me to heal a blind beggar sitting nearby. I still remember his triumphant smile as I slunk away humiliated. I wondered if God was taking a perverse delight in making me, his representative, look like a fool. Then the wife started digging through an old trunk to produce a prescription for a hearing aid. They had taken the child to Ankara the previous year but didn't have the money needed. I told them to give me those papers.

Later that week it clouded over. My host told me that unless I wanted to stay till spring I had better depart for soon snowfall would render access to or exit from the village impossible. Early the next morning a boy and I double rode a horse down to Beytüşşebap. While he turned around and rode the beast back home I checked in with the military police.

At a roadblock on the way back to civilization they took my "Christian propaganda", a few brochures I had with me, and waved them in my face. "You're a missionary," the officer spat out, wagging a minatory finger under my nose.

"Sir, do you see my beard?" I asked unctuously, stroking my facial hair with gentle dignity.

"What about it?"

"Well, sir, because I am bearded people think I'm a Muslim, I carry this literature with me to explain to them why I am not."

The man laughed. "You people always have an answer, don't you? Take your stuff and go!"

I made my way to Istanbul, where a dealer informed me that the prescribed hearing aid cost 65,000 Turkish Liras (±US$250). I didn't have that kind of money so departed empty handed. When exploring the sights of Istanbul, however, I struck up a conversation with an American tourist. He suddenly started asking lots of questions, then asked if we could meet again. We did so on the day before he left and he gave me his leftover liras; you couldn't change liras back into foreign currency back then. The amount was exactly what I needed for that hearing aid.

However, I had also become alive to the risks of ministering in Kurdistan.

> "More than ever I know the dangers, and in some ways I go back with loathing. A verse that has really burned its way into my heart is Luke 9:62, *"No one who puts his hand to the plow and looks back is fit for service in the*

Kingdom of God." Pray that I may firmly grasp the plow and keep both eyes on the goal. Pray that God will quicken my brain with respect to language learning. Let us pray above all that we may live a life of spiritual power, a life of close, constant walking in fellowship with our Lord."[58]

---

[58] Report for WEC Canada, Jan. 6, 1984.

20

1984

*"Men can only be happy when they assume that
the object of life is not happiness."*

George Orwell

■ ■ ■

1984 WAS A GOOD year from both a lingua-cultural and spiritual perspective. Because I mixed much with people I absorbed Arabic sufficiently to know intuitively what was right and what was not. I felt increasingly at home culturally, though not yet to the point where all my social needs were met by my Arab friends. "But may the Lord enable me to see things more and more from their perspectives, from their backgrounds, standing in their shoes."[59] Re-reading my correspondence of 1984 is interesting; Christian biographers write hagiographies based on that kind of stuff.

> "Oh Lord, you know my struggles even to utter a prayer. But you will not let me go because you are faithful, and others are praying on my behalf... Oh, more than anything else I want to be a man of God. When I see how His hand has been on me, well, it's enough to bring tears to my eyes. May we go and bear fruit, fruit that will last. First, the fruit of the Spirit in our lives, and then see that fruit reproduced in others."[60]

> "Entering a new culture, struggling with a strange language, facing situations you could never have imagined brings to the surface things which you didn't know live in you...

---

[59] Letter to Peter and Grace Vermeer, March 16, 1984.
[60] Letter to Peter and Grace Vermeer, February 12, 1984.

107

However, the exposing of this selfishness, fear, lack of love, irritability, home-sickness, loneliness, or whatever the thing happens to be at that particular point not only enables us to deal with it through confession and seeking the Lord's forgiveness, it gives a sense of permanent dependency on Him. Indeed, the Lord has been good, and I face the future with joy and assurance."[61]

"The only way the church of Jesus Christ is ever going to be established in these parts is through life-time commitment to the task. I went through a bit of a thing recently when it seemed as if the Lord was saying, "Peter, do you have any other secret ambitions? Are you prepared to spend the rest of your life here? Well, it was bit of a struggle, but I can now rest in the fact that He has called me to lifetime service among the Kurds, or until He shuts the door."[62]

Everything I wrote was most sincere. Much of it was untested and would fail the tests that were coming.

I completed Kelsey's program in March and made my way to Istanbul, where WEC's leader arranged for room and board with an old widow and her son Daoud. They offered me a lumpy sofa in the frowsy, smoke-filled living room of a tiny fourth-floor apartment in a sketchy part of town. I put my foot down, insisting on Daoud's microscopic bedroom; he could sleep on that stain-filled couch.

Like Arabs, Turks love hanging out late into the night. My hosts wondered what I did alone in that frigid bedroom after 9 PM—but those few square meters of private space kept me sane. Living with them was ideal from a lingua-cultural perspective. The old woman didn't know a word of English but loved to talk, while Daoud, with whom I got along well, knew some. They fed me breakfast and supper, usually something greasy and odd-tasting, but there was always plenty of it. Although at times my stomach churned, I never got sick.

[61] Letter to Peter and Grace Vermeer, March 16, 1984.
[62] Letter to Peter and Grace Vermeer, August 14, 1984.

At first I lost my bearings in that run-down, working-class warren of narrow, cobblestoned streets. "I live in a bad part of town; a real hooker district close by."[63] Pornography was ubiquitous; I didn't know how to escape it. At one point I didn't want to step outside the house for fear of being unduly affected by it. Not until the Islamist Ak Party came to power in 2002 was the raunchy media pushed from that urban shadow land.

For three months I studied Turkish part-time at a small language school. "I'm breaking my brain trying to pick up some Turkish. It is very difficult... However, we simply plod on."[64] I'd leave the house at the same time as Daoud, a tout in the covered market, and wouldn't return home until evening. After class I'd pick up lunch somewhere and spend an hour at the British Council to do homework. After that I'd saunter casually to the nearby Hilton, read the Reuters news printout on the bulletin board, order a glass of tea and finally accomplish what I really came for: sit on a clean toilet blessed with toilet paper! For the rest of the afternoon I indulged my passion for exploring.

I might take an overcrowded bus to a historic district, like the old Constantinople of Sultan Ahmed, or to Eyüp, or the Covered or Egyptian Markets or to Pera on the other side of the Golden Horn. I'd poke around the back streets by the Saint Sophia, the nearby Blue Mosque and the Egyptian obelisks. I'd buy a *lahmajun*, thin flatbread with minced meat, from a street vendor and drink tea in the garden tucked between the old book bazaar, the Beyazit Mosque and the stepped square before Istanbul University's imposing gate. Or I might take the clanging subterranean funicular from Karaköy to Beyoğlu and reconnoitre the warren of cobblestone streets and shops around the Galata Tower, to emerge on Istiklal Boulevard, then Istanbul's high-end shopping district. From there I could walk to Taksim Square, watch a Gipsy beat his mangy bear to get it to dance and take an evening bus home. Or I might take a ferry

---

[63] Letter to Peter and Grace Vermeer, May 26, 1984.
[64] Letter to Peter and Grace Vermeer, April 6, 1984.

across the Bosphorus to Chalcedon while sipping a cup of *sahlep*, a hot, milky drink made from orchid tubers and be entertained by high-octane vendors selling unrivaled lemon squeezers or the world's best shoe laces as Istanbul's magnificent, minaret-filled skyline slipped by. Sometimes I'd simply ride a random bus to the end of the line. Beyond its historic heart the vast city was, by and large, a sadly unglamourous sprawl of working-class tenements and *gecekondu* slums of muddy streets filled with mangy curs, skinny cats, thin-lipped women in black, wily, worldly-wise guttersnipes and bow-legged babies wandering aimlessly in sagging diapers. Gobs of electrical cables slung precariously from one building to the next, and after the dismal grind of a working day men filled the tea-houses.

Back then cheap coal was the main source of heat so winter pollution was terrible. From December to March a sulfuric haze enveloped the city and everything was covered with a sooty grime. Water, cold only, ran for about 2 ½ hours a day, and I developed an appreciation for the local communal Turkish bath. I connected with a small church of ex-Syriac and ex-Orthodox Arminian Christians and joined a Turkish choir in an Armenian church. Some basic Turkish fell into place: "I have my landlady in stitches sometimes. But we really communicate."[65]

One afternoon while sitting on a park bench idly watching the great unwashed pass by, a flock of sparrows fluttering greedily around some fragments of bread and a gurgling pigeon strutting coquettishly, puffing out its breast and curtsying manfully before its sweetheart, I heard someone call my name: "Petter? Petter!" There, rubbing his eyes and looking thunderstruck, was the very Hassan with whom I was nearly arrested on the Iranian border.

"What a reunion! That was surely of God! He was supposed to be in Van, eastern Turkey, and then to run into each other in Istanbul, a city of 6 million people! We

---

[65] Letter to Peter and Grace Vermeer, May 26, 1984.

had a good time together, and I had a wonderful opportunity to share the gospel with him... I'm meeting him again tonight, and hope to catch up with him in July. He was dumbfounded with surprise at seeing me sit there... I'm convinced God arranged for us to meet..."[66]

When the middle-man who purchased his village's chestnuts defrauded them the elders had ordered Hassan to kill him. While they negotiated blood money with the middle man's family Hassan went in hiding. The best place to hide is in a crowd and Istanbul, by any definition, fits that bill.

After we parted I purchased the hearing aid for the deaf boy in his village. A technician showed me how to adjust the thing and gave me a pocketful of ear pieces; one was bound to match the ear in question.

"Pray with me that this boy was born deaf for the sake of the Kingdom of God. Oh, that he may hear, and that this may give me real acceptance and favor in the eyes of the family and that whole village of 170 people, thus making it possible to learn the language and so communicate the truth in word as well as deed."[67]

In June I said goodbye to the widow and Daoud and headed eastwards. I'd been warned repeatedly against returning to the region. Banditry had increased and the PKK, the Kurdish guerillas, had started showing its teeth. It was becoming a war zone.

"Pray… that the Lord protect me from bandits."[68]

"Pray that the authorities may not enter the villages I'm frequenting, as these are really nationalistic Kurdish villages, the men freely carrying Klashnikovs, etc. If the authorities entered suddenly I would be suspected of

---

[66] Letter to Ken Getty, May 23, 1984.
[67] Letter to Peter and Grace Vermeer, April 6, 1984.
[68] Letter to WEC Canada, May, 23, 1984.

having betrayed them, and who knows what the end will be then. Sometimes I'm afraid."[69]

I took a train to Ankara, a bus to Diyarbakir and a minibus to Beytuşşebap, the town nearest Bezal, the Kurdish village with the deaf boy. Someone told me there was no-one in the village. They were semi-nomads who led their flocks to summer mountain pastures where grass is abundant, the air fresh, the water clean and they were far from the reaches of the government. I was despondent. Who should I run into, however, but the same wiry old man, Hassan's uncle, who had led me to Bezal the first time! I showed him the hearing aid and that afternoon he led me for hours along a narrow trail over the northern reaches of the Zagros mountains. At long last a stunningly verdant plateau opened before us, the sun painting the surrounding snow-covered peaks pink, a scattering of black goat-hair tents etched against the lush green of the dale, sheep and goats gamboled cheerfully in the evening gloaming, and I was warmly welcomed.

The next morning I laid the deaf boy's head in my lap, plugged different earpieces into his ear and fiddled with the volume. Suddenly he winced! Tears flowed down my cheeks as I lowered the volume. Using pebbles I taught him to count to ten in Kurdish.

One night someone roused those with whom I shared a tent. A caravan of donkeys carrying weapons for the Pesh Merga had arrived and needed unloading: AK 47s, boxes of ammo, and hardware I didn't recognize in the dark. I pitched in, knowing that if the Turkish military showed up my goose was cooked.

I caught the end of an era. Trays of stunning slides I took then and during two subsequent trips record the final chapter of centuries of Kurdish nomadic pastoralism: women in colourful, multilayered clothing forming a V through which the kids drove the flock: each would grab a sheep's teat and milk it as it made its way through the human chute. Women squatting,

---

[69] Letter to Peter and Grace Vermeer, May 26, 1984.

weaving goat-hair into a bedouin tent or making *mast*, a sour
yoghurt drink in a sheep's skin suspended from a tripod.
Children at play. Men in costume on horseback. Someone
playing a bag-pipe-like instrument made from a complete goat
hide. Someone took my camera and shot me washing myself
outdoors in a tub of water over an open fire, and then in
Kurdish dress. That photograph graced the cover of a booklet I
wrote after my crisis of faith.[70] After a week I was ready to move
on but they prevailed on me to stay a few more days. The
reason became clear: while I was enjoying village life the deaf
boy's mother had been busily weaving a unique prayer rug with
two crosses embedded in it for me. It now graces our living
room floor.

I spent some ten days with them, then trekked for six more
weeks through the region re-connecting with old contacts and
trying to make new ones. My vision was of a circuit route of
villages where I was befriended, trusted and welcomed.
Eventually I walked across no-man's land to Qamishly, Syria,
revisited the dreary towns of Deir ez-Zor and Raqqa, then to
Palmyra, across the desert to Damascus, south to Dera'a, and
across the Jordanian border.

Then I became sick. I could swallow neither food nor water
and felt weak as a kitten. Hepatitis. It was bound to happen; in
Kurdistan I had eaten and drank whatever the tribesmen gave
me. "My eyes and skin are the strangest colour yellow—like
grapefruit skin, but other than feeling totally debilitated there
are no real aches or pains."[71] I was housebound for six weeks, a
lonely time as my house mates had not yet returned from their
peregrinations. Church women fed me while I memorized
screeds of Arabic. My friend Basil dropped by regularly for
games of chess.

That autumn I enrolled in the University of Jordan's
advanced Arabic program where I befriended one Salih Güven,
a Turkish army captain studying Arabic on a scholarship. Salih
had also enrolled in a course at the Islamic Law College, and

[70] *Letter from Kurdistan*, WEC Publications, 1992.
[71] Letter to Peter and Grace Vermeer, August 29, 1984.

knowing my interest in religion suggested I tag along. He wasn't sure if Christians were allowed in but proposed we walk into the lecture hall together speaking Turkish. It worked like clockwork. "I'm attending a lecture a day in the Islamic law college. Very, very interesting, as you can imagine."[72]

The teacher, a tall charismatic fellow, lectured for an hour during which students could jot their questions on a slip of paper and pass that forward. He then spent half an hour answering the queries which had landed on his desk. He once maintained that the root of distrust which exists among Christians goes back to Judas Iscariot's betrayal of his master and fellow disciples. "Ever since there has been an inextirpable strand of mistrust and suspicion among Christians," he pontificated.

A student raised a hand. "Sir," he asked, "Is this teaching not offensive to Christian ears?"

"Any Christians here?" the professor demanded. I raised my hand, then stood up. He looked at me, several hundred pairs of eyes following the direction of his gaze.

I smiled and made a disarming gesture. "Sir, I do not relate to anything you are saying," I said.

"Let's talk after class," he responded. I nodded and sat down. We exchanged pleasantries afterwards.

Our Arabic teacher once told us to write a hundred words on the subject of Allah. I wrote Islam's ninety-nine names for God in neat columns, then added, *And in addition to all of these God is love (Bible: Romans 8:39)*". He gave me a perfect score. I sat my exams that December and received a diploma in Advanced Arabic.

Christmas Eve, 1984. The church youth decided to go carolling and asked me to chauffeur them in Kelsey's car. One young fellow wore a cheap Santa Claus outfit. As we drove from one church family to another singing carols at the tops of our voices the police stopped us and arrested our Santa Claus. I insisted on going along to the station; in the dark they didn't notice that I was a foreigner. We were seated on a hard bench

[72] Letter to Peter and Grace Vermeer, November 6, 1984.

and told to wait. There were four or five other despondent Santas, their beards in their laps or dangling from their hands. I noticed to-ing and fro-ing into a particular office, and when the door swung open caught a glimpse of someone with heavier epaulets sitting at a desk. I got up and stepped through that door. The officer's head snapped up. I nodded politely and asked if I could please take my Santa home. He then realized I was a foreigner, and told me I was free to leave.

I made my eyes twinkle friendly-like. "Sir," I said firmly yet with a smile, "I came with Santa Claus and I'm leaving with Santa Claus."

"We can't let you have Santa Claus," he said. "We have word of an imminent terrorist attack by someone dressed like Santa."

"Do I really have to believe that, sir?" I laughed. "Isn't this about harassing Christians? Listen, sir, just give me my Santa. I know him and can assure you he's no terrorist. He's the only one I'm asking for. You'll never hear from me again." The man looked me over, gave an order and released the young man into my care. "When other people were opening Santa's presents, I was trying to get him freed! It was really pretty funny, when you think about it."[73]

---

[73] Letter to Peter and Grace Vermeer, December 26, 1984.

21

Anna

"One day you will ask me what is more important? My life or yours? I will say mine and you will walk away not knowing that you were my life."

Khalil Gibran

• • •

April 2, 1984

"I do have one other tidbit of information... I think I may be in love. Don't worry about my making any rash decisions... I've not so much as kissed her... I'd always thought that here was one girl absolutely out of my reach. However, it appeared that she'd been a little 'taken' with me for some time too, which was gratifying. We'll see what happens. She's going to the Sudan, I'm not."[74]

April 15, 1984

"Yes, I'm in love, and what a delicious feeling!... Her name is Anna Kennedy. She is Irish... and she loves me! More importantly, she spurs me on to stick with the vision I believe the Lord has given me. She has blue eyes, very curly hair (natural curls) a real servant, organized, smart as a whip. She is good linguistically... What with her going to the Sudan who knows when the wedding bells are going to ring... In the meantime, it's good to be in love."[75]

---

[74] Letter to WEC Canada, April 2, 1984.
[75] Letter to Pete and Grace Vermeer, April 15, 1984.

May 23, 1984

"I'm still very much in love with my Irish girlfriend... She is leaving for the Sudan in 10 days. We are simply going on following the Lord, trusting Him to work things out. Don't worry. I have no desire to compromise on the calling to the Kurds... for either love or money."[76]

May 26, 1984

"I spelled out what my ambitions were and what I had to offer: insecurity, constant travel and movement, a desire to reach the unreached, no finances or earthly securities. I was so certain that she would break up that I'd already resigned myself to the fact. However, praise God, she didn't. Now she knows what she is getting into, and still she is more than willing. Poor thing! But I do love her very much."[77]

August 27, 1984

"I don't know how the Lord will work things out between myself and my dear Anna. However... the Lord does all things well for His children. What rest and comfort there is in that. A true, active, resting faith in His all-sufficiency is sufficient to carry you through any crisis or circumstance."[78]

November 6, 1984

"Yes, I am still very, very much in love with my Anna... Frankly, I expect to get married sometime during the early days of 1986. Still a long way away, but then there is so very much to do between now and then."[79]

---

[76] Letter to Ken Getty, May 24, 1984.
[77] Letter to Peter and Grace Vermeer, May 26, 1984.
[78] Letter to Peter and Grace Vermeer, August 27, 1984.
[79] Letter to Peter and Grace Vermeer, November 6, 1984.

December 23, 1984

"Yes, I am still very much in love. How I look forward to seeing her again next month."[80]

January 10, 1985

"I feel my rear end aching somewhat. Just came back from the hospital to get a tetanus shot. Also got cholera and yellow fever shots. This way I should come back alive and well from the Sudan. The political situation there is terrible right now... To tell you the truth, I'm not even sure if Anna is still in Southern Sudan or not. I have not heard from her in about three weeks because of the communications breakdown there. However, we will soon find out the truth of what is going on."[81]

The Sudanese embassy stopped issuing tourist visas so we rendezvoused in Kenya. I scraped together the coinage for a ticket by, among other things, selling my bedframe; a mattress on the floor is also comfortable. Anna met me at Jomo Kenyatta International Airport. A missionary guest house became our base camp. We both love exploring so after breakfast we'd hail a *matatu* (minibus), head for some as-yet unexplored district of Nairobi and wander. "God protects his foolish ones," the house manager clucked after we'd described a seedy district we'd reconnoitred. "You're lucky to come out alive."

A well-connected British contact persuaded Sir Charles Mugane Njonjo, Kenya's first attorney general and one of the nation's richest men, to let us use his holiday residence. We were given an address, spent several hours on a bone-rattling matatu and got off at an intersection of dirt roads alongside a lake. The driver pointed up the coastal road. We walked till we came to a beautiful chalet. It was locked. No one about. It was late afternoon, we were tired, hungry and in need of a shower. I noticed that the back door's hinges faced outward. Using a rock

---

[80] Letter to Peter and Grace Vermeer, December 23, 1984.
[81] Letter to Peter and Grace Vermeer, January 10, 1985.

and a rusty nail I had knocked the pins out of the top two hinges when a very black man exploded out of the woods, arms waving alarmingly. Breathless, he, gasp, explained, gasp, that he, gasp, was the doorman and, gasp, had a key. He let us in through the front door. While we admired the beautiful vista from the front window the man rushed from room to room opening windows to air the place out. Suddenly, a crash and pained cry from the back. We dashed over to find the poor chap, yellow-tinged eyes rolling in distress, picking himself off the ground. When he flung open the back door it jumped off its top pin-less hinges and, ripping the bottom one off the frame, came crashing down. Its weight pulled our man through the doorway, down the step and onto the grass. Other than loss of dignity he seemed alright. Together we hung the door back onto its top two hinges.

Next an older gentleman materialized. Would we kindly furnish him with our provisions, he asked, as he was the cook. Anna handed him a plastic bag holding a loaf of bread, a pot of jam, a packet of *La Vache Qui Ri* cheese and a can of tuna. His eyebrows shot up and the corners of his mouth drooped. "Very good, madam," he murmured stoically. "I will ring the bell when supper is served."

We unpacked in separate rooms and freshened up. A light tinkling summoned us to a table arrayed in fine chinaware. Feeling very colonial, we took our places. The gentleman cook entered and left us staring open-mouthed at the tray discreetly placed before us. Our simple fare had metamorphosed into unrecognizable delicacies. Before retreating he pulled the drapes and lit the fireplace. We struggled to suppress our laughter. Early morning he was at the lake's edge pulling in fish. We ate well. On our second or third evening, in the crimson gloaming on the shores of Lake Naivasha, I asked Anna to marry me. I had to project my voice as a nearby hippo began bellowing just as I kneeled before her.

A day later several luxury vehicles pulled up. We welcomed Mr. Njonjo and his entourage, thanked him for the use of his house, and explained the splintered doorframe. "A man with initiative!" he boomed in a voice like the last trump, a beefy hand smacking down between my shoulder blades. "There are not enough of you. I'll send the bill to the Canadian government. You've got more in you than Joe Clark". He'd met our chinless prime-minister and, like many others, been underwhelmed. "You'll visit us in Nairobi," he announced. A week later we called on him and his wife in their palatial home. We nibbled dainty biscuits and listened to a child scratch a tune on a cello.

Next I phoned Northern Ireland. A gentle voice answered in Ulster Scots. "Hello. This is Aghadowy 292. Rita Kennedy speaking". They still had three-digit phone numbers over there.

"Mrs. Kennedy, my name is Peter Pikkert, and I'd like to invite you to a wedding."

"Oh? That will be nice..." A little hesitation. "Whose wedding?"

"Your daughter Anna's. I've asked her to marry me, and she agreed."

Another hesitation, then, "Oh. That will be nice..."

We took the overnight Jambo Kenya Deluxe—better known as the Lunatic Express—to Mombasa. Watching impalas and giraffes gamboling over the veld while sipping coffee in the restaurant carriage with your girl is magic. The conductor discovered we were not married and wagged a finger. "No hanky-panky!"

Mombasa: Best coffee ever in an old-town backstreet café. Arab dhows bobbing in the harbour. Fort Jesus. Thousands of crabs taking over the beach as the sun set. We were in love. Still are...

After two glorious weeks I flew back to Amman.

22

A Denouement

"She wants me to bring her some apples: where shall I get her apples? If I were a farmer I would have planted her a garden of fruit."

Ilham Al-Madfai

•••

I DECIDED THAT more formal schooling would not benefit me linguistically so made the British Council's snug library my base. I kept working on my Arabic but at a more leisurely pace: "the higher classical literature and slang needs work. My goal is still absolute fluency"[82] When not reading Arabic I lifted Tennyson off the shelves, as well as Yeats, T.S. Elliot, and the Romantics Blake, Wordsworth and Shelley—I was so taken with Ozymandias I memorized it. Once when stretching my legs between the stacks I noticed Bertrand Russell's *Why I Am Not A Christian*. I read it, concluding that if a generation's premier philosopher could do no better than that, Christians have nothing to fear intellectually. I was never again intimidated by the jaundiced prejudices and dispositions of the narrow academic mind.

> "They had me preach in church the other week, and when it was over I marveled. It is amazing to hear yourself ad-lib in front of a congregation in Arabic! Oh, it is thrilling. Am hopelessly in love with the language and, really, studying it is no hardship... I'm really biting at the bit to get going on Kurdish."[83]

•

---

[82] Letter to Peter and Grace Vermeer, April 16, 1985.
[83] Letter to Peter and Grace Vermeer, March 27, 1985.

March 27, 1985

"My relationship with Anna is as strong as ever. How I look forward to her return to Jordan. She will be coming here in June, on her way to England... She is very, very special."[84]

March 31, 1985

"Life in Southern Sudan is terrible. I really, genuinely fear for her safety. However, I also believe that the Lord will keep us safe and sound for each other."[85]

.

I grew to love and appreciate my Jordanian friends, particularly Akram and Basil. Being accepted as one of them, sensing that the Arab/foreigner barrier had broken down, was satisfying indeed. On the streets I was frequently taken for a Circassian, a Lebanese, or a Kurd, and I developed an appreciation for the hurdles and obstacles my friends faced. "It is not easy being a young person in this society, caught between the progressive and the traditional. My heart goes out to some of these guys who are trying to change their circumstances against all odds."[86]

.

April 16, 1985

"I miss her. Sometimes I'm worried to death about her there in the Sudan. Things are not so rosy where she is. War, famine and a cholera epidemic. We can do nothing but cling to Psalm 91. I firmly believe that the Lord will eventually lead us together."[87]

.

---

[84] Letter to Peter and Grace Vermeer, March 27, 1985.
[85] Letter to Peter and Grace Vermeer, March 31, 1985.
[86] Letter to Peter and Grace Vermeer, April 16, 1985.
[87] Ibid.

I ran into the quirky pioneer Lionel Gurney. Born in 1910, he arrived in Aden in the early 1950s to found the Red Sea Mission Team. I'd heard him speak at Prairie and been impressed with his call to that blisteringly hot, desolate place, well nigh impossible to enter, let alone develop a ministry in. His small band travelled where they could, distributing Christian literature when they dared. They didn't plant churches for Dr. Gurney deemed any church with a foreign missionary presence as insufficiently indigenous.[88] The epitaph on his grave stone reads: "Islam Shall Hear". Some of God's greatest pioneers were colossal oddballs.

I also ran into Brother Andrew of Open Doors. They were starting to strategize about reaching the Muslim world. He tried to recruit me but I was "more determined than ever to wholeheartedly pursue the goal the Lord has given me: Kurdistan! That's what it is all about!"[89]

•

June 20, 1985

"My dearly beloved Anna finally arrived from southern Sudan. She arrived a day late, and I was worried! I kept going to the airport, meeting every flight coming from Cairo. She arrived first thing the next day. Oh, but I am hopelessly in love..."[90]

Actually, our relationship suffered a blow before we'd even left the terminal. I was munching an apple when she walked through the gate. She was very thin. I tossed the half-eaten fruit into a bin in order to take her single suitcase. She flinched, then withdrew. She'd just left a famine where her co-workers survived on a single meal a day. She hadn't seen an apple in a year and would have devoured the half I had just chucked. How

---

[88] https://danmission.dk/photoarchive/area/aden-yemen/?lang=en. Accessed June 6, 2022. The RSMT is called Reach Across today.
[89] Letter to Peter and Grace Vermeer, March 31, 1985.
[90] Letter to Ken Getty, June 20, 1985.

could she marry someone so profligate as to throw out apple cores? Thankfully, talking resolves most issues.

In conservative Muslim societies it is not easy to find secluded places where unmarried couples can be alone together, but I knew of a wooded area near a small Circassian village outside of Amman which, I thought, fit the bill. One afternoon we took a minibus to this village, strolled alongside a bubbling brook into the woods and settled comfortably on a flat rock sheltered by the overhanging branches of a large willow. We were just getting tactile when a swarthy native brandishing a machete materialized out of the ether. Waving his weapon like a scimitar he rained down curses from Allah while accusing us of being filthy pigs polluting their youth.

The situation called for sang-froid diplomacy. "God forbid, sir," I parlayed gently while making slow, soothing up-and-down hand motions. "Please hear me out, sir. The reason we came here is so that we would NOT pollute the youth. That is the last thing we want to do, sir. We thought this place was deserted, safe. Clearly, I was in the wrong. But, sir, if you know of a better place, please lead us there..."

The man relaxed slowly, as if he'd swallowed a sedative, the machete wielding arm dropping loosely to his side. He puckered his sable brow and I could see the cogs behind them churning. *"Ta'alu. Itba'uni!"* (Come. Follow me).

He led us to a derelict building and beckoned us inside. He then positioned himself in the open doorway facing away from us, the machete held upright. Circassians comprise the king's body guard and this individual manifested rich experience in that occupation. But feeling awkward, we called it quits. The man led us to the main road and, grinning dumbly, we caught a bus back to the city. One-on-one dating would have to wait.

Soon after we shouldered our fardels for the next stage of our pilgrimage. "I'll be traveling with a harem!"[91]

---

[91] Letter to Peter and Grace Vermeer, March 31, 1985.

23

The Holy Mountain

"We start the imitation of Christ with Holy Baptism, which symbolizes the Lord's Burial and Resurrection. Virtuous living and conduct in accord with the Gospel are its intermediate stage, and its perfection is victory through spiritual struggles against the passions, which procures painless, indestructible, heavenly life."

St. Gregory Palamas

. . .

SAYING GOODBYE was not easy for I'd come to love my Jordanian friends. "My own social needs were fully met by them. And they too sensed that there was no foreigner in Jordan that was closer to me than they were."[92]

It took about a week for Anna, two girls on a short-term mission trip and myself to travel overland to Istanbul. We headed first for Damascus, then took a side trip to Palmyra, then to Homs. On the bus to Aleppo an Arab Sheikh plunked down beside me. "Are they yours?" he asked, jutting his chin at the three girls.

"They are," I responded.

He pointed to a particularly cute one. "I'll give you twelve camels for her," he said generously.

"Felicia, he's offering me twelve camels for you!" I exclaimed in English.

"You're..." Her pipsqueak voice quavered then rose an octave. "You're not going to leave me here, are you?"

We crossed into Turkey, bussed to Gaziantep, Adana and Ankara, then took the overnight train to Istanbul. I moved back in with the old widow and Daoud and started a six-week refresher course in Turkish. Anna left for England and the others flew back to Amman.

---

[92] Letter to Pete and Grace Vermeer, July 14, 1985.

When I had to exit and re-enter Turkey for visa renewal purposes I decided to visit Mount Athos, partly out of curiosity, partly to settle a nagging question about mission strategy: should Evangelicals seeking to plant churches in the Middle East work through the existing churches?

Most of my Jordanian friends were evangelicals whose ancestors had converted from Orthodoxy as a result of Protestant missionary activities in the 19th and early 20th centuries. They were, however, strangely reluctant to reach their Muslim neighbours with the gospel. This, I learned later, was because decisions made in the early 19th century has colored the enterprise up to the present. It's a complex story; I'll keep it short and simple.

The 19th century was an age of empires. The sun never set on the globe-spanning British Empire, the Hapsburgs controlled central Europe, the Russian expanded to the Okhotsk and Bering Seas and the Ottoman Turks reigned over south-eastern Europe, the Middle East and North Africa. Sparked by an English Baptist in India called William Carey, that century also saw the awakening of unprecedent missionary fervor in the Anglo-Saxon world. In 1810 American Presbyterians and Congregationalists formed the American Board of Commissioners for Foreign Mission ("the Board"). Since India was a British show they decided to target the Ottoman Empire, under the illusion that "the Musselmans are a kind of heretical Christians"[93]. Though naïve, they approached the task with praiseworthy thoroughness.

From 1818 onward—when David Livingstone was a lad of six and the famed Arabist and explorer Richard Burton as yet unborn—big-thinking, genial Americans like Pliny Fisk and Eli Smith proceeded to survey the Ottoman realm. They discovered a bewildering number of ethnic groups and tribes who already self-identified as Christian: Greek and Bulgarian Orthodox churches in the west, Armenian Orthodox churches all over

93 Newel, Annual Report of the ABCFM, 1814, p. 111. Quoted in Pikkert, *Protestant Missionaries to the Middle East: Ambassadors of Christ or Culture?* Ancaster, Alev Books, 2008. p. 51.

Anatolia, Maronites in Lebanon, Copts in Egypt and smaller groups of Syriacs, Nestorians and a few Roman Catholics scattered hither and yon. In some regions the majority population consisted of people who had clung to their Christian identity throughout the vagaries of Middle Eastern history. Most were poor peasants, serfs bought and sold with land owned by their Muslim Turkish or Kurdish aghas.

This revelation led Board strategists to float the idea that they should not target Muslims directly but these poor, benighted and exploited Christian minorities instead. This became official policy in 1828, when the Board decided *not* to start a Protestant church. "If true piety could be restored to these (ancient) churches... if it could bring back to them the native simplicity and purity of the gospel, one of the greatest impediments to the conversion of Mohammedans to the Christian faith would be taken away."[94] Reforming the Orthodox churches would, they believed, lead eventually to the salvation of the Muslim world.

It did not work out that way. Knowing that the Protestants didn't accept them as "real Christians", the ancient churches turned against them. The missionaries now found themselves on a narrow path: they were not welcomed by the Orthodox churches and unable to work with "the Mohammedans" directly, at least not on their own terms. They responded by forming western-style evangelical churches from those who converted from the ancient Orthodox traditions.[95] The vast majority of Protestant churches in the Arab world today trace their history to this 19th century rending of the ancient persuasions, and up to the present the missionary community pours most of its resources into these Orthodox background Protestant churches—even if the last thing most of them want are Muslim converts in their midst. The walls of prejudice and

[94] Temple, *Missionary Herald*, 1835, p. 222. Quoted in Pikkert, *Protestant Missionary to the Middle East: Ambassadors of Christ or Culture?* Alev Books. Ancaster. p. 53.
[95] Blincoe, Robert. *Ethnic Realities and the Church: Lessons from Kurdistan. A history of mission work, 1668-1990.* The Presbyterian Center for Mission Studies, Pasadena, CA, 1998, p. 34, 62.

fear which have existed between the Christian and Muslim communities for over a millennium are simply too high to scale.

The Board developed an extensive network of schools for the Greek, Bulgarian, Chaldean, Syriac, Armenian and Arab *millets* (recognized minorities). At the apex were the Syrian Protestant College (The American University of Beirut today) and Robert College in Istanbul (Boğaziçi University today). These schools, it was hoped, would "create the conditions for preaching the gospel" by introducing a higher culture which would "facilitate the acceptance of the higher religion—Christianity"[96]. This approach became known as "The Great Experiment", and the Board stuck to it like Gorilla Glue.

Though the idea of loving their Muslim enemies and reaching them with the gospel was not on the Christian *millets'* agenda, they were delighted to have the missionaries educate their children, employ their graduates and defend their rights. That is still the case. However, this advancement of minorities who'd survived for centuries by keeping a low profile had catastrophic consequences. Not only did the missionaries' empowerment of Christian minorities fail in terms of evangelizing the Muslim majority, it was a factor in a series of massacres which culminated in the Armenian genocide of 1915.

By educating the ethnic minorities in their own languages (Armenian, Greek, Bulgarian and Arabic), the missionaries sparked a cultural renaissance. As their students were exposed to Western social values and political thought they began agitating for ever greater political freedom. Graduates from Robert College, for instance, played a massive role in the Bulgarian nationalist movement, while a secret printing press in the Anatolia College of Marsovan (Merzifon today) churned out vast quantities of Armenian revolutionary literature. Furthermore, the fact that intelligent, skillful, industrious graduates from the missionary colleges soon outstripped their

---

[96] Bosch, David. *Transforming Mission: Paradigm Shifts in Theology of Mission*. Orbis Books, New York. 2003, p. 297.

Muslim neighbours in terms of commerce and business acumen aroused deep envy and hatred.[97]

Neither the local aghas nor the Sultan, whose empire was crumbling at the edges, wanted to see their Christian minorities empowered. They perceived the missionaries as friends of their restive minorities, agents of western interests, and pawns of their own government's political agenda. In 1895 the Turks destroyed the Euphrates College in Harput and "from September that year until the end of December one massacre followed another through the empire."[98] In 1914 the Young Turks plunged their empire into the World War on the wrong side, and under cover of that bloodletting eliminated Anatolia's ancient Christian communities.

The Great Experiment had failed, spectacularly, terribly, because the missionary community had been incapable of separating Western culture, Christendom, from Christianity. By identifying Christianity with Western cultural norms and values channeled through their educational system they had tied their cart to the wrong horse. Certain of their own cultural and religious superiority, they were convinced that Islam would crumble under its weight. They were wrong, and the results of that mistake continue to haunt the Middle East. Western civilization fell short—as it was bound to do.

I am convinced that in spite of some very dark periods, post-Renaissance Western European culture in general, and Anglo-Saxon Protestantism in particular, has contributed more to the over-all wellbeing of mankind than any other socio-political or cultural system. But it was still "the world" from a biblical perspective, one into which the church should have spoken prophetically, not co-opted into its missionary enterprise.

In 1920 the allies dismembered the Ottoman Empire but, phoenix-like, the Republic of Turkey rose from the detritus. Its former Arab provinces became a patchwork of territories

---

[97] Ross, F; Fry, Frank & Sibley, Charles Luther. *The Near East and American Philanthropy*. Columbia University Press. 1929, p. 165.
[98] Meyer K. *A Clash of Swords*, Grand Junction, CO. Friends of Turkey. 1986, p. 52.

controlled by the French and British which eventually gained their independence, to become the monarchies and unstable dictatorships with which we are familiar. The Protestant churches established there by those pre-World War I missionaries survived and gladly absorbed most subsequent missionary attention. In fact, their continued existence there marks the great missiological difference between Egypt, the Levant and Turkey.

In the 1980s there were about 100 Protestants in Turkey, virtually all from non-Muslim minorities. The Board, a shadow of its former self, still ran two high schools and a printing press. Then it lost those too, and was reduced to a single, small private library where they kept their archives, and in which I would write my doctoral thesis. Soon afterwards that too closed, those precious archives disappearing onto the vaults of the Ottoman Bank.

For half a century the global church forgot about Turkey. Not until the late 1960s did 20th century interdenominational evangelical agencies like OM and WEC pave the way for the modern evangelistic effort to the country, a movement in which we played our small part. That new generation of missionaries was—and largely remains—unaware of the failed Great Experiment of our pre-WWI predecessors. However—and this is important—because of the virtual elimination of the ancient Protestant churches in Turkey we were forced to target Muslims directly; there was not enough of a Christian community left to build on. As a result, a viable Muslim background Protestant church has emerged there.

As a young missionary I didn't know all this history, but did entertain the same question that first generation had posed: should I work through the existing Christian community, such as it was, or seek to reach the Kurds directly? During my peregrinations in south-eastern Turkey I had visited the monasteries of Deir ul-Zafaran and Mor Gabriel, and left wondering about their life, doctrine and aspirations. I hoped to learn more at that rampart of Orthodoxy spirituality, Mount Athos.

.

The train shuddered to a halt in no-man's land. The Turkish locomotive decoupled and eventually a Greek one took its place. Scruffy border guards rummaged through our luggage. A jolt accompanied a blast from a whistle and we resumed our leisurely journey across Macedonia to Thessaloniki. Someone at the Greek embassy in Istanbul had given me scrap of paper with the address of the Pilgrim Office there and upon arrival a kind soul pointed me in the right direction. I told the monk in charge that I was researching Greek Orthodoxy. He had me fill in some forms and told me to return in four days. I spent that time exploring, the highlight of which was finding a deserted beach and lolling alone in the azure Aegean.

Upon receiving my *diamonitirion*, or special visa, I took a bus to Ouranoupoli, the last town before the Sacred Mount. The next morning a small ferry shuttled me and some black-clad, heavily bearded monks to Daphni, Mount Athos' tiny point of entry. It boasted a small minimarket, a tiny police station and a post office. I showed my papers and started hiking, first upward, then southward, along a coastal path. I arrived at the gates of the Monastery of Modesto and knocked. A monk with piercing eyes let me in, took me to a small room and poured out a glass of *ouzo*, neat. I'd never before tasted this overpowering, ghastly-tasting yet roborative beverage and struggled to suppress a coughing fit. I stayed for lunch: bearded men in dusty black garb slowly, silently spooned simple vegetarian fare while someone read from a large book in a sing-songy voice. I understood nothing, but during that cantillation grasped from whom Islam had learned its tedious Qur'anic reciting style.

I departed after the meal and for the next couple of hours worked my way up a steep path and then along a high ridge, the sea roiling and foaming far below. Suddenly I stopped in my tracks, reached for my camera and started shooting. There, perched on a huge rock high above the sea, towered the majestic Monastery of St. Peter. With every forward pace I felt I stepped back in time, into the Julian calendar, into an era which pre-dates the great schism of 1054. I knocked on the door. A monk opened up, pointed to a bench, offered another glass of vivifying ouzo and led me to my cell. I washed up, went to the dining hall, ate supper in silence with the brethren and slept as if drugged.

For a week I hiked from one monastery to the next. At 4 AM a monk would thump on the cell door to rouse me for morning prayers. I'd be the only spectator to a complex performance which began in the dark with a single chant and gradually rose to a crescendo, the song rising as ever more monks participated in a choreography which involved lighting ever more candles to symbolize the light which had come into the world, their flickering making the golden icons shimmer. Sometimes there would be a bench for me to sit on, sometimes wall hooks held me upright by my armpits. After about two hours the ritual would wind down, to be followed by a long liturgy. When that eventually concluded we headed for the dining hall to partake of vegetables, olives, sour wine, fresh bread and butter, all the while listening to a nasal chant in Greek from the *Philokalia* or some church father. At the monastery of St. Panteleimon everything was in Russian. After a well-deserved siesta the monks attended their respective duties—cooking, baking, gardening, icon restoration and other such activities—while I collected my satchel, filled my water bottle, and headed for the next monastery.

One day a horny, wild-eyed eremitic pursued me for hours down those dirt trails making sexual advances every time I glanced back. Not since 962 A.D. when, so I was told, the Virgin Mary came for a visit, has a woman graced the place—the bros even ban female goats and burros from the Holy Mount. Instead of snuffing out the sexual impulse this legalistic approach had obviously pushed it in different directions, at least in the foul-grinning troglodyte chasing me. I was pretty sure I could best him if push came to shove but was, nevertheless, relieved when I arrived untouched at the next cloister.

There was no signage anywhere. When crossing to the east coast, I got hopelessly lost. It was late afternoon and I had no idea which way to turn. I stumbled on a deserted chapel with a large bell dangling from the portico, hesitated but a moment, then yanked the clapper. A succession of canorous peals receded into the distance and minutes later an irate fellow in black robes came running. He pointed me in the right direction.

I longed to strike up a conversation with one of the more balanced looking cenobites, but none spoke any language I knew. Then my luck changed. I don't remember his name nor which monastery it was, but one afternoon a gentle monk with restful eyes and a graying beard—I'm looking at his picture as I write this—welcomed me in unaccented American English. He was happy to spend the rest of that afternoon and part of the next morning with me for he'd had no meaningful conversation with anyone for a long time. He was an American of Greek parentage. He'd joined the community nine years earlier, had not left it since, spoke no Greek, and had no idea what was going on in the world.

I informed him that one Ronald Reagan was President of the United States, that someone called Michael Gorbachev was trying to reform the USSR, that there'd been a terrible earthquake in Chile and a devastating cyclone in Bangladesh, that a Lebanese terrorist group had highjacked a plane, that Sikh terrorists had downed an Air India flight, that a dam had collapsed in Italy, and other such things. He nodded slowly as I spoke, clucked his tongue at times, made some vague hand motions and then asserted quietly that "the world out there" was an evil place. A kindly spirit in monk's garb can make banal inanities sound profound. I didn't mention his debauched colleague just over the hill, but suggested that evil is always close at hand.

What had brought him to the Holy Mountain, I asked. He'd come seeking salvation, he shared, a process that was ongoing. As he spoke I was reminded of my mother's complex spiritual struggles towards assurance of salvation from the penalty of sin. Her brand of hyper-Calvinism and the Eastern Orthodoxy of the gentle monk with respect to the doctrines of salvation, sanctification, sin and the nature of the will were, at the dogmatic level, poles apart. Yet their struggles were sadly similar: he too sought an existential yet unquantifiable experience of his own sinfulness, in his case through endless repetitions of the Jesus Prayer: "Lord Jesus, Son of God, have mercy on me a sinner". He too saw salvation not as the starting point but as the goal of the Christian life. He too struggled with lack of assurance. He too was convinced that salvation outside the church was not possible. For him too the church provided cultural continuity for his people. Both, I felt, were in thrall of a legalistic and condemnatory, hope-snuffing and life-sapping old covenant religion.

I told him I believed in a single, unilateral act of divine, regenerating grace granting the conviction that sins were paid for in full by the crucified Christ, and that the authenticity of the experience would be attested ever after by a changed life.

I asked him if he ever read the Bible; he confessed he didn't possess one. I promised to mail him a copy upon my return to "the world out there." I left the Holy Mountain convinced that reaching Muslims through the existing Christian community, whether Orthodox or Orthodox background evangelical, was a lost cause. If we were going to reach Muslims with the gospel of God's grace in Jesus Christ, we would have to do so directly, not by proxy.

24

Things Gel

*"The few whose delight is in meditation and understanding;
who yearn not for goods, nor for victory, but for knowledge;
who leave both market and battlefield to lose themselves in the
quiet clarity of secluded thought... these are the men of
wisdom, who stand aside unused by the world."*

Will Durant

. . .

SOON AFTER MY visit to the Holy Mountain I headed for
Kurdistan. Hoping to reconnect with old contacts as well as
make new ones I expected to be on the road from late August to
November. After that it was off to WEC's UK headquarters "in
time to see Anna accepted into our weird and wonderful
organization!"[99]

I didn't have an appetite for that eastbound trip; I wanted to
head west, for I was madly in love: "How I thank the Lord on
my bare knees for having given me a girl like that!"[100] But we
stuck to plan. "There is no need to write me for the next few
months as I will have no fixed address. Not even Anna will be
able to send letters."[101]

I struck up a conversation on the bus out of Aleppo with a
typical-yet-intelligent looking Kurd: lean features, soup-
strainer moustache, sparkling jet-black eyes, a clean dress-shirt
and baggy shalwar trousers. Salah Saida had always wanted to
go to university but when his father died he took over the farm
to provide for his younger siblings. Near the dreary town of
Amuda he signalled that he wanted to get off and invited me to
join him.

---

[99] Letter to Ken Getty, July 17, 1985.
[100] Letter to Ken Getty, August 21, 1985.
[101] Letter to Pete and Grace Vermeer, July 14, 1985.

We walked across a patch of dusty desert to a two-room, flat-roofed, adobe house like thousands scattered across the Syrian desert. He introduced me to his young bride, a cheerful, open-faced girl with a shawl draped loosely around her head, offered me a white plastic chair and fetched a Pepsi. I looked around the simple room and noticed something unusual: bookshelves. One sagged under the weight of dog-eared Arabic novels, translated western classics, a few history and sociology texts and an old encyclopedia set with a couple of missing volumes. Another shelf was filled with archeological artifacts: an ancient oil lamp, some painted pottery shards, part of a cuneiform tablet, some Ottoman coins, a worn mortar and pestle, small amphora jugs, a little marble bust with a missing nose and like miscellanea—all told, quite a collection, all the more remarkable for its unexpected whereabouts. Salah informed me that everyone knew he was interested in history, so whenever their plows turned up a stray artifact they passed it on to him. He could tell me what was Assyrian, Greek, Roman, Arab or Ottoman.

I looked with fresh interest at this home-grown intellectual. Just as every village has its idiot each one also has its book-lover, its thinker, its questioning man. It dawned on me then that these were the ones I should be pursuing since there is no hope for those with no questions. Why waste time on them? I needed to find the village savants—but how?

In a Jezidi (i.e., Devil worshipping) village elsewhere I met another intelligent local who made me feel welcome and, "for the first time I felt that reaching the Kurds was not an impossible dream, but within the realm of reality."[102] I crossed back into Turkey and made my way to Bezal, the village with the deaf boy. There a bright-looking youngster of about 12 or 13 whom I'd not met before loitered around me. I beckoned and asked him to tell me about himself. He explained that he was home for the summer from Iran, where he was studying to become an imam. He'd already memorized the Qur'an and was

---

[102] Letter to Peter and Grace Vermeer, October 10, 1985.

working on the Hadith. Bingo, another village prodigy. We spent much time together hiking and talking. I "had a SUPER time, and feel that the Lord will bless the time and testimony left behind."[103]

After Bezal I tramped back down to Beytüşşebap and found a *dolmuş*, or shared taxi, for Şirnak, the nearest town with a bus terminal. I threw my satchel into the back and took the window seat behind a young, long-haired, wild-looking driver. A policeman had taken the front passenger seat. A skinny Kurd with halitosis (they all had that) eased in beside me and we took off. An hour or so into the journey the vehicle turned spasmodic. It refused to down-shift and with fits and starts the cursing driver managed to coax it to the top of a hill, where we stopped. No amount of fiddling could budge that stick out of third gear. After consulting among ourselves we decided that we'd drive as fast as possible downhill in order to gain sufficient momentum to take us up the next incline. We piled in and shot down that mountain. That Kurd took those dirt hairpins like a demented racing ace, laying on the horn in villages, inevitably located in the valleys when we were going at top speed. I have distinct memories of chickens, goats and children scattering before us. The skinny Kurd beside me got carsick and hung out the window scattering a tail of vomit. The policeman prayed, his cap on backwards, his head bobbing up and down like a piston. As the car spun around another hairpin it clipped a pack-horse carrying a bundle of firewood. The beast jerked forward, pushing the chador-clad woman leading it over the edge into the ravine.

"Stop," the policeman cried. "You've killed someone!"

"If we stop here, we'll never get going again," the driver fired back through clenched teeth.

"Drive as close to the edge as you dare and I'll see if she's OK," I shouted. The driver gunned the car to the brink of the abyss while I hung out the window as far as my torso stretched. The unfortunate woman was lying on her back in a brook, arms

---

[103] Letter to Peter and Grace Vermeer, October 10, 1985.

and legs oscillating back and forth, her mouth moving staccato-like.

"No broken limbs, able to speak," I reported. The driver looked at the policeman. He nodded grimly and the car lurched forward.

I was on the road from late July to mid October. I fell sick several times—once from eating bad mutton and "when I finally came back here (to Istanbul) was totally worn out both spiritually and physically"[104].

> "Sometimes the ways of the Lord are rather difficult to figure out, but I too am seeing more clearly that no matter what the circumstances, it doesn't change a few foundational facts: that He came and died in my place and rose from the grave and now sits at the right hand of the Father with all power and authority and glory in heaven at his feet. Someday we will see things clearly, and on that day both the Lord Jesus and his children will be vindicated before the powers of the evil one. I draw comfort and strength from these thoughts quite often."[105]

I wasn't expected in England for another month, and the old widow was done with boarders. I hopped on a bus to a poor district hoping to find a place to stay, elbowing through the crush of passengers until I stood next to a young man holding an Arabic newspaper. Clutching straps, we swung in tandem as the bus careened this way and that. Our eyes met. I smiled and nodded. He nodded back. I asked him where he was from. Lattakia, Syria. I'd just been there, I said. We started chatting. He asked where I was going. I told him I was looking for a cheap place to lay my head for a couple of weeks. He suggested I move in with him and his fellow Syrian students—there was still room on the couch. We got off at the last stop and Mohammed Abu Kaf, geology student at the University of Istanbul, led me to a tiny apartment he shared with two others. The couch was clean and firm. I said I'd take it. I dropped my

---

[104] Letter to Peter and Grace Vermeer, October 10, 1985.
[105] Letter to Ken Getty, August 21, 1985.

satchel and bought a tray of baklava. That appeased the others when they showed up.

> "I moved in with some Syrian students... That arrangement was certainly of the Lord. We have many, many long hours of conversation, often late into the night. I gave them the book "The Balance of Truth" which really made an impression on one guy in particular."[106]

Finally westward, direction Anna! A non-stop 46 hour journey bus filled with Turkish guest workers and a couple of hippies took me as far as the Netherlands. I'd taken a jar of olives to sustain me and couldn't stand the sight of stuffed manzanillas for months afterwards. A ferry to the UK, another bus, and we were reunited! "Yes, I am still very much in love with my Anna... So level-headed, yet so tender and loveable."[107]

Bulstrode, WEC's magnificent Buckinghamshire mansion, was Eden and every day, rain or shine, we strolled around its beautifully manicured demesne. "It is obvious to the whole world that we are hopelessly in love."[108] We were treated like royalty. Little old conservative ladies gave us the keys to their flats when away for the weekend and the international director the key to his office so we'd have a place to duck into after hours. Kissing your woman in the CEO's office felt wonderfully mischievous; Anna's being a good sport in the tactile department has contributed wondrously to our long and happy marriage.

During the day she worked in the kitchen while I collected everything pertaining to Kurdish I could lay my hands on. I fired off letters to every possible source, visited the School of Oriental and African Studies, and purchased a small microfiche reader. WEC filmed an entire Kurdish library so I could smuggle it back into Turkey. At the same time an idea that had germinated while on the road started to gel...

---

[106] Letter to Peter and Grace Vermeer, October 10, 1985.
[107] Letter to Peter and Grace Vermeer, November 28, 1985.
[108] Letter to Ken Getty, December 9, 1985.

Most missionaries to the Middle East embraced "friendship evangelism". It is based on the presumption that if we live Christianly people we befriend might start asking questions which would "open doors for the gospel". I didn't think much of it. To me a friend is someone I like to spend time with, with whom I click, who doesn't drain me socially and to whom I am loyal even if they are not interested in Christianity and never convert; the idea of befriending people for the purpose of converting them felt vaguely duplicitous. As a "fisher of men," a single pole-and-line with myself as bait also struck me as pathetic. I needed something bigger, a net which would pull in thinking, questioning Kurds—the village savants.

One day it came to me: an unapologetic Christian publication. Under the rapid urbanization taking place during the Turgut Özal era, Turkey had become one of the most media-saturated countries in the world. The burgeoning urban population created nervous netherworlds of anonymity in which it was difficult to identify friend from foe. In that context the flood of cheap, ribald newspapers, inexpensive magazines and fly-by-night news sheets, each with its own ideological slant, let people with shared religious or political worldviews find each other.

The magazine I envisioned would lead us to thinking, questioning, intelligent Kurds. "We are praying about starting a Kurdish gospel broadsheet that might be published monthly, or 10 times a year 2 to 2 ½ years from now."[109]

I suddenly had lots of questions for WEC Press' computer guru. He suggested I get an Apple with a mouse. He showed me a newly arrived, smallish, hard-plastic ivory-colored box with an integrated black-and-white screen below which was a slit. A tiny picture of a rainbow-coloured apple with a bite out of it graced the bottom left corner. A cable ran from the back to a keyboard and a thin wire ran to the top a small beige box with a large rectangular button. "This is an Apple Macintosh. Only came out last year. It's ideal for your purposes. When you move this wee box, called a mouse, that arrow there glides over the

---

[109] Letter to Ken Getty, December 9, 1985.

surface of the screen." The man made some subtle hand movements and I could see the arrow moving about. "Position it over the appropriate command, there, at the top of the screen, click the button on the mouse with your index finger and voila! Child's play! No more abstruse codes! You'll want a WYSIWYG (What You See Is What You Get) program and Bob's your uncle! Can't help with your foreign fonts but that shouldn't be a problem, not with Macs." He patted the top of the machine kindly, then launched into a technical explanation way over my head on the reasons why that was so.

Wow! This was cutting-edge! Not cheap, but within reach. The long-suffering man assured me that if I sent him my final products on a floppy disk, "one of these things, which you push into that hole, like this", along with pictures I wanted inserted, they'd be happy to do the printing. Creating a magazine for thinking Kurds was actually feasible! "I'm already beginning to collect little articles and starting a photograph collection."[110]

Anna was accepted into WEC that December. During her final interview I pulled up a chair and sat beside her. Someone asked me what I would do if they rejected Anna. "If WEC can get things that wrong I'll resign," I responded. There were gasps, but WEC was not that foolish.

There was a brawl on the bus from London to Glasgow, one fellow attacking the bus driver, and then three others wrestling him to the floor while the bus weaved on but "we arrived in Glasgow none the worse for wear."[111] We then took the ferry to Northern Ireland to arrive safe and sound. "Anna has a lovely family; good solid dairy farmers."[112] My memories of that Christmas consist of a wee trolley weighed down with insane amounts of food and playing Poor Puss, Paddy from Cork and other such ridiculously wholesome Irish parlour games. January was spent visiting her friends and relatives, preparing for the wedding, speaking at various churches and mission-halls and keeping up my Arabic studies.

---

[110] Letter to Peter and Grace Vermeer, December 27, 1985.
[111] Ibid.
[112] Ibid.

February 1, 1986. Anna was radiant, resplendent in a simple white dress, holding a luxuriant bouquet of red roses. Weddings and funerals are major social events on that island nation, her family was well known in the community, and she was a missionary—a genus still esteemed there. Her brother suggested we have an open reception as we would never know who had supported her in which way.

The church was full. The Reverend Whyte officiated, WEC's International Director made interminable exhortations of which I remember nothing, and my mother's hilarious speech at the reception afterwards made no allowances for Northern Irish sensibilities. She was remembered long afterwards. My best man, a Dutch cousin, cracked jokes while I was drinking orange juice. The pulpy liquid shot down the wrong hole and I nearly choked to death. Instead of slapping my back or attempting the Heimlich, those dairy men stared at me like docile cows while I made squeaky sounds, tried unsuccessfully to suck in air, nearly lost consciousness, but then had a saving coughing fit. Afterwards Anna said she wondered if she'd be widowed before we'd had a chance to consummate matters.

Honeymoon in the back-country of county Donegal. Only the pubs were open that February, but when those cheery publicans learned that a Canadian had married a local girl it was, "Ach, that's brilliant. It's on the house, so it is!" Anna hand-carried the top tier of our wedding cake to Canada. I proudly introduced my bride to my Dutch-Canadian family and home church, held a second reception at the WEC HQ and roomed there for the next three months.

> "Married life is just great; we have such fun together and are not only lovers and sweethearts but also best friends. We thank God continually for His gift of one another and marvel at His goodness to us... People say Peter hasn't changed... just as crazy as ever! – though a few gracious souls say he has 'matured'"![113]

---

[113] Letter to Pete and Grace Vermeer (Anna writing) March 17, 1986.

Part 3

Early Ministry: 1986-1990

*"No amount of falls will really undo us if we keep
picking ourselves up each time.*

*We shall of course be very muddy and tattered children
by the time we reach home. But the bathrooms are
all ready, the towels put out and the clean
clothes are in the airing cupboard.*

*The only fatal thing is to lose one's temper and give up.
It is when we notice the dirt that God is most present in us;
it is the very sign of His presence."*

C.S. Lewis

25

A Bit More Context

"In all these countries, (Özal swept his hand across the map from Afghanistan to Algeria) too many people have too little hope."[114]

Turgut Özal

* * *

WE SETTLED IN Istanbul as newlyweds in May of '86, in a dingy apartment two floors below street level. The building was on a hillside so the bed- and living-rooms had a window through which we caught a glimpse of the Bosphorus. The kitchenette, dining area, bathroom and tiny second bedroom were dark as a root cellar with the lights turned off and smelled no better. We spent mornings scrubbing and painting and afternoons nosing around second-hand furniture shops. The place became home and we were happy there, except when the place flooded with sewage from the backed-up system.

In the 1980s our district of Cihangir was the epicenter of Istanbul's gay and transvestite demimonde, a demographic with whom Turks have a counter-intuitive relationship. Though strongly condemned by Islam, some of their most iconic musicians, like Zeki Muren (what a voice!), Bülent Ersoy (the Diva) and Mabel Matiz were flamboyant gender-crossers loved by fans across the political and religious divides. Muren even became a national artist, an honorific awarded by the government. Still, the bravura and faux-exuberance, the gaiety and glee of the colourful people around us struck me as contrived, as fabricated. I felt sorry for them.

One of Anna's gifts is hospitality. We'd just settled when my Jordanian friends Basil and Akram visited for a week.

---

[114] Comment to Strobe Talbott during an interview for *Time* (Jan. 28, 1991), and related by Talbott during *The Washington Institute's Second Annual Turgut Ozal Memorial Lecture.*

"When they left they said they were refreshed physically and spiritually. How we hope and pray that many may come and stay with us and find spiritual and physical rest!"[115]

However, we decided not to welcome just anyone—not, for instance, other expatriates. To connect with a culture built on sharing we could not be perceived as part of that self-sufficient expat bubble which exists in all major cities. A flow of foreigners would communicate to our neighbourhood that we didn't need them, and that would stifle one of the basic ingredients of friendship: the meeting of needs. If we wanted to connect with, to give as well as receive from the community, we had to let ourselves get lonely. So we asked our fellow missionaries to leave us alone. That didn't go down well with some but we promised to attend and occasionally host the required bi-weekly team meetings.

Subsequent weeks felt lonesome. Then, one day, the doorbell rang. I peered through the peep hole and saw the doorman's wife holding a plate. Anna opened up, smiled, and said "nose, nose". The Turkish for welcome is *buyrun* and nose is *burun*; she hadn't yet mastered the "uy" dipthong. The woman smiled back, handed Anna the platter, and left. Together we stared at the mucous okra-based goop.

"Would you eat that?" Anna asked.

"It... it doesn't really appeal to me."

"Not to me either."

"I'll flush it down the toilet."

She looked aghast. "Would you do that?"

"You have any better ideas?"

Turks do not return plates empty so days later Anna filled the dish with freshly baked chocolate chip cookies. I watched greedily as she made for the door. "Don't worry, I left some for you," she said. Irrespective of creed, colour or culture, everyone

---

[115] Letter to WEC Canada, August 3, 1986.

loves chocolate chip cookies. Anna had made her first connection.

I sat the entrance exams and was accepted into Istanbul University's Turkish Language and Literature program. That took care of visas. Anna enrolled at a private language school and also took sewing, macrame and cookery classes at a local girls' school. Others innately trust her, and soon a young married woman invited us over to their place. I noticed a chess board and asked the husband if he played. He promptly set it up. We were fairly evenly matched and Oğuz invited me over for a revanche. I learned later that his father had been a member of parliament, that he owned a coal mine, and was treated with some deference in the neighbourhood. My relationship with him never moved beyond the occasional chess game but the association raised our profile: we were suddenly perceived as friends of Oğuz Bey (Mr. Oğuz). We must be of some importance!

I befriended a big, well educated, fearless Kurd who had come to faith and worked as a Bible translator—a bold move as Turkey was going through one of its periodic let's-persecute-Christians spells by deporting missionaries and banning the Bible.

> "One of our workers has had to leave the country, apparently because she had some contacts with Kurds... They are unbelievably sensitive on this issue. They have also banned the Bible, though the sale of the New Testament is still permitted. However, there is a court hearing in June in which, I understand, they hope to put the New Testament on the banned book list as well. There are evil men in this country who are attempting to frustrate the work of God. Pray that their schemes may be confounded."[116]

---

[116] Letter to Peter and Grace Vermeer, February 26, 1986.

Our situation as Christians was mild compared to that of the Kurds. The war in the south-east had flared up and the junta's draconian response was to reject the notion of Kurdish ethnic identity altogether. The idea of producing a Kurdish Christian magazine under such circumstances was impossible so we decided to pursue a Turkish version which would appeal to Kurds. First, however, I needed to master Turkish!

Turkish is a Ural-Altaic language. It is agglutinative, meaning you can create extraordinarily long words with entire relative clauses embedded in them. *Vazgeçemediklerimiz-denmisiniz*, for instance, means "aren't you one of those of us whom we can't give up"? It has vowel harmony, meaning that sounds in which the airflow is not diverted have to match the last syllable of the root word, giving the language a melodic quality. Sentences typically end with the verb. As with Arabic, I found the formal language learning approach sterile and ineffective so, once again, started doing my own thing: reading comic books, listening to children's programs and finding places where I could more or less understand what was going on. A left-leaning university class-mate introduced me to some student haunts, hazy dens filled with pimply would-be revolutionaries puffing cheap roll-your-owns and arguing the merits of various socio-political panaceas and utopian chimeras while planning their next demonstration. The highly politicised atmosphere at the time evoked the spirit of pre-revolutionary Moscow, or Cairo after Nasser's coup. Turkey was undergoing a social and economic revolution, and the seemingly affable, short-statured man-with-a-paunch sporting window-frame glasses who drove it gave those chippy students much fodder about which to debate and demonstrate.

As with many intelligent, ambitious people born in humble circumstances, Turgut Özal saw education as the key to a better future. He completed high school with honors, then went to Istanbul Technical University, where he met future politico and supporter Süleyman Demirel. He studied in the States and fell in love with American know-how and can-do-ism. When his university pal Süleyman Demirel became prime minister he was appointed to the State Planning Organization.

The 1970s were a very unstable period in Turkish politics. Shaky coalitions failed to turn a tanking statist economy around, Turkey's invasion of Cyprus in '74 left it isolated and left- and right-wing terrorists groups fought running street battles. A military coup in '71 ousted Demirel. Özal headed for Washington to work for the World Bank, then went into business. Demirel was re-elected in '79 and Özal became his economic adviser. Özal pushed for radical changes, shock measures designed to create a market-based economy by opening the country to foreign investment and competition and by allowing inefficient state-supported industries to fail. He devalued the lira, let prices soar and controlled wages. Waves of strikes followed one after another. The following year the junta again seized power and decreed that anyone who'd been elected in the past was ineligible to run for office again. They retained Özal, who'd not held elected office, and promised him the five years of political stability he said he needed to turn things around. When the military allowed elections in '83 Özal formed his own party and, to the junta's consternation, won and became prime minister.

Nothing could stop this seemingly easy-going yet fast-moving, risk-taking, mesmerizing, preternaturally active wheeler-dealer with his incandescent vision of a modern but socially conservative Turkey. He survived a catastrophic plane-engine failure and an assassin merely nicked his finger. He deftly managed the generals and concentrated on the economy by stringing power- and telephone cables across the country, promising a fridge for every household and encouraging tourism. Anatolian entrepreneurs, risk-taking, pious Muslims like himself, took advantage of the new opportunities and flourished. Foreign companies responded to his overtures and slowly, steadily, Turkey shed its enervating statism and began pullulating with energy. A nouveau-riche of unctuous Muslims emerged, corruption became rampant, and charges of nepotism flew. Özal lost his popularity, had himself appointed president and usurped powers no previous president had enjoyed. He was now "the little Sultan". By the time he died in 1993, probably by poisoning, he had transformed Turkey beyond recognition.

In spite of the Iranian revolution next door, and though Özal was a devout Muslim, Islam would not become a major force in the country until later. The left feared it while the fascist junta hated it—you couldn't even sport a beard if you were a man or a headscarf as a woman if you worked for any level of government; even I had to shave off my beloved bristles to get into the university. Yet Özal surreptitiously unfettered an Islamic revival by allowing private schools, including religious ones, to set up shop.

All that to say that there was plenty of fodder for hyperventilating students in smoky haunts: the democratization of education, the free-market economy, the rise of popular Islam, the Little Sultan himself and much more. Demonstrations usually happened after Friday prayers on Beyazit Square. After the final Amen the devout spilled from the eponymous mosque onto the cobble-stoned expanse across the University to vent their spleens. They would be joined by angry trade unionists, embittered mothers whose sons had disappeared in custody and those disaffected students. Their only commonality was dissatisfaction with the regime. They would wave balled fists and shout "Allahu Akbar!", "God is great!", intermingled with insults and obscenities at the ranks of riot police. When they started hurling paving stones the police, wielding hard plastic shields and billy-clubs and backed up by water cannon, would charge.

I sometimes watched the excitement from the tea garden beside the mosque. While sipping a glass of Rize I once saw a large military helicopter hover ever lower over the crowd, its downwash creating such a dust-storm that demonstrators scattered in all directions.

26

Tears

"You have taken account of my wanderings;
Put my tears in Your bottle. Are they not in Your book?"

Psalm 56:8 (NASB)

. . .

Dear folks,[117]

... On June 14 Anna started bleeding quite badly, and we feared that we had lost the baby. She was two months pregnant. We rushed to the hospital and, indeed, she miscarried. However, the doctor suspected that there was something else wrong, although he was mystified as to what it might be. He did exploratory surgery, suspecting either a tubal pregnancy or that one of her ovaries had burst. Much to his surprise he found that her appendix was at the point of bursting. They removed it.

We spent the rest of the week in the hospital. I say we, because nursing care is so bad in this country a member of the family stays with the patient to change ped-pans, walk the patient, etc. We came home... Anna was doing really well... Last week we went back for a check-up and just as we were walking through the gates of the hospital a car hit us. I was basically unharmed but Anna, who could barely walk, was badly shook up. The incident really set her back. However, no broken bones or lasting damage, although she is only now starting to move about again.

So, we have had an exciting month, one not without a few tears. However, we have seen the hand of the Lord in these events...

---

[117] Letter to WEC Canada, July 2, 1987.

When we first found out that Anna was expecting we were reading from Malachi. That day we read that the Lord was seeking a godly seed for himself. We prayed that night that if our child was not going to grow up to love and fear the Lord, that He would take it. The Lord did so, and in doing so saved us, and particularly Anna, much more pain and trouble.

The doctor said that her appendix would have burst in two days' time. We were to have been in a little village on the Black Sea where there are no medical facilities. The Lord's ways and timing are perfect. Sometimes we see the reasons for His ways, or at least part of the reason, and we praise His name, and sometimes we don't... (but) we believe, and remember His faithfulness in days gone by.

Pray that we may continually be found walking quietly and steadfastly in the will of the Lord.

Sincerely,

Peter Pikkert

27

Heroes, Antiheroes and Heretics

"A funny thing happened on the way to my potential..."
From *A Thousand and One Nights*

. . .

DURING THE FALL of 1988 a remarkable group of people met in our subterranean appartement. Future church historians who ignore their stories and overlook their methods are merely scratching the surface of their subject for in the following decades those people became titans of the Turkish church. We gathered to talk about founding a church in which ex-Muslims felt welcome since the few existing churches run by ethnically Christian minorities were not places where Muslim seekers and converts felt at home.

Mike and Deanne were the only ones who'd been around long enough to master the language. I met Carlos at Istanbul University, where we sat next to each other. A skilled graphic artist with an impish streak, he'd sketch caricatures of teachers, sparking much muffled mirth as these were passed from student to student. He and Rosemaria were from Spain and, as yet, spoke no English. Brian and Deanne arrived around the same time we did. They'd had a rough start for, as unilingual Americans, were in the worst possible position to learn a new lingua-culture.

Language learning tends to be unidirectional, dictated by the relative economic strength of the communities involved. In order to get ahead in life, ambitious tribal people will learn the national language, Turkish or Arabic in the case of the Kurds. Smaller tribes like, say, Syriacs in Kurdistan, will speak Aramaic at home, the regional language, i.e. Kurdish, as well as Turkish. And, of course, everyone wants to learn English;

teaching English as a second language (ESL) is big business. Native English speakers, at the top of this totem, do something unnatural when they start learning a national language, and in politically and religiously oppressive countries people get suspicious: "Why do you want to learn our language? You must either be with the CIA or a missionary!" I myself have faced that accusation numerous times.

It didn't help that Deanne was pregnant and that Istanbul was much hotter, dirtier and chaotic than Washington State. Nor did it help that Anna, a keener sitting on the front row in the same language class, had already learned Hausa and Arabic, and that life in Istanbul seemed almost Edenic to her. There was another Spanish couple at that meeting, but they left within two years. Their place was taken by a remarkable American couple, brethren missionaries George and Donna.

Mike and Deanne were too busy translating the Bible and leading the mission team to join the pioneering church planting venture. Anna and I also declined, wanting to stay focused on Kurds. The others began meeting regularly at Brian and Deanne's house. Over the years that initiative overcame tremendous odds to become the *Beşiktaş Protestan Kilisesi*, the Beşiktaş Protestant Church, the first church in the country led by ex-Muslims.

Those successful pioneers had a number of things in common. Firstly, they learned the language well and took on the culture of the more disadvantaged. This fact, in-and-of itself, turned our American friends into top-notch missionaries for in doing so they broke the stereotype of the ugly American. Instead of seeking to turn others into images of themselves they set aside their own cultural trappings to cross the lingua-cultural hurdles by asking, "what is it like to be you? I'd like to experience what life is like for you as much as possible". In other words, they didn't parachute into the country and expect to be taken seriously. They recognized they needed to start at the bottom and earn the right to be heard and respected. They allowed themselves to go through the process of maturing linguistically and culturally all over again, to be, as it were, reborn as Turks, to grow and mature until they were perceived as Christian role models able to speak into people's lives with clarity and authenticity. There are not many who manage this; those who do become great missionaries.

Secondly, they persevered. Carlos, who also started the Istanbul Protestant Church, the first officially recognized church since the establishment of the Republic in 1923, is still there. It has spawned a number of daughter churches across the region. George and Donna stuck with the Beşiktaş church until retirement, when they finally bade a tearful farewell to a generation of Turks they'd nurtured in the faith. Another young couple of that era, Swiss Hans-Peter and Anna, moved to Antalya, a city on the south coast with no Christians whatsoever. They too became persevering heroes who mastered Turkish, embraced the culture, and saw a strong church of Muslim background believers come into being by following up correspondence course contacts and beginning a home Bible study. After decades of heart-breaking ups-and-downs that study evolved into a stable Muslim background-believer church with its own indigenous eldership and pastors[118].

Thirdly, these titans were theologically conservative, standing in the age-old tradition of those who interpret the Bible as normal Christians would with any other piece of ancient literature: based on its literary genre, historical context and how the original recipients would have understood it. Much as they sought to adapt to the local culture, they rejected anything that was unbiblical. They recognized that church life and the personal lives of believers must be purged of the sinful values of the prevailing culture.

My heroes didn't fudge the doctrine of hell nor the fact that salvation is found solely in Jesus Christ's atoning sacrifice. They taught that those who had not embraced God's gift of salvation in Christ would face perfect divine righteousness for eternity, while those who accepted the offer of salvation with

---

[118] The story of the Antalya church is told in *The Story Continues*, published by the Antalya Evangelical Churches, 2021.

life-transforming faith would live forever as objects of divine grace.

Fourthly, my pioneering friends shunned politics. Laser-like they focused on the church. That is what Christ died for, so that is what they lived for. Church life was about "preaching the unsearchable riches of Christ" (Eph. 3:8), the communal worship of God and Christian fellowship by people who, under other circumstances, have nothing in common.

Sadly, a disconcerting percentage of missionaries are not heroes, are, in fact, antiheroes. Herewith a few examples—just a few—drawn from my own experience and observations.

Some are so mulish they'd reject advice from the archangel Gabriel. Stubbornness is, of course, a prerequisite for pioneer missionaries; I've been accused of it myself. Without that attribute we wouldn't be where we are, doing what we do. But some are incapable of compromising on any issue. You cannot put them on a team for they leave a trail of broken relationships in their wake. A disturbingly high percentage of these specimens are of either Dutch or Korean extraction.

Others seek to foist some doctrinal hobby-horse on the rest of the community. If you don't hold to their particularly rigid, inflexible form of monergic Calvinism, or dispensationalism, or their strain of fundamentalism, you're an "evanjellyfish". Many a new church plant has been weakened by strong-willed ideologues drawing the gullible into their orbits. After wreaking havoc these bulldozers typically move on to create chaos elsewhere. Others, on the other hand, are so theologically dull they cannot explain the gospel in any language. I once had keys cut with a colleague who, I'd been told, had the gift of evangelism. As the locksmith ground out the object my colleague asked him if he knew Isa (Jesus). Though not common, Isa is occasionally used as a man's name. I could see the man's eyes go squinty as he racked his brain trying to remember if there were any Isas in the neighbourhood.

"You don't know Isa?" the missionary repeated.

"No, I don't think so," the man shook his head hesitantly while I paid for a shiny new key.

"You've got to know Isa or you'll go to hell," my friend asserted as we left. He'd "shared truth" with a Muslim and felt good about himself.

Some claim they are in the country "because they love Turks". That makes no sense to the Turks themselves, who are not only ambivalent about how they perceive themselves but are convinced the rest of the world is out to get them. In any case, "Turks" is an abstraction. We like or dislike particular individuals. I liked my friends Mahmut and Numan and didn't like Ekrem and Ayshe, though for the sake of the gospel put up with them.

Some are all raw emotion. I was responsible for one such an individual in his early years: unconstrained fervor collided with North Sea Calvinism. He'd wander the streets crying "Günah! Günah!" (Sin! Sin!) whenever he saw anyone doing anything wrong, of which he saw plenty since he could wander till dawn. When asked to share a devotional he'd metamorphose into an ancient prophet, leaping across the podium excoriating our lukewarmness, dissolving into tears while describing visions of hell as a gargantuan vortex drawing the Turkish nation into it, and challenging us to remedy the situation. Powerful stuff, though he must have skipped hermeneutics classes as his exhortations were only tangentially related to texts alluded to. However, he persevered, learned the language, married a sensible girl and, in the end, had an effective ministry. His emotional appeals were a hit with Bible school students.

Then there were the syncretists, a group known collectively as "the insider movement". Popular for a while, they sought to make the conversion of Muslims as easy as possible by fudging the deity of Christ and making public worship resemble that of a mosque. I was once invited to a "7:20 Conference" where they gave seminars on how to pray, act and worship like Muslims. Building their missiology on 1 Corinthian 7:20, *"each person should remain in the condition to which he was called"*, these "cutting edge" folk appropriated the apostle Paul's advice on marriage to encourage converts to stay inside Islam, to continue self-identifying as Muslims by praying in mosques, affirming the Five Pillars and repeating the Islamic creed that there is no God but Allah and that Muhammed is his prophet. They encouraged converts to think of themselves as Muslims with a special affinity for Jesus so they could stay within their own social networks and thus reduce the chance of persecution. They even published a Bible which excised notions Islam objects to, such as Jesus being the son of God, replacing "son" with words like "vekil" (deputy) or "God's Messiah". "Our Father" in the Lord's prayer becomes "Our loving, heavenly Lord". The fact that fundamental Christian doctrines were obfuscated and compromised and that Muslim suspicions of changes to the Biblical text were confirmed didn't seem to bother these folk. In fact, the ones I knew personally had a chip on their shoulder against those who didn't share their syncretism-celebrating Arianism. They looked down on us old-fashioned gospel-preachers who sought to contextualize the application of the message while remaining loyal to the Biblical text and the great creeds of the church. Thankfully theological truths are ancient and enduring and most errors and innovations ephemeral—as the insider movement proved to be. It is now largely passé though the damage they did, including the splitting of major mission organizations, remains.

Muslim converts I knew hated the insider movement. They had lived their lives in the dark cellars of Islam and had come into the light. They had joys and certainties to sing about—something never done in the mosque. They started writing music and praying spontaneously. They didn't want to bow and genuflect like fearful slaves anymore. "They want me to pray like a Muslim again?" one Iranian student of mine burst out. "There is nothing worse than having the guy in front of you pass wind when your face is in his butt. Oh, the joy of sitting and standing and clapping when singing and worshipping!" Later, after I'd become a theology teacher in the Middle East, I once asked my students to do a comparative study of angels and jinn in the Bible and the Qur'an. A recent convert, a young woman still wearing the chador, begged me to excuse her from that assignment: "I've just been saved from all that, from the false teachings of Islam and the Qur'an. Please don't make me read that stuff again!".

Some missionaries swung to the opposite extreme, refusing to accommodate to the culture at all. These types came in three varieties. The first insisted on the same lifestyle they'd had back home. A medical doctor and his wife missed all the perks of home. They rented the best apartment they could find and we did our best to make their life as easy as possible, yet the complaints never ceased. One day a neighbour phoned. Something was wrong, she said, and we'd better get over there. The front door was unlocked, a freshly cooked meal in the fridge, food and dirty plates on the kitchen table, along with a scribbled note "we've gone home". The man had gone to the bank, withdrawn money, bought tickets and got on the first plane out. He wanted us to ship their furniture after them. We sold it and sent the money instead.

The second type insisted that the way they practise their Christianity back home is how it should be exported to the ends of the earth. Korean Pentecostals I knew would scream and shout when praying, as they apparently do on their prayer mountains back home. Suggesting they modulate things so others might feel more comfortable had no effect. It was, in fact, almost impossible for non-Koreans to work with Korean clerics of any kind: the latter's sense of spiritual and cultural superiority could be overwhelming. "We are a proud people," one of their Presbyterian missionaries once warned me.

The third type are the escape artists. They will do anything but come to grips with the host culture and language. Some became potterers in their homes, making up for their failure by fixing this and mending that, then trying to improve what they just repaired. Some devoured every scrap of news about Turkey. They knew all that was going on in society but failed to engage with it. Some became involved in innocuous ministries, like the fellow who played the guitar in church and boasted about his worship ministry in his prayer letters. Some became wanderers. They called it prayer walking but they were basically full-time Christian tourists. Some escaped by going to every conference on offer. These were the self-styled mobilizers, networkers who recruit people for things they avoid doing themselves. Then there were home-schoolers, where father too spent inordinate amounts of time teaching the kids. Yet others exhibited bizarre behaviour: they wouldn't touch national food or let their children play with local kids. Others got caught up in some kind of innocuous activity, like stuffing envelopes for the correspondence course, photography, videography, or writing books (my problem). Others escaped from local realities by over-communicating with friends and family back home, phoning, writing and, after the advent of the internet, spending enormous amounts of time on Facebook, Twitter, Instagram, emailing, writing blog posts, or posting Youtube videos. One, a former helicopter pilot, spent hours a day at his computer flying a virtual helicopter. He later submersed himself in the expat community. Others were so scared of getting deported they did very little—you wondered why they bothered to stay at all. Some older missionaries, well past their best-by dates, hung around because they had some status in the local Christian community and feared becoming non-entities back home. Home churches, of course, support them all, naively accepting their glowing reports at face value. Some missionaries abandon the Christian faith. I know of several who became Muslims. Two co-workers committed adultery.

There is, of course, a final category. These are the ones who struggle bravely to learn the language but never master it well enough to teach or preach; they simply don't have the gift of tongues. Yet they refuse to throw in the towel and return home. They make friends with their neighbours, teach ESL, hand out Christian literature when appropriate, invite people to church, help new missionaries get settled, serve as field treasurers, give pastoral leadership to teams and serve in a thousand invisible ways. These are the humble saints of whom the world is not worthy, heroes too, who live exemplary lives before a steadily expanding circle of local friends and acquaintances. They form the back-bone of the evangelical missionary enterprise.

28

Plodding On

The moving finger writes, and having writ,
Moves on: nor all thy Piety or Wit
Shall lure it back to cancel half a line.
Nor all thy Tears wash out a Word of it.

Omar Khayyam

. . .

TWO YEARS OF unspeakably tedious rote regurgitation in Istanbul University's Türkology department was all I could stomach. Dominated by right-wing fascists and nationalists, teachers there still peddled the de-bunked Sun Language Theory, which holds that all languages stem from proto-Turkish, supposedly the language of the Sumerians.

I decided to teach ESL. The principal of the private institute which hired me liked missionaries for we did our job cheerfully and for little money; all we wanted were as few teaching hours as needed to get that coveted work permit. Some Turkish colleagues, working long hours to make ends meet, did not share her enthusiasm. One once cornered me in the staff room. "Pikkert," he demanded, towering over me while I sipped a glass of tea, "tell us what you're really here for". I could not admit I was a missionary—which everyone knew to be the case—as that would get me fired and possibly deported. The room fell silent; everyone looked in my direction.

"Ismet, you want to know what I'm really here for?" I asked forcefully.

"*Evet!* (Yes!)"

"Well, I wanted to live out my Christian faith in the most non-Christian environment possible, and I can't think of a better place than right here, with you," I said, pointing at his chest. After that I was left alone.

I was assigned top-level conversation classes. Though not allowed to touch the subject of religion directly, creative thinking sparked many a worthwhile conversation: "Today we'll talk about foods. Favorite foods, national dishes, that sort of thing". Soon someone would ask if I ate pork.

"Hmm... Jesus Christ once said that it's not what enters a man's mouth that makes him unclean, but what comes from it. What do you think about that?" Vociferous arguments on both sides of the argument would erupt and I'd had another successful lesson. "Reports from the school director and students clearly indicate that Peter has a gift for teaching... Oh that he had the freedom here to be a teacher of religion rather than of English!"[119] That would happen in due course.

On July 31, 1988, Anna gave birth to Owen Klaas Pikkert in Northern Ireland. Upon our return to Istanbul Anna started having horrible nightmares of Jesus and Satan wrestling. The recuring dream became increasingly distressing until, one night, Satan won, deeply shaking my ever sensible, stable wife. Then it occurred to me that during our absence something from the dark side had gained entry into our apartment. We turned the place up-side-down looking for we-knew-not-what. Finally, at the back of a drawer, I found the small, golden "evil eye" my students had given me before we left for Ireland for the birth. Turks pin these things to newborn babies to ward off the *jinn*. We destroyed the vile object and prayed in Jesus' name that whatever evil spirit was associated with it be driven from our home. Anna slept well again.

Although Owen was an easy child, full of cackles and smiles, it had been a difficult delivery and it took Anna a long time to regain her health. One breast infection after another, colds and the 'flu left her drained. "Then she developed a most horrible cough. Diagnosis: pneumonia! We did think she had a real humdinger of a cold!"[120] But that too passed.

---

[119] PL July 27, 1989.
[120] PL January 14, 1989.

"If Peter's gifts are in teaching, language, writing and literature, mine are perhaps in home-making and household management. I sometimes lament the fact that I have so little outside ministry, but then am reminded that I have a contented husband and a secure little boy who are happy to share their home with others. Peter is more in the public eye, forges ahead in the languages and is involved in several different ministries, while I try to be the 'suitable helper' at home. Though our roles are distinctive, we are a team and it works well."[121]

And so we plodded on, rejoicing in every assurance of God's presence and prepping for the day when the Spirit of God would work with unprecedented power in the Middle East by drawing great numbers of Muslims to Himself. We felt free to believe this because in the wake of the Iranian revolution an increasing number of Christians started praying for the Muslim world, and we were convinced that God does not give burdens like that in vain. Our mission team grew exponentially; there were now 23 of us from 6 different countries involved in a range of ministries: the Bible correspondence course, outreach to Central Asian Turks, Bible translation, literature distribution, personal evangelism, discipleship and language learning for newcomers.

We were elected to the field committee, led a weekly fellowship group and became "big brother and sister" to new missionaries. This meant helping them find an apartment, getting them into a language study program, showing them around, guiding them through culture shock, meeting with them for prayer and fellowship on a weekly basis and helping them get adjusted to life in the Middle East. Our Kurdish friend, the Bible translator Mahmud, came for supper once a week after which I'd give him an English lesson in return for a Kurdish lesson. "Pray that nothing may hinder the continuance

---

[121] PL July 27, 1989.

of these Friday night lessons as a better language helper could not be found."[122]

Owen developed into a serious, quiet, healthy and lovely child who "brings much joy as he scoots around in his little walker, getting into everything."[123] When he was a year old, "his strong will required careful channeling... The Turks just love him with his big blue eyes and fair hair, and he attracts many comments on the street."[124]

Politically things were unstable. The government fared poorly in elections yet clung to power. Inflation was out of control, bombs exploded far and near ("one nearby almost made me fall off the couch")[125], students rioted and a member of parliament shot and killed another in the chamber. The authorities stepped up their harassment of Christians. Several missionaries were arrested and their houses searched. We learned that the authorities were after a couple on our team and invited them and their three boys to move in with us.

> "Life is a bit hectic with so many of us in this two-bedroomed apartment but we are glad to have them stay with us. They are victims of the increasing police harassment of Christians and had to flee their home. People of weaker faith would have caught the first plane home but they have decided to stay and take legal action. It is an extremely difficult time for them and the least we can do is provide a roof over their head. Pray continually for us in dealing with the authorities—it requires great wisdom, much grace and endless patience."[126]

Our Turkish improved and the long years of preparation were drawing to a close. As word got out that we were pioneering a work among the Kurds others joined the effort and we established Kurdish Outreach Ministries (KOM). We also

---

[122] PL July 27, 1989.
[123] PL April 10, 1989.
[124] PL July 27, 1989.
[125] PL April 10, 1989.
[126] PL July 27, 1989.

laid the groundwork for a Christian magazine. "Learning how to use the computer on which we typeset, design and print out the master copy, writing articles, making a photograph collection, collecting thousands of addresses, and a host of smaller, related jobs have kept us busy."[127]

We came up with a name, *Yeni Yaklaşım* (New Approach), and pulled a team of writers together. We all chose pen-names. I called myself Tarik Kemal.

> "Pray that *Yeni Yaklaşım* may be used by the Lord to help clear the boulders of misunderstandings which clutter the vineyard and set forth Christ crucified in an understandable, forceful manner. Our vision is that... it will put us into contact with people who have an interest in spiritual things, enabling us first to begin a correspondence with them and then, if they so desire, follow them up with personal visits."[128]

The magazine would be illegal so it had to be produced and distributed on the sly. I would prepare a master copy on my newly purchased Macintosh and send the diskette to the WEC Press in England. They would print it and a volunteer there would send bundles of freshly printed magazines with address lists to a distribution network of youth groups, churches and individuals across the UK and Canada. These people would stuff a specific number of magazines into envelopes, hand-write the addresses on those envelopes, buy stamps and mail them back to Turkey. Recipients wanting to receive it on a regular basis had fill out a coupon and send that to a P.O. Box in Switzerland. Our co-workers there would smuggle these back to us during their periodic visits. Opposition dogged each step of the way.

> "We are engaged in a spiritual battle and Satan does not willingly let go those he has held in his clutches for so long...

---

[127] PL January 14, 1989.
[128] Ibid.

We are not the first in Turkey to see uncanny things happening to vital equipment. The hard disk on our computer mysteriously broke down when we were away for a few days. At first we thought we had lost all the information stored on the computer and thus had worked for many long months in vain. Peter almost wept. Now, after endless frustrations and no little expense we have managed to retrieve the information, though still cannot function properly until a repaired part arrives from the States. Getting the printer to cope with the special Turkish letters had been another headache and is as yet unresolved."[129]

We doggedly pressed on and one after another the hurdles were overcome.

---

[129] PL July 27, 1989.

29

Jebel Sima'an[130]

*Malak Ta'us (i.e., the Peacock Angel) existed before all
creatures... I (Malak Ta'us) was, and am now, and will
continue unto eternity, ruling over all creatures... There is no
place void of me where I am not present... The other angels
may not interfere in my deeds and work:
Whatsoever I determine, that is.*

From the *Keteba Jelwa*

. . .

THERE IS AN enclave in north-western Syria called Jebel
Sima'an, or Mount Simeon, named after a 4th century Byzantine
ascetic who spent decades there perched on top of a stone
pillar. This brother Sima'an, known as Simeon Stylites in
English, kept raising his lofty platform until it towered some 60
feet over the landscape. There he genuflected and preached
down to passersby. Admirers placed foodstuffs in a wicker
basket tied to a long rope. Other ascetics mimicked his
performance and in the course of time some 120 pole-sitters
dotted the landscape, "shouting down their theological
pronouncements from their little elevated balconies to the
expectant crowds below or giving personalized advice to those
favoured enough to climb the ladder and join them on their
little platforms".[131] The practice did not catch on further north,
where winters are harsh, nor further south, where summers are
blisteringly hot. After three-plus decades atop his pillar Simeon
died and the emperor of Byzantium built a magnificent
cathedral around his column.

---

[130] Details of this trip drawn from trip report written in August 1989
for WEC.
[131] MacCulloch, Diarmaid, *Christianity: The First Three Thousand
Years*. Viking, New York. 2009. p. 208.

Over time that pillar was ground one little chunk at a time into medicinal drinks by those who believed it had recuperative powers. When I visited the place it had been reduced to a stump about my height from the top of which I surveyed the ruined church around me.

After the Arabs conquered the region in the 7th century other theological convictions took root and flourished, so much so that the districts surrounding Mount Simeon—Antioch, Alexandretta and Aleppo—would become one of the most religiously diverse places on the planet. Greek Orthodox, Syriac Orthodox, Chaldean and Nestorian communities lived cheek by jowl with Sunnis, Alawites, Twelvers, Ismaili Shiites and Yezidis.

What interested me was the fact that although it is not contiguous with the rest of Kurdistan it has a high population of Kurds. It was also accessible. The medieval historian Sharaf ad-Din al-Bitlisi notes in his *Sharafname* of 1597, the earliest source of Kurdish history, that Kurdish *beys*, or landlords, had spread to the region, the northern part of which came to be known as *Kurt Dagh* (Kurdish Mountain) and the southern region towards the Mediterranean as *Jebel il-Akrad* (Mount of the Kurds). In the late 1930s a large number of Turkish Alawite Kurds fled there in the wake of the Turks' massacre of Kurdish nationalists in Dersim. They added their own colour to the regions' religious pastiche.

It was the Yezidi Kurds, commonly known as Devil worshipers, who intrigued me the most. They have a long history in the area. In 1599 one William Biddulph, a British chaplain serving in Aleppo, noted that "Coords" who "worship the devil" live there.[132] Whether they actually worship the devil or not is difficult to establish; the idea is offensive to the Yezidis themselves. In their cosmology *Malak Ta'us*, the Peacock Angel, is the first in a heptad of angelic beings, known

---

[132]   https://referenceworks.brillonline.com/entries/encyclopaedia-iranica-online/*-COM_1252Yazidis i. General" See also Biddulph, *The Travels of Foure English Men and a Preacher* (1609). Accessed Jan. 19, 2023.

collectively as the *Haft Serr*, or Seven Mysteries, into whose care God entrusted the world. Every so often these seven beings incarnate into human form, something called *kiras gehorrin*, or "changing of shirts". Their holy book, the *Keteba Jelwa*, or *Book of Illumination*, which they take as the words of *Malak Ta'us*, states that he is responsible for all blessings and calamities. Just as the Hebrews refuse to say Jehovah, their covenant name for God, so Yezidis refuse to speak the word Shaytan (Satan), with whom *Malak Ta'us* is somehow associated. In fact, they won't say any words which contain the "sh" sound for fear of mentioning his name in vain. This makes them readily identifiable.

I wondered if it might be possible to practise speaking Kurdish in Jebel Sima'an as this was still illegal in Turkey. I also wondered how open the Syrian Evangelical Church was with respect to the evangelization of the Kurds in that region; my earlier contact with Pastor Butrus in Qamishly had given me hope. So, although the family was down with food poisoning, we decided I should go ahead with that long-contemplated trip to the region. I took the night train to Ankara, booked a hotel room, headed for the Syrian embassy, filled in the application forms, handed over my passport and spent the rest of the day and night in bed trying to recover from the food poisoning. The following afternoon I picked up my passport-with-visa and snagged a night bus to Antakya (Antioch). I puked my guts out upon arrival, felt better and hopped on a bus to Aleppo. As the crow flies the journey from Antioch to Aleppo takes about two hours but we spent at least that much time at the Turkish side of the border and again on the Syrian side while the guards nearly dismantled the bus looking for contraband.

The next morning I headed for the Bible Society, to be informed that the director could see me on Saturday morning. It was Thursday. I got a haircut, took in a Duraid Lahham movie and went to the evening Bible study at a little Evangelical church. It was poorly attended but I met one Ahmed Junaid, a converted Yezidi. We hit it off. The following morning we travelled together to his village of Basufan, a Yezidi stronghold, and I spent a wonderful time with him and his brother Muhammed, who'd also become a Christian. I was deeply moved by this evidence of God's Spirit calling people to himself in that forgotten backwater.

The Bible Society director and his son gave me a very cool reception. They communicated in clearest terms that the Syrian church had no need for foreigners, that all we did was create problems. They were against any outreach to the Kurds, the son asserting that just as his forefathers had spoken Aramaic three centuries earlier but had since integrated into Arabic society, the Kurds ought to do the same. I asked if we should wait for three centuries before reaching them with the gospel and was rewarded with a contemptuous snort. When asked if there was anything Christians outside of Syria could do for them, he repeated that the best we could do was to leave them alone. I asked if we could pray together; I did. They kept silent, then sent me packing without the obligatory cup of coffee. The odious attitude of most ethnic Christians towards their Muslim neighbours never ceased to perturb. But I understood. Nothing was allowed to jeopardize their lovely Bible bookstore, church and medical clinic. Of the thousands of posters plastered everywhere of Hafez al-Assad, Syria's strongman, the most beautiful one graced their office. Unlike the eccentric St. Simean, up high and visible, these gentlemen preferred the low and discreet.

Next I visited a European couple who taught ESL which, they assured me, was a viable visa platform in both Damascus and Aleppo. They led a weekly Bible study in their home, had numerous opportunities for personal witness and rolled their eyes when I shared my experience at the Bible society. I left encouraged.

The overnight train carried me to Qamishly, in time for the morning service. Pastor Butrus, his wife and one of the elders of the little congregation of ethnic Christians invited me for supper. We talked at length about reaching the Kurds. Though cautious, they were much more receptive than the well-heeled folks in Aleppo.

The next day I learned that the eye of the *mukhabaraat*, the secret police, was near omnipresent. They questioned me closely, though politely. They knew exactly where I had been and who I had seen and wanted to know where I stood politically (when in Canada I usually vote Conservative) and what I knew about the Muslim Brotherhood (only what I'd read in books and the press). When they released me I walked across no-man's land to Turkey, caught a bus to Diyarbakir and home from there.

I concluded that it was possible to practise the curious Yezidi form of Kurdish in Jebel Sima'an for brief periods of time and that it might even be possible to set up shop in Aleppo and visit the region from there. All would have to be done without informing the city's leading evangelicals.

30

First Issues

"Give us wings to open the horizons of ascent, to break free from our confined cavern, the solitude of iron walls. Give us light, to pierce the deepest darkness and with the strength of its brilliant flow we will push our steps to a precipice from which to reap life's victories."

Fadwa Tuqan

■ ■ ■

WHO CAN DESCRIBE the emotions when the first issue of *Yeni Yaklaşım* rolled off the press? I'd been pregnant with her for years and had given birth at last. She was beautiful! True, it was a simple black and white production printed on a dot-matrix printer, but still... twenty pages of gospel truth, 3000 copies going to random addresses we'd assiduously collected from the four corners of Turkey. The lead article was on humans being created in the image of God and the ramifications which flow from that. There were articles about the unity and tri-unity of God, the power of the written word, the reasons why Muslims misunderstand Christianity, the trustworthiness of the Biblical text, God's final sacrifice in Christ and the first in a series on 1 John. Nothing like it had ever been produced in Turkish—but would anyone read and respond?

Several anxious weeks later our colleagues in Switzerland told us the first reactions were dribbling in. Then we heard from them again: multiple letters every day! We were elated! All those years of planning and prepping were bearing fruit! Some asked for free subscriptions, some for New Testaments yet others for answers to spiritual questions.

"Pray that we may have wisdom as we answer this correspondence."[133] A sampling:

"I am so happy that Y.Y. has opened new horizons for me." **Tahir (Kayseri)**

"I invite myself to the feast provided by Y.Y.!" **Ibrahim (Adiyaman)**

"I read your magazine slowly and carefully and cannot tell you how pleased and happy it made me. The subjects you touched on brought me much rest." **Isa (Mardin)**

"I want to tell you the good news! I am not a Muslim. I have rejected Muhammed. I have accepted the teaching of Christ. I want to continue my spiritual struggle here in my own country until I am put to rest beside my forefathers. Let us see the bells of the old churches ringing here again. I am weeping even as I write this, because I saw Jesus in a dream." **Mustafa (Diyarbakir)**

"I want to thank you for thinking of me, a guilty sinner. Although I have nothing in life and am forgotten in a corner of this prison, I want to thank you for sending me, your sinful brother, your valuable magazine." **Hamdi (prisoner in Turkish penitentiary)**

Someone in Switzerland ordered 1300 copies, so we printed 4000 copies of the second edition. The number of volunteers in the UK, Switzerland and Canada who posted the magazine back to Turkey kept increasing and we hired someone to help with typesetting. "Pray that all this effort may be in the strength of the Lord, rather than in the energy of the flesh, for then we can be assured that our labour will not be in vain."[134]

"For years I was an atheist. When I realized what Islam was all about I knew I couldn't accept it. I started reading the Bible in 1986. A long time has passed since then but

---

[133] PL September 20, 1989.
[134] PL November, 1989.

now I feel ready to become a Christian. Because when I read the Bible something moves within me... There is much joy in my heart but unfortunately there is no one here I can share this joy with or ask the many questions that fill my mind. I feel as though I'm by myself in the middle of the ocean. Would you be able to tell me if there is a group of believers here I can have fellowship with?" **Iclal (Izmir)**

"I found your magazine accidently in a rubbish bin. When I started reading it, it struck me as convincing. Your magazine's new approach caused me to change my mind about Christianity." **Aslan (Ankara)**

"I want to thank you for shedding light on issues that have been eating away at me. I have felt myself to be suspended in emptiness for a long time, searching yet not able to fill the emptiness within me. Your magazine crossed my path accidentally and I began to see some light. I've been thinking about what I've read for days and have come to the conclusion that it is the truth." **Alpaslan (Eskisehir)**

We printed 7000 copies of the third issue. Letters continued to pour in, convincing us that there was a deep spiritual hunger among Turks and Kurds, even if not every response was positive.

"Oh you poor bird-brained people, imprisoned by a twisted ideology and not knowing how or what to live for. Your labours are in vain. You cannot take our faith (Islam) away. Stop meddling in the affairs of Muslims or your end will be evil. Long live HELL for the oppressors." **Mesut (Dortyol)**

"You sons of bitches, are you all maniacs? While knowing that Islam is the only true way how can you believe in these idiotic homosexual Christian magazines? Your address has been forwarded to the Muslims in Switzerland. In the near future you will receive a surprise in your mailbox! Ha ha ha! You are all maniacs, sons of bitches. We're going to get you, you foolish drags. You'll soon be receiving a surprise in your mailbox... Farewell world!!" **(no name, no address)**

It was impossible to avoid the colds and 'flu which seemed to plague every resident of Istanbul that winter. Poor quality heating coal and the wet, foggy weather meant that the blanket of smog enveloping the city was unbearable at times. "Oh for a breath of fresh air!"[135] I still taught English two days a week and continued working on my Kurdish. We remained committed to our little Turkish fellowship and tried to carry out our mission responsibilities. And all the while the responses kept coming!

"I cannot believe how much I have been affected by what I have read. I can now say with ease that I am not a Muslim anymore. I've always had a fear of God in me but was never able to accept Islam. I was always searching. The fact that God had you cross my path must mean something. I want to learn more about Christianity. Unfortunately, I know so little. I guess the first step is to get a New Testament, the money for which you will find enclosed. Please help me. I want to walk in the way of God and Jesus Christ." **Kemal (Antalya)**

"I read your Spring and Summer editions and have come to realize that I really know nothing about Christianity. Please send me a New Testament that I might learn more." **Hamza (Istanbul)**

"I was amazed when I read Y.Y. I was unable to escape the many questions that came to mind. Although I read through the magazine many times I was unable to get rid of the turbulence in my mind. I had my family and acquaintances read the magazine and they too were amazed.

However, among ourselves we have nothing but questions, questions, questions... Well, we figured that

---

[135] PL November, 1989.

the way to get answers was to fill in the subscription coupon as fast as possible. If you have any other publications please send those as well." **Yasar (Trabzon)**

Owen developed rapidly and often had us in fits of laughter. He loved books, the cat which sat in the window sill, clanging saucepan lids and exploring those areas we thought were out of his reach. "What a joy the 'wee man' is to us!... Lord willing, next May he will have a little brother or sister to keep him company. Yes, Anna is expecting another baby."[136]

"Your magazine passed into my hands for the first time and I really enjoyed it. First of all you do not simply condemn people but talk about forgiving and forgiveness. It also pleased me that you are respectful of those who think differently. Enclosed please find the money for a New Testament." **Olgun (Kutahya)**

"When a friend gave me a copy of your magazine I determined to get in contact with you. I never understood anything about Islam until I'd finished high school. Then I joined a Qur'anic class but the rote prayers in a language I don't understand struck me as foolish. Nor could I agree with the textbook we used. It said that if the Qur'an were translated it would cease to be the Qur'an, and that we are to love Muslims because they are Muslims and hate infidels because they are infidels. After reading that I was turned off by Islam." **Erdal (guard in a Turkish prison)**

---

[136] PL November, 1989.

31

Blowback

"If you are going to walk with Jesus Christ, you are going to be opposed... In our days, to be a true Christian is really to become a scandal."

George Whitefield

■ ■ ■

WE KNEW THAT Yeni Yaklaşım would be contested and assumed that the line of attack would come from the Turkish authorities.

> "Yeni Yaklaşım will be like lighting a fuse—we don't know how long the fuse is, but sooner or later there will be an explosion. When that happens we will either be put in prison or deported."[137]

We hoped we'd sense when the authorities closed in on us so we could skip town prior to arrest as a clean police record would enable us to re-enter later on tourist visas for follow-up work. "Plead with the Lord that... when it inevitably falls into the hands of the authorities they will be unable to trace it back to us. Pray that I, especially, would not fear the consequences,"[138] Anna wrote prior to the first printing and, afterwards, "Pray for the Lord's protection. We know the authorities have read Y.Y. carefully—a copy in which the secret police had underlined in red all those parts they didn't like was returned to us in a roundabout way. There was lots of red!"[139]

We were wrong about the line of attack. The opposition, fierce, unrelenting and determined, came from fellow evangelicals who feared government reprisals. It manifested itself in ugly ways.

---

[137] PL January 14, 1989.
[138] PL July 27, 1989.
[139] PL November 1989.

"We have been the subject of threatening conversations and telephone calls. We expected opposition to come from the authorities (and no doubt that is still to come), but are deeply disappointed by the negative reaction of some Turkish believers... Motivated by fear, (they) seem determined to put a stop to the magazine at any cost."[140]

All the while the readers' letters flowed unabated.

"May the mercy and blessing of God be with you for publishing this magazine. I praise God for this publication and would love a subscription." **Hamdi (Ankara)**

"For as long as I can remember I have been an atheist. However, I want to thank you for publishing such a lovely, useful magazine. I'm beginning to see that your religion, unlike Islam, is not a heavy burden." **Ahmet (Adiyaman)**

"I am an irreligious Kurd. I know all about Islam but nothing about the Bible and Jesus Christ. I want to learn more, so I hope you will continue sending me your magazine." **Gurgin (Van)**

I was summoned to a meeting of church "leaders", mostly highly vocal individuals who spoke for themselves—there were hardly any churches to lead back then—and mission representatives.[141] Those who had written articles stuck with me. The attackers, one in particular, turned on them as well. I promised I'd refrain from using the words Kurd and Mesih İnanlısı (Evangelical) and embrace any limitations they asked for. I suggested they form a committee to proofread each issue before it went to press. I wasted my breath; nothing satisfied them. There was no room for debate, no margin for

---

[140] PL January 1990.

[141] This meeting led to the recognition that the missionary community and local churches should liaise on a regular basis and led to the formation of the "Leaders Advisory Counsel" which continues to this day.

compromise; if I didn't close shop they would inform the police. It was their way or prison and deportation.

I was reeling. Still naïve enough to believe that self-confessed Christians could resolve differences through prayer, looking to God's word, trusting the Spirit in each other and dialogue, I wasn't prepared for such ugliness. After that fateful meeting Mike, our laconic field leader, took me to a café. "Mike, I'm throwing in the towel." I struggled to supress my tears.

"I'd be disappointed in you if you did," Mike replied slowly. That was a long sentence for him for if he could say something in one word instead of two, he'd opt for the single utterance. And if he didn't have to say anything, he'd go with that. He hadn't said a single word during the meeting; none of the mission leaders had and I felt betrayed. "Peter was deeply hurt and disappointed by the manner in which the meeting was conducted."[142]

"OK Mike," I sighed. "I'll keep going." The WEC team, the KOM team, several Turkish church leaders and other missionaries all urged me to press on. One of the titans, George, procured a laser printer, an enormous hard plastic and stainless steel contrivance with hot rollers which pumped out sharp originals.

"A few months ago Peter was pleading with the Lord to take him a step further in his walk with Him. This present trial is probably designed for that purpose, so pray that he may persevere in it with patience, love and wisdom."[143]

And all the while letters streamed in:

"I want my friends to read Y.Y. as well. Enclosed you will find their addresses. Please send them a copy." **Sabah (West Germany)**

---

[142] PL March 1990.
[143] Ibid.

"I am a university student. I used to be an atheist but since reading your magazine have begun to realize what a big mistake that was. Here everyone is Muslim, or says they are. I used to be afraid to argue with them. Now, however, I know why and what to defend. My desire is that you will always be able to publish your magazine."
Erkan (Eskisehir)

Owen developed into a healthy, happy lad. "He is full of mischief though not really naughty. He still loves his books... We are very glad that he will soon have the companionship of a little brother or sister."[144] However, Anna developed pregnancy problems due to very low blood pressure. After a battery of tests the cardiologist advised bed rest and no stress! Hah! Our apartment's heating system, water pump and elevator broke down repeatedly and we had another stream of sewage bubbling its way through the hallway, dining area and bedroom. Two opera singers moved into the flat above and late night concert rehearsals and amateur singing lessons tried our patience. More than once I thumped on their door late at night to complain about the noise.

"Do we sense we are under attack? Yes, and almost literally too—Peter was attacked by a huge monkey. What next?"[145] Whether that ape, a chimpanzee, had escaped from an organ grinder or the zoo I do not know, but when we locked eyes on Taksim Square the beast leapt at me, latched itself onto my left leg, looked up and pulled its lips back to reveal large pink gums and an arresting set of incisors. I whacked it on head with my briefcase, whereupon it let go and bounded off.

"Life was certainly much more comfortable before Yeni Yaklaşım! Peter has never before experienced such heights of elation or depths of despair as in the last three months. We can scarcely contain our joy when we read letters from all over Turkey... Yes, life was easier, but

---

[144] PL March 1990.
[145] PL January 1990.

duller before. With the Lord's grace and your faithful prayers we press on—and that with joy."[146]

The mission's leaders concluded that we should continue the production of Yeni Yaklaşım as well as assume responsibilities as deputy field leaders for Kurdish Outreach Ministries (KOM) from somewhere in Western Europe. We hoped to last in Turkey until the end of summer 1990, go on a short furlough, and then set up shop elsewhere. Through an intermediary we informed the chief attack dog that we'd leave of our own volition, so please not to inform the police on us even though, "humanly speaking it is only a matter of time before the authorities catch up with us."[147]

The decision to move was confirmed by a new ruling requiring English teachers to be properly qualified. I wasn't, and thus forfeited my work permit. We now had to take the long bus journey to Greece every three months and re-enter on fresh tourist visas—not much fun with a toddler nor very safe in late pregnancy.

On June 1, 1990, the heavens opened and snagging a taxi when it rained in Istanbul was well nigh impossible. Drenched and frantic I ran from one street to the next trying to flag a cab. Nothing. "Lord," I cried in desperation, "we need transportation! NOW!" A taxi pulled up, two women stepped out and I hopped in. We picked up Anna. She was in advanced stages of labour. Traffic was reduced to a crawl; the chance she'd give birth in that cab was real.

"What's your name?" I asked the driver.

"Yavuz," he said.

"If it's born in your taxi we'll call it Yavuz," I said as Anna's contractions picked up speed.

"No, no, no... we'll get there in time," he squawked nervously and laid on the horn.

We made it, but only just. When they let me into the delivery room Anna was looking down at a little bundle in a pink sack.

---

[146] PL January 1990.
[147] Ibid.

She looked up at me tired but smiling. "It's a girl... it's a girl," she said dreamily. "I wanted it to be a girl..." We called that 8 pound, 5 ounce bundle Rita Joy. Rita after Anna's mother who'd come from Ireland to help out, and Joy because we were joyful. Actually, baby Rita was a joy during the day but suffered from colic at night. Anna cared for her until midnight, and then I'd take over. Cradling her on my forearm I'd pace up and down, up and down, until she eventually dozed off. Owen was "really tickled with his baby sister!"[148]

A letter from the doctor enabled us to extend our visas until mid-August. This meant we would not have to do another visa-renewal trip to Greece before furlough. God does all things well: losing my work permit was his solution to creating enough time for me to prepare several issues of the magazine in advance.

"I 1989 I read an article in a newspaper written against you people. I got your address from that article, but was afraid to write you until now. But some of the articles in your magazine really spoke to me, and I want to learn more about walking the pure and holy way of Jesus." **Erdal (Izmir)**

"I want to thank you for preparing this magazine. You have explained in the best way possible many things I never understood. Your magazine is practical and enlightening. That is why I want a subscription." **Levent (Hatay)**

"I am a teacher to 150 high school students. I have just finished reading your autumn edition and have learned much from it. I see it as my responsibility to teach the things I've learned to others. Of course you are well aware how difficult that is over here. Please show me how I can teach these things in the best possible ways. 150 students are waiting your support. I want them to know and understand the truth as well." **Ali (Diyarbakir)**

---

[148] PL June 1990.

Part 4

The Wilderness Years,
1991-1996

*"Bare heights of loneliness... a wilderness whose burning
winds sweep over glowing sands, what are they to Him?
Even there He can refresh us, even there He can renew us"*

Amy Carmichael

32

Move to Europe

"To be commanded to love God at all, let alone in the wilderness, is like being commanded to be well when we are sick, to sing for joy when we are dying of thirst, to run when our legs are broken. But this is the first and great commandment nonetheless. Even in the wilderness – especially in the wilderness – you shall love him."

Frederick Buechner

■ ■ ■

WE BADE FAREWELL to the great city of a thousand minarets with mixed emotions. We'd arrived as newly-weds carrying little more than suitcases and hearts full of vision and left as a family of four saying goodbye to our home and many close friends. The vision, at least in part, had become reality but at a cost. "It hasn't always been easy, but we have tasted and seen that the Lord is good and, resting in Him who does not change, look forward to the future."[149]

We moved into a missionary guest-house run by a spunky old saint. It took time to readjust; Canada's materialism and sexual flaunting seemed so upfront, so in-your-face. Letters from Yeni Yaklaşım readers were forwarded to us. "Reading and responding to them is a continuous thrill which follows us everywhere..."[150]

"I saw your magazine on the coffee table at a friend's house. I read it with pleasure and want to profit from it. Please send it to me regularly." **Huseyin (Malatya)**

---

[149] PL June 1990.
[150] PL October 1990.

"I was very pleased when you sent me your magazine. Through it I've reached true knowledge. The dark corners of my soul have been enlightened." **Huseyin (Kars)**

We shared about the work with friends, family and supporting churches, all of whom "fed our spirits, encouraged us to press on... and caused us to move up a size in our clothes!"[151] I also spoke at various Christian colleges, churches and conferences.

Owen, a gentle, loving child with a sensitive nature, made progress in talking and potty training. He even learned to dive into other kids' toyboxes rather than cling to mummy's skirt. Rita, chubby, cuddly and full of smiles, was more outgoing than her big brother—and potentially more defiant—yet never failed to charm.

Our team decided that after furlough we should settle in the Flemish mining town of Genk, 10% of whose population of 60,000 hailed from Turkey, half of whom were Kurds. As Flemish resembles Dutch I would not need to learn another language. However, securing a Belgian residence visa proved well-nigh impossible until someone suggested I resurrect my Dutch citizenship. A telephone call to the embassy followed by two trips to Toronto and, voilà, I was the proud owner of a freshly printed Dutch passport! We could now settle anywhere in the European Economic Community. That Dutch passport came in handy on a number of occasions.

"The missionary life, for us at least, is one of constant goodbyes. Yes, we are on the move again, this time from Canada to Europe. A new year, new friends, and a new location but, thankfully, two things remain the same: the God we serve and His call to us to take the gospel to the Kurds."[152]

---

[151] PL January 20, 1991.
[152] Ibid.

We flew to Switzerland for our annual WEC conference. Then I took a train to The Netherlands, purchased a used car from an uncle, headed for Genk, arranged temporary housing in a small apartment above a Baptist church and drove to Switzerland to pick up the family.

The cost of living in Europe was shocking. Our support had held up but not increased—and life in Belgium was much more expensive than in Turkey. We could not pay both rent as well as food and energy bills, a predicament resulting from Christian obedience, not from sinful behaviour: "God, do something... fast!"

One day my eye fell on a "For Sale" picture of an old house hanging in an estate agent's window. It was cheap! I went in, and the man showed me the portfolio of a three storey, semidetached brick house. "What's the catch?" I asked.

"The place needs work. No heating. Roof needs replacing. It sits on an old mine shaft. The government doesn't allow building in the area because if that shaft ever shifts your house will shift with it," he replied candidly. "It's down a dead-end street on the edge of town."

"I'd like to see it."

The house was worse than described. The kitchen was an addition at the back built over a well with a handpump feeding into a knee-high sink; the owner's wife, recently deceased, had been a dwarf. In spite of reasonable windows, it was gloomy; replacing the outside patio roof with see-through hard-plastic panels would fix that. The bathroom, added later, was OK. There were small, separate dining and living rooms, three bedrooms upstairs and an attic. The owner had raised pigeons—a quintessential Belgian pastime—and the backyard was crammed with foul-smelling, dilapidated coops filled ankle-deep with slimy, nacreous green, gray-tinged poop.

I smacked the building's outer walls with the flat of my hand: solid brick, though one section needed repointing. I stuck my head out the attic window: an inch of moss covered the slates, some of which were cracked. If cleaned and tarred they might last a couple more years.

"The government will pay half your costs when you renovate these old homes," the agent volunteered. "They're also going to run a gas line down the street this autumn".

"Can you help me fill in the appropriate application forms?"

"Sure. The place comes with the furniture."

I went home, told Anna what I'd seen and we did the math. We'd tithed and saved, so had a teensy bit of money in a savings account. We'd also received a small inheritance some months earlier. I revisited the friendly banker who'd helped us open an account upon arrival.

"I realize we're new in town and have no credit history, but this is what we've got for a down-payment," I said, and handed him the portfolio. "Will you loan us the rest?" The room fell quiet while he glanced at the papers, then at me.

"Okay," he said slowly.

"Could you add half the price of a central heating system?"

"Okay," he nodded. "I know some boys just getting in the business. They'll do it cheap."

Anna hadn't yet visited the place and wasn't feeling well when we did so. All she saw was filth, gloom, some dysfunctional renters and a huge German shepherd. "You're going to have to trust me on this one, Hon. Sign here." She did.

> "Never in our wildest dreams did we imagine that within three weeks of arrival in Belgium we would be possessors of a semi-detached house. An imminently suitable one came to our attention and then everything moved at lightning speed. Since the mortgage payments are considerably lower than monthly rent the only sensible thing was to buy."[153]

The renters promised to move out by August and did so in October, and a servant-hearted handyman helped us turn that sad fixer-upper into a cheerful home. We demolished those foul dovecotes, ripped the roof off the outdoor patio and knocked

---

[153] PL April 1, 1991.

out an interior wall. Pokey living and dining rooms combined into a single cheerful space with natural light streaming in. We tore out the knee-high sink, purchased cheap kitchen cupboards and ran water lines from the bathroom; we now had a real kitchen with running hot and cold water. I tied one end of a rope to the car's tow hook, tossed the other end over the roof ridge, advised Anna to not take the vehicle for a spin, climbed out the attic window and tied the rope end around my waist. I spent days sliding up and down that steep, mucous incline removing matted layers of moss with a paint scraper, then liberally lathered the whole with a tar-based goop. Soon we were entertaining overnight guests.

The one unresolved problem was heating, and as October rolled into November we huddled ever closer to the glowing coal stove. The HVAC chaps had delivered pipes and radiators but could do no more until the city ran that long-overdue gas-line down the street. I came home one day to find a middle-aged man in a cheap suit fussing with space heaters and measuring the electricity meter. Using body language Anna communicated that I was to say nothing. After the gentleman made his apologetic escape she explained how she'd put Owen and Rita into their winter gear, taken them to city hall, found the office that dealt with gas lines, tried to explain in her few Dutch words that she simply couldn't take the cold any longer and had burst into tears. No amount of previous phoning and cajoling on my part proved as effective as that lachrymal moment! Within days a yellow backhoe had dug a trench right up to—and no farther—than our house. By the end of January we were warm!

Most of the family was now engaged in language learning. Rita, at 10 months and cutting 8 teeth, struggled to say "da-da" while Owen and Anna tackled Flemish. She went to a school where that language was spoken in the classroom and Turkish in the corridors. Owen went to a local kindergarten. Unknown to us at the time he spent that year sitting by himself in the cloakroom next to the toilet. He never complained and, somehow, had learned Flemish by summer. My time was spent prepping Yeni Yaklaşıms and answering letters. We now had over a thousand subscribers.

"We read your magazine with pleasure and amazement, and haven't been able to forget it. We wondered what had hit us! If you are able to send us a New Testament and other useful books we will be very grateful. We want to become Christians as soon as possible." **Ali (London, England).**

"Hey Yeni Yaklaşım pilgrims, I read you magazine. I read it again and again and again. It was as though sweet spring water was poured upon my dry soul... The magazine showed me that my Islamic faith was an empty system of man's teachings. I used to be a teacher of the Qur'an. But I had a terrible fear of death. Whenever I considered death I nearly went crazy, but because I was a teacher of religion I couldn't share my fear with anyone. Sometimes I would faint with fear as I lived with this dread in solitude. But your magazine says, 'he who believes in JESUS will never die but live forever'. When I read that I fell on my knees and prayed to God in JESUS' name to take away my fear. God heard my prayer. I saw JESUS in a dream, and he has since then worked miracles in my household. He has brought peace, happiness and blessing, because JESUS took away my fear of death. I haven't been filled with fear since then. Truly God gave me and the souls of my household new life while still living in this world. Praise His glorious name. I wish that the new life JESUS gave me and my household be given to the rest of the Islamic nation. Amen." **(Yasar, Istanbul)**

33

Operation Provide Comfort[154]

"Stories, we all have stories. Nature does not tell stories, we do. We find ourselves in them, make ourselves in them, choose ourselves in them. If we are the stories we tell ourselves, we had better choose them well."

James Orbinski

● ● ●

ON AUGUST 2, 1990, Iraq invaded Kuwait and occupied it. We had prayed that God would destroy the spiritual powers dominating Kurdistan; the Gulf War destroyed much more as an American-led coalition bombed Iraq into a pre-industrial age. A ground assault retook the emirate and the allies crossed the border into Iraq. Instead of pressing through to Baghdad and oust Saddam Hussein they stopped partway and declared a ceasefire.

Encouraged by the President of the USA, the Shi'ites in the south and the Kurds of the north rebelled and for a few heady weeks everyone thought they'd succeed. But Saddam regrouped his forces and turned on them. While Bush the Elder fiddled Iraq burned. Ba'athist loyalists regrouped to round up and kill anyone they suspected of disloyalty. The rebels, both north and south, were defenceless against helicopter gunships.

Hundreds of thousands of Kurdish refugees fled for Turkey that Spring of 1991. It left them to fend for themselves in a mountainous border region cordoned off by the Turkish military. Still, though strafed from the air and risking their lives crossing mine fields, the chaotic deluge of people poured in. They came on foot, on donkeys, crammed into trucks or sitting in the scoops of tractors.

---

[154] Significant portions of this chapter appeared previously in my booklet *Letter from Kurdistan*.

While the flood of refugees made its way to Turkey from one end I was wending my way from the other in the comfort of my Toyota. Our newest recruit filled the passenger's seat, his worldly possessions the rest of the car. It was early morning, darkness ceding to first light. The roads were deserted. We'd passed Plovdiv, Bulgaria, and turned onto the E80. A couple of hours would take us to the Turkish border. I'd done all the driving and couldn't keep my eyes open any longer.

"You awake?" I asked.

"Ja," he replied. Dani was Swiss.

"Can you take over? I'm getting drowsy." We changed places and I dozed off. Next I felt the car swerve uncontrollably. Dani was asleep. I shouted. The car slammed into the metal guardrail running down the middle of the highway and bounced backwards onto the shoulder.

"You OK?" I asked. No answer, but Dani seemed intact. I took a deep breath, stepped out, and examined matters. The front left fender had crumpled over the tire, the headlight smashed. No leaks.

"Can you help me try and pull the fender off the tire?" But Dani was in shock, shaking like jelly in the wind. I pulled and yanked at it myself until I'd freed the tire.

"Move over, will you? Let's see if she'll start." She started. I put her into first gear and we drove off.

We got to the border. The Bulgarian official looked askance. I told Dani to pray like he'd never prayed before.

"Guten morgen." I can morph Dutch sufficiently to be understood in German.

"Guten morgen," he responded. "Sie hatten einen Unfall. Hast du eine Anzeige von der Polizei?" (You've had an accident. Do you have a police report?)

"Nein, habe ich nicht. Es war sonst niemand beteiligt." (No, I don't. There was no one else involved.) I explained what happened.

"How do I know you didn't kill anyone?" he asked.

"I assure you we didn't hit anyone," I repeated.

"Warten Sie hier" (Wait here). Dani, who'd stopped shaking, prayed silently. I stood by. Eventually the man reappeared. "Go ahead," he nodded. As we crossed into Turkey I exhaled long and deep through pursed lips. The Istanbul team took both the traumatized Dani and the damaged vehicle under its wing.

I headed for the Dutch embassy. "I speak Dutch, English, Arabic, Turkish and some Kurdish, and wonder if I might be of some use in the refugee crisis," I told the secretary.

"Wait here," he said. A few minutes later a woman appeared. She began talking to me in Arabic with a Dutch accent. She was good and we had a nice chat about Jordan and learning Arabic. She suddenly switched to Turkish and we continued our conversation in that language. After a while I asked her if she'd like to switch to Kurdish.

"You've got me beat," she smiled. "Give me your contact number and we'll be in touch."

The next day I was part of Operation Provide Comfort, the allied attempt to assuage their consciences and atone for their sins.

Ankara > Diyarbakir

The embassy connected me with the Dutch branch of Medecins Sans Frontiere (MSF, Doctors Without Borders). They'd just arrived, had taken a number of rooms at the Ankara Sheraton and were unpacking. "I'm the translator the embassy told you about," I said as I walked through the door.

"Good. We're trying to set up an office. Need a fax machine, photocopier, paper, some furniture." Clearly, money wasn't an issue.

"Sure." I borrowed a phonebook from the lobby and called an office supply company. Everything arrived chop chop. MSF was impressed.

"We need to get to Diyarbakir. The embassy said that the individual who can give us permission to enter the refugee camps will be there tomorrow.

I called around. All flights to Diyarbakir were booked—every relief agency was making its way there. I phoned a company chartering private jets; their representative showed up promptly with a manual credit card machine.

The following morning some of us climbed aboard a corporate jet for the 1 ½ hour journey. We landed, taxied towards the terminal building but stopped short.

"What's the matter?" I asked the pilot.

"The prime minister and his entourage are in that helicopter" he pointed. "I can't approach any closer until they've taken off". Something clicked in me.

"I think the guy we want is in that helicopter," I told the MSF director.

"We gotta get to him," he said.

"Can you open the door?" I asked the pilot. "We'll walk."

"Tamam" (OK). He opened the door and the steps unfolded.

"Follow me," I said. We disembarked but instead of walking toward the terminal I headed for that helicopter. Its rotors spun slowly, lazily, the bay doors still open. A team of blue-bereted commandos surrounded it.

"Acil Durum! Acil Durum!" (Emergency! Emergency!) I called out. The soldiers stepped back and let us through. I stuck my head into the chopper; 4 or 5 men wearing dark suits and strapped to their seats looked questioningly at me.

"Hello, Prime Minister," I smiled and nodded at Yıldırım Akbulut. His arm was in a sling. "Geçmiş olsun." That's what you say when someone has hurt himself. He nodded. I looked around. "We're trying to locate Mr. Necati Utkan." An elegantly dressed, silver-maned gentleman leaned forward. "That's me," he said.

"We're from Sınırsız Doktorlar Heyeti (Medecin Sans Frontiere). According to the Dutch embassy we need your permission to enter the camps..."

A hesitating split second? Then, "See me tonight at 8 PM in the Plaza Hotel." That evening we received the requisite papers.

MSF can move fast. We rounded up some journalists ("You want a story, stick with us"), rented white Suzuki jeeps, slapped MSF stickers on the sides, threw a tent, some cots and bags of rehydration fluid in the back and headed for the camps. Four hours through mountains I knew well and we reached the long line of armed soldiers preventing the Kurds from entering further into Turkey and everyone else from reaching the refugees.

"Boys, start filming," I told the journalists as the soldiers closed in on us. I shouted "Sınırsız Doktorlar Heyeti" with bravado while the director waved our permission in the air. Once again the soldiers stepped back and let us through.

After topping a little ridge we descended into the surreal world of the main camp. The eerie mist rising from the ground and the penetrating rain shrouded a myriad of multicolored sheets housing over 100,000 people. The overwhelming stench of carcasses and human feces wiped away the fleeting impression of a huge, grotesque family campground. Thousands of blackened tree stumps appeared to pin the camp to the steep degree slope. Rain had turned the clay into a squelching quagmire. We found a flat area, quickly pitched the tent, assembled some cots and hung the MSF flag. Presto! Our first patients were rehydrating. Subsequent memories collide and merge like patterns in a kaleidoscope.

Turkish-Iraqi border: Işıkveren Camp

MSF is well-connected and well-heeled. Chartered aircraft delivered supplies to Diyarbakir airport and rented trucks hauled the goods to the base camp, where the relief agencies had their supply tents and the army its encampment.

Our truck passed through the line of soldiers and into the teeming mass who, mad with hunger and thirst, fell on us like crazed vultures. A muscular relief worker climbed into the back and, cursing and swearing, beat off the marauders with a stick. When he couldn't manhandle the vultures any more I joined him, pushing and shoving people off the truck with a sturdy piece of timber. Suddenly the tarpaulin ripped loose. Bottles of water and loaves of bread fell off to be crushed in the omnipresent muck. The driver increased speed dangerously. We arrived at the clinic exhausted. The army guards helped unload what little remained of our cargo.

MSF was the first NGO to gain access to the camp. As the world became aware of the Kurds' plight, however, the allies organized a massive aid operation to provide relief for the millions of exhausted people pouring across the border. I watched those exhausted souls struggle on foot past long queues of abandoned vehicles, climbing down the pass and to the camp. The weather was awful, foul, sub-zero. Many, particularly the very young and the aged, died of dysentery, hunger or exposure and were buried alongside the road. The camp's cemetery was right behind the MSF clinic—little consolation to the long line of dry-breasted mothers waiting in the rain, nursing their dehydrated babies. Our shovels were in constant demand.

The clinic became a 40 bed hospital. Latrines were dug. The weather improved. Progress! As long as you refused to think of the vultures as fellow humans you didn't mind beating them off the truck.

Turkish-Iraqi border: Yeşilova Camp

We'd only just arrived. The Kurd's leg was gangrenous, the bullet still lodged in the slimy appendage. The doctor, someone from a rival organization, set up a collapsible table along the creek separating Turkey from Iraq, donned a chartreuse coloured surgical gown, attached various accoutrements to his patient, and put him under. I moved to a knoll overlooking the site to better witness my first amputation.

The doctor was almost finished when a huge double-bladed Chinook helicopter descended over the operating table. Bottles, medicines, surgical clamps and other attachments and accessories disappeared in a violent cloud of dust and dirt. The doctor struggled to keep his table and patient from following the rest of his gear into the creek. The helicopter jerked back up and everything went strangely quiet. The patient had died.

Mr. Big Shot

As one of the few who could communicate with everyone I was in demand. People admired me because I spoke many languages and got things done. Nothing was impossible, no order too large: depots, landing rights, meetings with officials; I arranged everything with apparent ease, as though my entire life had prepared me for this.

In the middle of it all I did a quick trip to Belgium to complete the purchase of the house. I drove non-stop across Europe, signed the papers, and flew back to Diyarbakir, back to the big adventure! Fueled by adrenalin, I felt alive! I had stature, was sought after, successful, a somebody!

The Dutch army made a helicopter available. The aviator, a girl about my age wearing an air force flight suit, handed me a headset and we climbed aboard. We ascended and, following the contours of the Tigris River, headed for Zakho, Northern Iraq.

"You like excitement?" she asked.

"Sure do..." The Alouette plunged earthward, then skimmed above the surface of the river, swaying this way and that as she maneuvered the machine between the ochre cliffs as if we were in an immersive video game. "We never get to do this back home. Too many regulations."

I was ashamed of the futile efforts of the Christian agencies. If their personnel hadn't mooched ration packs of the US army they'd have been as famished as the refugees. Our secular organization, on the other hand, operated efficiently and on a large scale. Our doctors, nurses and logisticians were true medical adventurers. I admired them. Intelligent, innovative, courageous, gladly sacrificing comfort, they were people I related to. They seemed refreshingly different from my missionary colleagues.

Darkar, Iraqi Kurdistan

After the allies established a no-fly, war-free zone in Northern Iraq they packed the refugees into trucks and shipped them to newly established resettlement camps. We followed, hoping to relocate our hospital in one of the camps. The allies had, however, already set up excellent medical facilities. We were left with nothing to do and a multi-million dollar grant to do it with.

We made contact with the Kurdish guerillas. They led us to Darkar, a village which had somehow been overlooked. While the villagers watched we opened a clinic and a well. We hauled in pipes, pumps and generators and got water flowing up to the village. While we sweated to get electricity going the villagers used the water and the medicines and continued to watch us work.

We asked the village chief if he would send someone to cook lunch for us and someone else to clean the latrines. He served us tea and thanked us profusely in the name of the Kurdish people, the Kurdish Democratic Party and his village. Two days later we went back to renew our request. He served more tea and thanked us even more profusely. After two more days we gave up and got our own cook. The villagers continued to watch us passively and use latrines piled high with their own excrement. I figured we'd be able to spend those millions when cholera broke out. And, sure enough, it did.

Potiphar's Wife

In the evenings we sat around our satellite dish and chatted. My colleagues didn't believe in God and made mincemeat out of my well-formulated arguments for his existence. They were existentialists: life is a challenge worth living for the sake of it. I understood. I too was living to the full, living on the cutting edge, soaring like proud Icarus. As I felt my Christian convictions ebbing, alienation from my fellow missionaries grew apace.

I wasn't the only translator. The other one, like myself, was also Dutch. She admired me because I spoke Arabic and Kurdish as well as Turkish; she only spoke Turkish. Though she was beautiful, it was her voice which bewitched me. I would get her to speak, ply her with questions, just to hear that warm, melodious voice. Her answers didn't interest me. In that rough, evil world her soft, caressing voice was like balm on my wounded spirit.

She knew I was married and had two children; she didn't care. We'd had supper together and were wandering through the dark streets of Diyarbakir back to our lodgings. Suddenly she stopped, reached into her handbag and showed me the depot key. It normally stayed with the logistician. She looked up at me and I felt her breath quickening.

"Let's go to the depot..." Those shining eyes looking into mine, that winsome smile and her caressing voice were the complete antithesis of the ugliness we'd witnessed. The Hollywood film I'd been living was reaching its inevitable climax. My will melted and my heart pounded. The stuffy heat closed in around me.

I closed my eyes and took a deep breath. That instant I had a vision. I saw Joseph running from Potiphar's wife. I saw it as clearly as if I were there. Suddenly I understood. He wasn't running from Potiphar's wife at all—he was running from himself. He couldn't resist her any more than she him. Another instant and he would have taken her. Suddenly the awful realization of what he was about to do came to him and he fled, not even trusting himself to pick up his cloak.

I looked into her expectant eyes, turned and ran. I could feel her eyes piercing into my back. I ran through the dark streets to my room, closed the door, but didn't have the will to lock it. I flung myself onto the bed hoping she'd followed me. I wanted her to walk through that door. She didn't.

.

The Lufthansa jet lumbered through Ankara's infamous smog and took off, pressing me against the seat. The smog enveloped my heart and soul, my sluggish mind barely comprehending that P. Pikkert, once proud pioneer missionary to the Kurds, had been brought to the brink of adultery and apostasy. I stared dumbly out the window, a desolate void in my chest stifling harsh self-recriminations.

I was spiritually bankrupt, my zeal burnt out, my faith dissipated. How could I preach the new birth when it made no significant moral difference? How could I face my wife? How could I continue as a missionary? How could I preach a loving God after witnessing his total lack of concern? I felt betrayed, deluded. Had a decade of fervent missionary work been based on a lie? The lie of a loving God? Something profoundly meaningful—that which had been the driving force of my life—was gone, irretrievably so, it seemed, leaving me extraordinarily lonely and fragile.

34

The Final Price

"Only He who gives faith can maintain it."

Anonymous

• • •

I, WHO'D HELD his struggling co-workers in mild contempt, had been weighed and found wanting. I was the weak and worthless one, not they. My faith had failed when the fires grew hot, not theirs. A decade of missionary work had been based on a lie—not the lie of an unloving God but on my self-delusions. The ugly reality of what I was and am had sunk its clutches into my soul and dragged it to my conscious attention. All was black.

The Lufthansa jet landed in darkness. Anna was waiting at the airport. Her love never failed. I'd feared I'd lose her love and, worse, her respect if she knew all. But she, in whom there is no guile, knew me too well.

I was exhausted, an emotional and spiritual wreck. For days, weeks, I'd wake after a restless night, eat breakfast, and tumble back into bed. After lunch I tried to fulfill some team responsibilities or putz on next Yeni Yaklaşım—but it all felt fraudulent. The self-recriminations took on a nightmarish quality, scrolling in my mind like a loop tape for endless hours. Anna had me back physically but not spiritually or emotionally. I gradually confessed everything. She didn't claim to understand but her unqualified, unmerited love, her prayers and her respect for my honesty restored some equilibrium.

In Iraq I'd lost my faith in a loving God and in the reality of my spiritual experiences. Still, the fact of Jesus Christ haunted me. He had to be who he claimed he was: the crucified and risen Son of God who'd come to take away the sin of the world. That was the bottom line. Why? Because there is no alternative. To claim he never existed is absurd. To assert that, like me, he was a deluded liar is sacrilegious, obscene. To ignore him is too dangerous.

One morning, months later, an innocuous event at our annual conference disclosed a second, intensely liberating truth. The Gulf War and Operation Provide Comfort had prised open Iraqi Kurdistan, and various agencies, including ourselves, had rushed in and set up shop. A missionary on our newly formed Iraq team led worship. "Guys," he said, "I'd like to teach you a worship song in Kurdish composed by a Kurd who recently came to Christ." He handed out the lyrics, fine-tuned his guitar and we began to sing.

At that I began to grasp a profound reality: He, God, was willing to pay any price, the ultimate price, for his elect. Any price! I'd doubted God's love because he let the innocent suffer and die. Yet he was willing to pay any price to save some. Any price... The ultimate price. I struggled to grasp it. An awful, unchanging, almighty God deliberately orchestrating the centuries to lead to the crucifixion of the second person of the Trinity for the sake of some. That was the ultimate price. But the ultimate price wasn't the final price. Light dawned in the darkness. A truth which became a bedrock of my theology emerged from the murk.

The ultimate price, the divine torment of Calvary, reconciled God and man, opened heaven's gate. But we, like forlorn sheep, need to be driven through that open gate. That is why the ultimate price is not the final price. The sovereign God continues to orchestrate the centuries to drive home his chosen ones. The suffering, the agony of the millions will continue until the some are driven through that gate. Then the end will come.

The world might have been a huge Disneyland where everyone, oblivious of his need, has a jolly time. But then, on the day of judgement, all would be damned for sin and would be unatoned for. And a Calvary in Disneyland is a travesty, an atonement unapplied. Do not the troubles of today drive home our utter helplessness and hopelessness? Is it not sovereign grace when some, brought to the end of their resources, cast themselves on him, whose abounding grace is manifest in the divine torment of Calvary? Is it not sovereign grace that drives some through the open gate?

This I knew from experience. As I was on the cusp of plunging into the moral abyss God gave me a vision of Joseph. When my faith lost its grip on him, he grabbed hold of me, confronted me with Christ. He would pay any price, the ultimate price, to save me from myself and from a Christless eternity. Since, for some inscrutable reason, I too was of the elect, a covenant child, absolutely nothing could separate me from the love of God. God intervenes on behalf of some! How awesome, how humbling. That kind of love demands worship and compels holiness and glad obedience.

The innocent men, woman and children perishing on that mountainside on the Turkish-Iraqi border appeared to me God-forsaken. Yet their suffering was not meaningless for that mountainside burdened many saints to intercede on their behalf, to give of their money and to commission their sons and daughters to missionary service. Saddam's victims did not suffer and die in vain for that mountainside opened the door for the gospel. And the gospel, even if shared haltingly in broken Kurdish by struggling missionaries, is powerful. It can convince God's elect of their utter helplessness and crowd them to Calvary. And now Kurds were singing and writing worship music to him who'd given his all, his life, for their eternal well-being.

35

Salmagundi

*"Our work appears to consist of a jumble of disparate pieces
which we sometimes struggle to combine
into a harmonious whole."*

Pikkert Newsletter, February '93

• • •

THE TRIUNE GOD allows us to be disappointed in him if that
contributes to him drawing his own to himself. Although that
shaft of theological light enabled me to regain my footing the
Belgium years were not easy. In the sterile solitude of a home
office the teeming multitudes of Islam were distant phantoms.
Within a year I wrote that "I'm restless. This sterile Western
world isn't for me. I long for the throbbing streets of Istanbul
and the virile mountains of Kurdistan—places where men fight
for survival instead of mow the lawn."[155]

We did not doubt the Lord's leading nor were we bored. A
variegated salmagundi of activities kept us hustling. Yeni
Yaklaşım burgeoned. Eventually eighty dispatch groups in eight
different countries mailed out 4000 to 5000 copies a quarter[156]
and I carried on a lively correspondence with those expressing
an interested in the gospel or had testified to God's grace in
Christ. The volume of mail the long-suffering postman hauled
up the street for us every working day astonished the
septuagenarian couple next door who emptied our box when we
were gone.

> "Looking at the stacks of letters and parcels on their
> dining room table I (Anna writing) had a mixed reaction:
> personal letters, over a hundred Y.Y. responses—these all

---

[155] PL November 1992.
[156] See KOM Conferences Reports for 1993 and 1994.

bring much joy. Bills and business letters reminded us that we had a month's work to catch up on."[157]

Anna kept track of the dispatch groups and juggled the various accounts, currencies, and exchange rates, trusting the Lord to match income to expenditure. "Finance has been a recurring issue, though we have seen the Lord working miracles for us"[158]; "if we had known when we moved to Europe what the end of year accounts revealed yesterday we may well have panicked".[159]

∎

"My dear brothers and friends of God, I am a Muslim, a servant of God. I was very pleased with the magazine you sent me. I would love to receive a copy of the New Testament as well. However, I am a Muslim, and not one of those secular, democratic Muslims either. I am a Muslim who believes with heart and soul in the Qur'anic law. However I thoroughly enjoy your magazine as it teaches me more about Christianity. Should you ever come to our town I would be very pleased to meet with you." **Arif (Mersin)**

∎

Kurdish Outreach Ministries grew to 25 individuals representing 10 different nationalities. Our folk in Belgium, Germany and Switzerland were involved in Bible translation, the production of radio programs, evangelistic videos, magazine production and administrative work while the Middle East contingent kept busy with language learning, personal evangelism and discipling new believers.

"Pray that God would make Peter and I wise assistant leaders."[160] Coaxing a rapidly growing, multi-cultural team of strong-willed people came with its own challenges. "Kurdish isn't the only culture we have to adjust to! Pray for deep unity

---

[157] PL November 1993.
[158] KOM Conference Report, 1993.
[159] PL February 1994.
[160] PL November 1993.

as the team expands"[161]; "adjusting to one another on the team is almost as difficult as adjusting to the Kurds."[162]

•

"May God bless your service in the Messiah's cause and may His help be with you. I want to thank you and to let you know that I am praying for you. I am learning much about the Messiah from your writings. Yeni Yaklaşım should be read by everyone!" **Ugur (Ankara)**

•

Although my heart was in the Middle East I could at least study Kurdish in Genk without the risk of deportation. I spent Thursday afternoons in a Kurdish teahouse playing chess with Nuri, whose brisk bishop or lurking knight frequently pinned my king and rook, carried on animated discussions on a range of topics with the other regulars and exploited opportunities to talk of spiritual things. Hassan, the owner, was the only one who ever showed an interest. When he suddenly died of a heart attack the place closed up.

The sole Belgian to frequent Hassan's was his burly, straight-talking book keeper. Once while imbibing chai with him I complained that the government was putting me out of business. Officially self-employed, I paid an astronomical amount into a social security fund.

"Take 'em to court," he advised.

"How do you do that?"

"Swing by my office and I'll give you the forms." I swung by his office, filled in the forms, sent them off and forgot about it.

•

"I curse you all. You are thickheaded, spidery fanatics spinning your evil webs. You do not preach the original Christianity but a lie. I curse you all. We have chosen for Islam and, if Allah wills, will live as Muslims until we die.

---

[161] PL February 1994.
[162] Letter to Macosquin Presbyterian church by Anna, May 25 1995.

I don't know from where you got my address, but I never want to receive a letter or magazine from you again. Don't bother me with your trash." **Nabi (Gaziantep)**

.

While I was making friends in the Kurdish community Anna gave up trying. This was a difficult decision but her friends were the women in her Dutch class, particularly a Brazilian and Belarusian, the latter of whom she led to the Lord. Beside learning Dutch, running the household, tracking our personal finances, raising two kids and handling ministry logistics, her real gift was, and always will be, hospitality. "Last year 48 people stayed at least one night in our home, and one couple spent 7 weeks with us. Hospitality is an aspect of our work which combines business and pleasure."[163]. That was Anna's take. Mine was more nuanced: "Peter says that having guests is three times as much fun as not having guests: you have the pleasure of anticipating their arrival, of having them with you and of seeing them go!"[164] Once eleven people filled our every nook and cranny. When the crowd finally departed I was at the front door waving them off with gusto and cheer.

One day the self-same pastor who'd advised me years earlier to "go to Bible school, maybe they can straighten you out" showed up, sent by his denomination to help our little Belgian Baptist church. For three weeks Lambert and his wife lived with us while we got them settled. Having two mature Christians around did us good and the kids enjoyed having surrogate grandparents.

Upon our return to Canada decades later I chanced upon Lambert one last time. I heard muffled noises emanating from the sanctuary during a prayer meeting and wondered what was afoot.

"A visitation," someone informed me.

"Anybody I know?"

---

[163] PL February 1993.
[164] PL May 1995.

"Probably not. He was a former pastor, before your time. His name was Lambert Baptist." There were not many visitors just then so I took time thanking God for the big, cheerful, godly, unconventional man who'd once inhabited the waxen cadaver before me.

·

"Yeni Yaklaşım first drew my attention when I saw it at a friend's house. I want to learn more about Christianity. It is almost impossible to learn about Christianity here in Turkey, and any publications which do deal with the subject are very biased, so I decided to write to you. I am a historian and want to increase my knowledge of Christianity. Please help me." **Turgut (Elazığ)**

·

The Mesut affair... Two days before Christmas 1993 a stocky, hirsute Kurdish acquaintance phoned in a panic: "My parents discovered I'm a Christian. They've taken my passport and ticket to Turkey and are after me. Can I come?"

Mesut was born in The Netherlands but had trained to be a Muslim religious teacher back in Turkey. He had been to Mecca but then became a Christian. And he wasn't just a friend—he was in love with one of my numerous Dutch cousins. I'd sent her to Turkish acquaintances in Istanbul to learn a little of the language and culture to help ease her into that relationship. Mesut was on the cusp of flying over there to ask her to marry him when his family found out. They broke into his flat, stole his passport and airplane tickets and threatened to kill him if he didn't denounce his faith in Jesus. The father spoke of hiring someone to do him in.

He showed up tired, dishevelled, not knowing what to do. We phoned his family but to no avail. We phoned everyone who might know where he was to warn them not to pass on any information. Then he wrote a long letter home in which he revealed how he'd been a secret follower of Jesus for three years, had tried to hide it, but now openly declared his allegiance to him who was life itself. Christmas came and went.

He managed to get a temporary passport and we put him on a plane to Turkey. That, we figured, would be the last place his parents would look. He could then marry my cousin as soon as possible which, we hoped, would relieve some of the pressure as his parents could then tell the Muslim community that he'd become a Christian for the girl's sake.

He arrived at midnight at the old Atatürk airport and was promptly arrested. I felt responsible; it had all been my idea. Rarely have we prayed with more fervency and never did I make such desperate phone calls to the police and the Dutch consulate. Eighteen hours later he was released and on New Year's Eve asked my cousin to marry her. She said yes.

Then another desperate phone call: "Peter, my brother is in Turkey looking for me. Where can we hide?" His family had extracted his whereabouts from a room-mate back in The Netherlands. They moved to another friend's house and two days later a Turkish pastor friend married them. As we had assumed they would, his family eventually came to terms with the situation.

·

"In the name of God, the merciful, the compassionate. Oh you foolish people! First you fool yourselves, then you make it your business to fool us Muslims. But we Muslim youths do not swallow the nonsense you foreign missionaries propagate about Jesus in your magazine. Jesus was never God's son, he was a prophet and we accept him as such. We love Jesus more than you, because our religion teaches us to respect him." **Gurhan (Istanbul)**

·

Three of us established the Kurdish Literature Committee (KLC), and hired Jemil, a godly Kurdish man, to work for us.

"Faith has been compared to a muscle: you have to exercise it for it to grow. Two other missionaries and myself are exercising ours so vigorously we sometimes fear spiritual hernias... For the three of us to financially support Shahin[165], his wife and 9 children is no small thing."[166]

The KLC proved to be a Spirit-led endeavor. Jemil spent his life in Bible translation, preparing other Christian literature, doing personal evangelism and leading Bible studies. He also prepared a weekly radio program for Trans World Radio. We never knew how many people tuned in to those 15 minute broadcasts but years later a Yezidi from the Caucasus contacted him. He'd listened to the program for years, had come to Christ, and wanted to meet the person behind the microphone.[167]

■

"Permit me to express my gratitude to all those who work for Yeni Yaklaşım. I would love to receive a Turkish New Testament, because I feel stuck in a religious cul-de-sac. I am unable to find answers to the many questions whirling around in my head and would love to correspond with you." **Nesrin (Hatay)**

■

Every so often I took the train from Genk to the Gare du Nord in Brussels, walk down the seedy, brothel-filled Rue d'Aerschot running behind the station then through the Quartier Brabant to Little Anatolia, the immigrant-filled streets and alleys around the Chaussée de Haecht. There I'd saunter among the Turkish and Moroccan restaurants and shops, praying and dreaming. Gradually an idea took shape: a library with a quiet meditative atmosphere decorated in classic Middle Eastern style—carpeted floors, cushions to sit on, Arabic calligraphy on the walls—filled with Christian books and other publications in Turkish, Arabic, Persian and Kurdish. It would, I believed, "attract disorientated, disillusioned refugees who have much time on their hands, establish our identity, enable

---

[165] Shahin was the code name we used for Jemil back then.
[166] PL November 1992.
[167] Personal email from Jonathan Gutknecht, dated Dec. 13, 2022.

us to market Christian literature and, most importantly, give us immediate personal contact and opportunities for witness."[168]

I repeatedly presented the idea at intermission meetings in Brussels. We eventually formed a committee to formulate our purpose, specify target groups and tackle potential problems. YWAM provided us with a superbly located venue and, stepping out in faith, we set Saturday, Dec. 11, 1993, as the grand opening. "Other than a building, an opening date, reckless faith and boundless enthusiasm we don't have anything. And a Study Centre without books is a silly thing indeed!"[169]

Many responded to the plea for suitable books, enabling us to pull together a substantial library of Bibles, Bible commentaries and books on Christian ethics, pre-evangelism, marriage and family life, apologetics, philosophy, as well as some scientific books and general books on Islam in Arabic, Turkish, English, French and Dutch. Belgian friends transformed a dingy room into an attractive reading room. A shiny copper plaque announced the existence of the Bible Study Centre for Muslims in four languages.

Fifteen people showed up on opening day, including five Moroccans who'd responded to invitations we'd handed out on the street, and then... nothing. "Though many people read the sign on the door we have not seen many Muslims come— indeed, we are happy if someone shows up at all!"[170] But slowly things improved. A year later we praised God "for the 30 people who requested a Bible from the Study Center in Brussels recently, and for a Moroccan who returns every Saturday to discuss what he reads."[171] Whenever we distributed flyers offering free New Testaments we could expect 15-20 people.

"Some Saturdays Peter sits there the whole afternoon and absolutely no one shows up. Then the next week some Muslim drops in and spends several hours discussing spiritual things and it seems so worthwhile again. Yes, the

[168] Report by Peter, December 1990 for KOM.
[169] PL June 1993.
[170] KOM Field Report, March 1994.
[171] PL November 1994.

work is slow and the center may as yet only be a flickering little light but if it were to shut down then there would be nothing but darkness in that immigrant and red-light district."[172]

•

"I am a Muslim Kurd who wants to accept Christianity. I want to become a Christian. Please tell me what to do." **Murat (Elazığ)**

•

I began taking courses in history and the social sciences at the Open University as that "beats watching TV when my brain needs to unwind."[173] My first exposure to the internet took place when my OU supervisor proudly demonstrated how his computer utilized the phone to access information stored on other institutions' computers by means of a screeching, squawking box he referred to as a dial-up-modem. I dimly grasped that this development might be of future importance.

•

"I curse each and every one of you. You are a shame to religion. Do you really think you can get us Muslims to swallow your nonsense? Islam is the one true religion. Every time the call to prayer rings from Istanbul to Mecca, remember that your work is in vain." **No name, no address**

•

Finances became so tight that I saw no way forward. I had to find a part time job. Interpreting is big business in Brussels, the European Union's de facto capital, and I didn't think it would be difficult to find work in that line. "But," I burst out disillusioned, "before I do I'm going to slap two 2x4s together into the shape of a cross, plant that in the front yard, and hang

---

[172] Letter to Macosquin, 25 May 1995.
[173] KOM Conference Report, 1993.

a sign on it: 'Here lies buried the life of faith'. Why does it always have to be so difficult? Couldn't God cooperate a bit? It's his work after all! We came because we, all of us, believed this was where the Lord would have us—and he failed us! It's cruel, man! It's not fair!"

"Listen to me," Anna took me by the arm. "Give the Lord six weeks to come through," she said gently. "If the situation doesn't change, go to Brussels and find a job."

"Six weeks... OK. I'll give him six weeks!" I responded glumly.

Soon after I received a summons to appear in a Brussels courtroom. At first I could make neither heads nor tails of it but then it dawned on me. This was an invitation to present my case against the state in response to the forms I'd filled out a year earlier, the ones the big Belgian book keeper had given me. WEC faxed over a print-out with a letter affirming that we were members in their employ, and on the appointed day I made my way to Brussels. It took some searching but I eventually found a room in a sky-scraper which matched the address given. There was hardly anyone there: two men in suits behind a raised desk and a woman with a steno machine at floor level.

I stuck my head through the door. "Am I in the right place?" I asked.

"What are you looking for?"

"A court room which deals with labor related matters."

"Are you Mr. er," one of the men looked at a dossier, "Peter Pikkert?"

"That's me."

"Do you have anyone representing you?"

"No, I'm representing myself."

"Please show me some I.D." I showed the man my driver's licence.

"Go ahead."

I launched into an ad-hoc oration in my best Dutch establishing the fact that my dear wife and I were long-term members in good standing with an interdenominational organization which had sent us to serve churches in various places—here sir, is proof of that, along with ten year's worth of salary statements, which till now, has always been sufficient for us to faithfully pay our bills; we've never taken a penny from any government—but because the state now forces us to pay the most exorbitant social security fees we simply cannot make ends meet anymore. Do the authorities really want us to draw unemployment insurance, become wards of the state? After eight or ten minutes of elocution in this vein I ran out of steam.

"And that's all I have to say, sirs," I concluded while the woman clacked away at the steno machine. "What do I do now? Find a waiting room and await your verdict?"

"No, you can go home," the judge smiled. "You'll hear from us in due course. Leave those papers with us." I walked up to the bench, handed over the WEC statement and print-outs and left. A couple of weeks later, but still within Anna's six-week deadline, the postman delivered a very substantial cheque. He did so again a week or so later. The court had decided in our favor and refunded us all we'd paid into that social security fund, an amount which, over the years, had totted up to a very tidy sum.

After dealing with some urgent bills I walked into an investment bank and bought dot.com stocks. The dot.com boom of the '90s was booming, as I'd gathered from my Open University supervisor, and we rode that wave. It was awful. As those tech shares shot skyward I became consumed by the idea of quick money. I tried to make sense of the business section of the paper, trying to figure out when this ride would end. Those shares increased about 40% that year. I cashed them in and breathed a deep sight of relief. A couple of weeks later those self-same shares plummeted precipitously. That was the first and only time I put money in high-risk stocks. I hated what it did to me, how the prospect of quick wealth had consumed me, and what—but for the grace of God—potential folly it could have been.

We never again experienced dire financial straights. Never again did we have to cry out to the Lord to help us make ends meet. He never again tested us at that level, though I wonder at times how he graded me on that one. Though grateful it ended well, at times I feel wistful, a tad nostalgic, for those days of utter financial dependence on the Lord. After we left Belgium our old house's rental income made all the difference to our personal finances, and when we finally sold it it's value had increased more than three-fold. The old subterranean mining shafts we'd been warned about had been stabilized and the municipality had opened the district for development. Upscale red-brick bungalows grew like amaryllises around it and the area rose in value, just like that tech bubble, but without bursting.

·

"I apologize for answering your letter so late. I have been spiritually very confused. However, I have decided that I want to keep on reading your magazine. In a world full of violence your magazine points people to that which is good and beautiful. Your efforts are worthy of praise. I want to thank you and want you to know that I shall look forward to reading your publication with pleasure."
Ayhan (Osmaniye)

·

I have loved Anna since before we married and will until the day I die. She is the "suitable helper" of Genesis 2, the wife of Proverbs 31. I neither josh nor exaggerate: without her sensible, godly, intuitively right advice and industrious partnership my life and ministry would have been an abject flop. I know God loves me for multiple reasons. The top two are his gifts of eternal life in Christ, and Anna.

Besides being gifted in administration and hospitality, she is fun, gutsy and with an impish streak. She'd been a missionary to Nigeria's Muslim north, where she'd helped administer a chain of health clinics around Lake Chad. She'd also served in Southern Sudan. The stories the kids pried out of her could fill a book: "One Sunday morning worship service, during a period of tribal warfare, a naked warrior ran across the front of our church—an open structure with a thatched roof—followed by a posse of other naked warriors in hot pursuit" or "well, I killed that rat with my broom," or "it was hot, so I hung my hammock and mosquito net from a tree outside. The leopard circled around me. I photographed its tracks in the morning," or "the pilot strayed into Ugandan airspace. She became really uptight as straying planes were apt to be shot down in that contested area, handed me a road map and told me to figure out where we were".

Perhaps her greatest gift is rightly intuiting how people feel or what they are thinking. Trying to hide anything from her is wasted effort. She also has a natural, unaffected empathy for others and ere long people bare to her their unvarnished souls. She'd leave for someplace and arrive home late. "What took you, honey?"

"I met someone..." and she'd tell of said someone's trials and tribulations. We walk into a cafe and soon surreptitiously nods in someone's direction. "Look at that woman. I just want to put my arm around her. She's really hurting."

"Waddayamean? She's just sipping a Frappuccino!"

She'd enter a food court, order a cup of tea, find a lone woman, ask if she can join her, and soon the stranger is spilling her innermost secrets as if in a confessional.

Anna spent twelve days in hospital for a hysterectomy. "My many visitors caused the patient beside me as ask, 'How can you have so many friends in just 2 years in Belgium?'"[174]

She traveled to Ireland on several occasions, once for a month after her younger brother was diagnosed with a malignant brain tumor: "this situation weighs heavily on me."[175] During another trip, in which she'd hoped to spend time with her mother and renew contact with her home church, "the Lord had another reason for me being there. The morning after I arrived my brother-in-law took seriously ill and his condition remains extremely grave..."[176] He too died young of cancer.

---

[174] PL February 1993.
[175] KOM Field Report, March 1994.
[176] PL November 1993.

After four years of form-filling, medicals, police reports from Belgium, Ireland and Turkey, photographs, application fees and what-not, she was finally granted Permanent Residence Status for Canada—the only snag being that she had to land there within two months to claim that right or forfeit it. Pleas for an extension were flatly refused, so off she went.

Whenever she was around Owen, Rita and myself were happy and secure. When she was away the house turned into a sepulchral, joyless box into which my lame attempts to infuse order and faux fun fell flat. As she put it after one of her absences, "Peter and the children managed (or at least survived!)." [177]

.

"Your magazine contains much valuable information and I want to congratulate you for faithfully carrying on with such honourable work. I have been reading the Bible for nearly a year. Most of my life I blindly followed the religion of my parents but have come to realize that important issues as these need to be looked into personally. Let me give you an example: we people are standing on one side of the ocean, and God is standing on the other side. For years I tried to swim across while beside me a boat was waiting to carry me across. That Boat, that Light, that Power, that Being that Son is Jesus Christ himself! Only through Him can we reach God. God's peace be upon you all." **Hakan (Mersin)**

Upon our return to Turkey years later this selfsame Hakan, along with his wife Selma, became close friends.

---

[177] PL February 1993.

36

Follow-up Snapshots

"Only a disciple can make a disciple."

A.W. Tozer

. . .

MY ANNUAL HIGHLIGHT was the autumnal foray back to Turkey. I'd invite another missionary along and we'd scour the hidden corners of Kurdistan, searching for those who had written us and trusting the Spirit to use and lead us. Sharing the gospel of God's grace in person with our readers was a thrilling and at times risky business.

Turkish Kurdistan resembled the Wild West back then: the fastest gun-slinger won, the little homesteader didn't have a chance and the traveller was viewed with suspicion. Fear was palpable. Stuck between Kurdish PKK (Kurdish Worker's Party) guerillas and the equally ruthless Turkish army, villagers left the countryside in droves for the cities.

We inevitably swung through Diyarbakir, Kurdistan's unacknowledged capital. It still retained traces of the old orient, and I loved the place. You could survey the maze of streets and alleyways from its black basalt ramparts and pick out the various mosques, caravanserais, public baths—the Paşa Bath, the Camel Bath and the Çardaklı Bath—as well as the Yıkık (Broken) and Four-Footed minarets. Back at street level you'd thread through the buzzing, swirling, pulsating market to the Hassan Paşa Inn or the Sülüklü Han, or along narrow, shop-lined streets thronging with sharp-eyed urchins, suspicious-looking men and waddling women. You passed stalls and stores piled high with Anatolian carpets, colourful bolts of cloth, finely embroidered shawls, plastic water jars and shiny brass and copper cooking pots and bowls. You nodded at vendors selling soaps, attars, lanterns, umbrellas, shoes and bales of tobacco, their wares spilling onto the street. Pungent cheeses, briny pools of olives, mounds of almonds, sacks of cardamom, ginger, cloves, cumin, cinnamon and myrtle imparted a tangy, intoxicating quality to the air. Pushcarts laden with pyramids of bright oranges, stacks of shiny red apples, silver squashes, yellow gourds, piles of green spinach and heaps of red and green peppers lined the sides of the throbbing streets. There were stalls selling dried foods, different kinds of rice, corn, mounds of shelled almonds and baskets of lentils. Money changers, their cash stored in upright safes behind them, were ready to exchange your Liras, Dollars, Sterling, Syrian Pounds, Dinars, Rials, Marks, Franks and, after January 1, 2002, Euros.

All the peoples of the Zagros Mountains mixed and mingled on the streets of Diyarbakir. Kurdish women chattered happily as they haggled with a harried vendor, their menfolk looking on—though by then I rarely saw the women wearing the colorful multi-layers of clothing they wore back in the village and few men wore the towering turbans and cummerbunds they sported in the mountains as these were symbols of Kurdish nationalism which the government sought to crush. Syrian Arabs in dark blue or brown dishdashas with red and white keffiyehs and black egals at rakish angles atop their heads swished past swarthy farmers ambling along, thin leather belts holding up baggy, lolloping trousers. The Turks were generally short and squat, their wives either covered in black or dressed western-style, depending on how seriously their husbands took Muhammed. They typically worked for the government or in the medical profession. The governor, judges, lawyers, police, teachers, soldiers, officially licensed doctors, midwives, nurses, dentist and pharmacists were mostly Turks back then.

Though still ethnically diverse, the city was less so than it had been half a century earlier. The ethnically Christian Armenians had been massacred during World War I and the once thriving Jewish community had packed up and moved to Israel in the 1940s and '50s. The few remaining Syriacs—almost all of them goldsmiths—still lived in their own quarter in the west of the city near the Mardin Gate, from which vantage the

Tigris looks like a brown rope looped along the valley floor. The centre of their world was the historic Mother Mary Syriac church.

I remember spending a delightful afternoon with two Yeni Yaklaşım readers in Diyarbakir. They were full of questions, and we were able to put them in contact with other believers there. "Is this the breakthrough we've longed for in this city?"[178] While standing under the collapsed dome of the large 19th century Protestant church I could not imagine that within 15 years a vibrant Evangelical church would re-emerge in the heart of the old city.

The secret police lurked in all quarters. When cab drivers attempted to run up the meter by taking me via some circuitous route, I'd first warn them, then inform them I'd open the passenger door in mid-traffic and, if there was still no response, do exactly that. That always triggered a rapid, curse-filled maneuver to the side of the road in order to keep the door from being ripped off by a passing vehicle. I executed this operation once in Diyarbakir. The car had barely ground to a halt before several plainclothes officers had yanked the cabbie from his vehicle and spread-eagled him over the front hood. They thought I was being kidnapped.

We once lodged at a two-dollar-a-night Diyarbakir hotel filled with police cadets. On learning we spoke Turkish they plied us with questions about Christianity and invited us to share more the following evening. We left the city on a high.

When visiting smaller towns or villages I normally planned two visits per day, one in the morning, after which we'd bus it to the next town or village to meet the next person. In theory that should have enabled us to meet 50 to 60 readers in the course of a month, but that never happened. Sometimes long bus journeys led nowhere; we once wandered for two days around ancient Edessa without meeting anyone. We usually connected with about half the people we'd lined up. Some would not be at home while others paid the postman to hold their mail until they could pick it up in person, thus avoiding

---

[178] PL November 1993.

awkward questions from nosy family members. Sometimes, knowing we were being followed and fearing for the safety of our contact, we passed them by. Once a bus leaving Mardin hit a PKK landmine right after our vehicle had passed by on the other side of the road. It killed 26 innocents. That night we fell asleep to the sound of gunfire and volleys of artillery.

I once traveled with two Christian men making a promotional video on the Kurds. Everything went flawless until we got to Diyarbakir. We were filming the market when two plainclothes policemen asked us to step into a nondescript van. After cooling our heels for some time in the police station we were ushered into the presence of a jovial chap, Police Chief Öztürk.

"What are you guys doing?"

"Filming, efendim."

"What are you filming?"

"Efendim, we started at Mount Ararat and are working our way across the country filming various cultural and historical sites. We are producing a documentary. Feel free to look at everything we've filmed so far, efendim."

"For which T.V. station do you work?"

"We're a private video crew, efendim."

"Do you have permission to film in Turkey?"

"Efendim, we inquired about that. The Turkish embassy in Brussels assured us we didn't need permission, efendim."

When you're in a pickle over there you cannot overuse the word efendim which, if you pronounce it right, means "sir" or "ma'am" (Turkish has no gender distinction). Change the intonation and the word can mean "pardon?" or "you see...". Practise makes perfect.

The questioning went on for some time. I tried to be polite, beat around the bush and appear straightforward all at the same time. Tommy the cameraman smiled naively and cradled his Betacam like a baby while Norman prayed through pursed lips with the tripod dangling between his legs.

Mr. Öztürk scratched his stomach, reached for the phone and called a superior. "We picked up this foreign film crew. You won't believe this, but starting at Mount Ararat they filmed their way here. No, no permission or anything... What? Throw them out of the country? Hmmm." He put the phone back on the hook, rubbed his chin, lifted the handset a second time and dialed a different number. "... What do we do with them? Yea, they seem pretty harmless. Let them go? OK."

"Gentlemen, you are free to go." Mr. Öztürk stood up and held out his hand. I shook it.

"Efendim, it has been a pleasure to meet you and I appreciate your efforts on our behalf. Do you happen to have a business card you could give me?" Without thinking he reached into his pocket and handed me a finely printed *carte de visite*. The next day in the next town the police accosted us again. Before they could take us away, however, I pulled out that card.

"Before you mess with us maybe you should phone police chief Öztürk in Diyarbakir. Here is his card," I said politely but without the efendims. They turned the little credential over two or three times then looked at each other.

"Sorry efendim. Have a good day."

"You too."

Once we tried to locate two people who had written very positive letters from Batman, an oddly named oil town on the Tigris. After a long search we concluded that contact #1 had disappeared. By nightfall we'd located contact #2 and spent a pleasant but inconsequential hour with him. When we got back to the hotel three plain-clothes policemen were waiting. They knew exactly where we'd been and who we'd visited and were obviously looking for an excuse to arrest us.

"Your papers are not in order."

"What is the matter with them, efendim?"

"Your entry stamp should be in your passport not with your identity card."

"Efendim, maybe you should inform the border police of that."

"What is your work?"

"I'm a writer, efendim. I work for a magazine called *New Approach*." I used the English translation of Yeni Yaklaşım.

"Writers need special permission from the governor before they are allowed to travel in this area."

"Efendim, we both know we haven't broken any laws." Then I hardened my voice and dropped the efendims. "However, if you are looking for an excuse to arrest me, don't bother. Just go ahead. It will enhance my next story." I held out my wrists so they could snap on the bracelets.

'No, no, no, we don't want to arrest you and please don't write things like that!" Turkish policemen are allergic to writers. They questioned us some more about whom we had visited and left, taking our passports.

They returned the documents the following morning. It wasn't difficult to figure out why they'd postponed our departure by twelve hours; that was the amount of time needed to interrogate our new acquaintance.

Yüksekova, the absolute dead-end of Turkey. We were afraid the police would again create trouble for our contact, so prayed that God would lead us to him without our having to ask for directions. After wandering around town for some hours we found the street. This time our contact was a teenager who shared the magazine with his best friend. Together they discussed the contents with an imam, a Muslim religious leader. They were thrilled to receive a New Testament.

Samandağ, i.e., Haystack, a singularly appropriate name for that labyrinth of unnamed, unnumbered streets and alleys of poorly constructed four and five story cinder block apartment buildings. It took time but when we eventually found the needle we were astonished. Surely those deep letters didn't come from this thirteen-year-old boy? No, they didn't. The boy's crippled grandfather dictated the letters. Grandfather would love to see us. Wouldn't we like to visit grandfather? A laborious journey in a minibus up a mountainside and a hike along a goat trail took us a spotless cabin with spectacular views of the valley below. The reward: supper with a sprightly mountain man with a crippled right hand who read Yeni Yaklaşım and the Bible, listened to Turkish Christian radio broadcasts and loved the Lord.

Time and again our destinations amazed us. Take the shoemaker. He lived in a dusty town I'd never heard of before and used the magazine to evangelize outlying Kurdish villages. In another town three friends read and discussed it together. Two were into the New Age movement but the third was a sincere seeker. A wonderful letter from a city on the Syrian border led us to an individual who astounded us with his depth of knowledge and love for Jesus.

Once I wanted to visit some old friends in Bezal, the village with the deaf boy, but decided against it when we learned that the Turkish government had imposed a food embargo. The military only allowed enough food into the area to feed registered residents so that the villagers would have nothing left to share with the guerillas—nor, we decided, with missionaries. Who should we run into in a city 10 hours travel further up the road? The very friend we'd hoped to visit!

> "Peter had a very worthwhile trip to Eastern Turkey. He travelled more than two thousand miles by bus and visited many of the readers of the Yeni Yaklaşım magazine who had written to us. God gave him tremendous opportunities to explain the gospel, but there was also considerable opposition from the authorities. The police were often on his trail and, at one point, threatened to arrest him. Kurdistan as a whole remains a Muslim stronghold, intolerant of Christian witness. Within it, however, God is calling out individuals unto Himself."[179]

Divine appointments, close shaves, interminable bus journeys, squeamish stomachs, vomiting, diarrhea... "Are these follow-up trips worth the expense, the sacrifice, the danger? Your theology will determine your answer. We will, by God's grace, return."[180]

---

[179] Anna writing to Macosquin Presbyterian Church, August 6, 1992.
[180] PL November 1993.

37

"Did God really say...?"

"But the challenge is always this:
Are men and women going to allow the Word of God to sit in
judgement on their puny minds, or are they going to make
their puny minds the judges of the Word of God?"

Alistair Begg

. . .

DURING THE REFORMATION Protestantism embraced the
doctrine of *sola Scriptura*, that is, the scriptures alone. This
dogma accepts the 66 books of the Old and New Testaments as
the authoritative word of God. It also holds that Scripture must
interpret Scripture, i.e., that it is self-explanatory. Among other
things this means that irrespective of the individual books'
various literary genres and historic development they contain a
mutually re-enforcing, coherent metanarrative pertaining to
salvation history which culminates in the Christ event and
speaks to Christians everywhere and throughout the ages. This
logical consequence of *sola Scriptura* is known as the doctrine
of the perspicuity, or clarity, of Scriptures.

Many skeptics—notably progressive theologians—have
derided this teaching, disparaging it as naïve or as a failure to
appreciate God as a transcendent mystery which cannot be
reduced to human words, or because they maintain that the
Bible reflects a particular historical and social context which is
impossible to reconstruct or fully fathom. And doesn't the
multiplicity of denominations offering widely disparate
interpretations prove all this?

More recently the doctrine has been condemned as a
powerplay by white males seeking to impose their values on
gullible "people of colour". Others hold that it is a violation of

contemporary literary theory. These savants reject the possibility of determining the author's intent—any author that is, but themselves. According to them, written texts only convey such meanings as are imposed upon them by the readers, who subconsciously superimpose their own peculiar values, prejudices and predilections. So, while their own assertive manuscriptions are to be accepted as the sober reflections of serious scholars, others people's compositions, they insist, have multiple meanings allowing for a multiplicity of responses. It takes a lot of interpretive gymnastics and sophisticated ivory tower ruminating to conceive of propositions such as these which, if applied to real life, would lead to complete communicative gridlock.

Sadly, these erroneous lines of thinking have had a monumental impact on the missionary enterprise. The assertion that readers impose their own meaning on the text based on their own social context is particularly corrosive. If true, the gospel message would be nothing but a socially determined construct, ultimately mere meaningless psycho-babble. Sadly, pseudo-evangelical scholars have attempted to integrate these trains of thought into their already wishy-washy Christian worldviews. The result is devasting though refutable, if not by cold logic, then through common sense and experience.

Take, for example, our multi-cultural missionary team. At our peak we represented a wide range of social, cultural and linguistic backgrounds: South African, Hong Kong Chinese, German, Swiss, Northern Irish, Dutch Canadian, Australian and Americans of both East and West Coast varieties. Some of us were in our twenties, others in their late fifties and everyone else in between. Some were singles, others married with children. Some were Baptist, others Presbyterian, Lutheran or Pentecostal. A few, like ourselves, had been professional missionaries since college while others had been farmers, engineers, or baristas. Each of us had a different conversion story. Some had become Christians at their mother's knee, others by reading the New Testament later in life; some because someone had witnessed to them, others through a TV program.

Although each person's story was different, the ancient Biblical message impacted each of us in much the same way: we had come to realise that we were sinners in need of a Saviour, that Christ was that saviour, and that he accomplished that salvation by virtue of who he was and what he did. He was the God-man who had met the demands of the divine law on our behalf in his life, and then died on behalf of those who could not earn their own way into God's good graces. Accepting these basic New Testament teachings had had a life-transforming impact on each one of us. Death had lost its sting, we had commenced a lifelong struggle against sin and shared a desire to communicate this great gospel news with others, particularly with those who would not normally be exposed to it. In a nutshell, we were a widely disparate community of communicators captivated by the same old world-view, one drawn from the translation of an ancient book written in three languages and, as a result, now shared a common set of hopes, aspirations and values.

What about those Yeni Yaklaşım readers with whom we sought to communicate our message of hope? What were they like? What hangups, values, predilections and cultural milieu did they share? Or were they so diverse that they too had virtually nothing in common? And what impact did all that have on their understanding of the ancient message?

If it had been possible to gather the different types of Muslims with whom we corresponded or visited around the dinner table—which, due to their mutual animosities, would not have been possible—and have them tell their stories, each would relate a tale in which the others were the monsters, the fiends. The mountain Kurd would relate stories of armed resistance to the hated Turkish oppressors and the city Kurd tales of exploitation and passive resistance. The nationalist Turk would narrate a string of grievances pertaining to western exploitation and Arab dastardliness. The religious Sunni, as convinced of his moral superiority as first century Pharisees—

though deeply insecure in that conviction—would relate a well-rehearsed list of perceived injustices experienced by fellow Muslims at home and abroad. The secularist would denounce the Sunni for suppressing the nation's democratic development while the hard-pressed Alevites, the country's largest religious minority, would complain about forced assimilation. A few in each category would be wealthy, a few more starving artists. There would be some lower-middle class folk doing their best to feed their families and educate their offspring and quite a few would be university students, some highly politicised. Though most faced Mecca when genuflecting and mumbling their prayers they lived in radically different social and cultural milieus.

But they all had one thing in common: each one had begun to nurture doubts and each one had become a reader, a thinker, a searcher. And therein, at the human level, lies the secret of missionary success. When people begin to query their own worldview, when they start asking their first tentative but probing questions, there is hope! And then when we, a culturally and linguistically varied team operating within the confines of our limited lingua-cultural understanding of the host culture, manage to interpret those ancient texts of God's grace in Christ to these questioners, not a few begin a new journey.

> "I am learning much about the Messiah from your writings." **(Ugur, Ankara)**

> "I gave up on Islam years ago. I am glad I discovered your magazine." **(Bulent, Izmir)**

> "I am serving a sentence in a prison for a crime I committed. I first ran into a New Testament here in prison in 1987, though I didn't start reading it until 1993. In 1994 I came to faith in Christ and have since tried to convince others to do the same, as a result of which some of my friends also believe in Christ. We have a request to make: we have several friends here in prison and we would appreciate it if you would send them your

magazine as well. May God's grace be with you."
(Berkay, high security prison in Turkey)

And thus in spite of threats and opposition the gospel takes root and begins to grow. Proceeding from widely divergent points of departure these questioners moved towards the same focal point: the cross of Christ. There they met, found life and, with missionary help, formed small Christian fellowships. These little churches soon resembled evangelical churches across the ages for these new Christians now aspired to become "like Christ" and to be integrated into the larger "body of Christ," the global church. In that process they became more like each other as well. As they started singing together—for they suddenly had much to sing about—they began looking and acting like genuine Christians everywhere, in all ages. And now, quite naturally, these disparate people found themselves gathering around a table to share a meal: first around the Communion Table and as they grew in faith in each others' homes. They had become brothers and sisters in Christ.

History demonstrates that wherever Bible-believing missionaries have gone a church is born. It might take them 16 months, sometimes 6 years, sometimes 16 years, but rarely longer. The Bible itself gives the reason: God's word is living and active (Hebrews 4:11) and will not return to him empty. It will accomplish what he desires and achieve the purpose for which he sent it (Isaiah 55:11). This inherent power of the gospel message never fails to amaze me. We missionaries may be faltering communicators but God wills to use our stumbling ancient words to draw people from totally other lingua-cultural backgrounds to himself and to integrate them into the universal body of Christ.

Yes, God still speaks. Yes, he still uses his word, the Bible, when written, preached and taught in a local language to communicate his supra-cultural message of eternal life through repentance and faith in Christ. When we first landed in Turkey there were less than 100 national evangelicals in the country, most of them converts from eastern Orthodoxy. Now, at the time of writing in 2025, there are some 10,000 of them, the vast majority Muslim converts, and the movement continues to grow.

The duffers who deny that the Bible contains universal truths which can impact anyone anywhere in much the same way are tragically mistaken. We, the conservative Christian missionary community, have proven that empirically and repeatedly over the course of centuries in Latin America, Africa, Asia, Europe and in the Middle East as well.

38

The Iraq Debacle

"A lowly person is a teachable person... Many of our spirits are too arrogant: they can teach others but can never themselves be taught."

Watchman Nee

• • •

OUR LAST YEARS in Belgium are a difficult skein to untangle. Rhyming God's omnipotence, omniscience and love for the lost with the facts of daily life can be baffling. Our biggest trial was Iraq. Our gentle Swiss leaders, true to their country's predilection to negotiate for conformity through compromise, tried valiantly to get our more contumacious missionaries there on the same page, but to no avail. They themselves were worn out and in dire need of a sabbatical. Anna and I took over.

I'm essentially a project person. Producing magazines, organizing a study center, addressing audiences from the safety of a platform, witnessing to Muslims and trekking through Kurdistan gave satisfaction. Field leadership, however, meant servanthood. It meant supporting others, helping them develop their ministries. It meant listening, counseling, organizing. It meant letting others increase while your own precious projects decrease. I feared it, yet also looked forward to it "because I want God to grant me that servant heart I envy about our WEC leaders and home church pastors. Though I don't relish the process, I look forward to serving our KOM team."[181] At the time we were 21 full time and several short-termers.

---

[181] PL May 1994.

"All are strong personalities otherwise they would never have made it there, and you can imagine the stresses not only of adapting to Turkish culture but also to one another... the potential for conflict is huge, and there is a great need for daily grace."[182]

Two couples and three single women in Shaqlawa, Iraqi Kurdistan, ran a center where they taught English and preventative health education. The team in Southern Turkey did Yeni Yaklaşım follow-up as well as discipleship training with a small group of believers. The German team was involved in the production of Kurdish literature, radio programming and evangelistic outreach and we were still in Belgium.

No sooner had we taken over the reins when the couple engaged in follow-up work in Turkey suddenly had to return to their home country, leaving just four single girls of which only two were committed for the long haul. Then the couple spearheading our outreach in Europe returned to the States due to health concerns. To top it all off, "the sudden closure of the Iraqi border and the police calling on our folk in Turkey showed us that more exciting days were ahead."[183]

When the Turkish government closed the crossing into Iraq to organizations not registered with them—which we were not—those wanting to enter the country were left cooling their heels in Turkey while those inside Iraq couldn't leave as they would be refused re-entry. I headed over in January 1995 to see what could be done.

All attempts to register with the Turkish authorities failed. "In the ensuing confusion it is a real comfort for Peter and I to know that God is our real leader, and that he is the one who has the ultimate responsibility for the closing or continuance of the work."[184] After much hassle we obtained temporary registrations with other groups, thus enabling our folks to cross the border for the time being. To create a stabler solution we

---

[182] PL January 16, 1995.
[183] Anna writing, Letter to Macosquin Presbyterian church, May 25 1995.
[184] Ibid.

established a new humanitarian aid organisation registered in The Netherlands. "Pray that the Turkish authorities will not turn us down this time."[185] They didn't.

However, the real problem, the one which would lead to the demise of the Shaqlawa ministry, were the toxic relationships which developed between that team's more mule-headed members. "Pray for better interpersonal relationships on the team. The enemy continues to attack on this level."[186] Later: "Pray that... they learn to support each other and function better as a team".[187] And later yet, "KOM faces setbacks... The three ladies who run our study centre in Northern Iraq are unable to make a 'beautiful integrated whole' of the ministry there."[188]

> "People, pray for KOM! Though I do not understand the relationship between our prayers and the works of a sovereign God, Scripture is clear that such a link exists. We are also keenly aware that Satan is frustrating our every effort to create a beautiful spiritual edifice among the Kurds. Pray, people!"[189]

Relationships became so noxious that I asked WEC's Middle East regional directors for help. They too recognized that the situation had become untenable and "were immediately struck by the loveless attitude and almost constant sniping at each other. This seemed to have become a normal way of relating."[190] Newly arrived recruits were not merely unsupported but faced unwonted criticism, leaving them physically and spiritually at the end of their tethers. To top it off, those running the center had become involved in the political aspirations of their Kurdish friends, as a result of which the place was perceived as pro-PUK, one of the main political parties. I travelled back and

---

[185] KOM Personnel Update, June 1995.
[186] Ibid.
[187] PL July 1995.
[188] PL September 1995.
[189] Ibid.
[190] KOM Family Letter, November 1995.

forth wishing Anna could accompany me, but she had to care for Owen and Rita. Counseling single women was not my most obvious gift!

During a follow-up visit in June we presented the team with a set of conditions they were to meet before I showed up again. If there was no progress we would shut them down. Instead we witnessed further deterioration. Newly arrived missionaries threw in the towel and moved to a different city just to get away from the Shaqlawa team. Then that team began making major ministry decisions unilaterally—including signing new contracts—without reference to WEC leadership. "There was nothing which might be construed as a breakthrough"[191] and in October we asked them to close down the ministry.

That decision weighed heavily on me, especially in light of the fact that the place was highly regarded by many. Up to 100 people made use of it on any given day, those running it did so efficiently, they had distributed numerous gospel tracts and had persevered in very stressful circumstances. But when we could not send them new personnel, when others refused to work with them, when they themselves refused to admit there was a problem and when they were perceived as politically biased, we felt we had no choice. We gave them a month to sell such inventory as was needed to cover debts and to put the rest in storage. We met with them for the last time in November. One responded almost cheerfully, with a "where do we go from here" attitude. I was deeply touched, and she would have a long and fruitful career in cross-cultural missions. The other two left embittered. I never from heard of them again.

> "KOM has gone through some deep waters. We hope, however, that we will emerge as a more unified, more sharply focused platoon of disciplined soldiers of Jesus Christ."[192]

---

[191] KOM Family Letter, November 1995.
[192] Ibid.

39

The Boil

*"To be a Christian means to forgive the inexcusable,
because God has forgiven the inexcusable in you."*

C.S. Lewis

. . .

"Peter found the experience (of field leadership) very difficult... While most KOMmers quietly got on with the job, field leaders, like priests and accountants, are confronted daily with the worst aspects of some of their clients. Trying to keep everyone happy was an impossible task and taking the necessary measures was not easy. Peter was left disappointed and hurt by some of our missionaries and nearly resigned from KOM."[193]

.

HAVE YOU EVER had a boil? One of those painful inflammatory sores full of pus? That's what that year of field leadership left me with. It was a great big one and it was awful. I suffered with it for weeks. I went to sleep with it and woke up with it. I catered to it, protecting it from bumps and scrapes, occasionally lashing out at anyone who came near it. It started to dominate my life. At first I hated my boil but eventually grew used to its tyranny. Then, one day, things came to a head. It happened at our annual conference when the team got together to pray, evaluate, and plan.

---

[193] KOM Annual Report, March 1996.

It was crowded in that conference center. People kept bumping into my boil. After a while I couldn't stand it any more. Things got so bad Anna fetched one of the brothers to see what he could do. This faithful man informed me that my problem wasn't others bumping into my boil but my unwillingness to lance the ugly thing. Without further ado he grabbed me firmly and pierced my precious boil. The problem, he pointed out in no uncertain terms, lay with me, not with those who hurt me. They had done what they did—so be it! Move on! Let go! Stop nursing your bruised ego! Die to self! Get over the fact that you were badly done by—so was Christ! Forgive those who don't seek forgiveness in order to release their hold on you. Did I believe in God's sovereignty over my life or not? You're becoming a joyless prig!

Man, did that hurt! You should have seen the puss squirt in every direction! All the hurt, misunderstanding and bitterness which had built up during the previous months flowed freely. Wow, was that ever an ugly sight! The Lord met me and I wept buckets.

My boil was gone though the area remained sensitive for some time. The ordeal left me exhausted and I looked forward to furlough later that year. I hoped that some time off would allow me to regain my strength and spiritual equilibrium. I never wanted to cater to and protect an ugly, festering boil again!

I was so emotionally and physically drained that I had little appetite for ministry. I even struggled to keep Yeni Yaklaşım going. We did not stand for re-election. We recognized that a large part of leadership at that stage consisted of matters I had little or no gifting in, like administration and counselling. Nor did we believe that those were our God ordained tasks.

There is an unhealthy yet almost inevitable process of advancement in mission agencies in which "the experienced missionary" gets ever deeper involved in such worthwhile activities as literature development, Bible translation or radio work. That's nice because projects are quantifiable—you sense instant accomplishment. Then he or she is elected to the field committee where they might become the secretary, the treasurer, or even the leader. That's nice too, because it strokes the ego. However, "the experienced missionary" is now drawn into a vortex of projects, personnel problems and conferences and may then be operating at his level of inefficiency.

Projects and personnel problems take up time. Lots of it. And a day only has 24 hours! As a result "the experienced missionary" spends less and less time with those locals who helped him learn the language and introduced him to the customs, cuisine, music, poetry, and history of his host country. The dear ones who figured so prominently in those early prayer letters are replaced by progress reports.

Projects verses people. We need to have leaders, and we have had some excellent ones who were capable of pulling off that balancing act. But when that tension goes and the balance is lost "the experienced missionary leader" either withdraws into his ivory tower or runs from one intransigent person to another without having the time or mental energy to formulate a clear strategy and gently lead forward those who are trying to get on with the job.

After extricating ourselves from it we henceforth politely refused to take on any official position of leadership in the mission.

40

Return to Turkey

"I shall be telling this with a sigh
Somewhere ages and ages hence:
Two roads diverged in a wood, and I—
I took the one less traveled by,
And that made all the difference."

Robert Frost

. . .

CHANGES WERE AFOOT. We were returning to Turkey! This was no surprise to anyone: "Peter longs for the day when the Lord will lead us back to the Middle East. Pray that both Peter and I will walk closely with the Lord and sense clearly when he is moving us on."[194]

We did not question the Lord's leading us to Belgium where, by his grace, we'd managed to keep Yeni Yaklaşım going and saw the Kurdish Literature Committee and the Brussels Bible Study Center become realities. We'd led KOM through a challenging period and materially the Lord had miraculously provided all our needs. Still, I was unhappy. I found peanut-sized Flanders boring, its people uneffusive and difficult to befriend. There is a limit to the quantity of good beer, chocolate, and fries one can consume, while such icons of Belgian culture as Tintin, Asterix, The Smurfs, Hercule Poirot and Adolphe Sax, inventor of the saxophone, were French speaking Walloons. I longed for the vibrant dynamic of the Middle East. I had an affinity for Arabs, Turks and Kurds which I failed to develop for the self-contained Flems.

---

[194] Letter to Macosquin Presbyterian Church, May 25, 1995.

Added to this was the sobering fact that we had failed to break through in Turkey, the country with the largest Kurdish population. Something had to change: we'd lost five couples there and were down to two single women. Two new couples were in the pipeline, but without adequate support we feared we'd lose them as well. At our 1995 conference the idea that we form the nucleus of a new team sparked much thinking, praying and dreaming.

Then, on one of my trips to Istanbul, two prominent believers — including my former fiercest critic! — asked if I would help them establish their own in-country magazine. I was nearly brought to tears at this textbook case of how things move in missions: foreigners start a ministry in the face of opposition, eventually locals catch on, at which time foreigners face a choice: press on alone or support the national church's endeavor, even if they do things differently. The textbook teaches submission, which meant the end of Yeni Yaklaşım. The new magazine would have a different name, be printed in Turkey and not contain articles in Kurdish. I would turn over our subscriber database and contribute practical expertise. My friend Isa would become the editor.

I feared that the brothers would run out of steam, in which case we would be left with nothing as I did not think that we could resurrect our distribution network once disbanded. However, I was running out of oomph myself; the idea of continuing to produce a magazine almost singlehandedly weighed heavily. I was bereft of ideas while a crate full of unanswered correspondence made me feel inadequate, even guilty.

Returning to Turkey excited me more than Anna.

"I am excited about returning to the Middle East, believing that is where the thrust of our work should lie. Anna has mixed emotions about going back—she and the children have settled very nicely here in Belgium... Pray with us that we are not carried forward on the force of my emotions or will or sense of adventure."[195]

We put the matter to the Lord, the team and our supporting churches, and received unanimously positive responses. "Anna's attitude changed to measured enthusiasm and the children are excited about it."[196] Of course Owen and Rita, at eight and six, didn't have a clue what they were excited about. "For them Belgium is home, Flemish their second language, and leaving will be a big adjustment."[197]

KOM decided to reboot in Adana, the gateway city to southeastern Turkey. Our brief was to support a newly forming team there until it could function without us. We committed three years to make this happen.

I had stepped down from the Kurdish Literature Committee when we took over as field leaders and a Turkish church in Brussels took over the Bible Study Center. We threw a farewell party for our Baptist church and Anna said goodbye to her Belarusian and Brazilian friends.

I sighed with relief when we boarded the plane to Canada for furlough.

"Although we sometimes refer to the five years in Belgium as 'Peter's desert experience' we rejoice in the knowledge that we have been in God's place for us. Peter is overjoyed, however, at the privilege of returning to grass-roots ministry in the Middle East and Anna will gladly follow him anywhere!"[198]

---

[195] Personal letter to Pastors Payne and Muller, July 3, 1995.
[196] Ibid.
[197] KOM Annual Report, March 1996.
[198] Ibid.

41

Piece of Cake?

"Christ's words from the cross are written in sharp-edged terms across some of the most inexpressible tragedies of history: 'They know not what they do'".

Martin Luther King, Jr.

• • •

HE WAS A little man wearing a large trench coat, his face half hidden behind a grey scarf. I didn't notice him until he shuffled to his feet halfway through Q & A, waved his arm to draw my attention and said, "It must be nice being a missionary. Work for three years—if you can call that work—then take a year's holiday!" He looked smugly at the congregation, craning his neck first to the left then to the right, before looking brazenly at me.

What did this man know of furloughs? How could I communicate in a sound-byte about the tensions and pressures we'd endured when leading a team of strong-willed missionaries in places where only the strong endure? How could this man understand the emotional toll of constant change, the sense of rootlessness, the need to continually readjust to new situations? What did he know about starting all over again in friendships, something which had plagued Anna since saying farewell to Belgium. Could he appreciate what it means to travel 15,000 kilometres and speak at more than 55 meetings across Canada during our 6 months at home? What did he know about home schooling, which Anna had begun in preparation for the move to Adana?

Is it possible to communicate to such men something of the fear and anticipation which filled us as we contemplated going to a new city on the edge of Kurdistan—a city of two million with possibly eight other Christians? How could this man appreciate the trepidation and thrill of seeing nationals take over "our" magazine ministry, knowing that their expectations were totally unrealistic and that the whole thing might collapse within a year or two? How could I tell in one sound-byte the joys and sorrows of communicating God's grace in places where it is unwanted?

"If missionary work is such a piece of cake," I replied with some asperity, "please explain two things: why don't more people do it and why is there such an abnormally high drop-out rate among career missionaries?"

The little man sat down hastily and disappeared inside his oversized coat.

·

You moil and toil and pray and plead in some forsaken place for three or four years then get on a plane to spend a year back home. The system harked back to the 19th century, the age of sail, when it was a long way from, say, Iowa to Istanbul or India.

The concept of missions was very different then. Victorian man, comfortably secure in his cultural and religious superiority, felt morally obliged to raise poor natives everywhere to his own Anglo-Saxon Protestant levels of development which were, without dispute, far ahead of the rest of the world in scientific, philosophical and educational terms. The desire to reshape the world into its own image was—using words as they did back then—the white man's burden. This impetus was backed by a theological notion now largely out of favor (though, oddly, making a bit of a comeback recently): post-Millennialism. It taught that the missionary endeavor would gradually transform the world into an increasingly better place until it eases into the Edenic kingdom of Revelation, at the end of which Christ would return.

Missionaries back then sought to discharge their burden through education. From the get-go, Protestant pioneers like Bartholomew Ziegenbald were zealous educators, and with the arrival of the Americans this compulsion went into overdrive. The American Board of Commissioners for Foreign Missions

("The Board") established impressive networks of schools all over the place. Some of the best universities in the Middle East today, like Bosphorus University in Istanbul and the American University of Beirut, began life as Board schools where "natives" could imbibe Christian enlightenment values while studying mathematics, history, physics, geology, business, engineering, botany, psychology, philosophy, ethics, general history, history of religion, English literature and various European languages.

Those educational facilities had a tremendous impact on the Middle East. Their graduates became the region's first generation of modern-style teachers, doctors, lawyers, bankers, merchants, authors, editors, interpreters and civil officials.[199] It also absorbed the bulk of missionary resources and personnel. Sadly, those schools drifted from the Christian fold within a generation, and in terms of church planting the massive effort proved misplaced and ineffective.

The other pre-WWI big ticket item was the establishment of medical services. Initially designed to meet the needs of the missionary community, facilities soon expanded to serve the general public. Agencies like The Board established hospitals, surgical wards, out-patient clinics and dispensaries, often in close proximity to the institutions of higher learning.

The establishment of schools and hospitals next to each other led to the development of the now much-maligned missionary compound, "isolated Christian communities modeling a form of western Protestantism which might be envied but which was in no way imitatable by the surrounding people."[200] These compounds could take on very quaint characteristics, totally out of character with the surrounding culture. Often built on hilltops from where they commanded beautiful views of the surrounding countryside, they were perceived as "walled villages of another race established in

---

[199] See 2008. Pikkert, P. *Protestant Missionaries to the Middle East: Ambassadors of Christ or Culture?* ALEV Books, Ancaster. p. 58.
[200] Pikkert p. 60.

these surroundings by some unexplained cause... An American walled village at that."[201]

All that to say that the work which kept most 19th century missionaries busy allowed them to return home for one year in four. With the collapse of those educational and medical ministries in the wake of World War I however, conservative Evangelicals were forced to rethink mission theology and praxis. Firstly, the post-World War I economic crises triggered a precipitous drop in recruitment and finances, forcing agencies to reduce their ministries to a fraction of what they were before. Secondly, a missiology based on Teutonic theological liberalism and Anglo-enlightenment proved theologically and socio-politically bankrupt. Put another way, the Great War showed that such concepts as "reason" and "Western civilization" had failed the missionary. Thirdly, the carnage resulting from Protestant nations (Anglican Britain and Lutheran Germany) fighting each other in the bloodiest conflict of all drove home the point that missionaries were not going to be midwives ushering in a new global Edenic era. Mission schools and hospitals were taken over by new, post-colonial nationalist governments or shut down due to lack of money and personnel. Ceasing to be perceived as heroic and worthwhile back home, public perception turned against the missionary movement.

Men like Samuel Zwemer and Kenneth Cragg responded by reconceptualizing mission strategy and practice. They re-focused theologically on man's original dilemma: sin leading to estrangement from a holy and sovereign God who provided the answer to his otherwise irreconcilable attributes of wrath and mercy in the person of Jesus Christ. Then they sought to develop a contextual apologetic and a culturally relevant proclamation based on God's revelation in Christ.

Building on their work the interdenominational missionary movement which emerged in force after World War II, and of which we were a part, refocused on church planting and making disciples. Missionaries were to become bi-cultural by developing abiding relationships with national brothers and

[201] Ibid.

sisters with whom you walked through life. This meant that leaving for long periods of time was out of the question, for the heart of discipleship is that the gospel be imitated if it is to be followed. Local Christians could understand visits home lasting for weeks, even for a couple of months—they themselves might return to their home villages for that long. Leaving them in the lurch for a whole year, however, was too disruptive relationally.

In any case, furloughs were strange, discombobulating times. You are 'home' but where is home? You are an outsider in your own country. Some there idolize you, others pity you, no one is indifferent to you. People expect you to say sagacious things without actually wanting you to share deeply about your passions and work. They have no idea what to ask, nor how to relate to you. You make them feel uncomfortable; you stoke vague feelings of guilt.

On January 1, 1997—tickets were cheap on the first day of the year—we stepped on a plane for Istanbul, and from there to Adana.

Part 5: 1997-2018

From Pioneer to Pedagogue

The Road goes ever on and on
Down from the door where it began.
Now far ahead the Road has gone,
And I must follow, if I can,
Pursuing it with eager feet,
Until it joins some larger way
Where many paths and errands meet.
And whither then? I cannot say.

Bilbo Baggins

42

Boomtown

"Every record has been destroyed or falsified, every book has been rewritten, every picture has been repainted, every statue and street building has been renamed... And that process is continuing day by day and minute by minute."

George Orwell

. . .

ADANA... A CLASHING cacophony of crazy traffic, squat palm trees, shouting street vendors, hawking street urchins and bustling masses of friendly people. An estate agent took us to eight different flats and we agreed on the first one he showed us. It had three spacious bedrooms and inspiring views of Lake Seyhan and the Taurus mountains.

A rapidly expanding wild-east boom town of hastily built, shoddily constructed high-rises and uneven pavements, it was difficult to imagine the place as having a history deeper than, say, mid-19th century Chicago. Yet it is one of the oldest continuously inhabited places on earth, mentioned in the Epic of Gilgamesh, on Hittite tablets and in Homer's Iliad. Its district of Yüreğir was ancient Mopsuestia where Theodore of Mopsuestia, one of the finest exegetes of the early church, developed the grammatico-historical hermeneutic the Reformers adopted eleven hundred years later. Little remains of that rich past. Hidden behind a Quranic school, a tea house and a Mukhtar's office is a neolithic tumulus, a dusty mound upon which bored archeology students carry out desultory excavations. Down the hill a Roman bridge spans the Seyhan River and, well, that's about it. There are some Ottoman buildings and the inevitable Atatürk Museum. Like the rest of the country, the city was in denial about its pogrom-filled, genocidal past. It looked forward! There was money to be made and people to be exploited—not least those Kurds fleeing the turmoil of civil war in the south-east.

·

Money... We arrived with 5000 Canadian dollars in our pockets and within weeks those pockets were turned inside-out. It took this miserly Dutchman's breath away but hey, that's how things were done in Adana! That wad of pretty paper paid for a year's rent up front (an Adana custom) and got us launched. The house wasn't yet cozy but we were welcoming guests.

On February 1, a month after arrival, we celebrated our eleventh wedding anniversary. The restaurant was pleasant, the food Turkish cuisine at its best. Soft brown curls framed those blue, smiling, Irish eyes. "It feels almost like coming home, doesn't it?" she said.

"I love you, Anna."

·

The Cold... True, outside the February chill wasn't as cold as in Canada but indoors there was no escaping it. A gas heater kept the worst chill out of the kitchen and dining area, elsewhere we shivered. Oddly, the orange trees gracing the sidewalks were in full fruit. You could reach up and pluck a frozen Washington Navel on your way to the grocery store.

The neighbours assured us we'd soon long for the shivers. They were right. Adana has but two seasons: winter and summer, with only a week or two between. The heaters disappeared, carpets rolled up, quilts and woolen sweaters washed and stored away. The solar system now spewed scalding water. The onslaught of heat sparked another round of shopping: balcony furniture, fans, window blinds.

·

Homeschooling... A friend back home carved Anna a shield called "Pikkert Private Academy" with a singularly appropriate motto: "I can do all things through Him who gives me strength" (Phil. 4:13). Anna didn't really home-school, she ran a school at home. At 9 AM a tinkling bell announced the start of the school day, whereupon she went into schoolmarm mode. The bell also tinkled for recess and lunch. Mornings were spent on English and Math, and the hour after lunch on Bible, history, geography, science or creative writing. At 2 PM Anna reverted back to mum/wife mode. Art and craft were left to the children's own initiative while music consisted of listening to classical compositions. Foreign language was Turkish and physical education covered by riding their bikes or, for Owen, dribbling a basketball with neighbouring kids. In spite of the inevitable struggles Anna remained sane and, in the end, even found it a satisfying experience.

> "I can honestly testify to the fact that when the Lord asks you to do a job He also equips and enables. Here we are three quarters of the way through this year's school curriculum and the children are right on target."[202]

It helped that Owen and Rita were bright, reasonably disciplined and loved to read. "Making learning fun, maintaining a good attitude, being creative, ensuring adequate social interaction; these are the things that wear me out" (Anna writing).[203] My contribution consisted of reading Newberry Honors Books before bedtime—hours which morphed into cherished memories.

.

Kids... Afternoons were spent exploring "Fossil Hill", an empty field where they hunted for fossils and fed a wild turtle living in a cave. They rode their bikes, played Civilization on the computer, read, did crafts or re-watched one of our three or four English videos. They never want to see Black Beauty again. "They don't miss out academically though some days I sense their loneliness and longing to belong to a group or club of some kind."[204] The nearest other home schoolers were 500 km away. We enrolled them in a Saturday afternoon gymnastics

[202] Letter to "Folks back home", May 3, 1997.
[203] PL March 1997.
[204] PL December 1997.

club but after two months of Soviet-style workouts pulled the plug on that.

There were no girls of Rita's age and the boys wouldn't let her play with them. Seeing her sitting forlornly on the stoop, clutching her stuffed rabbit by the straps of its denim coveralls while watching the boys play soccer nearly broke Anna's heart. "Rita was like a closed bud who would undoubtedly flower when we return to Canada."[205] Yet with numerous adult guests of every nationality passing through we didn't need to worry about the kids becoming maladjusted socially. We also became a close-knit family.

Rita had the most beautiful, silky-blond hair which Turks could not resist stroking, affectionately pinching her cheek in the process. She didn't like that, but Owen saw an opportunity. "Dad, if I took Rita to Atatürk Park and put up a sign saying 'For a Lira you may stroke my sister's hair' we could make a lot of money!"

"Hmmm. Not sure about that. Ask Ayhan Bey (Mr. Ayhan, the neighbour) what he thinks". He came back pumped. "Dad, Ayhan Bey said he'd pay double!"

"Hmmm. I still don't think it's a good idea. It's a bit exploitative."

"But I'd share the money with Rita!" Thankfully, sister didn't rise to the occasion, though later she became the most business savvy of us all.

One day she was marching ahead of me, hands in her pockets, when she stopped in the middle of the sidewalk and waited until I'd caught up. "Isn't it amazing?" her brow was furled, her sparking eyes thoughtful.

"What is?"

"All these nice people and none of them know Jesus!"

"You're absolutely right, Sweetheart. It's amazing..." The question would haunt her later in life.

.

---

[205] PL December 1998.

Hakan and the birth of LACE... Owen and Rita's great frustration was their inability to communicate with local kids, so I developed an intuitive language learning program for them. I roped in Hakan, a Yeni Yaklaşım reader who had come to faith, as a language helper.

Hakan was a *hamal*, a public porter. A profession perfected in the long ago, *hamals* carried their burdens on their backs by means of a *semer*, a hard leather cushion strapped over the shoulders and resting on the hips. Hakan's speciality was appliances. He would stoop forward while store flunkies dropped a newly purchased fridge, stove or washing machine onto his *semer*.

The secret to being a good *hamal,* he explained once, was finding the right poise and balance. Once that was achieved he'd follow the client home through the city's melee, clutching one end of a short rope, the other end of which was wrapped around his burden and tied to the bottom of the *semer*. "It is an interesting study to watch the muscles of the *hamal's* legs distend and his veins dilate as, nearly bent in two, he treads leisurely along, groaning under a weight which it would take two ordinary men to carry."[206]

I paid Hakan to give the kids Turkish lessons. Afterwards he and I would sit on the balcony, read the newspaper and talk about current events. He was intelligent, remarkably well informed and a natural teacher. As I kept developing the language program he started using it to teach other foreigners. The Language Acquisition for Cross-Cultural Effectiveness (LACE) course was born and is still used to train missionary candidates the principles of lingua-cultural acquisition.

·

Local Friends... "Pray that God will give us friends in Adana in whom our social needs are met—and to whom our Christian faith will mean something."[207] Though establishing deep

[206] Julius R. Van Millingen. *Peeps at Many Lands: Turkey*. London. Adam and Charles Black, 1911.
[207] PL June 1997.

relationships took time, the Lord quickly provided local acquaintances. Ours was a new apartment complex so relationships were not yet fixed. We clicked immediately with our neighbours. They were not only man and wife but, as was common, first cousins, part of a large close-knit clan.

Ayhan Bey and I often sat on the balcony to discuss eternity. They were Alawites, an oft persecuted sect who felt they had more in common with us than with the Sunni majority. "Pray that Christ in us will change this lovely family's standing before God. We have nothing else to offer."[208] Anna did not need to step out the front door to look for woman friends for every two weeks or so the ladies had four-hour long afternoon tea parties which she joined.

I got into my old groove of mornings in the home office and afternoons with people. I found a chess club, played billiards in a local pool hall and discovered a tea house to my liking. Our devout neighbours were markedly different from my more-Marxist-than-Muslim tea-house acquaintances. With no major projects and programs on the go I had time to devote to extra prayer, so twice a week I pushed through bushes and brambles up a low hill where I'd sit with arms wrapped about my knees, my back resting against the bole of a gnarled olive tree. There, in the shade of its canopy, the wind sighing among the branches, I interceded for my family, for the city spread before me, for the Kurds and for our team, three godly, diligent, tenacious, gifted couples and a single guy. The couples had babies and the single's fiancée stayed with us for six weeks prior to marriage. When two other missionary couples began meeting regularly with a few local believers for worship and Bible study I started interceding for them as well.

·

The missionary community... Two German couples joined Kurdish Outreach Ministries. They settled in well, approached language learning with Teutonic discipline and had a long and

---

[208] Personal letter to "Family and Friends" May 22, 1997.

fruitful ministry. Soon after a number of other agencies also started sending personnel to Adana.

> "New workers with other organizations look to us for some guidance and support. Peter seems to have developed a kind of advisory/pastoral role for several young men finding their way in the Middle East. An open home where folks are accepted and encouraged is a real need for many."[209]

"I've learned (Anna writing) that a welcoming and peaceful home, a listening ear and a slice of apple pie can go a long way!"[210] We hosted a weekly prayer meeting for our team and a Sunday service during which we gathered around the coffee table, opened in prayer and sang a couple of hymns. Owen read the Scripture, Anna raised topics for intercession, and we took turns praying. I'd read a chapter from a Christian book in lieu of a sermon. Owen suggested he be given pocket money so we could take up an offering.

As the number of Christians meeting for worship at our place grew we began dreaming about establishing an international church. I started meeting with the team leader of another evangelical agency to pray and plan about starting an 'Adana International Fellowship' which we hoped would be the forerunner of the first Protestant International church in modern times in this vast gateway city. "About twenty people attended our first meeting on the occasion of American Thanksgiving, and the next one is planned for Christmas. Pray for much wisdom in this new venture."[211]

■

Travel... We did not own a car so either walked or used the minibus. We'd put the kids on a minibus to our co-worker Cornelia's house and tell the driver where to let them off. Rita, age 7, once got a city tour before the absent-minded chauffer

---

[209] Ibid.
[210] PL September 1997
[211] PL December 1997.

realized he'd forgotten the little blond girl nervously watching the world passing by. He dropped her off on his next round.

To help Isa with Turkey's new Christian magazine I took the fifteen-hour bus trip to Istanbul so frequently the stewardess (yes, intercity busses have stewardesses over there) would welcome me aboard with a warm smile, hand me my favorite newspaper and come around with a cup of coffee just the way I like it. I dealt with some of the technical aspects of magazine production early on and provided Christian news from around the world, "but the project is the responsibility of Turkish believers and we want to encourage them to run with it."[212] The new magazine "looks so good it makes the old Yeni Yaklaşım look primitive!"[213]

.

Happiness... When was the last time you were happy? I don't mean the last time you experienced pleasurable feelings because one of your senses was titillated but something more elusive: real happiness.

Whenever I looked at the snow-capped mountains from our balcony it struck me afresh: I am happy! Neither food poisoning nor extremes of temperature nor computer crashes nor police raids on co-workers nor the belief that our phone was tapped—nothing shook that happiness. "Peter is happy here in Turkey and feels more at home in the Turkish than in the Belgian culture."[214] Belgium was necessary but not necessarily nice. Yes, the standard of living was higher there but it was an environment for which I was ill suited, in which I struggled with tasks for which I was ill gifted. All that had changed.

Aristotle held that happiness is a way of doing things, not something one arrives at. There is much more to it than that. Happiness includes both being what God wants you to be and doing what he has set aside for you to do. For us that meant

[212] Anna writing, Letter to "Folks back home" May 3, 1997.
[213] PL December 1997.
[214] Anna writing, Letter to "Folks back home" May 3, 1997.

being Christians in a Muslim environment, being a support to other missionaries, being a faithful friend to a select few and being a writer. It meant not letting other people's expectations rule our lives and resisting the temptation to be anything but lowly missionaries.

Owen: "Mum, did you want to come to Turkey too or did you really come because Daddy wanted to so badly?"

"The Lord led us here, honey, so we came."

43

Summer Past;
We Were Not Deported

*"Princes, kings, and other rulers of the world have used all
their strength and cunning against the Church, yet it
continues to endure and hold its own."*

John Foxe

• • •

THE POLICE STORMED into Cornelia's apartment, searched it minutely, interrogated her, took her diary and computer diskettes and threatened to deport her. Sometimes we missionaries were accused of working for the CIA or of supporting the PKK, the Kurdish separatist terrorist organization, and sometimes because, well, we were missionaries. The first two accusations were impossible to prove since they bore no relation to the truth. The third was true. Although it was not a criminal offence to be a Christian the word "missionary" had—and continues to have—negative connotations in Turkey, and that for good reasons.

I noted earlier that the main thrust of the 19th century missionary enterprise was establishing schools. Though misplaced as a church-planting strategy this effort did not generally have long term negative consequences on the host societies—with the glaring exception of Turkey. This is because the educational institutions established during Ottoman times chiefly empowered the Arab, Greek, Bulgarian, and Armenian minorities.

Pliny Fisk, one of the earliest American missionaries to the region, stated in 1825, i.e., during the middle of the Greek war of independence (1821-1829), that "the (Greek) nation is roused... The time of political revolutions should also be a period of religious reform. Americans should undertake this mission... There is no time to be lost."[215] Hence in 1828 the missionary community decided not to focus on the Empire's Turkish majority but on the Orthodox Greek, Bulgarian, and Armenian minorities, wistfully hoping that once revived these ancient churches would take it upon themselves to evangelize the Turks. They followed this misguided policy for the rest of the 19th and into the 20th century.[216]

Understandably, the Ottoman Turks had little sympathy for the Greek, Bulgarian, Armenian and Arab nationalist causes, nor for anyone espousing the welfare of these restive minorities. The last thing the Sultan wanted was that his unruly Christian subjects and Arab provinces be educated in Western social values and political thought—yet that was exactly what the missionary educational system accomplished. Wittingly or not, they empowered those distinct minorities. Armenians who formerly only spoke Turkish began using their native tongue and the linguistic standardization promoted by the missionary presses enabled them to communicate with greater ease across the empire. This led to the missionaries being perceived by the Muslim majority as friends of the Christian minorities, agents of western interests, and pawns of their own governments' political agendas. This had colossal and dreadful consequences. It not only failed in terms of evangelization but triggered a series of pogroms. In 1895, for instance, the Turks attempted to destroy the Euphrates College in Harput "because they regarded it as the means of enlightenment and strength to the Armenians"[217] It culminated in the Armenian genocide of 1915. In short, Turks to this day hold missionaries at least partly responsible for the collapse of the Ottoman Empire; little wonder the word "missionary" sticks in their throats.

[215] Fisk *Missionary Herald* 1827:267, quoted in Pikkert, *Protestant Missionaries to the Middle East: Ambassadors of Christ or Culture?* ALEV Books. Ancaster 2008, p. 51.
[216] For an extensive overview of early Protestant missionary work to the Middle East see Pikkert, P. *Protestant Missionaries to the Middle East: Ambassadors of Christ or Culture.*
[217] Ibid, p. 79.

Among Cornelia's stuff the police found a paper with the evil word Kurdistan on it and opened a court case. Cornelia visited our place frequently and we were glad to help her during those difficult days. As a result, however, we fully expected a similar raid so purged the house of everything which could be remotely construed as incriminating. While her court case was ongoing she went home to Switzerland for a family visit and was refused re-entry upon her return. "That was a real blow to us."[218]

A Mennonite family moved into a neighbouring apartment complex. They too were often in our home. Soon the police showed up there and turned their place up-side-down. They found nothing incriminating so gave them a liberal three weeks to pack up and get out. That was pretty good: sometimes they just showed up, told you to fill a few suitcases, stamped your passport *persona non grata* and escorted you to the airport.

Next the police visited another newly arrived missionary couple and inquired about me: "Is Peter Pikkert in town?" The couple pretended not to know.

> "Keep praying that we can stay and be bold in our witness to Jesus without foolishly attracting the attention of the authorities. Sometimes even so-called 'friends' turn out to be police informants. Constantly having to be careful becomes wearisome... Every day we have here in Adana is a bonus."[219]

Are we important? No. Expendable? Yes. However, we represented Jesus Christ in a place where he was not known and the enemy of mansoul was seeking to eradicate that testimony. Humanly speaking our expulsion would have been a blow to the work at that time for "the team looks to us not only for language and culture acquisition but also for Christian fellowship and planning for ministry."[220] The dark side would not prevail. God eventually established his church in Adana through his faithful servants. That, from the human side, was a

---

[218] PL December 1997.
[219] Ibid.
[220] Ibid.

matter of intercession, faith and obedience to the great commission.

Rita, looking worried: "Mum, what will we do if they arrest Daddy?" I was not raised in Mennonite pacifist traditions so planned to put up a fight. I found a secular-minded lawyer, explained the situation and kept her on a retaining fee. If the police showed up I was to call her immediately. She promised to run over irrespective of the time of day or night and open a case against them which she would spin out for two and a half years. That was the amount of time left which we had committed to helping our team get off the ground.

> "Pray that God will somehow, miraculously, enable us to stay right through to 1999. By then the team should be sufficiently well established in the language, the culture and in ministry to make a go of it on their own."[221]

At first our hearts missed a beat every time the doorbell rang. Eventually, however, life returned to normal; you learn to live with the idea that the police may arrive at any time. Knowing that the Lord was in control and that no human authority can thwart his purposes became a real and practical comfort. They never found us. The three-monthly in-out trips on different passports enabled us to stay on tourist visas, and since we had not registered at city hall our address was not on file. Like the Sodomites who "wearied themselves to find the door" to Lot's house (Gen. 19:11), Adana's police never found ours.

---

[221] PL September 1997.

44

Tentmakers Inc.

"Frodo found that some explanation of what he was doing would have to be given. He gave out that he was interested in history and geography (at which there was much wagging of heads)."

J.R.R. Tolkien

• • •

MISSIONARY GUEST HOUSES are microcosms of the evangelical enterprise in particular regions, and I availed myself of them whenever possible. Often managed by kind-hearted American retirees, they are safe, comfortable oases for that interesting array of mankind which self-identifies as "kingdom workers". You will undoubtedly meet the preternaturally upbeat woman who strides your way, one arm stretched in front of her. "Ha, ahm Aymber from Alabama. Where are ya'll from? Ah just arayved from Tajikistayin." Then are the traumatized, those whose marriage is falling apart, those who have just been kicked out of a neighboring country or those needing emergency medical care. If you hang around long enough you'll meet the hyperactive, hyperconnected Egyptian seeking to learn all about you, and wondering where you stand on the Israel-Gaza conflict, or young folks on summer mission, or a quiet gray-bearded visiting professor minding his own business (latterly that was me), in town for some conference. There are usually several locals as well, scurrying about cleaning rooms, making beds, mopping or firing up the vacuum cleaner just as you settle into a comfortable arm chair.

In the past the vast majority of these "kingdom workers" were Anglo-Saxon. With the near collapse of missionary recruitment from that race however, and the increase of missionaries from the rest of the world, you now have Koreans,

Indians, Brazilians, Filipinos and Egyptians all dutifully tucking into Special K at the breakfast buffet set on the sideboard by that lovely couple from Kansas or Ohio. Suppers tend to be more authentic if they employ a local cook.

Dinner conversations in these places fascinated me for that is where you learn how people finagle their visas. "And where do you serve?" someone will ask.

"Afghanistan."

"Oh, how interesting. What do you guys do there?" The question pertains to the cover used to obtain that coveted work permit, not "kingdom activities".

"We run mental health clinics." Of course they do. They are in Afghanistan, after all.

"Kazakhstan. We operate an animal food business."

"Tunisia. We run a hydroponic farm."

I quietly listened while hunched over my food, deeply impressed with what these young people, bona fide "tentmaking" heroes, were pulling off.

.

Tentmaker was the metaphor we used for missionaries working at secular jobs in countries hostile to the enterprise[222]. The term was draw from Acts 18:3, which suggests that the apostle Paul and some friends supplemented their incomes by making tents.

Tentmaking has a long history. After their expulsion from Byzantium the Nestorians plied their professions as bankers, merchants, physicians, astrologers, translators, traders in precious stones and philosophers while they preached their way across Persia and India as far as China. Later the Jesuits, famous for their accurate calculations of planetary movements, ingratiated themselves with the Chinese royal court, which prized that sort of celestial foreknowledge. 18th Century Moravian and Basel missionaries practiced their trades wherever they went as well. Like Paul and the Nestorians, they did so to make ends meet.

---

[222] More commonly referred to as Business as Mission (BAM) today.

Today's tentmakers do not generally utilize their profession solely for fiscal purposes; faithful friends and supporting home-churches usually take care of that. They do it in order to obtain that elusive document, a residence permit which leaves you with sufficient time to develop friendships, engage in discipleship training, church planting, the translation of Christian literature and whatever else might further the cause of Christ in countries closed to classic missionary work.

Tentmaking for visa purposes was pioneered by Dennis E. Clark, an unsung pioneer of the modern missionary movement. I met him in the 1980s when he was a spry old man with amazing stories to tell.[223] As a young man he studied in Switzerland, where he mastered French and German and came to faith. In 1940, during the frenzy of World War II, he sailed for the Indian subcontinent, settled in Lahore and mastered Urdu. A remarkable linguist, he could pass as a local when wearing his pakol and shalwar kameez. He also learnt Pasthun, and was a gifted Bible teacher[224]. Like the apostle Paul, he was peripatetic; he could be found in Lahore, Rawalpindi, Karachi, New Delhi, Peshawar and who knows where else. He never stayed long and never took charge of the churches he helped get started. He prepared men for leadership, appointed elders and moved on. As with the apostle, some of his church plants were remarkably resilient.

In 1943 he and his bride Gladys moved to Peshawar, a largely Pashtun city on the Khyber Pass. There he established the Central Asian Trading Agency (CATA) which, he hoped, would open doors into Afghanistan. He imported Singer sewing machines, bicycles and other goods into the country and exported dried fruit. In 1946 he opened a CATA office in Kabul, but that only lasted for a month. He was deported for sharing the gospel with a local using a Persian New Testament. Clark

---

[223] I drew from a short article written in April, 1999 by the late Robert C.D. Brow to get my facts straight. See http://www.brow.on.ca/Articles/ClarkRev.htm. Accessed May 30, 2023.
[224] See, for instance, his book *The Life and Teachings of Jesus the Messiah*, Dove, 1987.

was my kind of hero: a gifted linguist, a grass-roots missionary, a flexible, humble risk-taker for God able to think outside the box and blessed with a wife who stood with him through thick and thin.

His attempt to enter Afghanistan using a business venture sparked the imagination of Christie Wilson, who worked as a tentmaker in that country for over 20 years. His 1980 book *Today's Tentmakers* had an enormous influence on young guys like myself who dreamt of taking the gospel to closed countries.

Christie spurred mission agencies—not least WEC—to jump onto the tentmaking bandwagon. With gusto and zeal, and full of hope and cheer, mission-minded professionals and students signed up in the hope of penetrating the Communist and Muslim worlds with the gospel. We stopped referring to "closed countries" and started speaking of "creative access nations" (CANs) instead. After some years, however, it became clear that tentmaking in creative access nations required more than gusto, zeal, hope and cheer. In fact, it proved to be a disappointment. In the late 1980s and '90s hundreds of tentmakers drifted back home, and in 1997 my fecund ideator colleague Dan Gibson published *Avoiding the Tentmaker Trap*[225], in which he outlined the problems with which he, ourselves, and many others had had to grapple.

First, there was the time factor. Employers, assuming you are there to work hard and make lots of money, left you with little time for anything else. By the time you'd navigated the red tape, done a long day's work, traveled to 3 or 4 stores to buy food and relaxed a bit with family there was little time left for language learning, visiting nationals, discipleship and church planting. As a result few tentmakers came to grips with their host country's language and culture and even fewer developed a successful ministry outside of work.

Then there was the integrity issue. Some tentmakers claimed to be foreign experts in one thing or another but lacked the qualifications. One fellow I knew pretended to be an expert on

---

[225] Gibson, Dan. *Avoiding the Tentmaker Trap*. WEC International; 2nd edition. 1996.

oriental carpets, a complex subject of which he knew next to nothing. A talkative chap, I suggested he become an ESL teacher instead. He did so and has had a long, fruitful career in the Arabian Peninsula.

Next is the security issue. Most closed countries monitor foreigners' mail, phones and, later, emails and social media accounts. Though happy to welcome expatriate experts, even Christians, they become obstreperous when they suspect you of converting locals. Some expats became so paranoid their Christian witness was reduced to zero.

The temptations posed by the expatriate community was also a distraction. Since many of those early tentmakers failed to learn the local lingua-culture they integrated into the expat demimonde of international churches, sports clubs, youth get-togethers, cultural events, movie nights, etc. Expats are a colourful though often troubled subspecies of mankind: think of the surgeon whose scalpel slipped once too often, the wifebeater eluding a court case, the gambler who couldn't pay his debts. One WEC colleague landed in North Africa hoping to reach Berbers but decided to become pastor of the international church in order to minister to this needy demographic.

In Istanbul I had assumed the guise of university student and English teacher. In Adana we didn't think tentmaking for a residence permit was an option as submitting an application would draw attention to the police record we suspected I had for previous Yeni Yaklaşım activities, and that would lead to deportation or worse. For three years we quietly left and re-entered the country every three months on fresh tourist visas. Because we had dual citizenships we could take a ferry to, say, Northern Cyprus or a Greek island on one passport and re-enter a day or two later on the other—expensive, but involving a minimum of interaction with officialdom. Dubbed "the professional tourist route", it was used to great effect for many years by quite a few missionaries. This modus is not possible now, in the digital age.

Although we did not "make tents" for visa purposes, we still needed a cover. We had to appear to be doing something that made sense to those around us, for Adana was not a tourist destination. I presented myself as a researcher investigating the subject of "The West Through Muslim Eyes". We also exploited my love for writing. After years of penning Yeni Yaklaşım articles Calliope's craft was embedded on my DNA. It gave me professional satisfaction as well as the rebel's gratification of challenging conventional ways of thinking. "What we initially viewed as an interesting hobby now appears to be a God-given ability which Peter has been encouraged to develop."[226] So, in the mornings when other men left for work and Anna and the kids gathered around the kitchen table for home-schooling, I wrote. Whenever I published an article, or when the LACE course rolled off the press we'd ballyhoo the achievement with our neighbours. Of course I also contributed to the new Turkish magazine, but we couldn't celebrate that publicly.

"Doing research" seemed like the ideal cover. No one questioned it and it was tremendously flexible. It enabled me to make time for the team and for guests, as well as frequent trips to Istanbul. However, when Anna and I later reviewed our time in Adana we realized that it too had its limitations. A man's friends are drawn from his family, work colleagues and fellow churchgoers. We had no family or church to draw from, and writing, being a lonely profession, is not conducive to making friends. While Anna soon had more people in her life than she could cope with I only managed to get to know a few well. This became a source of frustration and resulted in a sense of failure. We concluded that in time I should become properly qualified for some tentmaking job, one which would give us a residence permit, allow time for Christian ministry, make sense to the neighbours and lead to ongoing contact with other men.

"Pray for a close walk with Jesus and personal holiness, for boldness mixed with wisdom when witnessing, for respect and acceptance in the local community, for divine appointments, for more labourers to join us..."[227]

---

[226] KOM Annual Report, March 1996.
[227] PL December 1998.

45

50 And Rising

"Time flies over us but leaves its shadow behind."

Nathaniel Hawthorne

. . .

"IT'S BEEN THREE MONTHS. Write a prayer letter!" she said. The thermometer rose to 50 Celsius (131 Fahrenheit) and still the red fluid kept rising. The world was an overheated sauna. We filled the bathtub and slipped into it when conditions became unbearable—air conditioning was for the rich. It had not rained since spring. Wildfires broke out nearby. Rita suffered from recurring bouts of vomiting and her budgie hadn't the oomph to lift its head. Neither did I. Stupefied and stripped to the waist, I nodded over my desk dripping like an alembic distiller. Even after midnight it remained in the upper thirties. And the humidity! They called the city "Turkey's armpit" for a reason.

Had three months passed since our last circular? What was there to report? We were still there, which we hoped was good news for the Kurds. We'd had a holiday in Northern Cyprus, and that had been good for us. I'd led two small groups, one from Belgium and one from Canada, around the country, hoping they would carry a vision for the Middle East back to their home churches. Our local team had grown to seven, including the single guy who lived with us that summer. We were grateful for unity and mutual support as we tried to determine what ministries they could engage in now that they were coming to grips with the language and the culture. How does one reach the Kurds without getting deported? That was the question!

What else? We'd survived an earthquake. Some were killed, many more injured. Many of Adana's buildings were damaged, many beyond repair. Our apartment too sported impressive cracks. Aftershocks continued for weeks. That, and the intense heat, encouraged many to flee for the mountains or the sea, leaving the city a ghost town. Death was on everyone's mind and it was easy to speak of eternity with those who remained.

After the earthquake Anna had escorted Owen, Rita and four other kids to a children's camp. She was still partly traumatized by the earthquake and vomited often during that ten hour bus trip along the serpentine coastal road. At a rest stop she fainted. Six foreign children stood over her, looking worried. When she came around a Turk held up her head.

"Take this," he said in perfect English, holding up a little white pill. She resisted; one doesn't take pills from strangers, not in Turkey nor anywhere else.

"Don't worry Anna," he said. "It is I." Then she knew it was the Lord or his angel, took the pill, felt better, climbed back onto the bus, and safely delivered the children. A missionary couple took her in and tucked her into bed. When she woke up her clothes, freshly washed, were neatly folded on a chair.

What else? We continued to lead Sunday morning worship services and mid-week prayer meetings for our team. I continued working on various writing projects and continued bussing to and from Istanbul to help with the new Christian magazine. However, life was an effort for the red fluid expanded until the thermometer burst and the liquid dribbled down the wall.

Eventually the awful, fiery sun relented. Summer passed and the trauma of the earthquake subsided as the aftershocks became milder and less frequent. Those who'd fled to the sea or the mountains returned. Rita regained some weight. Soon we would be able to reach for a light blanket at night. The calendar reminded us that another Christmas was at hand, an event celebrated by a handful of foreigners.

"Whenever I (Anna writing) hang out the washing on our back balcony and survey the endless rows of apartments I have two emotions: heartfelt sadness that no one believes in Jesus and a deep sense of the sheer privilege of being able to exalt his name in this city."[228]

Then she got sick. Two weeks of frequent visits to the hospital, endless tests and a biopsy suggested something untoward. The Lord gave us quiet hearts as we prayed for grace to accept whatever he had in store for us. *"Shall we accept good from the Lord and not trouble?"* (Job 2:10). Extensive tests for breast cancer proved negative and antibiotics and hormone treatment eventually beat the infection.

> "The drugs blur my brain, make me both sleepy and nauseous and mean I cannot accomplish as much in the day as I would like to... I like to be alert, active, strong and capable but at times the opposite is true and I just cannot dash about as I used to."[229]

One year rolled into another: another Ramadan, another Eid, another Feast of Sacrifice. Owen splayed out on the couch while black-bearded men sacrificed bleating sheep and panicky goats on balconies and down in the yard. "Ooooh... I'm gonna be sick." Outside Rita, squatting on her haunches with puddles of blood coagulating at her feet, watched the butchers do their thing. Owen refused to eat the jiggly cuts of red mutton arriving from neighbours, maintaining that it was meat sacrificed to idols. We shoved it into the freezer. Weeks later Anna turned it into stews. Thus we hung in there, blending and assimilating as best we could. Refraining from bold moves and brash adventures, we slipped in and out of the country every three months, thanking God for each new day.

A visiting missionary asked Owen what he wanted to be when he grew up. "A philosopher," he declared confidently. He mistook her somewhat startled look so furled his brow and leaned forward. "Auntie, do you know what a philosopher is?"

"Yes, I do," she nodded slowly. She reminded us of that exchange when he received his Doctorate in that field of study two decades later.

---

[228] PL December 1998
[229] Anna writing, personal letter to Nancy Wood, 24 October 1998.

Hakan, my one Christian friend and the kids' language tutor, decided to remarry the woman he'd divorced some years earlier. The ceremony took place in our living room. I preached a sermonette, he and Selma repeated their vows before a few guests and Anna provided cake and refreshments. He later joined the merchant marine, to be killed in an altercation in Buenos Aires.

Our three year commitment to Adana drew to a close, and we accepted an invitation to join the home office in Canada. The Lord had blessed in terms of building up a small team which could survive without us but I experienced a sense of failure in the area of evangelism. Although we enjoyed the company of our neighbours and sought to be consistent witnesses in our apartment complex no one came to faith.

> "They now know that Christians can be upright, moral (and even nice!) people who have a genuine relationship with God and claim to be sure of a place in heaven. This is indeed major progress... but will not suffice them on the Day of Judgement."[230]

We were disappointed with ourselves... and maybe also a little with the Lord. Still, seventeen years earlier no one was targeting Kurds. Now we were the largest missionary presence in Adana, demonstrating that it was possible to take new recruits to regional hubs, have them learn the language, adjust to the culture and get started in Christian ministry. Nearly a dozen mission agencies working in Europe, Iraq and Turkey were engaged in broadcasting, or translating the Bible and the Jesus film, or post-quake relief work, or church planting and discipleship training. Prayers for visas and safety in travel, for fluency in one, two or three languages, for meaningful relationships, for protection from the police, guerrillas and fanatics, for new candidates, mature leaders, finances, and growth in grace and wisdom were answered.

---

[230] PL December 1998.

Although we personally saw very little spiritual fruit in Adana, God's Spirit continued to work and today the city boasts several evangelical churches and a Christian bookstore.[231]

---

[231] Adana Umut Kilisesi (Adana Hope Church): https://adanaumutkilisesi.com/; Adana Protestan Kilisesi (Adana Protestant Church): https://adanakilise.com/; and the Adana Kurtulus Kilisesi (Adana Salvation Church).

46

"What Do You Do All Day In That Mansion?"

"Our relationship with each other is the criterion the world uses to judge whether our message is truthful - Christian community is the final apologetic."

Francis Shaeffer

. . .

EVER EMBARK on some venture you imagined impossible or an enterprise for which you were ill suited? Why did you do it? Peer pressure? The desire to impress? The need to prove yourself? How did you feel afterwards? Stupid? Brave?

Joining home staff? No sir, I'm a pioneer, a cutting edge kinda fellah. Don't fit easily into well-established teams. Find yourself some retiree for *that* job. Live communally? No ma'am, I'm an introvert, a private sort of person. We treasure family life and all that... Yet there we were, in Canada, doing something seemingly ill-matched. Why? There were pragmatic reasons: Anna needed three years of residency to claim citizenship and WEC was crying out for help. But there was more to it.

People might act out of character for a variety of reasons, for a limited period of time. They are, however, rarely able to sustain that for weeks, months or years. Eventually they slip into their old ways—unless they undergo a character change. The Lord must have reprogrammed something for at some stage I discovered I was at peace, even content—at least for the time being—in my new role. Maybe this too had something to do with that process theologians dub sanctification.

It was a long way from our concrete apartment and the hustle, heat and harassment of Adana to WEC's stately mansion on a hill among mature maples and sycamores in an up-scale cul-de-sac. We relished our religious freedom and marveled at Hamilton's beautiful waterfront, majestic trees and countless steeples. We adjusted from a formal to a casual society, from an intolerant to a hyper-tolerant environment, from viewing people as extensions of extended families to individuals in their own right. We explored libraries, enjoyed church camps, family reunions, and discovered our responsibilities as home staff members.

We occupied a large living room with a small kitchenette, two bedrooms, one of which we divided using closets, and a bathroom. "Pray for us as we adjust to living in a continually changing community of up to 25 people all living and working in a single large house."[232]

We soon fell into our new routine. Wake up, washup, devotions, breakfast, dishes, see the kids off to school. Walk to the ground floor and gather for prayer. We prayed a lot. From 9 to 10, three mornings a week, we poured over the latest batch of incoming letters and presented their contents before the Throne of Grace. Political developments in much of the world made it increasingly dangerous to be a Western missionary, so whenever an urgent request came in we'd pray for that after lunch or dinner. We organized days of prayer and fasting and hosted special times of intercession open to the public.

After prayers a coffee break and then to work. The director might be on the phone resolving some crisis in the Congo while his wife vaccinated a couple heading for Equatorial Guinea. Ancient Jack might tackle next year's MissionFest registrations while his eighty year old bride answered the phone and updated mailing lists. Dan arranged deputation tours and Suet Mei hummed in the kitchen. In the basement Jon #1, fingers flying, punched numbers into a calculator. Dawn changed bedding in the guest rooms or was off to the airport picking up newly arriving missionaries. Jon #2, the handyman, might be painting a room or taking the washing machine apart—again. Anna worked in the candidates department helping people find their niche in ministry.

---

[232] PL April 2000.

"I'm overworked and underpaid... and just love my job! It is fascinating to witness the wide variety of people whom the Lord calls, and rewarding to help them find the right place in missions."[233]

Those with whom she corresponded had endless questions and expected immediate answers: "I think God is calling me to Kazakhstan but how can I be sure?" "My parents aren't happy about me going, what should I do?" "I have no formal training but attend a good Bible-teaching church. Is that sufficient?" "Do you really need that many references?" "What should I cover in my testimony?" "How necessary are those medical and dental reports?" "How do I apply for a visa to the Middle East?" "What do I say I will be doing if I can't use the word missionary?" "What happens if I get sick?" "Are you serious about me having to write a will?" "Can men wear shorts over there?" "How much will it cost?" "Is there an organized program or do I have to initiate everything myself?" "What do you mean by being committed to teamwork?" "I was never any good at languages. Is there no place where I could use English?"

She received lots of inquiries from inexperienced young women looking to alleviate the miseries of the most traumatized kids in the poorest countries as well as from college kids who wanted to get their missions stint over with. Others indicated some vague notion about some day wanting to go somewhere, and then there were those who inquired about teaching when they had never taught anything to anyone before. Others asked how God guides or questioned if this 'faith principle' really works. And then, most infrequently, there was an inquiry which made all the sifting worthwhile: someone with adequate Bible training, clearly called by God to serve cross-culturally, ready to commit their lives without counting the cost, and with a solid church behind them.

Once she'd answered the basic questions she dealt with short-term, preliminary and final applications, references, medical forms, doctrinal statements, acceptance letters and

---

[233] PL Jan. 2002 (Anna writing).

advisory reports on each applicant for the Candidates' Committee. When our cook left for Bible college she also prepped an evening meal for 14-20 people once a week. Struggling at times to balance the needs of work and family, "she wants to be 'restfully busy.'"[234]

The Candidates Course had developed since my day. Now recruits didn't just learn about WEC's ethos, value system, doctrinal statement and practices, they also studied church planting and church growth, spiritual warfare, team development, computer use, cross-cultural life, discipling of national believers, conflict management and health matters. I taught Islam and Muslim Evangelism, Contextualization (i.e., how to make the gospel relevant to people of other cultures), Marriage and Family Life on the Mission Field, Language Learning Techniques and Security Issues in Closed Countries. I also developed a new WEC magazine and we each mentored a new candidate. This involved spending informal, one-on-one times with them.

Those informal times spent with candidates and returning missionaries were, at times, more important than our formal jobs. Anglo-Saxons are a goal-orientated, achievement addicted multitude. This is reflected at the home-bases of mission agencies in how we give account. Director's reports, department head updates, field leader summaries, prayer letters and mission magazine articles all tend towards the statistical. We talk numbers: the number of candidates applying, churches, Bible schools and seminaries visited, sermons preached, books sold, dollars donated, dollars spent, missionaries trained, missionaries lost, meals cooked, guests entertained, etc. That type of accounting is easy, the statistics empirically verifiable. Depending on the slope of the graph, the drop of the bar or the cut of the pie, the numbers either delight us, confirm our ministry, justify our existence and thus stimulate praise and general satisfaction, or they depress, causing us to question our validity and stimulate intercession. But graphs, bars and pies cannot measure the informal.

---

[234] PL April 2000.

How do you calculate the bonding that occurs while cooking, eating or washing dishes communally or when bagging the mound of garbage 25+ people produce every week? How do you report evenings spent sipping hot chocolate and discussing points of doctrine, child rearing, interpersonal relationships, culture clashes and the skeletons in the mission's closet? How do you quantify the unplanned tangents raised and pursued during lectures or the questions with which you are suddenly bombarded in the laundry room? The biggest impression on missionary candidates were not the carefully structured logic of lecture notes but those off-the-cuff comments when walking up the staircase together and the unvarnished testimony of life lived before them from morning till night. The crux of missions, notably the nature of each individual's relationship with God, with fellow missionaries, with home churches and supporters and with national believers and unbelievers is soon sensed—yet is incapable of reduction to a graph or statistic.

> "It takes supernatural strength to keep on welcoming each new arrival with joyful enthusiasm and equal excitement. Many are exhausted or discouraged on return from the field and need a lot of tender loving care."[235]

To our surprise we found ourselves doing an increasing amount of unrehearsed marriage and family counseling.

> "Pray that our words would be wise and helpful, and substantiated by our own family testimony... Pray for the informal hours we share with candidates and furloughing missionaries. That, often, is when the really important issues are raised and dealt with."[236]

Every year two or three of us trekked across the country to represent the mission at various churches and conferences. These were times of great camaraderie. For a month chauffer Rick ensured we arrived everywhere on time as we zig-zagged around the Great Lakes and across the Prairies from one

[235] Letter to "Friends in Macosquin" May 7, 2003.
[236] PL November 2001.

church or Bible school to another. We'd put thousands on the old van's odometer, stayed with numerous beautiful Christians, once helped deliver a calf, showed mission videos and spoke to countless students, farmers, pastors, elders, deacons and businessmen. We touched base with former missionaries, some of whom still struggled to re-integrate. We'd challenge people to commit themselves radically to God and we'd sense a lot of warm, fuzzy feelings towards us. However, the Holy Spirit operates according to his own time-table: "we met one couple who first heard me speak in Manitoba in '96; they expect to be on our Candidate's Course this fall... Sometimes God gave us glimpses like that just to stimulate our faith and encourage us to keep going."[237]

Anna labored in the office until 3:30, when the kids returned from school bowed down under heavy backpacks, hungry as bears, and ready for debriefing. In Turkey they had been conscious of their foreignness; they were still misfits.

> "Being a good student and exemplifying Christian character are virtues valued by their teachers but the subject of derision by fellow classmates. High marks and good behaviour just aren't cool! Owen has learned to weather the storm but Rita is still very sensitive to verbal abuse. Pray for them."[238]

At first Owen was bullied. I had him practise a Judo move on me: "Be quick, firm and carry it through without hesitating." Then I informed the principal that they may have to deal with a bully with a broken arm. When the kid came at him again Owen snatched his hand, twisted it rapidly into the wrist lock and felled him. He came home on a high and was not bothered again. I was proud of him.

"Dad, I'm gonna take my basketball to school," he declared one day.

"Go ahead son, but it may get stolen." It was a rough inner-city institution.

---

[237] PL March 2001.
[238] PL November 2001.

"I'll take the risk."

During recess he tossed it towards an immigrant kid and soon he'd gathered together a crowd of outsiders. He kept busy with the Student Council, Young People at church, strumming his pawn-shop guitar, unwinding with a good book, stroking his timid guinea pig Aristotle or playing basketball in a Roman Catholic house league (started flatfooted, became an all-star). He was voted emcee for graduation though he never found a kindred spirit—a problem which haunted him into his thirties.

Rita, our tomboy, came to be accepted by the girls in her class "but pray for her as she stands up for Jesus in this school."[239] Her latent fun side, her intelligence and multi-talentedness became increasingly evident. A piano teacher caught her plinking on the piano, recognized a gift we hadn't twigged on to and asked if she could teach her. She also played the recorder and ukulele, borrowed a clarinet and was soon playing it in the junior band. She didn't like dolls but loved soccer and Contrast, her hyper-active guinea pig. She threw herself into her studies, piano lessons, school band, swimming, soccer and athletics; with girlfriends at school, at church and at WEC, life was never dull. "Then, suddenly, she will stop and curl up with a good book for a weekend before the next whirlwind of activity."[240] On Sunday nights Anna and I focused our prayers on them and their future spouses, dubbed Johnie and Suzie for convenience's sake. "Pray that in the midst of this Piccadilly Circus we can create a healthy family life for the kids and ourselves."[241] On Easter Sunday, 2008, both testified to their faith in Christ and were baptized.

If you'd asked Owen and Rita about the most difficult aspect of living in a mansion full of comings and goings they would have replied "the hellos and the goodbyes". Still, raising them in an environment where they were surrounded by pilgrims going places for the Lord was ideal. For us too it was a privilege, a humbling experience, to work with the Argentinian lawyer

---

[239] PL January 22, 2002.
[240] Letter to "Friends in Macosquin", May 7, 2003.
[241] PL June 2002.

who'd shed his toga to don a T-shirt and reach out to gays in Madrid, or the former professor of Mathematics from Columbia heading for a little Bible school in Equatorial Guinea, or the electronics engineer who, with his Japanese wife, left for Nepal, or the family of seven who went to Fiji.

We usually had Korean candidates as well. Their English ranged from poor to virtually non-existent. Always having to speak slowly and listen intently was tiresome. When teaching I had to explain things in simple, idiom-free English and even then was surprised by outbursts of laughter at something which tickled the Korean but not the Canadian sense of humour. Sometimes we unwittingly offended, at times enriched, at times irritated.

On weekends the candidates were in charge of cooking. We'd leave church hungry, like everyone else, but instead of excited expectancy we'd motor home with nervous apprehension. You never knew what awaited you; it might be a few puny fish floating belly-up in soya sauce along with a bowl of lukewarm, pale goop garnished with raw carrots. I'd sigh, then force a couple of spoonsful down the hatch. When my stomach heaved I'd slip from the dining room to sneak upstairs for a peanut butter and jelly sandwich. That also worked the other way. The Koreans were pretty good about eating the Western fare they faced daily, though at times their portions were suspiciously small. Sometimes you caught them boiling sweet-potato noodles at midnight. "No, it's not always easy being part of an international team."[242] Sometimes I got "peopled out" and stood in need of extra grace to live and work with so many in such close proximity. "We have sometimes grown weary of community living but have experienced the Lord's grace in this."[243]

Sanctification is not mere growth in knowledge, in which case inquisitive souls would have a leg up on everyone else. It is growth in Christ-likeness, which equates to developing "the fruit of the Spirit", i.e., love, joy, peace, patience, kindness,

---

[242] PL November 2000.
[243] Annual WEC Conference Report, June 2003.

goodness, faithfulness, gentleness and self-control (Gal. 5:22-23). These attributes cannot be developed in solitude. Sanctification is—at times—a painful group project.

47

"Lord, I Just Want To Teach!"

"The easiest method of acquiring the habit of scholarship is through acquiring the ability to express oneself clearly in discussing and disputing scholarly problems."

Ibn Khaldun

. . .

I HAVE A ROMANTIC relationship with boats so became a member of the Hamilton Bay Sailing Club. Unlike most I liked being out when there were waves and the wind blustery. Because I tend to look at things from a slightly different perspective, certain people—particularly those who become queasy in rocking boats—consider me a nuisance. The way I'd tack and gybe, point the boat in an unexpected direction, veer off course to ride a wave or try to catch a squall which causes the boat to heel precariously yet sends it surging forward, makes them sea-sick.

> "Peter is known as someone who can see the big picture and dares to think outside the box. Some love him for this and others are disturbed when he rocks their boat!"[244]

After we'd been on home staff for a couple of years the old candidates' director retired. A young couple took their place. None of us knew them well. After they'd settled in I submitted a thought-provoking proposal. To my consternation I was informed that henceforth my suggestions were deemed irrelevant. As we hoped to return to Kurdish work in the Middle East, we were told, we wouldn't have to live with the long-term consequences of my ideas and so they wouldn't be considered. They then stripped me of most of my teaching responsibilities.

---

[244] Letter to "Friends in Macosquin", May 7, 2003.

I love teaching and when unceremoniously cast aside was at a loss. I was comforted by the fact that the other lecturers' involvement with the candidates—even that of the director—was abruptly curtailed as well; misery likes company. My desire to think creatively went into irons. I continued to nurture plenty of ideas and dreams but they now had little to do with the ministry of the sending base.

Alone in my office one afternoon I lifted my head to heaven. "Lord!" I cried, "I just want to teach!" and dropped my head onto the desk in discouragement and frustration. Suddenly an authoritative male voice filled the space. "Well then, Peter, you go and be the best teacher you can be!" it said.

I yanked my head off the furniture and looked around, wondering who had overheard my cry. There was no one, not in my office, not in the room next door, not in the hallway. The Lord had spoken. It was the only time in my life when God addressed me audibly—and the experience set me free. I had become so identified with the mission to the Kurds that the notion of stepping away from that felt vaguely treasonous. The Lord's voice that quiet afternoon set me free from nagging doubts and a deadening sense of obligation. It set me free to become a teacher, the best teacher I could be—even if rejected as such by some in my own agency.

Although I had done a lot of teaching I was mostly self-taught, and other than my Prairie B.Th. had no formal qualifications which an institution of higher learning would take seriously. I was an autodidact, a dilettante. True, I was an avid reader, but of books I chose for myself. There is an insecurity which comes from being an autodidact. Though I knew more about language acquisition, missions and theology than most around me, there were gaps in my knowledge, basic concepts I had not grasped, a lexicography of which I was only half-aware. What I taught had not been evaluated and ratified by qualified experts. I was untested, had not sat the examinations. In fact, I felt slightly fraudulent, a poseur who, because of his lack of formal instruction, feared meeting qualified experts and be caught out.

Years earlier I'd clipped an advert from The Economist for a hybrid program run by Syracuse University's Maxwell School of Citizenship and Public Affairs. I pulled it out and requested an application. I was turned down for my Prairie Bible Institute degree was not recognized. I appealed, adding copies of my Kurdish and Turkish grammars to the application package and was accepted on probation.

I loved the academic environment and spent happy summer stints with near-sighted, stoop-shouldered professors and eager fellow students. The program was demanding and intellectually stimulating—yet at times vaguely disquieting. There was much talk on that most boring of subjects, indigenous issues, and we had to attend a long lecture with graphic video given at the trial of a white man who'd killed a black youth in Mississippi. Or was it Alabama? I would not realize until years later that those privileged profs were drip-feeding the poisons of collective white guilt and critical race theory into the nation's public discourse. Those notions would coalesce into a multi-front assault against the most successful socio-political constructs of all time: Anglo-Saxon, Judeo-Christian civilization and its progeny, the liberal, Anglo-American world order which, for all its faults, became the freest in history which, for all its foibles, contributed more to mankind's wellbeing than any other and which, for all its vulgarity and kitsch, gave birth to unparalleled artistic and musical flowerings thus enriching the lives of virtually every human on the planet. While the Ivory Tower zealously sowed the seeds of destruction for the culture which had given birth to it I sleep-walked into their caustic woke/cancel future. But I'm running far ahead of myself...

I graduated with a Master of Social Science. Next was ESL certification and an Advanced Certificate in Applied Linguistics. I was now a bona fide ESL teacher; landing a job in the Middle East wouldn't be a problem. Next I enrolled in the D.Th. program of the University of South Africa. I also began teaching for Toronto Baptist Seminary, MissionPrep, Gateway Missionary Training College and the Center for Intercultural Training in North Carolina. I found myself lecturing to pastoral and missionary candidates from across the evangelical spectrum—everyone, it seemed, except WEC missionary wannabes. But that didn't really matter anymore for the stream of candidates there dried up.

"Sadly, western male missionary recruits have gone into hiding..."[245]

"Where oh where are the Canadians?"[246]

"On this current orientation course we only have three missionary candidates, all from Korea."[247]

---

[245] PL October 2002.
[246] PL June 2002.
[247] PL February 2003.

48

The Missionary Kid (MK)
Phenomena

"It takes a village to raise a child."

Yoruba Proverb

• • •

WHEN PREPARING OUR return to the mission field we, like many career missionaries, faced the agonizing decision about our children's education: home-school, national school or boarding school? Few subjects provoked more emotional participation among conservative Christians than that of family responsibilities versus work/ministry, for placing ministry ahead of family was deemed irresponsible and sinful. This was partly a reaction to the breakdown of family life in the culture at large and partly stemming from a nebulous feeling that earlier missionaries had sacrificed children for the sake of their work.

Responding to the general crisis in domestic life, agencies like Focus on the Family and Promise Keepers promulgated their "family theology" at conferences, over the radio waves, online, and through slick videos, books and magazines which demotivated young couples from contemplating cross-cultural missions: "I am willing to go overseas, but would never expose my kids to disease and danger"; "we believe God is calling us into missions but only where the right educational opportunities are available"; "we considered missions but have postponed that until after the kids have left home."

Homeschooling was all the rage while "packing the kids off to boarding school" was condemned by the opinionated as the abrogation of parental duties: "After God, your family MUST be your number one priority"; "We would NEVER send them away; God expects parents to raise their own children". But homeschooling missionary mums are also trying to learn a foreign language, adjust to a new culture and often live without modern conveniences. There is no library to draw from and no support from family or church. If there is a church, it will likely consist of new, immature believers meaning there are few—if any—Christian role models besides mum and dad. There is unlikely to be a kids club, no young people's group, no interaction with other Christian teens beside a few MK peers likely to leave at any time or who speak broken English because they come from Korea or Brazil. When the kids' only friends are Muslims, what do you do when your teenage daughter falls in love with one of them? Pack her off to boarding school? That will lead to bitterness and resentment.

In any case, kids sent to boarding schools are scarcely ever "packed away". They are entrusted to dedicated Christian professionals who live for the purpose of training and educating the next generation of Christian leaders. Standards of education and spiritual instruction at these schools are usually of a high caliber and frequently it is the younger children still at home, not those at boarding school, who feel deprived. Families reunite over Christmas, Easter, summer holidays and during parental visits in the course of the year. Many MK's at boarding schools spend more quality time with their parents when they are together than the average Christian kid who always has them around.

There is something askew with a simplistic "God comes first, then my family, then my work/ministry" formula. It pays lip service to the primacy of God but is, in fact, a form of family idolatry. It presumes that the injunction to "raise your children in the fear and admonition of the Lord" and the command to take the gospel to the ends of the earth are mutually exclusive. When the married state, home comforts and the education and happiness of children throttle missionary activity God is perceived as less than sovereign, as one who cannot be trusted to keep kids from the nasty influences of a pagan or disease-filled environment. After baptism or child dedication services many devout parents seem to snatch their children off the altar, look up to God and say, "Keep your hands off him. He's mine!" What does it say about our faith when we will not allow anyone—not even God himself—to interfere with our family life? Is it healthy to shield our children from evil social influences by minimizing their interaction with non-Christian peers, by pulling them out of the regular school system, by fostering a social life limited to the confines of the church? Does this kind of evangelical environmental determinism actually produce strong Christians who can serve God sacrificially in non-Christian environments?

Christ strongly rebuked those who placed family concerns ahead of himself. *"If anyone comes to me and does not hate his father and mother, his wife and children, his brothers and sister—yes, even his own life—he cannot be my disciple"* (Luke 14:26), he intoned. The Bible gives numerous examples of children raised at home by decent, even godly, parents who turned out rather badly: think of Ham, Aaron, Solomon, Jehoshaphat, Jotham, the prodigal son... Conversely, Christ strongly praised those who were prepared to leave their families for the sake of the Kingdom of God. He promised that *"everyone who has left houses or brothers or sisters or father or mother or children or fields for my sake will receive a hundred times as much and will inherit eternal life"* (Mat. 19:29).

The Bible is replete with examples of young people who were separated from their parents, some at a very tender age, often because of excruciating socio-political circumstances or, at times, because the parents voluntarily gave them up. Moses was separated from his family and thrust into a hostile, ungodly environment as a toddler. Joseph was sold into slavery as a teenager. Samuel's mother Hannah entrusted her very young son to a dubious religious community. King Joash, after losing his family at a very young age, was raised by the religious community. David was separated from his family to become a teen-age outlaw. Daniel, Shadrach, Meshach and Abed-Nego were teens when deported to Babylon. Esther, an orphan, was snatched from her uncle's house while a young virgin. All that to say that life's priorities do not line up in a neat 1, 2, 3 fashion, the family is not an end in itself and God's gifts and demands are not mutually exclusive. A loving family is a precious trust from the same God who gave the Great Commission, and our responsibilities fall into their rightful place when we put God first in everything, including family life. He wants us to seek his will, and then demands a faith-filled response. Of course his will takes into account the families he has entrusted to us! And, of course, the Deuteronomic injunction to *"teach them* (i.e., God's commands) *diligently to your children, and talk of them when you sit in your house, and when you walk by the way, and when you lie down, and when you rise"* (Deut. 6:6-7) cannot be dismissed. God established family in order to bring new people into the world, to provide for them, to prepare them for adult life and to teach them his ways. But he does not dichotomize or prioritize our responsibilities along the axis of ministry verses family, nor does he give incompatible commands.

If parents raised their children responsibly from the get-go should their teenagers not be sufficiently strong spiritually and emotionally to be entrusted to the larger "Christian clan"? MKs have been successful spiritually, emotionally, socially and vocationally in far higher proportions than the children of parents in other vocations. This is backed up by hard statistics.[248] Interestingly, those with boarding school experience were more likely to be religiously committed, more likely to choose missions as a career and three times more likely to return overseas as missionaries than non-boarders. The statistics went on to show that more of them had a "very happy childhood", felt that adequate time was spent with parents, that they read the Bible "very often", shared their faith, became missionaries themselves, were more satisfied with meaning and

---

[248] Raymo Raymo. *Marching to a Different Drummer: Rediscovering Missions in an Age of Affluence and Self-Interest.* Christian Literature Crusade, Fort Washington. 1998, p. 87.

purpose in life and were politically more conservative than non-boarders.[249]

Missionary education is an intensely personal thing. Some parents choose to home-school, some send their kids to national schools, some to Christian boarding schools, some leave the field and return home. Parent wrestle with these issues; there isn't a missionary kid who hasn't seen his mother cry when leaving him/her at a boarding school...

> "I (Anna writing), especially, struggle with the prospect of being separated from the kids, but believe that the Lord will enable when the time comes."[250]

After much discussion, prayer and debate, the elders of our home church asked that we delay our return to the Middle East by a year, until Rita turned 14 and was ready to move to high school. We believed the Lord had led them and were at peace. Time proved that to be the right decision.

Today the M.K. issue is not as acute as it was when Owen and Rita were teenagers. This is because the career missionary movement in the West has largely collapsed. Parents still weep at separations but sending one's kids to a quality boarding school is considered a privilege by the Koreans, Filipinos, Indians, Latinos and other non-Westerners who have filled the gap.

[249] Sharp, Larry. "Boarding Schools—What difference do they make?" *Evangelical Missions Quarterly*, January 1990.
[250] Letter to Macosquin, May 22, 2001.

49

Transition

"We find by losing. We hold fast by letting go.
We become something new by ceasing to be something old."

Frederick Buechner

. . .

IF YOU INQUIRED about the best thing we've done in life, we'd reply, "discipled a few key people in the faith". Christ did not merely instruct his followers to plant churches—promising to do that with them (Mat. 16:18)—but to make disciples. So that is what we wanted to do upon our return to Turkey. "I'd like to be involved in discipling, both by word and example, a few choice men. I've begun to intercede for them already—even though we have not yet met."[251]

In January 2004 I made a brief trip to Istanbul to scope out the landscape. I reconnected with the team, spoke to old friends and church leaders and caught a glimpse of what God was doing nation-wide. The news from Adana was particularly encouraging. The team had stabilized as people received work permits, the Bible Society opened a bookstore and the Adana International Church (AIC) its doors. A small group of new believers had formed the Turkish Protestant Church, called a young couple to be their pastor and joined forces with the AIC to rent a building. Of course opposition from within and without endured: local authorities still harassed and new believers were still sinners. The church had grown steadily elsewhere as well. Despite periods of persecution there was more legal scope for Christians to meet and worship. There

---

[251] PL October 2003.

were now about 2500 believers across the country willing to stand up and be counted; "still only 0.004% but growing!"[252]

I learned that an informal, intermission discipleship program was being re-organized into a formal evening Bible School, that they need qualified academics in order to gain accreditation, and that they'd love to have me join the team. I was elated.

> "While sitting in a ferry-boat crossing the Bosphorus in a winter blizzard... Peter had an overwhelming sense that this is where we belong."[253]

In Canada our status changed from Canadian staff members to "missionaries preparing to return to the field." We still persevered with our household responsibilities: cooking, telephone duty, washing-up and garbage chores. I pressed on with my studies, teaching and preaching, but stopped producing the WEC magazine. Anna pulled out of the Candidates' Department and started reading new books about ministry among Muslim women, along with her Turkish Bible and grammar book. We got our passports updated: four Canadian, three British, an Irish and a Dutch one. We re-organized our mailing lists, transferred paper files onto a hard drive, learned to do on-line banking, prepared a budget to present to supporting churches, booked medical check-ups, got the necessary immunizations, visited the dentist and optometrist, purchased health coverage, a year's supply of contact lenses for the kids, and scoured the internet for the cheapest flights.

> "Preparing to uproot yet again takes its toll on the whole family. Decisions need to be made about almost everything we turn our hands to. We need wisdom and grace for these unsettling months of transition."[254]

---

[252] PL October 2003.
[253] PL April 2004.
[254] PL. October 2003.

Five MK boarding schools had recently closed. Two in the Middle East had been shut down by the authorities, one in Pakistan had been attacked by Muslim gunmen, French troops had extricated staff and students caught in cross-fire between rebels and government soldiers at the International Christian Academy in Côte d'Ivoire, while WEC's school there was evacuated a day or two before the rebel army arrived in town. The schools still operating were overwhelmed with applications, forcing them to make hard decisions. We had no Plan B for Owen and Rita's education. "Join with us in the prayer of faith—both for their acceptance and for the necessary finances."[255] We saw their acceptance at Black Forest Academy (BFA) in Germany as the Lord's final nod of approval. "The kids are enthusiastic and Anna is willing!"[256]

> "When no-one is looking Peter catches himself skipping cheerfully at the prospect (of returning to Turkey). Sure, there is a dark side: next summer we will be parted from our family, friends, church and, worst of all, our children. The obedient Christian life is a piercing sweetness. While Peter skips, Anna contentedly puts one foot on front of the other."[257]

We sold the car, gave away our furniture and reduced our belongings to two suitcases each. Sight unseen we bought the entire household of a family leaving Turkey. Then came the farewells: family farewells, church farewells, youth farewells and the round of "we'd like to have you over before you leave..."

---

[255] PL. October 2003.
[256] Annual WEC Conference Report, June 2003.
[257] PL October 2003.

Part 6: The Best Years Yet

2004-2014

"Work is as much a basic human need as food, beauty, rest, friendship, prayer, and sexuality; it is not simply medicine but food for our soul. Without meaningful work we sense significant inner loss and emptiness."

Timothy Keller

50

A Rough Restart

*"All women speak two languages: the language of men and
the language of silent suffering. Some women speak a third,
the language of queens."*

Mohja Kahf

. . .

OUR NEW HOME was a ground-floor, older style apartment on
Istanbul's Asian side. It was dark but cool, and a mere twenty
minutes by bus from the ferry docks.

Although Turkey had made great progress on multiple fronts
the quality of workmanship remained substandard. A multitude
of minor trials tested our patience: a water pipe ruptured,
curtain rails fell, a shower head exploded, taps fell apart, new
shower head herniated and the new printer refused to print.
Drill bits buckled, screwdriver head bent, cell phone
malfunctioned, bank card blocked, water bill twenty times
overpriced, curtains fell down again, shower wouldn't stop
leaking... "I guess our adversary knows where to test the non-
handyman!"[258]

> "Pray for protection from discouragement due to
> loneliness, homesickness, enervating heat, corrupt
> officials, inefficient bureaucracy, stomach upsets from the
> change in water and food, effort of functioning in another
> language, many hours on public transport and being the
> odd balls in a foreign culture. May we be characterized by
> the joy of the Lord."[259]

---

[258] PL September-October 2004.
[259] PL July-August 2004.

Neighbours were friendly. We cultivated our relationship with them by helping their offspring with English. Before long Anna was drinking tea in neighbouring flats and nine women came to her house-warming party. Their verdict: her appearance was clean, her house was clean and her heart was clean. "What more could you want? Turkish women, however, have a habit of saying to your face what you want to hear. Who knows what they say about these infidels in our absence."[260] Years later, after our relationship with them had deepened, several confessed that they had been upset when they learned that "Americans" had moved into their complex.

That summer was clouded by the looming separation from the kids. Anna planned to help settle them in a dormitory, a converted farmhouse in a village somewhere in southern Germany. On the hunt for inexpensive tickets, I headed for a travel agent on the European side near Istanbul's famed Pudding Shop, an eatery popular with beatniks on the hippy trail to free love and cheap drugs in Nepal. There a poster advertising ultra-cheap flights to Cairo, Egypt, caught my attention. Instead of moping around the house without the family, a wee adventure, I reasoned, was the better alternative. I'd always wanted to explore the City Victorious and so, on a whim, purchased those cheapies for myself along with the ones for Germany for the others.

Late August Anna and the offspring headed for Germany. "Oh, the pain of separation is very keen, and tears come easily."[261] "When Anna left Owen and Rita at Black Forest Academy, she thought her heart would break."[262]

While Anna's heart was breaking I settled into the Anglican guest house near All Saints Cathedral in Cairo, an odd shaped building resembling a pineapple top. For the next several days I joyfully battled my way through the exotic tapestry of Middle Eastern and African humanity wearily crowding the sunbaked boulevard along the Nile, each specimen hiding the immortal

---

[260] PL November-December 2004.
[261] PL September-October 2004.
[262] PL November-December 2004.

spark. I avoided locking eyes with the hungry touts advertising jaunts on neon-lit, garishly festooned, sha'abi music-blaring feluccas, then moseyed aimlessly through the cobblestoned alleys of the Old City, a jumble of oriental seediness shaded in permanent gloom by the narrow buildings jutting overhead. I escaped the languorous fug of Al-Azhar's sacred precinct where students rocked to-and-fro reciting the Qur'an to stroll through the musk of Khan al-Khalili to Al-Fishawi, where Napolean Bonaparte, Jamal id-Din al-Afghani, Um Kulthum and Muhammed Abdu had drunk tea and swallowed rejuvenating sherbets.

I nosed around the Museum of Antiquities' musty collections, marvelled at King Tut's mask and wandered around the faded fin-de siècle elegance of the Khedive Ismail's "Paris on the Nile" around Tahrir Square. I sipped a restorative demitasse at the Café Riche, where Gamal Abdul Nasser and his cronies once huddled around a little wooden table to eat hummus and plot the revolution of 1952, and where Najuib Mahfouz and Taha Hussein received inspiration from the mass of humanity shuffling by on the other side of the window panes. I breezed in and out of Groppi's, its famed chocolate far exceeding my budgetary constraints. I took in a Sunday evening service at Qasr Dubara, the largest evangelical church in the Middle East and swung by the Presbyterian seminary. A taxi took me to Giza, where I sauntered around the Pyramids and paid respects to the Sphinx. Its neatly restored paws effected an incongruous and jarring contrast with the rest of the creature. Thankfully they didn't try to recreate its nose as well.

I returned home uncommonly satisfied with self—to find a wet-eyed Anna with a no-nonsense Northern Irish colleague at her side. My disconsolate wife had been at her loneliest when she'd returned to an empty house the day before and when Iris phoned to inquire how she was coping had burst into tears. That aging saint had bustled over, brewed a wee cuppa tea, the Britishers' default response to all circumstances of life, and taken her in for the night. The next afternoon she accompanied Anna back to our place to wait for me.

"Hallooo! I'm back!" I shouted cheerfully when I toodled across the threshold, dumped my bag in the entryway and pushed through the living room door. "How was German..." Then I saw Iris sitting upright on the settee. "Oh, hi Iris... How are you?"

She looked at me with a cold, reptilian stare. "Peter Pikkert!" The Northern Irish voice had the authoritative ring of a sergeant-major and her eyes pierced through me like hot gimlets drilling through Vaseline. "What do you think you're doing, leaving your wife like that? How insensitive can you be? You should be ashamed of yourself, so you should!"

She was absolutely right. I had abandoned my dear, gentle, courageous Anna, the love of my life, when she needed me most and suddenly felt terrible. I could only nod affirmations, head bowed at a 45 degree angle, look demurely at a spot in the carpet, and take it on the chin. I begged for, and was granted forgiveness but felt like a Neanderthal for days. Still, the city of a thousand minarets had cast its spell and beguiled me. I would return. One day, soon.

The women in our apartment soon reached out to Anna, sensing how she missed the kids: "Now we know you are a mother just like us. We didn't think you westerners had such strong family bonds..." How could they, when their only previous experience of us were the American soap operas on T.V.

Weeks later Anna's back went into agonizing spasms. An X-ray revealed a herniated disk. They kept her in hospital for some days, then prescribed a bottle of analgesics and released her.

"Anna's confinement to bed with her back problem brought the neighboring ladies crowding in with Turkish meals for the ailing. At Christmas she repaid some of their kindness by distributing seven plates of goodies with cards explaining that we were celebrating the birth of a Savior, not just New Years a week early!"[263]

---

[263] PL January-February 2005.

∎

The late Megan (not her real name) affair. Megan should be numbered among that company of highly intelligent female eccentrics England dispatched to the Middle East in the course of the 19ᵗʰ and 20ᵗʰ centuries: think Lady Anne Blunt, Gertrude Bell, Lady Evelyn Cobbold and Dame Freya Stark. Megan had arrived in Turkey in the 1980s and, like many of us back then, had obtained a visa by studying at Istanbul University. She stuck with the archeology department, eventually becoming an expert Urartologist. She learned Urartese and whenever an archeologist stumbled across a cuneiform engraving in that language was summoned to decipher it. She published a catalogue of Urartuan inscriptions and a book on Urartuan measures of volume, both highly esteemed by that paltry few who understand these matters. She was also the librarian of Hasat, the Istanbul-based theological training program which I'd been invited to join.

Hasat's leader was an older gentleman, new to the Middle East. One day, after I'd been with the ministry for a month or two, he informed me that I was fired. I was flabbergasted. The man then divulged that he'd received a serious complaint from Megan and felt compelled to terminate our relationship. I could not imagine what lay behind this hatchet job, and he refused to reveal the nature of the complaint.

Megan and I had never been close but we'd been civil—or so I thought. When cornered she debouched that "it was about how I'd treated Ming" (not her real name). I hadn't a clue what she was on about.

"Mick," I said to our field leader, "get to the bottom of this, will you." While I devoted the following weeks to my doctoral thesis and playing chess with a friend in a café, Mick dug. He also talked to Ming, who had no idea what this was about either. It transpired that Megan had wrongly mixed Ming into a highly garbled version of the Iraq debacle years earlier, had bottled this up for years and now, suddenly and without checking her sources (a major *faux pas* for scholars), exploded.

She was forced to write an apology and, humiliated, resigned from Hasat. The experience left me sympathetic to men who suddenly face accusations from intelligent women which purportedly took place years earlier. I took Megan's place on the leadership team and Anna her position as librarian.

Phew. At long last life and ministry to the growing church of ex-Muslims could settle into fruitful grooves.

51

They Lived By Faith

"Faith is like radar that sees through the fog the reality of things at a distance that the human eye cannot see."

Corrie Ten Boom

• • •

THE GESTATION PERIOD of the indigenous Turkish church was difficult and long. As already seen, prior to World War I there were significant numbers of churches, Protestant and otherwise, across Anatolia. None were ethnically Turkish. Misguided attempts to reach Turks by empowering the ethnic minorities had ended in genocide and deep anti-missionary sentiment.[264] For half a century after the Great War the newly formed Republic of Turkey languished forgotten by world Christianity. By 1960 the country boasted fewer than 10 Turkish Protestants.[265]

In 1961 two young chaps with Operation Mobilization (OM) entered the country. I never met Dale Rhoton for he only lasted a couple of years. His friend Roger Malstead, however, hung in there and, in spite of opposition and expulsions, a viable team grew around him. They pursued a three-pronged strategy: literature blitzes, i.e., the quick distribution of tracts at night using short-term teams, book distribution and a correspondence course. They were frequently targeted by the police and their efforts seemed to bear little fruit. Still they persevered.

---

[264] See Pikkert, P. *Protestant Missionaries to the Middle East: Ambassadors of Christ or Culture?* Ancaster. Alev Books. 2008.
[265] Johnstone, P.J. *Operation World: A Day to Day Guide to Praying for the World.* WEC International, STL Books, Kent, England. 4rd edition, 1986. P. 414.

WEC's first missionary was the delightful Jürg Heusser. He arrived from Switzerland in 1962 to be expelled a couple of years later. He then established Orientdienst which has been reaching out to Turkish migrants in Germany ever since. Later, when some in the missionary community sought to dissuade me from focusing on Kurds, he encouraged us to press on and not lose faith.

WEC's second missionary was Agnes Reinhard, also Swiss. She arrived in 1965, was expelled, re-entered and married Misak Gunay, one of the few local believers. We knew them well. Misak wrote for Yeni Yaklaşım and their daughter Deborah served as my secretary before we were forced out (see ch. 30). They lived in a tiny house in a seedy district of the city. Agnes once told us that one of the things she'd had to sacrifice for the gospel was the right to enjoy beauty.

The Finnish Lutherans arrived in 1969 and on November 1, 1971, our team leader Mike O'Donnell stepped off the train in Sirkeci, Istanbul. By then there were about 20 missionaries in the country.[266] The first missionary with TEAM (The Evangelical Alliance Mission) arrived in 1972. Slowly, unsteadily, numbers grew. People were expelled almost as fast as others arrived. Towards the end of the '70s the deportations eased off for a period and numbers rose to about 40. By then there were about 50 national believers, of whom about 5 were former Muslims.[267]

Some of those early workers, like the Malsteads, were tenacious. When deported, they would change passports in Greece or Germany and re-enter at different border crossings. Some got expelled so often they changed their names. George Burch, who first appeared in the '60s, was one such person. He first settled in Ankara, then in Trabzon, a very conservative-nationalist city on the Black Sea, then in the more liberal city of Izmir under a new name. His example encouraged others to move beyond Istanbul and Ankara. One couple moved to the

---

[266] Brown, C., Payne, M. & O'Donnell, M. *Fifty Years of Vintage Coffee*. Ebook, WEC Canada.
[267] Ibid.

eastern city of Gaziantep in the early 1970s, a very bold step. They hung in there for a couple of years before being pushed out. One of our single women, Norma Cox, also moved to Gaziantep. She was deported numerous times. In the late '70s OM sent some personnel to Adana, including David Goodman. In '79 a gunman knocked on his door and shot him dead. The first Western martyr of the modern era lies buried in a Muslim cemetery under a headstone describing him as an "İsacı", or "Jesus Person"; Turkish did not yet have a word for Evangelical Christians. The church later settled on Mesih İnanlısı meaning "Believer in the Messiah". Other missionaries boldly headed for Adana, only to be pushed out. Adana was a tough nut to crack. It would be without a long-term missionary presence until our team settled there.

During the 1980s more agencies targeted Turkey; it was back on the missionary map. Those of that generation who stayed possessed great perseverance and faith for those bereft of such qualities were quickly weeded out. We prayed, hoped and believed but did not witness any breakthrough. However the Bible was translated, literature distributed, gospel seeds sown and a few converts discipled. By the early 1990s, when the population of Turkey was 62 million, there were about 250 of them, roughly one per missionary.[268]

During the '90s the missionary community grew dramatically. In spite of deportations there were about 670 of us by the end of the millennium. We spread to new cities and launched numerous ministries. We created evangelistic internet sites, advertised in newspapers, sponsored concerts, ran children's camps, published magazines, started little church plants and regular Bible study programs which eventually morphed into accredited degree programs.

In the year 2000, some 40 years after the first missionaries entered the country, the number of national believers added up

---

[268] Ibid. See also Johnstone, Patrick. *Operation World: A Day to Day Guide to Praying for the World*. STL Books, WEC Publications. 1986. p. 415.

to about 1150, not quite two for every missionary present.[269] That would change dramatically during the Age of Erdoğan.

[269] Brown, C., Payne, M. & O'Donnell, M. *Fifty Years of Vintage Coffee*. Ebook, WEC Canada.

52

The Age of Erdoğan

"A political party cannot have a religion. Only individuals can. Otherwise, you'd be exploiting religion, and religion is so supreme that it cannot be exploited or taken advantage of."

Recep Tayyip Erdoğan

• • •

IT IS EASY to find Recep Tayyip Erdoğan quotes which sum up the man for he is very talkative, and much of what he says reflect *halk kurnazlığı*, or peasant cunningness. He eloquently strings truth-alleging phonemes together so they sound credible, pious or deep. Thinking men soon realize, however, that, like the quote above, much of it banal, hokey stuff which dematerializes upon examination. But Erdoğan knows his proletarian masses' ("my people" as he likes to call them) intellectual abilities, aspirations and inspirations. He would be the country's most prominent political figure for several decades, the man who dictated the fluid context within which we had to operate.

Born into a working class, religious family, he was a go-getter from the get-go. Pocket money went to bottles of water and day-old sesame seed buns which, reheated, were fobbed off as freshly baked goods to drivers stuck in Istanbul's infamously congested traffic. He played semi-professional soccer, joined a Naqshbandi Sufi order and earned a diploma in business administration. He is not altogether unprincipled for he is a devout Muslim. Fellow students called him *hoca*, i.e., religious teacher. He honed his oratorical skills in the youth branch of the Islamist National Salvation Party and became a convincing purveyor of classic Islam and corny ideas. I enjoyed listening to his compelling offerings of half-truisms, Islamic clichés, bromides and personal takedowns. When political parties were disbanded in the wake of the 1980 coup he entered the private sector and made lots of money.

In 1983, when the junta permitted newly formed parties to run for parliament, he joined Refah (Welfare). Ideologically Refah mingled Islam with Turkish nationalism (think anti-Americanism, anti-Europeanism, anti-Zionism, and anti-Roman Catholicism). It fared badly. Few Turks want an Islamic state; they perceive themselves as, somehow, European. As seen earlier, Turgut Özal's socially conservative Motherland Party won by a landslide. Erdoğan took note and bided his time. Eleven years later he ran for mayor of Istanbul and, against all odds, won.

Managing a megapolis with more people and greater industrial capacity than many nations is a good place to cut one's teeth if one aspires to run the country. Confounding the naysayers, the doubters, the elite, the snobs and the fascist generals, Erdoğan listened to his proletarian masses, rolled up his sleeves and went to work. He dealt harshly with corruption and repaid much of the city's multi-billion dollar debt. He solved chronic water shortages by laying hundreds of miles of piping and tackled the city's infamous air pollution by banning coal, laying natural gas pipelines and converting the city's enormous fleet of busses to environmentally friendly fuels. He reorganized garbage collection. He built bridges, overpasses, and expanded the subway system to alleviate the congestion; I pitied those who lived in districts through which he punched roads or subway lines. He would seize huge swaths of housing and, taking advantage of the Turk's centuries-old habit of vastly understating the value of their assets, paid owners a fraction of the market value.

Everyone but the leftists, the socialists, the secularists, those erstwhile home-owners and the generals were delighted. The latter, counting themselves heirs and protectors of Atatürk's anti-Islamic, secular/nationalist heritage, could not appreciate the fact that the upstart, pragmatic, Islamist populist permitted bus drivers to sport beards and female students headscarves. When he recited The Soldier's Prayer at a political rally they struck. The poem includes the lines, "The mosques are our barracks, the domes our helmets, the minarets our bayonets and the faithful our soldiers." They accused him of inciting violence, forced him to step down, sentenced him to ten months in prison and banned him from participating in future elections. The day he reported to prison he released an album entitled "This Song Won't End Here", a playlist of nationalist poems by Turkey's leading poets. It sold over a million copies.

From prison Erdoğan and his cronies planned their comeback. They realized that neither a purely Islamic nor a purely Nationalist party, nor one which combined both strands (like Refah), could win a national election. They formed the Adalet ve Kalkınma (Justice and Development) Party, AK for short, and presented it as democratic with socially conservative credentials—a Muslim version of the old Christian Democratic parties of Europe. This was the winning formula. AK won the election of 2002 overwhelmingly. It appointed an interim leader long enough for the ban against Erdoğan to be overturned and the age of Erdoğan was upon us. It became the context, the inadvertent backdrop, to the growth of the kingdom of God, i.e., to the really important spiritual stuff about to take place, things occurring well below the radar screen of the man himself.

The gospel writer Luke described the context of the life of John the Baptist, Jesus Christ, and the birth of the church as follows: "*In the fifteenth year of the reign of Tiberius, Pontus Pilate being governor of Judea, Herod being tetrarch of Galilee, his brother Philip tetrarch of Ituraea, and Trachonites and Lysanias tetrarch of Abiline, during the high priesthood of Annas and Caiaphas, the word of God came to John the son of Zacheriah in the wilderness*" (Luke 3:1-2). Luke recognized that God had raised up a particular godless cohort of political leaders to provide a suitable environment, the brutal *Pax Romana*, to unwittingly facilitate the ministry of a few people operating on the fringes who would, in the breathing space provided, become an unstoppable force. For centuries—from Malachi to Matthew—nothing budged and then, quite quickly, God moved various pieces around the board so that the gospel could surge ahead.

We'd already witnessed a similar dynamic in Kurdistan. We'd struggled against impossible odds for years. Nothing yielded, no breakthroughs. Then, quite suddenly, Saddam Hussein's idiotic civil war begat a new reality. Missionaries infiltrated and the subsequent war with ISIS created great spiritual hunger. Today there is a church in Kurdistan—small, struggling, but a church nevertheless. We saw that dynamic at work again during the Age of Erdoğan.

Islam extols strength and Erdoğan's Islamists quickly made their new-found power and influence felt. This initially led to a renewed period of persecution. Of course harassment of converts by the police, employers, family, neighbours and extreme Muslim and ultra-nationalist gangs had been going on for years. Those suspected of engaging in missionary activities ran the risk of deportation or were refused re-entry into the country. In 1997 Muslim fundamentalists bombed the Bible stand at a book fair killing a little boy and injuring 24 others. In 2001 eighteen Istanbul churches received letters from the municipality threatening legal action if they didn't close down. The churches lost the lawsuits and the appeal but kept meeting anyway.

In 2003, the year after Erdoğan's AK Party come to power, an Istanbul church was bombed and then raked with gunfire. Our pastor Semir kept a Bible with shrapnel embedded in it as a memento. Afterwards a Roman Catholic priest was shot twice as he was kneeling in the front row of the Santa Maria Catholic church.

"The lies the media propagate concerning what goes on in our worship services, and the motives and practices attributed to foreign workers are enough to make your hair stand on end. Some individual believers—both national and foreign—have suffered physical as well as verbal abuse. Pray that through this God would embolden the Turkish believers and impress on all of us the need to maintain a testimony that is above reproach."[270]

One of the main troublemakers was one İlker Çınar who for years posed as a convert to Christianity. He even became pastor of the evangelical church in Tarsus. Then, suddenly, he appeared repeatedly on television and in the press maligning Christianity and the Turkish church with the most vicious calumnies. Next he published a book the title of which translates as *I Was a Missionary; I Cracked the Code*[271], in which he revealed many missionary names and ministries. He turned out to be an intelligence agent who had operated undercover to spy on us.

"The negative publicity in the press and on television regarding the Turkish church and foreign workers here continues. Ironically one of the main instigators of all the trouble is a man in Tarsus who is wreaking havoc in the church and breathing out murderous threats against the Lord's disciples, just as in the Book of Acts. Pray for protection and for the growth of the church throughout Turkey despite all the opposition."[272]

In 2007 five young men attacked a Christian publishing house in the central city of Malatya and, in a gruesome assault, first tortured and then slit the throats of two converts from Islam and of our friend Tilmann Geske. Fear's cold tentacles clenched our hearts.

"One day eclipses all others since we last wrote to you. On April 18 a German friend and two Turkish brothers in Christ were martyred here. We are shocked and horrified by the tragic event's brutality, and are still trying to come to terms with it."[273]

---

[270] PL March-April, 2005.
[271] İlker, Çınar. *Ben Bir Misyonerdim. Şifre Çözüldü*. Istanbul. Ozan Yayıncılık, 2005.
[272] PL May-June 2005.
[273] PL May-June 2007.

The day after Suzanne and the other widow, Şemse Aydın, appeared on national television. Their spirit of forgiveness created shock waves. "Father, forgive them for they do not know what they are doing," they said, quoting Jesus' words from the cross. The attackers, caught red-handed, testified that instead of recanting the three had called out to Jesus. As the Geske's team leaders when they first arrived we'd wondered how they would fare; now we were in awe.

The police treated the murderers like VIPs. Though many Turks condemned the gruesome murders, others—including some of our neighbours—felt that they deserved their fate because they proclaimed Christianity in a Muslim country.

After struggling to find someone who would sell her a coffin Suzanne buried her Tilmann in a local Muslim cemetery. She then raised their three young children in Malatya, becoming the region's best-known Christian, a permanent reminder of the horror of Quran-based Islam to everyone in a region still in denial about their parents' pogroms against the Armenians. She is one of my heroes, as is the courageous Stone family who joined her almost immediately. They saw a beautiful church of former Muslims emerge in a city where none was before, a church which now sends Christian workers to still-unevangelized regions of the country.

Later that year an attack on the Protestant church in Antalya sent an old man to hospital, and then a 19 year old, egged on by an ultra-nationalist television series, knifed a Roman Catholic priest in the stomach.

> "According to a report by the legal committee of the Turkish Alliance of Protestant Churches there have been scores of attacks on congregations and church buildings in the course of 2006-2007. These are dangerous days in which to maintain a visible Christian presence in the Republic of Turkey."[274]

274 Pikkert, P. *Protestant Missionaries to the Middle East: Ambassadors of Christ or Culture?* Ancaster. Alev Books, p. 215. 2008.

When the persecution abated in 2008 the Turkish church was purged of nominal converts, leaving a smaller but healthier body of believers who looked forward with an amalgam of hope, trepidation and determination. The Heavenly Hand then exploited the proud politician as its unwitting tool to accomplish holy purposes. Erdoğan's new constitution, designed to lift the pressure from his Islamists, enshrined freedom of speech and religion. And so, in time—though only for a time—the courts fell in line with the new rights and freedoms provided. Bans on the use of Kurdish were lifted, people were permitted to change their religious affiliation and religious communities allowed to register as associations established for the purpose of teaching and worship. For some years the country even imagined it could join the European Union.

Reflecting St. Luke, an obscure German theologian once noted that world history is nothing but scaffolding for salvation history and that the Hebrew Bible, the TANAKH, categorising Joshua, Judges, Samuel and Kings as prophetic, recognised that history is not mere "once upon a time" stuff but an "operative word" which pushes the divine agenda forward.[275] Ugly Islamic extremism, first seen during the modern era under Iran's Ayatollahs, then by Turkish extremists and, later, by ISIS in the Arab world has led many sane Muslims to quietly question their religion and explore the Christian alternative. The legal breathing space, though narrow and frequently resisted at the municipal level and later screwed back by Erdoğan himself, created a window of opportunity which enabled the fledgling indigenous church to grow, mature, rent or purchase properties and develop its own Turkish identity and leadership.

The time to provide sound theological education to this newly emerging entity had come—and the Hasat team was ready.

---

[275] Sauer, Erich. *The Dawn of World Redemption.* 1951. Exeter, Paternoster Press. p. 94, 148-149.

53

The Photo Album

"Character, like a photograph, develops in darkness."

Yousef Karsh

· · ·

I'M BROWSING through the photo album Hasat presented us at the farewell dinner given in our honor. Letters saying nice things accompany the pictures. Everyone looks young, cheerful, energetic. They were ten wonderful years.

Hasat was not a residential school for few students had the wherewithal to engage in full-time studies. Instead, we teachers usually travelled to wherever there were students. My first course, Christianity, Pluralism and Secularism, was based on a book I was writing[276]. I had three students. Kaan, who became pastor of the first church comprised primarily of former Muslims, smiles benignly in one of the photographs. His sudden death came as a great shock and we wondered how the church would survive. It did. Ali later became the principal of Hasat and Murat the chairman of the board.

Before long I was writing and teaching courses on a range of topics: God's Plan for the Nations, Christian Ethics, Introduction to the New Testament, Old Testament Survey.

At first much of my teaching was at the Sunday-school-on-steroids level. Some churches used us to run their mid-week meetings. We even ran a class for Armenian women; the letter accompanying their photograph is long and cloying.

---

[276] *The Fall of Christendom and the Rise of the Church*. WEC Canada, Hamilton. 2006. Turkish Version: *Hrıstiyan Batı Efsanesi*. Istanbul. Gerçeğe Doğru, 1st printing 2009. 2nd printing 2011.

I encouraged inquisitiveness. Forcing new believers to examine what was biblical and what was cultural in their expression of Christianity often led to lively debates on the nature of non-negotiables and when and how they could flex. For those raised in an educational system which supresses independent thinking and squelches the questioning of teachers, this was new and—once they had gotten over their initial hesitancy—hugely liberating. At times I struggled to reign them in. "Peter had an enthusiastic bunch of mainly new students and enjoyed many lively discussions."[277]

I'm looking at a picture of Yakup. He is staring back at me with his wife and infant son. A keen young man, he started a youth movement, recognized the need for training and turned to us for help. The hours I spent tutoring him are one of my best investments. He went on to earn a M.A. through Hasat, then graduated with a M.Th. by distance education from Southern Theological Seminary. That youth ministry is now a nationwide phenomenon.

Converted from a conservative Muslim family, Refik took many Hasat courses and became an elder in our small Turkish church. In 2015 he and two others founded İlk Umut Derneği (First Hope Association)[278], an NGO providing relief to victims of natural disasters. He, his wife Linda, Anna and I are pictured on a ferry en-route to a youth conference. A photograph of that event shows some 60 young people, many of them Hasat students, crowding around us.

I loved teaching Systematic Theology. Students came with ingrained beliefs from their own religious background and cultural tradition so we compared their old cosmology with the Bible's teachings on, say, the nature of inspiration and the authority of Scripture, creation, the attributes of God, the person of Christ and the nature of salvation. I once had them do a comparative study on the biblical view of angels and demons with Islam's teachings on the jinn. A new convert, a woman still in full hijab, asked me with tears in her eyes if she could be

---

[277] PL March-April 2010.
[278] https://ilkumutdernegi.org/en/.

excused from that assignment. "I've just been saved from all that," she pleaded. "Please don't make me delve into that again". I never repeated that assignment. "Keep praying for wisdom in selecting content and insight to make it relevant."[279]

By 2005 we had over fifty people taking various courses[280], by 2009 sixty[281], by 2011 about a hundred[282] and our impact on the Turkish church became significant. Church leaders asked if we could provide training at a higher academic level so we made arrangements with a school in Scotland to deliver their Diploma in Theological Studies. As one of the few instructors with both adequate Turkish and a terminal degree I prepped ever more courses at ever-deeper levels: The Pentateuch, History of Christianity, Marriage and Family Life, The Prophets, Wisdom Literature, the Book of Acts, Theological English. Eschatology proved particularly encouraging for our tiny, hard-pressed Christian community.

> "They seemed to grasp the big picture of the end times and were sobered by the reality that the current upheavals in the Middle East may even increase as we approach Christ's return. They were encouraged, however, that God is on the throne and will continue to call out and preserve His church. Hallelujah!"[283]

Like the apostle Paul, we were not building on the foundations of others; what we laid down others had to build upon. Though an inter-mission ministry, Hasat recruited only theologically conservative teachers—until Dr. Tim came along. His photograph shows a long, aquiline profile turned towards me, laughing at some joke I'd cracked. A product of Princeton Theological Seminary, he was a *bone fide* Old Testament scholar. We co-taught a number of courses, as "Tim has a much greater knowledge of the OT; Peter has much better

---

[279] PL March-April 2006.
[280] PL. November-December 2005.
[281] PL January-February 2009.
[282] PL January-February 2011.
[283] PL January 5, 2008.

Turkish."[284] Bemused by my conservative evangelicalism, Tim had me to read the likes of Donald Bloesch and James Barr. I dutifully worked my way through all seven volumes of Bloesch's *Christian Foundations*. A delightful read, I found that kindly scholar straddling two horses: neo-orthodox notions of Scriptures and a compromised doctrine of the sovereignty of God along with a high view of Christ and pietist spirituality. Unlike Barr, the gentle Bloesch wasn't "saved out of" fundamentalism, and thus didn't have an axe to grind. Instead of engaging intelligently with contemporary conservative scholars, I found Barr's book *Fundamentalism* a caricature, a carefully curated take-down of a static straw man.

Tim made me a better teacher for we grow in understanding by interacting intelligently with those who force us to rethink our own presuppositions, who push us out of our echo chambers and prompt us to deal fairly with those who think differently. He was, however, mistaken if he'd hoped his books and our subsequent discussions would shift my conservative evangelical worldview. Instead, he unintentionally taught me to evaluate critically erudite men, some of whom pose as evangelicals. Reading Bloesch taught me to accept the limitations of my darkened mind instead of compromising the ancient teachings on infallibility and the ineffable. By clinging to the testimony of the Faithful One of Revelation I avoided the logical rachet effect towards neo-orthodoxy's enthronement of reason over revelation. As for Barr, he unwittingly taught me the imperative of portraying one's detractors without rancor or shrill tones, and in ways they'd recognize as true reflections of their positions.

In a word, I gradually evolved as a Bible teacher from one scrambling for survival to relaxed maturity and with seven unshakable convictions: God is sovereign, spiritual warfare is real, the Biblical text is trustworthy in all it affirms when interpreted according to genre and historic/grammatical hermeneutic, penal substitutionary atonement is the Bible's bedrock teaching on salvation, man's ability to accept that

---

[284] PL May-June 2007.

salvation for himself through repentance and faith is initiated by God and is a life-transforming experience, the allegiance of those who have undergone this experience now lies with that body of believers—the church universal—for which Christ died and, one day, God's will shall be done on earth as it is in heaven. These fundamentals were—and remain—the pillars of the sacred, living structure of Christian truth in which I dwell. I testify that, when embraced, they are profoundly liberating, meaning-providing, and peace-inducing. They are fundamental to me becoming a happy man.

Like virtually all churches under anti-Christian regimes, the Middle East's traditional denominations were uber-conservative. Perennially on the defensive, these dwindling communities deemed fresh thinking and the innovative as perilous threats to their identity, and thus to their survival. Now, suddenly, new missionary spirits burst old wineskins. Glossolalist charismatics, hard-core, divisive Calvinists (spearheaded by a Turk who'd studied at Westminster), the Anglicans (spearheaded by a grad from a liberal Anglican seminary), a Korean cult and cruel health-and-welfare preachers all contributed to the theological ferment. As the need for sound theology became increasingly acute, Hasat came to be trusted by most Protestant factions. "We have been asked to provide theological education for the whole Turkish Protestant Church right across Turkey."[285]

I now found myself on overheated busses or rattletrap planes to cities and towns across the country: Ankara (Galatia of old), Antakya (Antioch, where followers of Jesus were first called Christians and from where Paul launched his missionary journeys), Diyarbakir, Samsun... Some, like the church in Antalya, had over a hundred attendees on Sunday mornings; most were small, struggling works. Our regular trips to those isolated fellowships in far-flung outposts left them "amazed that someone would go all that way just to teach them."[286]

---

[285] PL January-February 2011.
[286] PL. March-April 2010.

"Peter is always preparing for the next teaching event. There were quite a few aha! moments in the ten weeks of seminars on 'God's plan for the Nations', particularly with respect to the nature of the church and its relationship with the world... Sometimes the hours of preparation, most of it in Turkish, can be a slog. At other times he is encouraged by sudden inspiration."[287]

Back to that photo album: I'm looking at pastor Orhan, a short, lugubrious Father Brown look-alike peering at me myopically. His small church in Samsun was the only one along the Black Sea coast, and opposition was great. A 24/7 bodyguard, a burly ex-policeman, followed us everywhere, ensured there were no known hot-heads in whichever restaurant we made for, checked that the car wasn't booby trapped and sat in on my classes. Pastor Orhan now leads a significant congregation from a beautiful sanctuary built with Korean money, and several new churches have been birthed along the length and breadth of the Black Sea coast.

Some courageous missionaries had found jobs in the Kurdish city of Diyarbakir and, at great personal cost, saw a church come into being there.

"It was a call to the Kurds that first moved Peter to the Middle East in 1982. At that time there was neither a single believer nor even a missionary in Turkey's largest Kurdish city, Diyarbakir. Not in his wildest dreams could Peter have imagined that in June 2010 he would be teaching the book of Revelation there in a church of about 40 solid Muslim background believers. Yet the Lord has done it and Peter rejoiced in the privilege."[288]

Yes, there were moments when Satan asked me what someone with my qualifications was doing there when I could land a much more prestigious seminary position back home. "Pray that we will remain true to what God has called us to do,

---

[287] PL May-June 2010.
[288] PL July-August 2010.

whether it amounts to anything in the world's eyes or not."[289]
Intensive teaching periods, including ongoing instruction of
new missionary candidates in Canada with MissionPrep, were
generally followed by tiredness, jetlag and feeling overwhelmed
by all the lesson preparation, the sermons, the devotionals, the
teacher training days and the conferences. "Peter is very tired
and needs supernatural power for this week... Pray for
rejuvenation!"[290] "Pray for fresh energy for another new place
and new group of students."[291]

Still, teaching spiritually hungry believers across the country
made the long journeys in the stale fug-diffusing, jam-packed
buses, subways, trains or planes worthwhile. And when
returning home from some grimy working-class district,
indistinguishable in dress and demeanor from the weary
laborers casting brief, incurious glances in my direction, the
winter rains lashing the commuter train's windows, or when,
late at night, I watched the lights of the great urban
conurbation hugging the shores of the Bosphorus and Sea of
Marmara glide by from the ferry plying its way back to Asia
through the flotilla of darkly silhouetted barges, cargo ships
and fishing smacks, their lamps twinkling in the dark, I knew I
had the best job in the world. I'd walk through our front door
still too adrenalin-filled to sleep, already planning the next
class. "It is hard work... but he loves it!"[292]

---

[289] PL November-December 2006.
[290] PL May-June 2011.
[291] PL May 3, 2014.
[292] PL March-April 2010.

54

More Snaps

"A pleasure is full-grown only when it is remembered"

C.S. Lewis

...

HASAT WAS LAUNCHED WHEN three university students asked an elderly spinster to teach them the Old Testament. Mary developed a basic curriculum, called it Bithiniya, the 1st century name for the Istanbul region, and started teaching. She didn't know Turkish well, so one of the guys translated. Upon her departure David took over. He is pictured smiling cheerfully at our dinner table, for Anna's dinners inevitably beget cheer. David's Turkish was also limited. His strength was recognizing his shortcomings and recruiting people to fill the gaps. In 2005 we changed the name to Hasat (Harvest) as Bithinya was too Greek-sounding for the Turkish ear. When David left my hero George, of whom the album contains numerous snapshots, took charge.

The problem with most heroes is that they shrink when scrutinized up close. Not so with George, whom I have scrutinized for decades. We first met in 1990, soon after I'd published the first Yeni Yaklaşım. That amateurish, stippled production, the best my dot-matrix printer could spit out, wouldn't do for George. He procured a huge laser printer—cutting-edge technology back then—which he somehow slipped into the country. George, I learned, was both enterprising and sacrificially supportive of whatsoever advanced God's kingdom.

Christ died for the church so George would live for its Turkish iteration. He learned to banter, joke, teach, cajole, gently rebuke and disciple new believers in their heart language. I know of no other with such love for and profoundly practical knowledge of God's word and the ability to communicate it in Turkish. The Lord used him, along with my erstwhile Istanbul University class-mate Carlos and friend Brian to found the Beşiktaş church[293]. The others moved on[294] but George stuck with those former Muslims, for he is faithful in friendship. He modeled Christianity over the long haul in ways Muslim converts could aspire to imitate.

George led our theologically diverse, multi-cultural team with wit and wisdom. He trusted the Holy Spirit in us, recognized and exploited our gifts and gently nudged us along. There is hardly a church leader in the country today whom the Lord hasn't touched through him. He and Donna are among the greats "of whom the world is not worthy".

■

The album's leading photograph is of the leadership team. We five met weekly to pray, plan, rejoice in the ministry's rapid expansion ("Hasat just grows and grows"[295]), and wrestle with consequent challenges. We hosted luncheons for pastors and elders to discuss how we could better serve them. Were we dealing sufficiently with the issues facing a church in a Muslim society? How could we better adapt our teaching practices to a learning style which excels at regurgitating facts but struggles to think and write critically? How could we assess practical application, the impact of our teaching on hearts and hands, on devotional lives and service to the church? Should we become a legal entity? Should we seek accreditation?

A handful of church leaders felt they would benefit from more in-depth studies so I was charged with exploring the feasibility of developing a Masters program. What might that look like? To whom might we turn for accreditation? After

---

[293] See chapter 27.
[294] Carlos Madrigal left to establish the Altıntepe Protestant Church, to which he devoted the rest of his life. It became the mother church of a string of daughter churches across western Turkey. See http://www.istpcf.org/our-churches/. He too is a genuine missionary hero.
[295] PL November 11, 2013.

several false starts the Lord led us to TCM, an American seminary in Austria. George and I sallied forth to Vienna and their principal visited us in Istanbul.

> "Pray that in all our meetings the Lord will make His way clear both to him and us... Pray for wisdom and peace for Peter; he feels that he is flying by the seat of his pants (is that the same as walking by faith and resting in the Lord!? Hmmm...). In any case, he feels out of his depth half the time and under time pressure all the time."[296]

We signed an MOU with them, recruited some qualified faculty and wrote joyfully that "it is thrilling to be able to offer theological education at this level."[297] We had asked the Lord for a minimum of three students and he gave us five.

There is a lovely photograph of myself, one of TCM's teachers and that first cohort. When they eventually graduated George and I headed for Austria to attend the ceremony. We were rightfully proud: one our guys was valedictorian. The program has been graduating people ever since.

.

A number of photographs were taken in the building we eventually purchased. Inexorable rent increases and the danger of expulsion by unsympathetic landlords led us to envision, then actively trust the Lord for our own office and library. I was appointed chairman of the building committee. Our early meetings consisted of little more than praying and day-dreaming: "We'd like to purchase an apartment—something that requires a wee miracle or two"[298] and "We have our first few pennies towards our goal of $275.000".[299]

Money dribbled in dismally slow. "You cannot do much... when you have less than 15% of the money in hand needed to buy a place."[300] Then, suddenly, it flooded in! After months of

---

[296] PL January-February 2011.
[297] PL September-October 2011.
[298] PL September-October 2010.
[299] PL May-June 2010.
[300] PL November-December 2010.

searching we purchased two derelict floors in an ideally located building. Close to public transportation, it looked down on an old, walled Christian cemetery run by the British embassy, an urban oasis of gnarled trees and dappled sunlight striking higgledy-piggledy headstones, marble crosses, a carved angel and a chapel. How we praised God who through the generosity of his people gave us more than we had dared hope for! A sympathetic contractor spent months transforming our dilapidated space into fresh, brightly lit offices, a boardroom, a kitchen, and the library/classroom featured in those photographs.

Next we decided to go legal. Providing instruction to Christians in churches was not illegal, but it struck everyone as a good idea to be pro-active with a government suspicious of religious activities occuring below its radar screen. After extensive consultations with lawyers and leaping numerous beaurocratic hoops and hurdles we became a legitimate association established for the purpose of supporting Turkish Protestant churches.

·

There are a several photographs of Anna sitting among piles of books. She was our librarian. Though not a book-consuming culture, Turkish now boasts an inordinate quantity of Christian literature because Western missionaries, hailing from more literate societies, cannot repress the urge to get their favorite authors translated. Converts too got on the gotta-publish bandwagon for, as a local proverb has it, "where the front wheel passes the rear wheel follows".

There were shelves of discipleship-in-four-steps stuff, spooky spiritual warfare and dramatic works on the end times (one of the earliest translated works was Hall Lindsey's *The Late Great Planet Earth*), gobs of advice on marriage and family life and a yard of guilt-inducing, legalistic Christian moralism. Some volumes were fabulous, like the NIV Study Bible and Grudem's *Systematic Theology*. "She (Anna) needs wisdom to devise the most user-friendly way of arranging books in the Hasat library. Western classifications don't always fit the Turkish mindset."[301] And "I just love sorting out a mess, so it gave me great satisfaction to see our 4000 books now catalogued and neatly shelved."[302] She then turned her tidy mind to the boxes of unorganized articles and book chapters translated over the years. "Neat little digitized files need to replace dusty old binders full of papers."[303]

When the academic program came on stream Anna coordinated the translation and publication of more robust works of theology and Biblical studies. This was a monumental undertaking, "something which requires almost daily communication with translators, checkers, correctors, proofers and stylists."[304] Some translators, also working on fluffier projects for others, frustrated her due to their inability to keep promises. "She feels the pressure of all the deadlines. The stress is usually first felt in her back."[305] Many hours at the computer led to carpal tunnel syndrome. "Pray for healing in her wrist and forearm."[306]

The translators had the language but not the requisite theology so their every sentence had to be back-checked against the original. Her greatest need was not for translators but for theologically qualified, native English speakers who were meticulous, fastidious, finicky and with excellent Turkish to check the accuracy of the base translations. "They are as rare as gold dust."[307] She herself did the pre-press proofs and the creation of Turkish indexes. "Pray for eyes to spot the errors!"[308], and "how much of a perfectionist should she be?!"[309]

∎

---

[301] PL November 1, 2012.
[302] Report to Trinity Baptist Church, Summer of 2011.
[303] PL September-October 2011.
[304] PL September-October 2007.
[305] PL January-February 2006.
[306] PL July 2012.
[307] PL September-October 2006
[308] PL September-October 2008.
[309] PL September 19, 2013.

Hasat graduations were joyful occasions. Some years there were just a few graduates, two or three, then up to five and six and then, "Praise God that we have 9 graduates this year, 5 of them in cities other than Istanbul."[310] Some were church-goers who'd progressed through our general program, others pastors who had worked through one of the academic programs. A convivial dinner was followed by flattering speeches jocularly applauded, intercessory prayers and the granting of diplomas. "Pray our graduates will serve their churches well."[311]

Those were happy years. We lived busy but deeply satisfying lives as members of a fantastic team engaged in work we wholeheartedly believed in, and which suited our gifts. We'd found our niche and complemented each other well.

---

[310] PL May-June 2012.
[311] PL May-June 2008.

55

Ah, the Church...

"The glory of the gospel is that when the church is absolutely different from the world, she invariably attracts it."

Martyn Lloyd-Jones

AH, THE CHURCH... that colony for whom Christ died, for whom God sovereignly controls the events of history and for which we should live. The New Testament paints grandiose portraits of her as Christ's body, or as a divinely indwelled temple constructed of "living stones" joined like fine masonry, or as a bride dressed in white whom the groom, Christ, loved to death and for whom he is planning a great feast, or as a golden lampstand designed to uphold "the light of the world" before mankind. Sadly, the churches we have served were, by and large, caricatures of the ideal, reflecting instead the down-and-dirty realities the apostle John describes in his admonitory letters to the churches of Asia Minor.

Take our first experience of "church" in Turkey. The attendees were descendants of ex-Nestorians and Armenians who, like all Middle Easterners, had phenomenally long memories. They could neither forget nor forgive how the Turks had treated them in centuries past and thus hated them without distinction. We met in the chapel of the largely derelict Bible House, former headquarters of the once mighty American Board of Commissioners for Foreign Missions.

The long Sunday commute across the conurbation we called home was never boring. A minibus took us to the docks on the Asian side of the Bosphorus, the waterway connecting the Black and the Mediterranean Seas. From there a charming old ferry, dodging tankers, container ships and fishing vessels, sailed past picturesque Leander's Tower, ancient mosques, Sultans' palaces and the St. Sophia, once the world's largest church, now a mosque. We disembarked in old Constantinople, walked past more mosques, a spice market and through a teeming oriental bazaar selling everything from fresh fish to frying pans, from pirated DVDs to condoms. Then we pushed through a half-hidden cast iron gate, climbed a staircase and, at long last, arrived.

An arthritic old man with tufts of hair growing from his ears played a wheezy organ so larghissimo you could yawn and only miss two syllables of a Fanny Crosby translation. A few regulars prayed, each emoting their customary ardor and emotion, and someone read a passage from the old Ali Bey translation of the Bible. Then various individuals arose to address us. One such, always first to mount the pulpit, invariably pontificated on the imminent return of Christ and the need to mortify the flesh. Next a barely literate orator challenged us to legalistic obedience, whereafter a third son of Adam rose to critique his predecessors. There was no elected leadership, no pastor, no sacraments, no membership, no church discipline, no financial accountability and no business meetings. Once in a while a convert from Islam showed up—there was little else in terms of public Christian worship in those early days—but as Turks or Kurds they were not trusted. They soon moved on. It was a Sardis church, having a reputation of being alive but, in fact, dead.

> "We almost gave up in despair... (However) Peter has now been asked to preach more often and longer(!) so pray for inspiration, anointing, cultural appropriateness and fluency in Turkish."[312]

In spite of our good intentions and hard work our presence became unsustainable when a wealthy, unbelieving family head determined we were no longer welcome. He had taken umbrage when I requested he stop his loud side conversations when the word was being preached. Hugely offended, the man asserted

---

[312] PL. July-August 2005.

that this was his church and that he would no longer tolerate outsiders.

> "Pray that the four leading believers will not continue to allow this unbeliever to dictate how the church should be run, as has been the case for many years now. The man either needs to be removed, to humble himself or, best yet, to be born again. Pray too that we may not sin in our response to this whole affair."[313]

However, the man was right: it was his church. The others informed me in private that though his behaviour was unacceptable they could do nothing because he was very rich. I learned he was a loan-shark to whom others were beholden and, as a Turkish proverb puts it, he who pays plays the pipes.[314] And so, after having given several years of our life to them we offered our nunc dimittis and moved on. Like Sardis, however, a few poorly taught but unsullied young fellows started taking Hasat courses. They eventually graduated, developed a heart for Turks, and—once their elders had moved on or died off—revitalized the group. But in the meantime we were churchless. "It does not feel right, nor good, to be without a church home so please keep praying for the Lord's leading. We want to serve in a local church."[315]

We started attending a small chapel on the grounds of the Swedish embassy, also on the European side of the city. They were a fluid group of starving artists, underpaid actors, a second-rate rock guitarist, a dental assistant, a model, an executive secretary, and a few university students—basically a grab-bag of unlikely marginals. Virtually all were single or divorced, and a different fraction showed up on any given week as consistent commitment was a foreign concept. They struggled with unemployment, penury, broken relationships, single parenthood, immorality and hostility from family. Some had only just begun their journey with Jesus, others remained

---

[313] PL Jan.-Feb. 2006.
[314] Parayı veren düdüğünü çalar.
[315] PL May-June 2006.

jaded Muslims. Worship was a lively affair generated by electric guitars and bongos. There was no elected eldership, membership or financial accountability, but we were warmly welcomed: "Please keep coming. We need an older, stable, mature Christian couple here." Indeed, they did!

> "We may look out of place, but we've become quite attached to our whacky little church group. After the Christmas service we all went to a dubious back-street café where one of the girls used to work as a fortune teller. Peter often receives invitations to preach and lead the midweek Bible study, and Anna has been called the Church Mama. Her baked goods disappear quickly after meetings."[316]

A suave Turk who had studied with Hasat and whom a Baptist mission agency, in their infinite wisdom, paid to study at an Anglican seminary, returned from overseas to lead the group. He insisted that he had no intention of turning us into Anglicans but proved to be an unabashed dissembler with respect to that matter.

> "We recently learned that he caused a church split with an earlier attempt to make the church Anglican. Undeterred, he went to Oxford to receive ordination. We are concerned about what might happen next."[317]

We don't mind giving our best to small, struggling churches of immature believers and to supporting leaders who are out of their depth, but my gorge rises at pastors who can lie like Ananias and obdurately "lord it over the flock." In spite of his multiple guarantees otherwise and despite everyone's misgivings, the man persisted in pushing us towards anglo-catholicim. "How far do we go in terms of compromising our interpretation for the sake of unity? What is negotiable, what is not? We need wisdom and love. May our worst fears not be

[316] PL January-February 2007.
[317] IBID

realized."[318] But they were. The man now wore robes, drank the left-over communion wine and, without explanation, unilaterally "cancelled until further notice" the midweek Bible-study and prayer meeting into which I had significant input. Sunday attendance dropped precipitously. "We are saddened as one by one these young believers are falling away."[319]

> "Deeply hurt and betrayed people want to meet with Peter to discuss what is, to them, a bewildering situation; he is in an awkward position and requires much wisdom and graciousness."[320]

I had no appetite for fighting with a duplicitous "national church leader" so with heavy hearts we too bid the remnant our adieu. It eventually shriveled and scattered and that, sadly, was the alpha and omega of a once lively group of Muslim converts.

A small fellowship of 20 to 25 people in a distant district where I had taught Hasat courses invited us to join them. In spite of the two-hour commute by minibus, ferryboat, tram (all 26 stops) and a stiff walk, we grew to love them, and when a supporter offered to help us purchase a flat we moved house to be close. We had scarcely settled before Anna was drinking tea with the young woman across the hallway.

> "*All my fellow townsmen know that you are a woman of noble character*" (Ruth 3:11). Our whole neighbourhood is Muslim and Anna the only foreign woman... Would the butcher, the grocer, the fruit and vegetable sellers, the fishmonger or the baker say this about her?"[321]

Our new little Smyrna church was poor yet rich, suffering tribulation and slander. Though tested by Satan, they remained faithful. Though nationalist extremists beat Pastor Semir to the ground, and though they shot the windows out of our venue, the core group didn't waver.

---

[318] PL March-April 2007.
[319] PL May-June 2007.
[320] PL November-December 2007.
[321] PL November 1, 2012.

Unlike other minority Christians, Pastor Semir had a heart for Muslims. He even gave his daughter in marriage to a young convert into whom I also invested extra time. Refik now co-leads the most significant Christian relief agency in the country.

I preached regularly and served as an elder. The women spent hours in the kitchen as most Sunday meetings concluded with a simple meal. After lunch plates were cleared off and washed and about half the group would gather around the table for a Hasat course. On Thursday evenings people dribbled in for homegroup where, after a restorative glass of tea, I'd teach through a book of the Bible. We then shared what was on our hearts and prayed out loud, all at the same time. Afterwards we'd eat, drink more tea and coffee, and chat till close to midnight.

Although we celebrated some baptisms, a Christian marriage and a birth, we marvelled at the depth of resistance to the gospel in society at large.

> "The church door is a revolving one; people come and people go. We have been praying for five people to come and stay. It looks like we might have one – a man who believed years ago but never had the courage to go public."[322]

Then number two arrived, a single woman who suffered from depression but found some joy after professing faith in Christ. The two new members weathered the storm when their families turned against them and they lost their jobs. After much prayer a Muslim convert's parents deigned to visit him and his new bride. Then three more people joined, though we longed to see more of the Spirit's regenerating power in their lives. "So often we are discouraged as they drift away after their enthusiastic starts."[323]

One winter's night a large cement slab from the underside of the apartment floor above our meeting room crashed down; the upstairs neighbours expressed their wish that we'd all been

---

[322] PL November-December 2009.
[323] PL November-December 2010.

crushed down there together. For months we worshiped and ate in the adjoining room, hoping the rest of the floor above would hold. We jerry-rigged a temporary ceiling in time for a simple but beautiful 10th anniversary celebration.

We cherish those memories of warm, Sunday and late-night fellowship when we consumed copious quantities of food, tea and Turkish coffee and prayed and studied the Bible with people eager to learn.

∎

The scripture's inspiring imagery of the church too often falls far short of current realities. We still live in that "not yet but one day" dimension which permeates Biblical promises and prophecy, but experience of good Christian fellowship and the vision of eventual perfection enabled us to focus laser-like on living life in her service.

56

Anna and the Neighbours

"Tell me who your friends are and I'll tell you who you are."[324]

Turkish proverb

. . .

LIFE TOOK PLACE against a backdrop of political instability and religious opposition. The grinding civil war with the Kurds stoked Turkish nationalism, the jingoism inflaming otherwise sane citizens. When Turkey sent ground troops into Iraq demonstrators filled the squares: "Turkey, love it or leave it!" Those not flying the flag and expressing outrage felt vulnerable. Christians again became scapegoats as memories of missionary empowerment of ethnic minorities during the Ottoman period were resuscitated. Both foreign and national Christians suffered physical and verbal abuse.

> "The Protestant community... continues to receive bad press, being labeled as 'destructive and subversive', out to 'divide the country' and 'turn it back into a Christian nation.' There is even a bus in Istanbul distributing free anti-Christian literature."[325]

The fat really hit the fire when a Danish newspaper published a cartoon of Muhammed with a bomb as his turban. Massive demonstrations by hot-blooded defenders of their long dead prophet tied up traffic, Christian friends were beaten, a Roman Catholic priest shot dead. Elsewhere churches were set ablaze, more Christians attacked, Western embassies stormed, and boycotts organized.

---

[324] *"Bana arkadaşını söyle sana kim olduğunu söyleyeyim."*
[325] PL July-August 2005.

A reward went to anyone who managed to behead the hapless cartoonist. "We pray, and seek to live peaceful, quiet and godly lives in high-strung days."[326]

One Eid and Christmas followed another. Ramadans, the month of fasting from dawn to dusk, were often times of intense untoward spiritual activity. People were more alive to the unseen world of the jinn, more expectant of dreams and visions, spent more time reading their Qur'ans, at prayer and in the mosque yet, understandably, were more irritable. I would be too if I hadn't eaten or drunk all day. Tempers could rise quickly, triggering mob violence against infidels.

Heaving quiet sighs of relief when life reverted to normal, we'd break fast with our neighbours, a melange of the devout, the nominal and the seemingly secular—until a crisis occurred, when all sought solutions in a cocktail of faith, cultural traditions and the endless superstitions of folk Islam. All were "decent, middle-class, middle-aged folk who would have no respect for anyone who'd betray their cultural/religious heritage"[327]. While I traversed the vast city and country teaching Bible and theology or jetted off to Toronto to train new missionaries, Anna endeared herself to them.

> "It is a strange existence, and not much fun, to have your husband in Canada and kids in Germany, but my neighbours have smothered me with friendship in their absence. For Turks it is unthinkable to be all alone with no immediate family nearby."[328]

She joined the women's tea parties, events designed to promote good neighborliness and raise money. Held on a rotation basis, the hostess cleaned house till everything sparkled and prepared a vast array of dishes. After food fortunes were told from coffee dregs, and then each guest would deposit an agreed sum of money in a glass bowl on the

---

[326] PL November -December 2007.

[327] PL November-December 2006.

[328] PL May-June 2005.

coffee table. With no access to banks, this was the hostess' opportunity to purchase that new carpet or appliance for her home. We ate leftovers and breathed stale cigarette smoke for days after Anna's turns. She rarely got a word in during those four-hour events as she served women who "watch her every action like hawks."[329] We prayed they would see she was different not merely because she was foreign but because she was a new creation in Christ. One December she read them the Christmas story. Some dismissed it out of hand, others said the Qur'an had abrogated it, one said it was beautiful and a few left thoughtfully silent.

Those jaded women came to cherish Anna, and whenever she was confined to bed with back problems they'd crowd in, Turkish meals in hand. She repaid their kindnesses at Christmas by distributing plates of goodies with cards explaining that we were celebrating the birth of a Savior, not just the New Year a week early. This, in turn, was rewarded with cuts of raw mutton during the Feast of Sacrifice or Noah's pudding during Ashura, the celebration of the landing of the ark which, according to their tradition, settled on Mount Judi. Supplies aboard had nearly run out, the story goes, so Noah instructed his family to scrape up the leftovers for a celebratory pudding. Once six different neighbours seeking merit with Allah each gave us bowls of wheat, rice, barley, beans and chickpeas cooked together and mixed with dried apricots, figs, mulberries, dates, raisins, currants, walnuts and almonds, flavoured with sugar, cinnamon, cloves and rosewater, and decorated with coconut and pomegranate seeds.

In time more opportunities to share the gospel opened up. One neighbour, enthusiastically reading her New Testament, wondered how could they kill such a man as Jesus. Another asked if he had really risen from the dead. A third warned Anna to keep her views to herself.

"She (Anna) has many opportunities to share the truth but finds their minds darkened by traditions of false

---

[329] PL March-April 2005.

teachings about Christianity. It is humanly impossible to break through; only God by His spirit ever will."[330]

Church debacles, dark winter days, missing the children, the disappointment of broken promises, menopausal blues, ongoing back problems, the human impossibility of the task, the lying endemic to the culture, nasty flu bugs, insufficient energy for the work and the ongoing disheartenment of living in an oppressive environment took their toll.

> "We have been challenged recently regarding our measure of faith. There are few tangible results in our line of work in the Middle East, and we need to believe that the Lord is at work in people's lives even if we do not see it. It is easy to be satisfied with being faithful, but we also want to be full of faith."[331]

The political situation stabilized, the economy expanded, the middle class grew and the cost of living soared. Up the road Starbucks joined McDonalds, Burger King, Pizza Hut and Kentucky Fried Chicken; we preferred the cheaper and tastier Turkish restaurants. The growing middle class began incorporating Christmas traditions into their New Year celebrations. The red and green tinsel, tree lights, Father Christmas, frantic shopping for luxury gifts, wines, chocolates and a turkey were all geared for New Year's Eve. December 25 passed unnoticed by all but the tiny group of Christians, making our celebration of the Savior's entry into the world even more precious.

"Keep praying for words, wisdom, boldness and, above all, for the Spirit to work in hearts."[332] Once Anna joined three friends in a mosque to listen to an imam droning dreary recitations from the Qur'an at a funeral. Afterwards she shared the gospel with one. "So you will never have to pay for your sins, Anna?" the woman asked amazed. The penny had dropped. She understood that Jesus had paid that price once

---

[330] PL November-December 2005.
[331] PL March-April 2005.
[332] PL September-October 2006.

and for all... but then quickly added, 'born a Muslim, Anna, die a Muslim.'"333 Once Anna dropped in on our neighbour across the hall when a stranger was visiting. The latter was suspicious and uncomfortable in Anna's presence. Nazan quickly assured her: "Don't worry, Anna too is a woman of faith." Words of testimony often elicited the response, "Anna, you be as good a Christian as you can be, and we will do our best to be good Muslims."

> "We keep pressing on and look to Him to do what we cannot possibly do—open the eyes of the blind that they might see."334

We do not know if any of those neighbour women ever looked to Christ for the forgiveness of sin.

---

333 PL March-April 2007.
334 PL March-April 2006.

57

The City on the Ping

"Events at home, at work, in the street –
these are the bases for a story."

Naguib Mahfouz

. . .

I DEPLANED AT A modest airport in Northern Thailand. John Kayser—the self-same John Kayser who'd suggested I read the book of Proverbs multiple times as young Christian—had asked me to write 24 film scripts on language acquisition for the Chinese church's Back To Jerusalem missionary movement. Both the project's sponsors and the "uncles" overseeing various underground church networks in country liked the result and, rather rashly, I agreed to direct their filming as well. This, I learned, would take place in Chiang Mai.

It was my first time in the Far East, and I was out of my comfort zone. I had two six-week time slots to make it happen, and was out of my depth. The experience forced me, as William Carey once put it, to believe great things of God and attempt great things for God. Though the event drained me, remembering how God came through at the time stood us in good stead when, years later, we were challenged afresh to step out in raw faith.

Faith, like a muscle, must be exercised for it to grow, and this divine adventure strengthened my conviction that God is utterly trustworthy and, as such, was an important event in my spiritual development. I will try to describe things as I experienced them in this chapter and the next.[335]

---

[335] This chapter is distilled from emails sent to the family between Nov. 2-5, 2008.

Someone drove me to the studio. The boss showed me around and left me in their guest suite. I made a beeline for the toilet. While sitting there I noticed a length of hose with a faucet attached to it, the purpose of which was self-evident. I braced myself for a cold blast but was pleasantly surprised; it's the tropics, after all. After experimenting with a variety of poses I discovered that the somewhat counterintuitive stance of leaning forward and squirting through the legs was much more accurate than twisting one's arm around the back and shooting blindly. Once used to the system I found it a massive improvement on our western paper-only approach. An agreeable squirt, pat yourself dry with a sheet of toilet paper, and your backside is as clean as a whistle.

The phone rang. Someone asked what I wanted for supper. I said I wasn't picky, though not overly keen on seafood. The line fell silent for a bit, then she said she'd see what they could do. The studio boss took me to an open buffet in 5 star hotel, at which point it dawned on me that in her eyes I was a VIP. "People are proving to be very obliging."[336]

Thais don't shake hands, they "wai" by bringing the tips of their fingers together under their chins, bow, and saying something unintelligible. Their response to me thrusting out my right hand was an awkward raising of the hands half-way to the chin and the beginnings of a bow, followed by a quick reverse and forward thrust so as to grab and shake my hand before it was withdrawn. I adapted. For a day or so the response was the exact opposite as before: forward thrusts of the right hand followed by a quick recovery into Thai wai. I found their way vastly superior. It has all the appearance of meekness yet is both efficient and hygienic. When entering a room filled with people you simply wai once from the doorway and make eye contact with all present. When passing someone you can wai without breaking stride and, as it involves no touching, there is no transfer of germs.

---

[336] Email to Hasat Colleagues, Nov. 9, 2008.

Nothing was scheduled for day two so I hiked into town. They drive on the left, which was not a problem for one familiar with Irish roundabouts. My problem was the swarm of mopeds and scooters which, like clouds of insects, attacked from all sides. I nearly came a cropper, and took to looking in every direction twice before crossing a street or stepping around the pop-up restaurants crowding the sidewalks. Keeping pace was a slow-moving pick-up hauling a large Buddha statue with a mega-watt sound-system blaring bombastic street-preaching interspaced with eerie piccolo music. Young women invited the desperate into dicey-looking parlors in high-pitched, sing-songy English, pot-bellied Western men wandered around with stone-faced Thai girls on their arms and saffron robed monks moved with an appearance of profundity.

I found a Starbucks, ordered a Latte, climbed to the covered terrace, settled into a wicker chair, and looked down on those packs of whizzing scooters. Students, crones, workmen, striking beauties, nattily dressed office workers, entire families, all focused on the few yards before them, raced pell-mell around an intersection. It was massively entertaining. The underpowered two-wheelers came in all colors and shapes: well-dressed women raced along on snazzy, spotless pink or pale blue models while young guys added headlights. One ruby-red specimen boasted nine chrome beacons. A family of four chugging by on a gasper was not unusual. I wondered how one could physically squeeze that many people on a vehicle designed for one, two in a pinch. Three on that little banana seat? OK. But four? When a family pulled up to the curb I saw a child's seat squeezed into the modicum of space which permits the steering wheel to swing this way or that. At the cost of maneuverability you could take the family, including Junior, for an outing. Junior's gripping both mirrors to keep from flopping excessively forward or backwards when dad suddenly braked or accelerated on that manic road didn't help. Others had baskets hanging from both sides of the steering wheel, yet others sported saddle bags, trailers or, most common, sidecars. These tended to be a large, metal cages filled with friends, family members, bolts of textiles, boxes of electronic goods or loosely packed construction material. Some were converted to ambulatory restaurants. Feet propped on the banister while nursing my drink, I felt like a colonialist surveying the scurrying natives. The heavens opened: late monsoon. A man with a patio umbrella welded to his moped stopped in the middle of the street, opened it up and kept going, albeit visibly less stable than before.

Though not as nasty looking as Egyptian restaurants most eateries struck me as rather insalubrious. Hunger eventually got the better of me. I stared at an incomprehensible menu then asked the waitress to serve me her favorite dish. She loves boiled rice with chicken floating in a watery, curry-like sauce. I asked about public transportation. Red pickups with canvas tops run specific routes; hop in the back and hand some cash through the rear window. The three-wheeled motorized tuktuks will take you anywhere.

I flagged down a red pickup, climbed in the back and shoved a few Bahts through the window. The nagging question of how one stops the thing was soon answered: when pressed a wee button causes a buzzer to ring in the cab which triggers a pull-over response. I clambered over the tailgate near the guest house, where Enoch, the main actor, and Susanne the translator were settling into their rooms.

That evening the studio boss took us to a multiple acre concrete slab with a tin roof on bare poles covering countless picnic tables and a staggeringly long eat-all-you-can buffet. The food was uncooked. A skinny waiter plunked a large metallic pot with flaming coals on our table upon which he placed a circular gully with a perforated mound in the center. He then filled the gully with water. You placed delicacies of your choosing onto the perforated mound to barbecue them or dropped them into the water to boil them. I wandered up and down that buffet looking for something, anything, to cook. Nothing among those stacks of South China Sea critters appealed. The smell was overwhelming, the din deafening with a thousand-plus people shouting and smacking loudly, a live band singing Thai pop and huge, blaring TV screens on different stations. It was sensory overload. I barbequed a few bits and pieces and manfully shoved them down my throat. The others were in their element. After several hours of that phantasmagorial smorgasbord under flickering neon we returned to the guest house where I collapsed into bed.

Early the next day, Sunday, a van swung by to pick us up. We saw the city's moat, various canals, a pretty University and, slightly out of town, a beautiful waterfall reminiscent of a Chinese pen and ink drawing: tumbling water, stone staircase, gnarled trees with exposed roots gripping massive boulders, dense tropical canopy. Leading up to the waterfall vendors sold fried worms and huge, deep-fried cockroaches.

Next we were driven to a church, a simple storefront painted in pastels. Thais love light shades of pink, blue, yellow, violet and purple. Even the plastic chairs were light blue. As guest of honor I was ushered to the front row, middle seat. The room filled with about 50 worshippers. Six girls in white gowns were dancers, not baptismal candidates, and for me their performance was the service's highlight. While the band played and the congregation sang they executed perfectly synchronized, exquisite routines. The main dancer was less than three feet from my nose while another was rivetingly ugly. The girls also banged tambourines with multi-colored pastel tassels and waved red flags with gold crosses. One swung a candle around. I could visualize them one day exercising their talents in heaven with me, in due course, swinging by for another look.

An Australian preaching through a translator orated about seizing the opportunity and pushing through the door to get what you want. Christ was altogether absent. During the fellowship meal someone handed me a plate of leach-like things. All the slimy sea creatures of the previous night's buffet, that unfortunate glimpse of roasted worms and cockroaches at the waterfall and some cute puppies in a cage outside a restaurant I'd seen earlier loomed before me. I couldn't do it; I just didn't have it in me. I sidled to the door, flagged down a tuk-tuk, negotiated a price and climbed in. Back at the guest house I downed a glass of milk and several slices of bread spread thick with Nutella.

Determined not to give way to jet-lag I hiked to the main road, hopped into the back of a red pickup, disembarked at an open market and inspected ebony, mahogany and teak carvings—some of startlingly high quality—silver jewelry, opium pipes, textiles, gross-looking/smelling foods, paintings— mostly mediocre but quality stuff as well—silks and copper ware. I came to a dazzling gold-plated wat, or Buddhist temple, and walked through the main gate. No-one batted an eye. The courtyard was abuzz with people cooking and eating and vendors selling jade jewelry, silver Buddhas, joss sticks and a variety of eclectic religious paraphernalia. I took off my shoes and entered the inner sanctum. A huge gold-covered Buddha, lots of reds and yellows, ornate carvings, burning incense. Buddha's life, laid out like the stations of the cross in a Roman Catholic church, was painted on the walls. The place gave me the creeps.

Praise the Lord, in the shadow of a skyscraper with an international hotel logo emblazoned on it I found a McDonalds, a Burger King and a Pizza Hut. A street juggler performed amazing feats with bowling pins while I staved off starvation with a slice of pepperoni and cheese.

I wandered to the Ping River, perambulating lazily along the stone steps leading to the muddy waters. Occasionally a sampan glided by, and the combination of stairs, boats and blushing sky creating an oriental tableau I'd hitherto only seen in National Geographics. Several ruddy tourists, lungs heaving like suction pumps, paddled feverishly to make it back to a rent-a-kayak facility upstream before the crimson sun retired for the night—a somewhat jarring effect on an otherwise sublime scene.

I flagged down a red pickup, pushed a few Bahts through the window and pressed the button at the appropriate moment. A shower, a sleeping pill and bed. I needed to be well-rested for the morning,

58

A Peculiar Adventure[337]

*"People are so strange and so complicated
that they're actually beautiful."*

Khalil Gibran

. . .

ENOCH IS ONE of the most intriguing human oddities with whom I've had occasion to interact. A wiry survivor frequently sporting a blue Mao suit, he'd been a talk show host in China. He'd played some role in the Tiananmen Square uprising, was imprisoned, escaped, and made his way via Laos to Thailand, where he'd come to faith in Christ. His English was poor and he spoke surprisingly little Thai. Launching him as the guru on language acquisition to the Chinese missionary movement was rather droll.

My scripts, which he called "Peter's scriptures"—correcting him on this was useless—consisted of two parts. First fictitious missionary Li Wei shared his early struggles and how he broke through when someone demonstrated various helpful techniques and methods. The videos then cut to a fictitious underground Bible school where teacher Jhang Dong explained the underlying principles behind missionary Li Wei's discoveries and experiences. I cast Enoch as teacher Jhang Dong. The Li Wei scenes were scheduled for later, with a different actor.

---

[337] For this chapter I drew heavily from lengthy emails written to my family between Nov. 2 and Dec. 6, 2008 and again between March 21 and April 29, 2009.

There were parts of my scriptures I could not get Enoch to understand, and he couldn't pretend to teach it if he didn't grasp it. When he did get it he couldn't retain his lines long enough to act authentically. One evening I informed the Lord that we had a problem, and wondered what was he would do about it. The answer came in a flash: do the voice recordings first and film later so that Enoch wouldn't have to memorize anything. The next morning I informed the studio boss that I didn't need the cameramen for a week but wanted a sound technician and an audio booth instead. I then had Enoch read his lines with feeling. Whenever he sounded too wooden or too dull or too whatever, we would correct him from the observation room. He took it well and there were lots of laughs. Whenever he or translator Susanne didn't understand a section I'd simplify it, she'd translate on the fly and Enoch would make the recording. As we got to more difficult sections I'd explain things the night before; even with the Chinese in front of them it took me two nights to demystify the basics principles of phonetics.

Nothing fazed Enoch. We might be running far behind schedule, the imperious Susanne might lose her temper—he took it all in stride. He wouldn't record a scene until he'd prayed at length. Like Orpheus, he burst into song at the oddest moments, his powerful, melodious voice ringing through the building. He liked martial arts and once gave a jaw-dropping display of kung-fu. He loved—even seemed to need—beauty and decorated the booth with plastic flowers, a red paper lantern and other bits of kitsch. He loved my trilled whistling; every so often he'd ask me to "do holy song", meaning he wanted me to whistle Jesus Loves Me or I Will Sing Of My Redeemer. Once, after stepping outside to clear his head, he returned stroking a huge, luminescent-green locust. He stretched on his back on the studio floor, the animal quivering on his stomach. He focused on it, gently stroking the creature for five or more minutes before releasing it back into the wild.

After completing the audio recordings we created a house church: calligraphed Bible verses, a world map, a cross, some books, a TV (not too dinky, not too fancy). I hadn't a clue what underground churches looked like but assured them ours was most authentic one I'd ever beheld.

At last we were ready to film and I called up the extras. When I learned they were only available for a couple of hours a day I fired the lot, including a wizened old lady not a day less than seventy, all dolled up to play her part in a movie. She was so crestfallen I had to supress my nasty Dutch habit of laughing at other people's minor miseries. I insisted on four or five 20-35 year olds with decent Mandarin available full time. The next morning four unwashed Chinese punks showed up. Three had greasy hair flowing past their shoulders, the fourth a multicolored Mohawk. One wore a cross-and-skull T-shirt with DEATH in Gothic letters on it and one sported tattoos up and down his arms. They looked like gangsters. One seemed retarded, or rather, mentally challenged as we are now encouraged to say. However you put it, I had a problem requiring immediate attention. I told the cameramen to take a break, had a skivvy hustle my stars to the nearest barber while another purchased fresh shirts; within the hour we were rolling tape. Thankfully, two were smarter than they looked, and I told the rest to pretend interest and intelligence: "Just look at the teacher, then doodle earnestly in your notebook for a few seconds—here are your notebooks—then look back up at the teacher. Easiest 300 Baht a day you'll make in your life". Two tatty girls showed up the following morning and I added them to the cast as well.

Using a boombox I blared the first audio file into the studio and urged Enoch to repeat and act. It was disastrous. Fixed to the spot like a graven image he whispered his lines, concentrating much more than warranted. I got off my director's stool and mimicked the Chinese recording loudly, with overflowing animation and body language. The penny dropped! It hadn't dawned on him that he could repeat his lines out loud and that we'd synchronise the audio with his moving-lips files afterwards. He then gave a demonstration which earned him an ovation.

Two days in my extras turned morose. I learned from their leader that the studio chauffer, charged with delivering them in the mornings, was taking 50% of their wages. After sorting that out we rolled tape again. I fed the extras their lines one sentence at a time and they grew into the job. Soon we had some usable footage. That Friday afternoon I bought tubs of ice cream and threw a party.

For a couple of weeks we progressed beyond my most sanguine expectations. We'd work till about 4:30, by which time Enoch was toast. I then caught up on emails after which I walked into town looking for supper. I struggled to find appealing gastronomic options until, one evening I stumbled across a night-market—and there it was, off to the right: O'Malley's! Oh, how marvelous, oh how wonderful! I perused the sybaritic menu at leisure, eventually settling on New Zealand pork chops. I was transported to 7th heaven and henceforth supped on pub fare while gazing languidly at a bustling oriental market.

Loy Krathong, a festival in honor of the Buddha and the goddess of water, saw Enoch, Susanne and myself by the river for a look-see. Swarms of celebrants, male and female, aged and juvenile, set little rafts the size of breakfast plates with lit candles fastened to them floating down the river. Long sticks protruding at acute angles from the river bank allowed the current to push the wee boats, some decorated with flowers and incense sticks, to the middle of the Ping to carry people's sins downstream. Others lit large cylindrical lanterns. About 70 cm by 1 meter and fueled by a burning mass, they operated on the same principle as hot air balloons. After sending one aloft you held your hands together, made a wish and followed your lantern's upward path. If you really wanted to make an impact you could buy a string of firecrackers from the monks and tie those to your lantern before releasing it, creating a spectacular type of slow-moving meteor effect. Hundreds of these lanterns filled the night sky; I found the spectacle sad, yet strangely beautiful. One got caught in a tree and set it on fire while an imbecile tourist deliberately set his ablaze before letting it go.

The flaming mass flew a dozen meters before crashing into the middle of an intersection, nearly setting alight a young couple on a moped.

There were several podiums along the river running various shows simultaneously. I watched a monk sporting a colorful diaper frenziedly beating a huge drum with knees, elbows and both ends of a stick and assumed the frenetic leaping and twisting was of religious significance, though my limited knowledge of Theravada Buddhism failed to make a connection. After absorbing it all I left the others, went home, drank a glass of chocolate milk, did a crossword puzzle and betook myself to bed.

Suddenly the relationship between Enoch and Susanne deteriorated. Sharp exchanges preceded her leaving in a huff. Then she refused to be in the same room with him, leaving me without a translator. That evening she knocked on my door and, obviously distraught, explained that Enoch was serenading her, picking her wildflowers, had bought her earrings and had tried to kiss her. Ah, oh... everything made instant sense.

The following day I took Enoch to O'Malleys and slowly, in halting English, he told me about his divorce two years earlier and of his sudden love for Susanne: "she godly woman, we very happy—maybe...", stringing each sentence together like beads on a string: she... she godly... she godly woman... she godly woman, we... she godly women, we very... etc. Slowly, spasmodically, the moonstruck fellow told me about the earrings and the kiss, his heart for the Lord and how it was possible to learn the mind of the Lord in these matters. Tears coursed down his tortured face as he was telling me all this. I offered to approach Susanne on his behalf. That mollified him.

There was, of course, nothing new I could tell her so we brainstormed reasons I could communicate back to him why she didn't think this relationship was right. I assigned her to the audio studio to help the sound technician synch the audio and video tracks. She also moved to different accommodations, which made Enoch churlish. He'd suddenly leave the set, lock himself in an unused room to engage in long, solo prayer sessions, leaving two cameramen, two sound technicians, a gaffer, the secondary actors and myself twiddling our thumbs, a situation which would have made Job irritable. It was time for another tete-a-tete. I grabbed my Chinese-English/English-Chinese dictionary (Google Translate did not yet exist) and took him out for another meal.

Enoch: "Why we not work team? God want us work team."

Peter: "You and Susanne two chemical. Chemical together is explosion. I keep chemical apart."

Enoch: "I very sad. God put flower in field."

Peter: "Many flower in God field..."

The conversation, one distinctly short on sparkling gaiety, continued in that vein for some time. He wanted the next day off to, as he put it unctuously, "do quiet think". All the while we were falling further and further behind. Even when we got going again he'd lock himself into a separate studio for long periods: "I not ready. I pray", forcing me to display monumental amounts of patience and self-control as I cajoled him back onto the set in my suavest manner.

One Thursday he informed me he would leave on Saturday. The lead cameraman didn't think we could complete all his scenes in the remaining day-and-a-half but I said he could leave on Saturday if he did as told on Friday. I canceled scenes meant to be taken in a computer lab and a garage and had a computer and a motorcycle engine brought to the studio instead. We managed to complete the remaining scenes, including one outdoors, for which I placed a small tape-recorder in a hat, pressed play, and clapped it on his head so he could repeat his lines.

I was glad to be done with the zany eccentric. Just as he couldn't leave Susanna alone, he couldn't let me be anymore either. Pretending an interest in the tormented emotional life of a lovelorn Chinese neurotic while trying to keep him focused on the next day's shoot was exhausting. The dark side, I was sure, had sought to undo the project but the Lord, keeping me utterly dependent on him, came through at critical moments to dispense appropriate dosages of grace.

Then, just as I was packing up, the country exploded. Things had been simmering for months, but now the knives were out as red-shirted populists fought yellow shirted monarchists in the streets. The Reds Shirts shut down the airport and, as someone at Thai Airlines affirmed, "you no leave Thailand". An American G.I. Joe (crew-cut, clean-shaven, army boots) who "worked in security" but spent inordinate amounts of time writing reports on a laptop at O'Malleys, told me the stand-off would continue until the government fell. Soon over a hundred-thousand people were stranded, with thousands added every day. G.I. Joe said the government was opening an information bureau for stranded tourists and gave me an address. I hoofed it over there, showed my passport and expired return tickets, was handed a slip of paper, told to move my belongings to room 1019 in the Empress Chiang Mai hotel and not leave the premises. The Ministry of Tourism would foot the bill.

Living in a top-tier hotel becomes tiresome quickly. The buffet, though large, consists of the same spread day in day out, the band plays the same 15 soft pop songs every lunch and supper, the same people wai and smile in the same, artificial way whenever you pass them.

The streets became increasingly violent. Every afternoon, however, I sneaked off to O'Malleys, which assumed the flavor of Rick's Café in Casablanca. G.I. Joe divulged that they operated a secret runway across the border in Laos and offered to fly me out from there but WEC's director put the kibosh on that. After a tumultuous week the airport re-opened. I snagged a flight to Bangkok and, surprise, surprise, they checked my luggage through to Istanbul. Hallelujah! Six weeks of a most peculiar adventure was half over. Filming the missionary Li Wei scenes would take place in the spring.

.

What struck me as odd, unique and oriental before appeared hohum three months later. My new lodging, a traditional teak wooden house on stilts with its own bathroom, air conditioner, double bed, cupboard and desk, was on a different level: I could

walk below it without hitting my head. Part of a compound
called The Juniper Tree, it was set among fragrant flowers,
beautiful trees, whirring cicadas, singing birds, tiny geckos
running erratically then stopping briefly to look around
quizzically, and black-winged chopsticks flitting about. There
was an outdoor pool, a rustic dining room with louvred
shutters, a small library, a lounge and prayer room.

The place was abuzz with missionaries and their offspring
from surrounding countries. Some came to have more babies,
some to holiday, others to attend a conference. One family,
newly deported from China, looked shell-shocked and a lonely
geezer latched on to me. I broke free and made for O'Malleys.
The political situation had stabilized, and Ken the proprietor
and the helpful spook were sitting on the veranda. It's always
good to meet old friends.

The man assigned to play Li Wei was a retired Chinese-
American with an impish streak and sparkly eyes. I recast him
as an older, experienced missionary sharing a life-time of
experiences with the younger generation. As before, we
recorded the audio files first. Although Johnson spoke fluent
English his Mandarin was poor, and he could not remember the
proper pronunciation he'd worked out with Susanne prior to
each paragraph. I had the technicians hook up a microphone to
his headset so she could feed him his lines one at a time. Soon
we'd found our stride. On the day we finished the audio
recordings the hard drive started knocking and they had not
made back-ups. I had them burn everything onto CDs. Next we
created two living rooms: missionary Li Wei's home in China
and his apartment in "Islamistan". We were rolling tape again!

The studio shut down during Songkran, a week of
pandemonium during which people throw buckets of water at
each other. The sponsors coughed up a ticket for Anna and she
joined me for that. I was dead tired. Directing, worrying about
props, the sets, the camera angles, acting (I had scripted myself
in as Mr. Ahmet, the language helper) had worn me out. While
I slumbered like a dormouse Anna chatted with the Juniper
Tree's wholesome clientele.

When I'd caught up on sleep we headed out. We got soaked, like everyone else. Then we sat cross-legged on a shelf in a low-ceilinged room with blood-red walls and forest-green carpet, ate steamed rice, fried bananas, fried chicken, curry, chilly, pork rind and cabbage while watching five or six musicians with whining strings and oriental drums accompany eight elegant dancing girls dressed in glistening silks. The Fingernail dance focused on the sinuous movements of fingernail extensions. The lights were dimmed for slow-tempo upper-body movements in which the girls gracefully waved lit candles. This was followed by the gentle sways of the Butterfly Dance, the Happy Dance, and various other stylized affairs whose names I have forgotten. Thai dancing is the opposite of Irish dancing, the former being mostly upper-body work, the latter legs-only.

We watched a herd of elephants stacking logs, dancing and playing the harmonica. One lifted Anna's hat from her head, then gently replaced it. Brows furled, eyes squinting, they painted colorful flowers, cypress trees, and self-portraits. It was amazing. Along with a belly-scratching German, his petite Thai escort, an Indian family and a young Italian couple we watched three monkeys (grade school monkey, middle school monkey and university monkey) do a weightlifting, basketball and bicycle routine so pathetic it was hilarious. Not far from the elephant show and the monkey school were the long-necks. For a fee camera-toting tourists can gape at pretty women with heads held aloft on grotesquely elongated necks supported by copper rings. We visited a silk factory, a jade factory, an oriental night market and ate at O'Malley's. We read books, ate meals we didn't cook, stepped into clothes someone else laundered, lounged around the pool and played Scrabble in our tree house. And then it was all over. She returned to Istanbul, leaving me with a wrinkled bed sheet, a light dip in the extra pillow and a kaleidoscope of memories. I loved her then and I love her now.

Johnson and I drove through the rugged Golden Triangle to Burma to renew our visas, and then we were rolling tape again.

I'd forgotten what shirt he'd worn for a particular scene and discovered that the tapes were all unlabelled; we had to spool through three or four before they found what I was looking for. We were back in business. Finally we got to the scenes in which Enoch does voice-overs. To my utter consternation the studio had wiped out all 25 of those audio files! That drive had got a virus, the technician decided to reformat it, couldn't remember what those particular files were, decided they were unimportant and wiped them out. And of course, in spite of my cajoling, no backups!

> "I can't help but think that this is just another one of Satan's fruitless little attempts to frustrate things, but that this will be another chance to see the Lord proving His ownership of this project."[338]

We recalled Enoch to re-record those audios during which time Susanna went into hiding. Then, with one day to spare, we were done! Twenty-four training films with their audio and video in perfect synch, each unit and scene clearly labeled to match my scriptures.

On the last day I went for a walk, turning left where I normally turned right, and found myself facing Queen Victoria gazing regally from an eight-foot pedestal clasping a scepter in one hand and a globe in the other. I pushed through a creaky gate and found myself wandering among the headstones of a neglected foreigners' cemetery. Some of the graves were ornate, others just a weathered piece of wood with a name and dates of birth and death in fading white or black. They were of missionaries, anthropologists, soldiers of fortune, rogues, paupers... Most were Anglo-Saxons. There was a sprinkling of French and German, a single Danish soldier and a freshly dug hole. Each an erstwhile adventurer, a world-traveler, a risk-taker, a story-teller who never made it back home to tell his tale, the shabby remains of their mortality forgotten in an untended grave far from home.

---

[338] Email to Anna, April 23, 2009.

I suddenly felt lonely, gutted, bone-weary, a stranger, a wanderer like those in the ground about me. I pushed through the creaky gate, hailed a conveyance to O'Malley's, sat near the window and ordered a valedictory fish and chips.

Postscript

By September of 2010 the DVD based missionary training series of which this project was a part had been handed to the leaders of seven different house church networks "who are very happy with it".[339] I was also informed that those networks represented some 30,000 home churches.

---

[339] Email from John Kayser, Sept. 14, 2010.

59

The Kids Grow Up

"By doubting we come to inquiry,
and by inquiring we perceive the truth."

Peter Abelard

. . .

WHEN ANNA SAID goodbye to Owen and Rita at Black Forst Academy. "She thought her heart would break—but it hasn't! God's strengthening power in answer to your prayers has been almost tangible."[340] Frequent emails describing new friends, the dorms' social interactions, school events and excellent report cards helped ease parental pains. Both kids recognized it was a privilege to be educated in that Christian-American bubble at the junction of Germany, France and Switzerland.

Rita, ever full of vitality, threw herself into music and sports. Owen enjoyed solitary hikes up hill and dale and was elected Student Body President. They would arrive at Christmas or for the summer months exhausted but satisfied, to return all too soon to their "insanely busy" lives.

As a coming-of-age present between their junior and senior years I took them on a trip, with them choosing the destination and doing the planning within strict budgetary restrictions. Owen opted for Cairo. I look wistfully at photographs of him sipping tea at Fardawis, the sweat beading on his happy face, fingering a tesbih at the sarcophagus of Ibn Tulun, arms crossed alongside the Sphinx, and partway up a Giza pyramid. We explored the great city's swarming, garbage-strewn alleys and markets, visited Al-Azhar, the Museum of Antiquities, that marvelous testimony to Christianity's enduring spirit the

---

[340] PL November-December 2004.

Mokattam Cave Church, and a raucous camel market somewhere in the desert. We motored through more desert to the Saqqara Necropolis, clambered up the side of the Red Pyramid then down a shaft into its inner chamber. We floated down the Nile and climbed the citadel. Owen shares both my romantic love for history and insatiable desire for knowledge. He looks fresh-faced in those pictures, yet grew up fast... He was wise beyond his years, preternaturally so.

Owen accepted an offer from McMaster, our hometown university, to do a double major in Philosophy and Political Science. On home leave that summer, we painted our Hamilton condo, scoured thrift stores and garage sales, spent time with my increasingly frail parents and visited supporting churches. To help the kids get going financially we established a "setting up for life" fund, a sum of money equivalent to four years of undergraduate tuition fees. Once spent they'd be on their own financially. We didn't have that much money in hand but figured it would become available as they needed it. All too soon we bade our son farewell and put Rita on a plane for Germany.

The summer after his freshman year Owen pressure-fried chicken for KFC, an activity so unsatisfying it convinced him he could do better reading books and winning scholarships. That strategy stood him in good stead right through to his PhD.

Rita threw herself back into life at boarding school until a heart rhythm disorder kept her from participating in sports. That hit her hard. The medication stopped working and Anna went to Germany when she was admitted to hospital for a heart procedure. There were complications. The initial diagnosis was confirmed but the needed procedure deemed too risky to be completed. She learned to live with the condition.

Interested in sun and fun, she chose Miami for her trip with dad. We settled into a boutique hotel in the bustling Art Deco district and sallied forth to accumulate memories of sunning on South Beach, people-watching, parrot-watching, hiking along the promenade, window shopping and returning to Big Pink for victuals.

Upon graduation she decided to study Bible and emergency medical training at Prairie, my old Alma Mater, but had to forgo the Bible bit to pass her EMT tests. In stellar MK fashion, she took things in stride when practicums didn't work out, moving into an abandoned trailer "to save tons of money". Upon eventually receiving her diploma she moved into our Hamilton condo with Owen, worked at a local coffee and doughnut joint and doggedly studied for her Ontario paramedic exams. Our hearts nearly broke when, after a brief furlough, we said farewell to her in that coffee shop. Her future was in the air and we had doubts about her spiritual wellbeing. She passed the exams and found work as a paramedic and in confined-space rescue work.

My mum died and dad became increasingly frail. My sister looked after him, allowing us to continue in missions. Anna asked him if he was assured of eternal life with Christ. "My girl," he replied, "I know the promises and they are good enough for me." Then he too died.

Upon graduation the university awarded Owen a fulsome scholarship to pursue a Masters in Philosophy. "Pray he will continue to walk in close fellowship with his Saviour as he reads extensively and thinks deeply about such issues as the nature of truth and ultimate reality."[341]

Unlike Owen, who was both intelligent and well-read in the humanities, Rita was merely intelligent, knocking off logic puzzles that stumped me. From the day she first asked me as a little girl how it was possible that we could be right and "all these nice people" wrong, she'd been a questioner. This was a trait I'd encouraged; I even taught a Hasat seminar on the art of asking questions. There is no hope, I maintained, for those who have no questions, and honest questions deserve honest answers. Rita would arrive home from boarding school with lists of questions which I then sought to answer to the best of my ability.

---

[341] PL September-October 2010.

While Owen had "increased opportunities to defend the Christian faith,"[342] experiences with self-styled believers who failed to live up to their calling combined with the siren call of the world led his sister to question the efficacy of Christian truth. She demanded Euclidian-like certitude before committing; the fact that historic realities do not share the same level of certainty as mathematics kept her from doing so. Like a puerile Descartes, she, with unregulated intelligence and typical vitality, doubted everything. She deconstructed apologetic works and arguments her brother and I fed her with razor-sharp logic while sinking ever deeper into a relativistic morass. "She is wrestling with some difficult spiritual truths,"[343] we wrote.

> "Peter has just finished teaching the Marriage and Family Life seminar. Did it go well? No, this one was a real struggle, not because Peter wasn't prepared or the students weren't intelligent or enthusiastic but because it coincided with a very difficult situation in our own little family. Rita's continued struggle with some difficult theological concepts has led to a deep crisis of faith. She is also recovering from a broken relationship... at times we have felt totally helpless... Please pray earnestly for her as she longs to reach a place where she can wholeheartedly love the Lord again."[344]

Our intercessions turned increasingly desperate: "God, do something!" Yet all the while she drifted further from us and back towards a boyfriend about whom we had grave misgivings. "Please continue to pray that the Spirit would enlighten her mind in her pursuit of truth and rekindle a love for Christ in her heart."[345]

.

---

[342] PL March-April 2011.
[343] Ibid.
[344] PL May-June 2011.
[345] July-August 2011.

January 20, 2012

Hey Riet,

... Why do I question the integrity of your "search for truth"? Because anytime the idea of a systematic, disciplined approach to a particular question that pertains to some critical aspect of Christianity is broached (textual issues, the person of Jesus Christ, the possibility of miracles, etc.) we soon reach a point where you shrug off actually coming to grips with the question on its own terms with simplistic sound bites the likes of: "since it took place a long time ago you cannot really know what happened"; "the events of the past are made of lots of probabilities added together, making the actual event in question even more improbable"; "since continental philosophers disagree with Owen's analytic approach to metaphysics Owen could be wrong and, that being the case, I don't need to take his analytic approach seriously"; "Islam has its experts. Are they all wrong?"; "Every field has its experts and they all disagree", etc.

Back in the Spring I offered to read with you, chapter by chapter, through some books dealing with the questions you were posing back then, to dialogue with you about those readings to, in effect, take you through those subjects as if through a college course. No response. Not that that matters anymore because subsequent dialogue has convinced me that your problem is not, in fact, intellectual but is a problem of the will... I do not think you really want to submit to that which isn't on your terms, including the need to submit to the rules of the discipline pertaining to the questions you are posing. You seem content to dabble in them on your own terms and with people of your own choosing, however actually ignorant of the subject in question these undoubtedly bright and interesting people may be...

There seem to be no real fixed points, no firm anchors in your life. That is, obviously, not true of us; we hold to a number of certainties, fixed points the nature of which you know all too well. You were raised on them. However, as you drift further and further from the fixed points on which you were raised your relationship with us will, of course, change. After all, there are things we don't approve of...

Please note that this does not in any way imply that I reject you. It simple means that I am not interested in engaging in a "search for truth" which takes place on your terms. If at some stage you are prepared to acquiesce to the demands of the field to which your questions belong let me know, and we can pick up this conversation.

Let me close by saying that in many ways I am really proud of you. You are a wonderful and winsome person, you are fun to be with, bright, spontaneous, hard-working, generous, a caring, loving daughter to us and sister to Owen... You are not a waffler. I deeply admire how, in spite of the odds, you managed to get your EMCA, how you have pulled yourself together after all you've been through, the way you have embraced your studies, your pro-active approach to finding work when out of a job, your dreams for the future... I am delighted to support you in these things, and want you to succeed in them!

Your ever loving, ever caring Dad

February 5, 2012

... However, the real question we need to wrestle with pertains to your place in our family. You, after all, have chosen to break loose from our family's values... We now live in two fundamentally different worlds. Mum and my core values begin at the cross, are lived in obedience

to the risen Saviour and end in resurrection life. Since everything of importance I would talk with you about are based on those values, which you have ditched, anything I say would be condemnatory. Hence I think it is better that I say nothing.

I will, of course, be happy to stand with you in things I believe in (as in education, career, etc.)... It also goes without saying that I will continue to intercede to the Lord for you, fully realizing that you may have to stray a lot further before coming back to the foot of the cross. When, eventually, you find yourself in that place I believe the transformation will be all the greater! Hallelujah!

Love, Dad

∙

On a brief visit to WEC's UK manor house God granted us a profound stimulus to faith. The building's top floor, undergoing renovations, was stripped to the studs. Light streamed through a window. Suddenly Anna heard a voice saying, "this is a work of construction." Those words would not leave her and she took them to mean that what God was doing in Rita's life would result in something beautiful—but not before things were stripped to the bare studs. We clung to that vision even when the divine deconstruction was so severe I told God that I wouldn't have the guts to do to my children what he did to his.

"We are deeply saddened by Rita's decision to walk away from Christ and return to a relationship with a non-Christian boyfriend. Please intercede for her and pray for great wisdom for us as parents. The Lord has strengthened us to believe that she will return to Christ one day... but may it be soon!"[346]

Separated by an ocean and a continent and feeling utterly impotent, desperation again crept into our prayers as we

[346] PL March-April 20212.

tracked her jumping around lopsided, like the confused movements of a knight in a losing game of chess. I told Anna that our intercessions had turned to foxhole prayers, full of panic, devoid of rest, and suggested we stop pleading until we could actively trust the Lord again. When we resumed praying for her a week or two later we were more at peace. "Rita still struggles with different aspects of the Christian faith. We feel we have done what we could and that now we must leave to the Lord that which we cannot do."[347]

Owen entered into the University of Toronto's PhD program. His first year was difficult. Already mentally fatigued, he was also emotionally drained. That summer he and I embarked on a recuperative road-trip through the mountains and canyons of Arizona and the deserts and mesas of New Mexico. In the mean time Rita, hurting from a second break-up with her boyfriend, remained "confused regarding the nature of faith and asks for prayer for real clarity."[348] Slowly, steadily, the Lord drew her back to himself. Slowly, steadily, she traversed the long, torturous road towards the recognition that Christian certainty is rooted in the relational.

Our prayers morphed from fearful intercession to being "deeply thankful to God for evidence of his ongoing work in her life."[349] She happily cruised around Ontario on her motorbike, dreamed of fostering troubled kids, enjoyed hair-raising safety and rescue jobs down storm pipes below the city of Toronto and high up factory smokestacks, then took her career to the next level by becoming a fire fighter. One spring she asked us to forward the following note to those who'd prayed for her:

"Thank you so much to all who have supported me, either through prayer or encouragement, during the past few years. I am still on a steep learning curve regarding what it means to be a Christian and have faith; perhaps that will always be the case. Despite this,

---

347 PL September-October 2011.
348 PL May-June 20212.
349 PL March 1, 2015.

I can now testify to the joys of a mind filled with peace that passes understanding, a transformative degree of trust and an awesome church community."[350]

Somehow she metamorphosed into a beautiful, balanced, mature, loving, capable woman who loves the Lord, his church, and hurting people, and who gives us great joy. I cannot explain the divine process that effected this transformation other than that she had an advocate with God the Father, Jesus Christ the righteous, who joined his perfect intercessions with those of our many friends along with our pathetic cries (1 John 2:1).

Owen, meanwhile, plodded on. He spent a semester at Yale, started lecturing, and "asks for prayer for mental stamina and, more importantly, that he will further cultivate the spiritual disciplines of the Christian life."[351] He'd show up on our doorstep whenever he attended some philosophy conference in Europe.

"The kids... need wisdom and fortitude as they interact respectively with philosophy professors who scoff at the idea of the existence of a personal God, and with rough alpha-male fire-fighters... We are much encouraged that both take their faith seriously."[352]

[350] PL. 3 May. 2014.
[351] PL 4 January 2016.
[352] PL 3 January 2018.

60

The End of An Era

"Man appears for a little while to laugh and weep,
to work and play, and then to go and make
room for those who shall follow him."

A.W. Tozer

• • •

WE RECALL THOSE FINAL bustling years in Turkey with
fondness, although the country moved in confusing, even
contradictory directions socially and politically. The low-grade
war with the Kurds ground on while the "Malatya trial" of those
who murdered our Tilmann and his two friends exposed a web
of lies and conspiracies. It was as if the missionary community
and not the accused were on trial.

> "Unlike the rest of society, these issues do not increase
> our blood temperature: we simply stand back, pray and
> anticipate that our sovereign Lord will use it all to draw
> unlikely people to Himself and build up His church."[353]

While Erdoğan's heavy-handed regime kept the lid on a pot
simmering with tribal and religious hates and resentments,
untold numbers of Syrian refugees fled the twin brutalities of
Assad autocracy and Islamic fundamentalism to flood the
streets of Istanbul begging or looking for menial jobs. And
every year we strove afresh with the bloated bureaucracy
hoping, praying, for yet another, ever costlier, extension to our
residence permits. Life became expensive. "We are tightening
our belts. Fish here is a lot cheaper than beef, so Anna has
discovered some great fish recipes!"[354]

---

[353] PL March-April 2008.
[354] PL November-December 2008.

Mission agencies do not publish their disconcerting attrition rates. Failure to master the langua-culture, the resultant inability to make national friends, spiritual dryness stemming from an inability to feed oneself spiritually in the absence of a vibrant church life, moral failure, doctrinal ambivalence and the low response rate all contribute to the problem. Regarded as experienced veterans, we served as "big brother/big sister" to some of the newly arrived, helping them settle into life, language study and, hopefully, into ministry. Even so we could not stem the outflow.

And yet, slowly, steadily, the Turkish evangelical church grew until we were almost 100 small fellowships. To celebrate the anniversary of the martyrdom of our three brothers Istanbul's churches met jointly for worship and fellowship. Praising God as a larger group proved such a blessed experience that church leaders organized more such events. I addressed over 100 young adults at the first inter-church youth rally in Istanbul, an unimaginable event when we first arrived 25 years earlier. "The struggles and harassment continue but, praise God, there is growth!"[355] That youth rally became an annual three-day retreat to which we were invited more than once.

> "We had a wonderful weekend as Papa and Mama to 80 Young Adults from the whole Marmara region. The Spirit took hold of Peter's messages and pressed them home. Wish you could have seen a new Muslim background believer worshipping with all his heart and boldly wearing a T-shirt saying 'Now I belong to Jesus Christ'".[356]

As the church grew it became bolder. One Christmas it held an open-air service, albeit in the city's most liberal, easy-going district. This was followed by a public ad campaign. Although the bus ads were removed after 10 days, countless people saw it.

Every autumn a fresh cohort of enthusiastic students attended Hasat classes, and we teachers were in ever greater

[355] PL November-December 2008.
[356] PL November-December 2011.

demand. My regular stops were Samsun, where Pastor Orhan soldiered on with his 24/7 bodyguard in tow, as well as Antalya, Ankara, Izmir and Antioch. One of my most popular courses was on the book of Revelation. The tiny, hard-pressed community of believers quickly grasped the big picture, were sobered by the reality that upheavals in the Middle East might increase as we approach Christ's return, but were encouraged that God would preserve and eventually reward His church. "A persecuted church rejoices greatly in their glorious future."[357]

With the passage of time, however, travelling around Istanbul crammed into overheated subways, buses or tramways became increasingly problematic. Though Anna's greying hair sometimes secured her a seat, the journey across the vast metropolis to the Hasat office wearied both of us. The things in which I was heavily involved, like securing legal status, acquiring a building and setting up a Masters' level program had all, by God's grace, been accomplished, and with the increase in Turkish teachers Hasat was in good hands. Anna had catalogued and shelved a thousand books, organized the wealth of articles that had been translated over the years, overseen the translation of various theological tomes, and had plodded on with the error-prone typesetter. She'd also served as team treasurer, ran the household, made sure I made it to my next engagement without forgetting anything, and served countless meals to numerous people.

We informed Hasat that I would step down from the leadership team in two years time. It was time to make room for younger people. The ten years we served with Hasat had been our happiest years of ministry to date. We had no idea what we would do next...

When Cornerstone, WEC's missionary training college in The Netherlands, invited us to join them we accepted. Training the next generation of missionaries was, we felt, a wonderful way to cap a missionary career.

■ ■ ■

---

[357] PL May-June 2010.

Istanbul, 29ᵗʰ June, 2014

Dear Friends,

I'm sad. In fact, this is my saddest birthday ever. A couple of days ago I walked around our lovely Hasat premises for the last time, said a quiet farewell to our closest colleagues and walked out feeling really down. Last week the Hasat family had put on a lovely dinner for us, presented us with a beautiful picture album and said all kinds of nice things about us, but the finality of handing over the keys and closing the door hit me hard.

The farewells are not over yet. Tomorrow will be our final day in church. We love that little group; they have stood with us through some difficult days, and we've stood with them. God has used them in our lives and us in theirs. It's hard not to feel sad.

Anna tells me that feeling sad right now is healthy. Imagine, she says, if we were happy to leave! That would mean that relationships were broken, the ministry was dysfunctional or that we were running from something. No, we are sad because, by God's grace, we are finishing well. Hasat is in good shape: a united team, a clear vision, legal status, financially stable and a wide acceptance by the Turkish church. And although our little church is very small we recently appointed two godly young men as elders. Finishing well may be sad but, as Anna says, it's a healthy sadness...

61

Goodbye To All That

"If we consider created reality as a whole we discover at its core not only a rational pattern but a meaningful one that is good, and this, too, is a sign of the divine."

St. Bonaventure

. . .

I SLEPT, DEAD to the world, till late morning, and again after lunch. In between I sat for hours, days on end, on a wooden bench staring over the guest house's ramshackle rose garden and across an Umbrian valley to the green serrated hills rising in the east. Drained physically and emotionally, I could not focus on anything. Reading was too much effort. Making simple decisions—like what I wanted for supper—was difficult. Anna prayed and waited. Every so often she'd sit quietly beside me to hold my hand.

Unlike the depression I slipped into after the Gulf War, I was not troubled. Not joyful, mind you—that would return later— just very tired. And relieved. Tired and relieved because, by God's grace, we had finished well.

Irrespective of their many years of faithful service, what local people remember is how missionaries finish. We wanted our testimony to remain unsullied for, after our salvation, it is our most precious possession. Although those final weeks in Turkey had been exhausting, we left with all relationships intact and no loose ends left dangling. Hopefully, people would remember us fondly.

I was also relieved to be out of the Middle East. I was suddenly tired of that proud, belligerent, insecure world. This surprised me as we had long since come to grips with some of its languages and cultures, had made deep friendships both in and outside the church and enjoyed years of fruitful ministry. Now that we were out, however, I realized how the prevailing oppressiveness had begun to weigh on me. I was tired of wrestling with a backward-looking civilization which, courtesy of an industrious Sunni scribbler of the Middle Ages called Al-Ghazali, holds that Allah's will is absolute, the sole, direct cause of all events. All things, so the imam stated in *The Incoherence of the Philosophers,* must be attributed directly to the unbound will of God, not to the normal rules of cause-and-effect. And now, over 900 years later, I was tired of a world which had become inimical to reason, questioning, and innovation, tired of an authoritarianism which discourages free, rational inquiry, where scientific development is moribund and cultural cross-fertilization viewed with suspicion. I was tired of a world in which busy fellows with bushy beards in madrassas gulled the faithful into believing that the Qur'an was co-eternal with God and contained the final answers to all possible questions, and who insisted on imposing their pestiferous lies and archaic notions on everyone else. I was tired of a world in which politics and religion leaned on each other for legitimacy. I was glad to leave a world which views women, Jews and us Christians as second-class citizens or, worse, as scapegoats, and which whips up fear of death for homosexuals, blasphemers and adulterers.

I was tired of a fatalistic anti-intellectual bravado which stifles individual effort, devalues personal freedom, restricts open communication and where human life is cheap. Tired of a world composed of subjects, powerful leaders and enemies. Tired of a world at the whim of a few wealthy families. Tired of despotic governments with their spies and informants and their aptitude for violence, where the rule of law "hung between the lips of one man", as a Turkish friend put it. Though all people are assuredly created equal and in the image of God—there is no hierarchy of races—the cultures they have manufactured, as every refugee and immigrant realizes, are far from equal. I came to see my Muslims friends as victims of their religion and respective cultures.

As I rested those ten days and let the relief of being out from under all that wash over me, the body responded. Tense muscles relaxed, breathing slowed, shoulders dropped. My whole self sighed repeatedly, releasing pent-up tensions and stresses, and the knot in the stomach slowly loosened.

We eventually ventured into a world which had embraced the Renaissance, the Enlightenment and the scientific revolution. We drove to Orvieto, anchored to its volcanic plug down in the valley, to sip lattes on the piazza before its magnificent cathedral and munch pizza at sidewalk cafes. We walked along the shores of Lake Bolsena and hiked up to Bagnoregio, the birthplace of the Medieval theologian Bonaventure. Unlike Al-Ghazali and his ilk, he and his fellow scholastics integrated revelation and reason, and sought new syntheses when the two appeared to move in divergent directions. They held that faith was rooted in grace and supported by reason flowing from the very nature of the God who'd created a wonderful universe for us to explore, measure, and chronicle its causes and effects.

The vagaries and vicissitudes of 800 years of Western history had failed to extirpate that intellectual heritage. Somehow it survived the bloodletting of the Thirty Years Religious War, the French Revolution's anti-clericalism and guillotine, Bonapart's megalomania, the senseless slaughter of Anglicans and Lutherans at the Somme, Marxism's crushing bipolarism, Stalin's Orwellian dystopia, Fascism banal wickedness, Nazism dehumanizing barbarism and the Holocaust's industrialization of diabolical evil so great not even the apostle John saw it coming. It had survived the misplaced dogmatism of the Inquisition, Enlightenment superciliousness, Darwinist disdain, cultural relativism, structuralism's straightjacket, post-modernism's fragmentation and Wokism's mendacious re-writing of history. MENE MENE TEKEL U PARSIN. Each had been weighed in balances and found wanting.

After a decade of ministry in an oppressive society I looked forward to re-engaging with a civilization which, as a result of brave theologians' celebration of grace and reason, and of a covenant-keeping God and an incarnate Christ, values the worth of the individual, encourages critical thinking, respects the inquisitive spirit, and where politics and religion are distinct and separate. Hallelujah! What a relief!

Part 7

The Long Recessional: 2014-

"You are old, father William," the young man cried,
"And pleasures with youth pass away.
And yet you lament not the days that are gone;
Now tell me the reason, I pray."

"In the days of my youth," father William replied,
"I remember'd that youth would not last;
I thought of the future, whatever I did,
That I never might grieve for the past."

"You are old, father William," the young man cried,
"And life must be hast'ning away;
You are cheerful and love to converse upon death;
Now tell me the reason, I pray."

"I am cheerful, young man," father William replied,
"Let the cause thy attention engage;
In the days of my youth I remembered my God!
And He hath not forgotten my age."

Robert Southey

62

Cornerstone Life

"Apply yourself wholly to the text;
apply the text wholly to yourself."

Johann Albrecht Beugel

...

ONE WINDOW OVERLOOKED a meadow with a small horse barn, the other an apple orchard. A book on the coffee table helped us identify the range of flora and fauna all around. The robins, warblers, orioles, woodcocks and turtledoves flitting about the trees, the rabbits gamboling among the greenery, and the melancholic nag gazing dolefully over the top of her Dutch door were wonderful; the grey skies and frequent rains less so.

Cornerstone, once a rambling nunnery in a comatose Dutch village, rang with the excited buzz of enthusiastic young adults from Germany, France, Switzerland, England, Wales, Korea, Australia, the US and The Netherlands. Community life was part of its ethos, and most of the sixty-some residents lived cheek by jowl in the main building. The two-minute walk from our tiny apartment across the courtyard to the main building provided us with just enough distance to stay sane. We ate the main meal together and everyone pitched in to run the place.

We were, once again, on steep learning curves. Anna figured out where to shop, furnished our new home and got her mind around myriads of other details, including her new responsibilities as guest services manager. I got us registered with the government, obtained health insurance, opened a bank account, got a Dutch driver's licence, purchased a used Renault, got cell phones and an internet hookup. Then I drafted four Theology courses and, later, two courses on Missions as well as Introductions to the Old and New Testaments. Courses were modular, each one lasting a week or two. When not teaching I was grading or prepping for the next course.

Most students were eager young professionals. All had spurned wealth and status, homes and jobs to train for full-time missionary work. They represented a wide range of denominations, levels of Bible knowledge and theological understanding; some "simply loved Jesus" while others held tightly to notions they grew up with which might not actually be biblical. The fact that, year upon year, the Holy Spirit continued to draw people to the cross of Christ—sometimes in very dramatic ways—and then generate deep desires in them to give their all to the Saviour and come to us for training was profoundly heartening.

I loved teaching the great gospel doctrines. We explored how they were understood in the course of church history and then grounded everything in the Scriptures. We delved into the concepts of inspiration, the doctrine of the Trinity, the attributes of God, creation, human nature and the fall into sin, the person and work of Jesus Christ, the cross and salvation, the person and work of the Holy Spirit, sanctification, the nature and mandate of the church and final judgment. God's Spirit seemed particularly present when we applied Paul's teachings in Romans 6 and 12 on breaking the power of besetting sin. I wanted them to leave well-grounded, with a balanced appreciation of what really matters, understanding how that can be transformative and why they can be sure of its validity irrespective of culture and context. In the missions courses we covered the Biblical basis for missions, the nature of hell, the history of missions, contextualization, business as mission, urban missions, money and missions and contemporary issues in mission. Seeing students well established in the faith and equipped to confront the questions posed by other religions or by the irreligious thrilled me.

Anna dealt with bookings and accommodations for guest lecturers, chapel speakers, visiting parents, prospective students, board members, volunteers, conference and seminar registrants, college reunions, WEC's annual field conferences and the "Explore Mission" weekends for young people. She was also responsible for grading students' comments on missionary speakers and regularly presented various ethnic groups— Kurds, Basques, North Koreans, Kosovars, the Bhutanese, Emiratis, the Turkmen of Central Asia—to the student body, reminding us of the injunction to "declare God's glory among the nations, his marvellous deeds among all peoples" (Psalm 96:3), and to prompt intercessory prayer for the spiritually lost.

We were assigned seven or eight mentorees whom we prepared for their internships and debriefed upon their return. Every spring they'd sally forth to their placements around Europe, the Middle East and Asia, to put into practice what they had learned in the classroom. Six weeks later they'd drift back, bursting to tell of being pushed out of their comfort zones and feeling stretched to their limits, about the frustration of not knowing the language, about stomach upsets, about new and, at times, disconcerting, insights about themselves, about the power of prayer and, above all, about the Lord's enabling grace and how they had experienced him in new ways. We'd listen to stories of protection, provision, guidance, of how they rejoiced over individuals touched by the power of the gospel, how they grieved over the unreached and the hard of heart, how they'd sought to minister to the downtrodden and how they had learned from their trials and errors.

> "The... students in our group have been in parts of Asia which are barely reached with the gospel. The couple who lived through the earthquake in Nepal will need special care. One guy needs direction in a relationship and the other girl needs grace to be single. The Lord has knit our hearts to these seven. They are our 'little flock'. We want to watch over them, serve them, and be an example to them."[358]

---

[358] PL May 7, 2015.

We also sought to help them discern what the Lord would have them do post-graduation: where to serve, in what kind of ministry and with which agency? Where would their support come from? How would all this affect their kids' education?

"Pray for discernment and gentleness in all our involvement with the students, whether that be in the classroom, the dining room, around our coffee table, or on walks along the dike. We long to be good models to these young people preparing to serve the Lord in long-term, cross-cultural ministry."[359]

Every December 5, at Sinterklaas, our Kenyan colleague would be offended by St. Nick's "Black Peter" companion, a Dutchman in blackface who threatened to stuff bad children into a jute sack and haul them off to Spain. Every July graduation rolled around: fifteen one year, twenty another, to disperse around the globe as career missionaries. Exhausted but satisfied, the staff would tie up loose ends and take a well-deserved holiday for all too soon a new cohort of eager missionary hopefuls would arrive to raise the decibels in the dining room.

---

[359] PL January 3, 2018.

63

Of Students and Staff

"The Protestant work ethic finds its application in many contexts in the twenty-first century. Perhaps the most obvious is the phenomenon of 'faith-based activism': religious groups using their faith both as a platform and a guiding principle for social engagement and voluntary work."

Alistair McGrath

. . .

FOR THE TWO years our mentorees spent with us we journeyed with them, offering a listening ear, general pastoral care and, without telling them what to do, seeking to coax them towards realizing their God-given potential. We encouraged them to take radical steps of faith with discernment and in fellowship with their home churches, offered pre-marital advice, marital counselling and tips on raising kids cross-culturally.

> "Some struggle with the pressure of assignments, local ministry and practical work. Some are challenged to think wider than their own, very strict denominational constraints as they prepare to work with an inter-denominational mission. One has little home church support and another is coming to terms with his calling to a very difficult country. A mother wonders how she will cope with small children when overseas. Pray God will give us 'the wisdom that comes from above' as we seek to help each one of them."[360]

---

[360] PL November 11, 2016.

We met on a weekly basis to share, pray and eat a meal in our tiny living room, while one-on-one times involved lots of coffee and hikes along a nearby dike. The German couple learned to live jammed together with the rest of the Cornerstone community, the English couple figured out where the Lord wanted them to serve, the single French guy wondered about joining staff, the Korean pastor needed to be humbled, his wife required gentle encouragement and the single Swiss girl dating the Dutch cook scrutinized our marriage. We enjoyed their youthful zeal and appreciated their myriad questions about everything and anything pertaining to Christian life and service. When particular needs or concerns arose mentoring could be very time-consuming, yet also most rewarding. During end-of-year interviews we touched on every area of their lives and were encouraged with their openness, the evidence of spiritual maturity, and an increased preparedness for overseas missions. "They are not perfect, but then neither are we."[361]

As student numbers grew the need for more long-term and, preferably, younger staff members grew apace. This problem kept us on our knees for finding suitable people willing to work without a regular salary was not easy. Every year we had to trust the Lord afresh for teachers, maintenance workers and kitchen and household staff. At one point we were so desperate that we took time off work every Wednesday to pray. "After a morning of prayer which focussed on this need our growing sense of desperation turned to one of confident dependency."[362]

The increasingly heavy work load began to take its toll, not least on Anna. The principal, a seasoned saint, recognizing her workload was too heavy, reduced her responsibilities and gave her a desk away from the bustle of the open-plan main office. "Pray for discernment and courage when we need to say 'No' – not easy when we are short-staffed."[363] Anna also suffered from periodic episodes of intense pain and immobility due to bone

---

[361] PL July 2, 2015.
[362] PL July 8, 2016.
[363] PL January 3, 2015.

degeneration in her lower back. "Pray for good results from physiotherapy, and that she may experience the Lord's grace and growth in Christ-likeness through this ongoing trial."[364]

The most immediate need from one year to the next was for cooks. They never lasted more than a year, yet someone always showed up at the last minute. One year a Swiss girl dished up plates of gnocchi, another year a robust Italian woman doled out piles of pasta. Another year was carnivore heaven as our man was an expert on the barbeque. Meat was less evident with the Italian pastry chef, though we enjoyed trays of dainty baked goods. That individual, a true Romeo who spoke neither Dutch nor English, managed to woo one of our students, a girl who spoke both those languages but no Italian. Once, when things were particularly dire, we were challenged by Luke 11:8 to pray with shameless audacity:

"If we were not confident in the Lord's provision we would be panicking—five full-time staff are moving on, and there is, as yet, no one to replace them. We boldly hold on to the promise that those who hope in the Lord will never be put to shame (Psalm 25:3). Pray with us for new teaching and managerial staff."[365]

Instead, a volunteer pulled out due to an undiagnosed illness, two potential staff couples fell through and Anna had more episodes of acute lower back pain. "The final blow came last week when our kitchen and household supervisor was diagnosed with cancer."[366]

We canceled all business meetings to devote ourselves to prayer. As we waited before the Lord we were encouraged by our unity and depth of fellowship, and ascertained that there was no "sin in the camp" hindering us. We recognized that it is normal that a place which trains young people to take the gospel to unreached places will, inevitably, be subject to Satanic opposition. We renewed our trust in the Lord and continued to

[364] PL September 5, 2015.
[365] PL May 2, 2016.
[366] PL November 11, 2016.

wait expectantly while praying for sustaining grace and a joyful spirit as we soldiered on until the Lord saw fit to provide. Then, wham: two full-time staff members and a volunteer had to be relieved of their responsibilities due to burn-out, and a faculty member took extended compassionate leave due to the sudden death of both parents. We were dangerously overstretched. We again set aside extra time to pray for replacements. At long last the Lord came through. Out of the blue we received several applications. Although one proved to be a dud, the others, along with a number of local volunteers, helped lift the burden. That autumn the staff room was almost full, and with younger faces. "We praise God for answering our persistent, sometimes desperate, prayers last year for more staff."[367]

---

[367] PL September 2, 2017.

64

Some Theological Convictions

"Anyone who has been to foreign lands longs to return to his own native land... We regard Paradise as our native land."

St. Cyprian

...

I HAVE IMBIBED a lot of Bible commentaries, Protestant theologies and church histories. Think of the three contemporaries Gerhardus Vos, Lewis Sperry Schafer and Louis Berkhof. Then there were A.W. Tozer and his contemporary, Cornelus Van Til, born in the same village as myself. I read Watchman Nee, Jacquis Ellul, Francis Schaeffer, whom I devoured, Carl Henry, Kenneth Scott Latourette, whose *History of Christianity* I read repeatedly, Leon Morris, John Stott, D.A. Carson, Alec Motyer, George Eldon Ladd, J.I. Packer, Millard Erickson, Wayne Grudem, Norman Geisler, Alvin Plantinga, Walter Kayser, Gordon Fee, R.C. Sproul, John Frame and such pastor/teachers as James Montgomery Boice and Ray Stedman, from both of whom I drew heavily when prepping sermons. Then there were my contemporaries, men like Roger Olson, whose histories of Christian theology I read repeatedly, Alister McGrath and Michael Horton, just to name some major influences. Most everything perused was at the pastoral, non-specialist level; not being conversant with the Biblical languages, the original sources were beyond my ken.

Still, I learned from each while forging my own theological convictions, initially via negation. I learned to disagree with the dispensationalism of the dispensationalists, the theonomy of the theonomists, the baptism and ecclesiology of the paedobaptists, the eschatology of the a- and post-millenialists, the nature of the will of the free-willers and, conversely, the absolute divine omnicausality of the hard Calvinists. As I read and ruminated my convictions lined up with classic evangelicalism.[368] However three unconventional theologians and a powerful experience led me to adopt a particular approach to Christian sanctification, forge a more nuanced position on the use to which God puts his divine sovereignty, develop a lofty regard for the church, and conceptualize the non-relationship between it and the state.

Dallas Willard wrote much about retraining the body by embracing solitude, silence, Bible study, prayer, service and worship. Do that, he advised, and you will eventually start doing the right things, the Christ-like things. It may feel artificial at first, but the physical retraining through the steady application of these disciplines will, he assures, lead to victory over sin and the exaltation of Christ in the body. Then—and this is important to him—the disciplines themselves become pleasant, metamorphosing into a "conversational relationship with God".[369] I sought to apply his teachings and experienced something of their truth. Still, something was missing, something pertaining to that elusive Pauline concept of identifying with Christ in his death and resurrection. The meaning of this was forced upon me during a retreat in a Benedictine monastery.

The cell assigned me contained an outsized crucifix. I found the dominating wooden Christ, with its twisted, near-naked body, the sunken-cheeked face with its agonizing expression, the nail-pierced hands and feet and the gash between the emaciated ribs, off-putting. I was about to remove the artifact from the wall and place it face-first into a corner when, suddenly, a startling impression, an utterance in my head, halted me in mid-motion. "Peter," it asked, "why does that crucifix irritate you so...? That's you on that cross!"

I looked afresh at the crucified Christ and considered the implications of that utterance. Then, quite abruptly, the apostle's teachings about Christians being united with Christ,

---

[368] See my book *Theology 101*, Alev Books, 2023.
[369] See, for instance, his books *The Divine Conspiracy* and *The Spirit of the Disciplines: Understanding How God Changes Us*.

being one with him in his death, burial and resurrection so they could live life to God's glory, made sense. When Christ was crucified, I was crucified with him! When Joseph of Arimathea and Nicodemus took his lifeless body from the cross, they took me down as well and placed us together in that cave. And on the third day we both rose to newness of life! All it takes is me "counting" (NIV), simply "considering" (ESV), myself as having gone through that process of death, burial and resurrection with him. On the basis of that act of identification "I am now alive to God in Christ Jesus", from which faith position I can rightly "offer every part of myself" to God as "an acceptable living sacrifice" for him to use "as an instrument of righteousness" (Rom. 6:13-14).

Ever since my devotional routine often includes visualizing Christ and me hanging together on that cross, us being taken down and buried together and then being raised to newness of life. Thereupon I "offer the members of my body as a living sacrifice" (Rom 12:1). I start at the top: "Lord, my brain is at your service today. Give me wisdom and discernment. Here too my eyes and ears—let me be careful what I look at and listen to." I work my way down, past hands and reproductive organs to my feet. Since the cancer I include my prostate and bones as well; it's all handed to him for the day, for him to utilize as he sees fit. This oft-repeated act of devotion transformed my Christian walk for, as Willard promised, frequent physical repetition gradually retrains the believer to delight in the path of righteousness. Now I do not worry about long-term victories over particular sins; my concern is the immediate, overseeable present. Tomorrow I'll count myself dead, buried and risen with Christ afresh and rededicate the parts of by body to him for that day's service so that "Christ is exalted in my body" (Phil. 1:20) all over again for that particular day.

∎

Stanley Hauerwas and William Willimon were two Duke University profs with whom I do not have much in common theologically—with one great exception. In 1989 they wrote a short treatise entitled *Resident Aliens: Life in the Christian Colony*[370] in which the two Wesleyans juxtaposed their bleak assessment of western society and historic Christendom with a vision of the church as a colony of unassuming disciples in hostile territory. The colony's values are shaped elsewhere, receives its directions from beyond and invites others to join it, but does not join them. It is confident of its ultimate victory, not because of its own innate strength but because it identifies with a kingdom bigger and stronger than itself.

This liberating analogy—a mere elaboration of the apostle Peter's insistence that Christians should count themselves aliens and strangers in the world—kept me from focussing overmuch on bettering the planet or from salvaging the West's erstwhile Christian consensus. I began viewing social and political developments with disinterested interest, much as I might watch a play: though interesting, it does not fundamentally affect how I live life. News broadcasts became mere background to the main event, to wit, God acting in judgement and salvation—events often difficult to disentangle as God draws sinners to himself, sees them steadily transformed into Christlikeness and playing the role he assigned them in his colony. The model allowed me to embrace that outsider status of which I was so keenly aware at times.

The beauty of the analogy is that it works in virtually every context. Teaching believers in the Middle East that they were now outsiders, citizens of a different world, aliens living temporarily in a foreign land whose values they no longer shared, made sense to them. Christ died for this colony, I taught, so let us live for it. As outsiders we were not expected to have the answers to the problems facing society nor expected to be agents of social, economic or cultural betterment. We didn't belong. Our loyalty lay elsewhere. We were to stay in tune with

---

[370] Hauerwas, S. & Willimon, W. *Resident Aliens: Life in the Christian Colony*. Abington Press, Nashville TN. 1990.

developments in our true home, heaven, and with what king Jesus was accomplishing in and through his colony.

The model also influenced my take on divine sovereignty and spiritual warfare. Events outside the colony—Satan's domain[371]—may be random, absurd and chaotic; to those within it they are not, as Paul affirmed in Romans 8:28, *"And we know that in all things God works for the good of those who love him, who have been called according to his purpose."* In short, all that occurs to the divine colony is designed to glorify the King, sanctify and strengthen us colonists and add to our numbers—much to the chagrin of despot Satan.

Years later, when conservative Christian acquaintances responded atavistically to the rapid social changes of the 2020s by embracing theonomism, the model again stood me in good stead. Though I too bemoaned the passing of Christian influence on public life in the Western context (and what a glorious historical anomaly that era was), it enabled me to remain outside the political dogfights of suddenly combative and abrasive pastors and elders—though at times I longed to shake them and shout, "Stop your political posturing! Let the measure of evil God permits the nation reach its tipping point.[372] Let him bring low the proud, punish those who kill the innocent, and raise his hand against those who raise theirs against his own![373] Stop trying to salvage Babylon; her demise occasions applause in heaven![374] Come out of her!" But I kept my peace knowing that nothing I'd say would make a whit of difference.

---

[371] 2 Cor. 4:4; Eph. 3:10, 6:12; 1 John 5:19.
[372] Genesis 15:13-16.
[373] See, for instance, Nahum 3:1-4, etc. Also Genesis 12:1-3 compare with 1 Peter 2:9.
[374] Revelation 18-19:5.

65

The Little Drummer Boy

"I was with book, as a woman is with child"

C.S. Lewis

. . .

BACK IN MIDDLE SCHOOL I'd look dreamily out the classroom window and fancy going up north, to a little cabin somewhere, and write. That urge to write never left. As a result I have patiently borne varied unsolicited appraisals of my scribbling, and even of the fact that I put pen to paper at all.

Early in our marriage Anna's idea of missionary work pertained to the immediate spiritual and socio-economic needs of people, not to writing. Penning prayer letters was good, inasmuch as it was necessary, as were write-ups for Yeni Yaklaşım, but when I wrote for the now defunct *Middle East International* she balked. Those with an elevated interest in the immediate concerns and feelings of people, I learned, may not appreciate the uninspired written word as much as I do. For me writing was a necessary crutch and remains an irresistible urge. When there was nothing to show for one's labours at the end of the day, the week, the month, banging on the old Remington and, later, a keyboard, provided satisfaction, a sense of accomplishment. It let me hold something tangible before others. Anna came to accept me as I am, and this too contributed to me becoming a happy human. I have, however, received miscellaneous other criticisms over the years.

"Real experts have written much better books on your subjects."

This zinger was aimed at my non-fiction. I believed there was value in restating consequential stuff for different audiences.

The Fall of Christendom and the Rise of the Church[375], penned to help the kids come to grips with a world they were about to enter, traced the marginalization of Christianity in western society. I'm not sure if it helped them, but others maintain they were blessed, challenged or educated. The Turkish translation, entitled *The Myth of the Christian West*[376], proved surprisingly popular, establishing me for a brief period as a Christian intellectual among that country's tiny evangelical community. I also doubt if those making the allegation have read *Protestant Missionaries to the Middle East: Ambassadors of Christ or Culture.*[377] My doctoral thesis, it made a little-known, now difficult-to-ignore connection between the missionary movement and the Armenian genocide. *Theology 101*[378], a restatement of classic evangelical teaching with supporting Bible verses written out in full, was critiqued for not contributing anything new. The point, however, was to encourage people to "seek the old paths, which is the good way, and to walk therein, so they find rest for their souls" (Jeremiah 6:16). Some missionaries find it a useful tool, those who struggle with lengthy prose find it helpful, and the Arabic translation is used as a textbook in the Middle East.

"What's the point? You hardly sell any books. No one reads 'em!"

That, sadly, is true for most authors. Still, *Letter From Kurdistan*[379] went through two printings and my Kurdish grammar[380] was a timely hit. Prior to the first Gulf War there was so little interest in the Kurds that publishers did not think the manuscript was economically viable. Convinced otherwise, I self-published it under the imprint Alev Books—a fortuitous decision as the Gulf War raised the profile of that hard-pressed people tremendously. Every mission group, military mission

---

[375] WEC Canada, Hamilton, ON. 2006.
[376] *Hrıstiyan Batı Efsanesi*, Gerçeğe Doğru Kitaplar, Istanbul. 2007.
[377] ALEV Books Ancaster, ON. 2008.
[378] ALEV Books, Ancaster, ON. 2023.
[379] WEC Publications, Bulstrode, Gerrards Cross, U.K. 1992.
[380] *A Basic Course in Modern Kurmanji*. ALEV Books.

and aid organization to the region must have purchased a
bundle. A Turkish grammar[381] followed, but it flopped. I don't
know how its Armenian translation fared.

In any case, it is not necessarily the number of people who
read books but the nature of those who do which makes a
difference. Take *The Essence and Implications of Missio Dei*[382].
Cornerstone, taking the apostle Paul as its model for missions,
focused on evangelism, church planting and 'making disciples'.
Influenced by a sunnier view of the natural man and embracing
a wider concept of missions than those of the apostle, various
guest lecturers began making the academic dean's and my toes
curl. They had embraced a paradigm called *missio Dei*, a model
which sees everything good and worthwhile as part of God's
mission, and that God invites his people to join him in
accomplishing all this good stuff. We saw it as a contemporary
twist on the old social gospel. Decades earlier it was greedily
embraced by mainline, liberal churches because it furnished a
fresh theological foundation for the social services they were
already providing. Now, it transpired, that demographic of so-
called "cutting-edge evangelical thinkers" who long to be taken
seriously by secular academia but never are, had jumped onto
the bandwagon and were pushing it in evangelical faculties.

> "Explaining the slippery subject of *missio Dei* to his
> (Peter's) students took considerable effort. Once they had
> grasped it, however, they saw how it has permeated the
> modern missionary enterprise, and how it deviates from
> the more classical theological basis for missions."[383]

I was asked to write a position paper on the subject. It
circulated widely. Both the dean and I then submitted separate
articles on *missio Dei* to the mission's internal newsletter.
Weeks, months passed, but no magazine appeared, nor did we
heard back from the editor. I expanded my paper into a little

---

[381] *A Basic Course in Modern Turkish.* Gercege Dogru Kitaplar.
Istanbul, 1999.
[382] ALEV Books, Ancaster. 2017.
[383] PL March 4, 2017.

book with the above-mentioned title. Not wanting to present any distortions, I sent the manuscript to one of its main proponents. Christopher Wright responded at length, amiably noting where he felt I had misrepresented him. After the requisite emendations a copy went to WEC's international director but instead of a commendation I received a strongly worded missive ordering me not to publish. I was flabbergasted! Why would the director of a mission agency shut down a rational conversation on contemporary trends in mission theology?

Early in my career I was personally acquainted with our international leaders, theologically astute men with an unwavering commitment to evangelism, discipleship and church planting. However I had paid no attention to the shifts and changes occurring in the head office. The bros now in charge, I suddenly discovered, were mostly medical doctors and engineers who'd served in hospitals, orphanages or other such institutions and were, I discovered, swept along by the latest propositions wafting across the evangelical world. They were pragmatists out to "bring us in line with the times." Former convictions and theological moorings, like the ancient Christian dogma that God became man primarily to save us from the penalty incurred by our sin and to prepare us for eternal life, were shifting, as were the priorities which arose from that. Little wonder they pushed the this-world paradigm of *missio Dei* and touted the half-truth of Christ's victory over the *effects* of sin on us (*Christus Victor*), and not penal substitutionary atonement. Some pitched annihilationism as well. The mission was adrift theologically.

> "We are deeply concerned about powerful, post-modern trends within evangelicalism which push the idea that the very essence of the message, notably the nature of the atonement, is culturally determined. Some of the latest books on missions make Peter weep."[384]

---

[384] PL May 12, 2018.

"In our previous letter we mentioned a paper Peter had written on *missio Dei*, a widely held contemporary theology of mission of which he is critical. While some recipients welcomed it as an eye-opener, others were less enthusiastic! The latter are anxious he not publish his concerns for fear that it would create tensions and division. The subject is, however, sufficiently important for the direction of missions that he feels he should go ahead. He needs to know how to balance truth and love. Pray!"[385]

Around this time WEC held a leadership convention in Germany. Tearfully I presented my concerns at a plenary session. We then met with the top dogs and I re-iterated my concerns. They listened politely and promised to establish a theological review committee to which I would be invited. That theological review committee was never appointed. However, the drift towards a full-on embrace of *missio Dei* was checked. The book was later translated into Brazilian Portuguese.

That affair permanently affected my relationship with an organization I once loved dearly. WEC now became a marriage of convenience: they channeled our support while I worked at the grass-roots level training the next generation of missionaries. Thankfully, those censorious Boomers are now gone and the theology they espoused appears hackneyed. More "old-path" focused younger leaders are taking their places.

"You write because you want to be famous. You're proud."

Sadly, there was sufficient truth to this that I stopped writing fiction. *Desecrated Lands* and *The Visitor* had Christian themes but my breakthrough novel, *The Infidel*, did not. Written under a pen name, published by a secular publisher and sold at bookstores across the country, it was my best piece of writing—and as soon as it hit the shelves I realized that Anna's fears were being realized: God had not called me to be novelist but a missionary. I vowed not to turn my pen to fiction again. When

---

[385] September 3. 2016, Letter to Donna Bristow.

the copyright reverted back to me I asked the publisher to remove it from the market. They sent me the last ten copies before destroying their remaining stock.

Henceforth I would write with an eye on the kingdom of God. A late-night program on a Turkish television station featuring newly published books praised the Turkish translation of *The Epic of God and Man*[386], an easy-to-read retelling of the Old Testament which highlighted the themes holding the narrative together.

A Comparative Dictionary of Religious Terms in Islam and Christianity[387] was also lauded by an unlikely source. While sipping coffee one sunny afternoon with a bright young Muslim scholar I suggested we collaborate on a religious dictionary: he'd write the Muslim understandings and I'd write the Christian versions. We'd publish our respective definitions side by side to show the different meanings we attribute to the same words. Numan eventually agreed, we wrote a memorandum of understanding, and got to work. He wrote in Turkish and I in English, and then we translated each other. The words were the same but the meanings often very different. I was repeatedly startled by Numan's understanding of such concepts as sin, salvation, sanctification, and of people like Adam, Abraham, and Jesus. Under reconciliation, for example, he states that this concept (at least with respect to man's relationship with God) only exists in Christianity.

> "The work highlighted the irreconcilable differences between Christianity and Islam. Both writers recognize that only one of them holds the truth, and both are convinced that he is the one!"[388]

Once, while working together on the subject of eternal judgement, Numan looked across the table and asked point-blank: "Peter, do you think I will go to hell?"

---

[386] ALEV Books. Ancaster, ON. 2015. Turkish version: *Tanrı'yla Insanın Öyküsü*. Yeni Anadolu Yayıncılık, Istanbul. 2020.
[387] Malkoc, N. & Pikkert P. Alev Books. Ancaster, ON. 2020.
[388] PL July 1, 2017.

"Numan," I replied, looking him in the eye, "nothing grieves me more than that idea."

"That's exactly how I feel about you, Peter," he responded.

We chipped away at the project for ten years, and I was elated when the first, beautiful copy reached me. I wanted the family to share my joy, so their ho-hum response—they've lived with my writing projects all their lives—pained me. That night, however, I had a vivid dream, a vision of angels in heaven rejoicing because someone had found Christ through the work. Soon afterwards I received an email from a Muslim scholar at the University of Qom, in Iran. An Islamic Channel there had featured the work and he requested a copy. We sent him one via a friend of his in Italy.

.

Like the little drummer boy, I will bang my drum; I cannot do otherwise. Some may not like the rhythms or the clamor but, remarkably, just enough people do to encourage me to keep me going. "None of Peter's books are best sellers, but we praise God that a few seem to be of great help to some."[389]

---

[389] PL March 3, 2018.

66

Church and Monastery

"If we are going to be for the world as Christ meant for us to be, we are going to have to spend more time away from the world, in deep prayer and substantial spiritual training—just as Jesus retreated to the desert to pray before ministering to the people. We cannot give the world what we do not have."

Rod Dreher

. . .

ROMAN CATHOLICISM IN The Netherlands is a tale of defeat snatched from the jaws of victory. After Dutch Calvinists won the war of independence against Catholic Spain in the 17th century, the country's "Papists" suffered systemic discrimination for generations. Barred from civic life and viewed as second class citizens by the Protestants beyond the rivers Waal and Maas, the Catholic south sank into poverty and an intellectual malaise. This changed in the late 19th and early 20th centuries, courtesy of the Dutch Reformed theologian and prime minister Abraham Kuyper. An ardent promoter of "sphere sovereignty", he let the Protestants, Social Democrats and Roman Catholics develop their own segregated sub-cultures. Seizing the opportunity, the Catholics founded newspapers and radio stations, organized trade unions, cooperatives, political parties, farmers' associations, and established schools, hospitals, sports clubs and the like. For half a century the church dominated life in the south through its role in health care, education and social welfare. Mass attendance was high while pilgrim shrines and monasteries blossomed. Each village boasted a huge church; the one in Beugen, built in the 1950s, was big enough to hold every person in the village while Cornerstone, just around the corner, was an erstwhile nunnery.

From the 1960s onward however, left-wing, liberal Dutch cardinals pushed a radical agenda which lead to polarization, disillusionment and a falling away of the faithful—though the Catholic social institutions and cultural trappings continued to exist. Anna became a member of a fitness class run by Beugen's Catholic Association of Seniors. During the annual Carnival, society revelled in the pre-lent inversion of the existing order: decorum was cast aside, authority figures mocked, boisterous celebrants in crazy, colourful costumes roamed the streets dancing, drinking vast quantities of beer and partying late into the night. Huge imaginative floats and marching bands commandeered downtowns. Though traditionally the last fling before the rigors leading up to Good Friday, there was a lingering undertone of past distress and hardship, of a population momentarily defying the dour harshness of an imperious Calvinist elite.

The other ancient institution which clung on was the monastery. Although monks received a bad rap during the Reformation, I had developed an appreciation for Christian communal life during my Prairie years and again at Cornerstone. Living cheek by jowl with like-minded students and model teachers is, I still believe, an important aspect of theological education and life formation, something which cannot be replicated by the mere transfer of information through distance education. The daily routines of devotions, study, work, and prayer create habit-forming rhythms which progressively disengaged one from the distractions and hurly-burley of the world. This is very liberating, and I came to believe that by abolishing the monastic movement the Reformers had deprived Protestantism of a powerful tool. Monasteries had been, after all, centers of education and mission, the repository and conduit of the learning and culture of the classical age which successive waves of barbarians had swept aside. It was largely because of them that Christianity survived the fall of the Roman Empire and the subsequent dark ages. The monks' vows of poverty and chastity, and their uncompromising Christian life of service kept the flame of

Christian truth and worship alive when everything else was crumbling or tumbling.

The western monastic tradition spoke to me more than the Eastern versions I'd experienced at Mount Athos and Mor Gabriel. Assurance of salvation (or rather, "divinization" in Easter Orthodox parlance) as the goal of the Christian life appeared too much like the experience-laden church tradition of my parents. Nor could I appreciate their emphasis on spiritual enlightenment, inner transformation, the cultivation of humility and the mastery over one's carnal desires through ascetic practices. The easterners simply did not have the same practical bent as their western counterparts.

Largely free from state interference, western monasteries followed the carefully structured rules of the St. Benedicts and Gregory the Greats. Little wonder the peasants of those turbulent early Middle Ages esteemed and admired the monks, for beside singing Gregorian chants and meditating on the sublime they labored tirelessly draining swamps, clearing forests and reclaiming land. The ordered complexes of chapels, workshops, beer breweries, inns and hospices ministering to the surrounding areas became symbols of the city of God serving the city of man. The monks' discipline and sanctification of work would become aspirational values in much of the western culture. Whenever I entered one of those gated communities I had the sense of passing from the fleeting busyness of this world into the restfully busy community of those who live detached from worldly things and in the light of eternity.

The monastery I came to know best was St. Agatha, since 1371 the uninterrupted home of the Order of Crosiers. Up the road from Cornerstone, I'd walk through its ancient gate into an other-worldly domain, into the realm of those who pursue purity, worship in harmony, serve with serenity and, it appeared, die in peace. I'd order a coffee and kloosterkoek (monastery cake) in the Gatehouse cafeteria, listen to the bells toll the Nones, then spend a quiet moment beside a stone-carved station of the cross in the high-walled, white-washed sanctuary or wander through the enclosed gardens. The connection between monasteries and gardens is old for the Bible describes paradise as a garden. St. Agatha brewed its own beer, grew many of its own vegetables, tended fruit trees, raised chickens, kept bees, painted icons and ran a research center on Dutch monasticism.

One day someone mentioned that one of the brothers was a bookbinder and pointed to a barn-like structure across the way. I returned home deep in thought. A week later I was back, pushed through a little gate with a "no entry" sign dangling from it and knocked on a back door. It swung open and a gray bearded, friendly-looking human appeared. The wispy tufts of white hair poking from the sides his dome gave him a somewhat whimsical appearance. Blue eyes squinted at me through metal rimmed glasses "Wat kan ik voor u doen?" (What can I do for you?) he inquired kindly.

"Sir, I teach theology at Cornerstone, just up the road," I said in my politest Dutch. "But I'd like to do something practical... Would you teach me the art of bookbinding?"

"Are you handy?" he asked.

"Sir, I build wooden ship models," I replied truthfully.

He stroked his beard. "I'll give you a month to prove yourself," he said at last. And that is how I came to work with Brother Edgard Claes, one of Europe's pre-eminent bookbinders. For nearly a year I spent delightful Friday afternoons working under his supervision among the pinch and sewing presses, guillotine, plough, computer-controlled milling machine, airbrush extraction unit and backing boards, creating beautiful wood and leather books, some of which grace our bookshelves today. Edgard's own polycarbonate covers were works of art, exquisite objects painstakingly created over a period of months to reflect the heart of whatever volume he was binding. The kindly monk stood in that profound, now largely lost, Christian response to social upheaval by being a wellspring of artistic and creative endeavors.

As our relationship grew, talk veered naturally to things eternal, and I was struck by the gentle monk's lack of certainty pertaining to eternal life. The monks do not, it transpired, die in peace as a matter of course. Though the monastery provided a powerful model of how the church might function in a troubled world, the dogmas which have given me such hope and happiness—penal substitutionary atonement, the imputed righteousness of Christ and the transforming reality of regeneration—were absent.

Finding a church which revelled in those teachings in that post-catholic region was, in fact, difficult. We eventually landed at a little pastorless Bible fellowship in a neighboring town. I joined the midweek prayer meeting, clicked with the four elders, and was soon preaching. "Peter especially continues to have a lot of input into the church, which he juggles with his Cornerstone responsibilities."[390] Anna served tea and coffee after the services and chatted with the women during our lengthy fellowship times. We came to admire those faithful couples leading that little evangelical church in a secularized wasteland.

---

[390] Letter to a personal friend, September 3, 2016,

67

Beauty

*"All my own small perception of beauty both in
majesty and simplicity is founded."*

J.R.R. Tolkien

...

WISE PEOPLE ADVISED us to repatriate to Canada earlier
rather than later. It takes time to rebuild life after spending
most of it overseas, they said, for erstwhile friends move on,
churches change pastors and societies metamorphose. So we
did.

As I relive those four satisfying years at Cornerstone the
word "beauty" jumps to mind: the beauty of a supportive team
committed to training enthusiastic young people making
radical decisions for Christ, trusting God together with them,
and then experiencing him coming through in unexpected ways
in response to prayerful obedience and faith.

We also revelled in the beauty of nature. After years in the
concrete jungles of Middle East we never tired of those glorious
autumn days when the magnificent browns, yellows and
maroons of oak, beech and sycamores scintillated in the
brilliant light of the sun breaking through the gray of a passing
squall. Or of sipping coffee at the Veerhuis café watching barges
putter down the gently flowing Maas. I walked much of the
Pieter Pad hiking trail in stages, meandering over dikes and
between hedges, across the fields of Montogomery's failed
Operation Market Garden, through forests filled with cheerfully
chattering birds and age-old towns with cobblestoned squares
surrounded by narrow brick buildings with crenellated roofs,
the flat land gradually giving way to rising and dipping as I
approached the Belgian border.

The kids came almost every Christmas; we covered half their ticket, they coughed up the rest. We'd enjoy leisurely days eating oliebollen and appel flappen (oily Dutch New Year treats), watch the candles flicker on the coffee table and chat endless conversations, bound by no schedules and no deadlines. Life doesn't get more beautiful than that.

During the summer holidays we indulged our penchant for exploring. Unlike Canada, Europe's varied natural and historic beauty is compressed; there are no great distances between one scene, one country, one tableau and another. We drifted back from Switzerland after officiating at the wedding of former students, savoring divers historic, natural and gastronomic experiences along the way. We fell in love with the rolling hills and ancient towns of Alsace so headed for the Vosges Mountains the following summer: relaxed devotional times, hikes around a 16th century chateau or mediaeval castle and motoring down the Alsatian wine route, stopping for the plat-du-jour at pavement cafés in picturesque villages and familiarizing ourselves with the local wines. Roast chicken or Quiche Lorraine pairs well with Riesling or Gewurztramminer.

Long weekends might find us dodging Amsterdam's hordes of bicycles, wandering among its canals and tall thin houses, contemplating Rembrandts and Vermeers at the National Art Gallery, or me oohing at ship models in the maritime museum. We explored Alkmaar and Edam of red-waxed cannon-ball cheese fame. We nosed around Den Bosch where, among the ninety-six stone statues gracing the roof of the Cathedral of St. John I eventually spotted the winged angel speaking into a single-key cell phone, her direct line to heaven. We visited long-lost cousins on the Veluwe and swung by the famed Kröller-Müller museum to stand before Van Goghs, Mondrians, Seurats, Braques and Gauguins. We spent our 30th wedding anniversary in Groningen tracing my humble roots. We renewed the lease on my grandparent's long unvisited gravesite and located their onetime candy-store, now a seedy student dive. I asked an old geezer puffing a gasper nearby if he remembered the "suikerbakker" (candy maker). "Sure! The boys would swing by after hours to buy illicit liquor from him."

Once when Anna visited family in Ireland I bussed around central Europe. The stones salvaged and reused in the restoration of Dresden's Frauenkirche cathedral retain the scorch marks of the allied fire-bombing. The only things which survived that war crime were the statue of Martin Luther and the relief carving of Jesus' agony in the Garden of Gethsemane. Prague was stunningly beautiful, its Romanesque, Gothic, Renaissance and Baroque architecture untouched by the war. Bibliophiles filled bookstores, buskers on the Charles Bridge were world-class, and food was cheap, tasty and plentiful. Budapest seemed plebian and Vienna priggish in comparison.

All things this side of glory terminate, including the beautiful Cornerstone interlude. Our faith had been stretched and God at times tangibly present through the beauty of his creation, the creativity of mankind, and his transformed people. It took five days to give away our stuff, vacuum and mop, pack suitcases and bid farewells. A kind colleague drove us to Schiphol.

68

Ugliness

"You sign your place and calling, in full seeming,
With meekness and humility; but your heart
Is crammed with arrogancy, spleen and pride."

Shakespeare, Henry VIII

. . .

THE SAGES WHO'D advised us to repatriate early were right for we scarcely recognized our native land. Aggressive, secular ideologies and movements had swept through the nations' media and cultural establishments, ridding it of its Judeo-Christian heritage. Society and church had become unrecognizably tribal.

The seeds of that fractionalization had been sown by the institutions of higher education much earlier—I was exposed to it during my time at Syracuse University. The fruit might have taken decades longer to germinate had it not been for the strains and stresses which the Covid pandemic of 2020-2023 engendered and the explosion of violence erupting when white policemen killed a black petty criminal. The ever-present racial and economic inequalities these events exposed seemed to demand a radical new approach to social renewal. Utopian visionaries demonized Christianity's legacy, violently imposing in its stead simplistic, quasi-religious notions of social justice and fluid personal identity along with their own dogmatic narrative: the world is divided into oppressed and oppressors. "Peoples of color" along with divers socio-economic and non-binary genderqueer folk are the oppressed, victimized by entitled white heterosexual oppressors. People can become whatever they decide to be by their own effort, while redemption and a socially equitable utopia is achieved by forcibly seizing cultural and political power from those entitled Whites. The movement had its own vocabulary: woke, intersectionality, critical race theory...

Like utopian visionaries throughout the ages they sought to crush perceived enemies. They allowed no margin for nuance or dialogue or compromise. Wielding the weapons of political correctness and "cancel culture" the woke crusaders sought to harm, humiliate and ruin the livelihoods and reputations of anyone standing in their way. Those who espoused the value of the unborn, embraced classic views on sexuality and marriage or held to a wholesome work ethic were shouted down, cancelled, fired, denigrated. The movement became so powerful that the ruling and corporate elites felt obliged to kow-tow to this simplistic, superficially attractive vision. The public space open to Christians shrunk alarmingly, with those serving in health care, education, law and government who vocalized their concerns dismissed as threats to the wellbeing of society.

Of course many people feel discriminated against, and not without reason. I too long for a society that provides equality, freedom and dignity for everyone. I recognize that those uncompromising, unforgiving ideologues were responding to genuine hurt and suffering, and that like past millenarian movements, they sought to upend society on behalf of the downtrodden. But unlike those secular utopians I regard people as created in the image of God and possessing an eternal soul. Their reduction of humanness to skin color, sexual orientation, ethnicity and position in society fails to recognize that happiness lies, in large measure, in the nurture and development of our transcendent spiritual nature. The new secular religion led only to new social fissures, discriminations, injustices and intolerances.

The greater ugliness, however, was that some Christians joined the political fray. Intimidated by the new ideologies sweeping the North American continent, those atavistic evangelicals became hard-core political warriors in their own right. Exhibiting little burden for lost souls and ignoring the transforming power of the gospel and the supra-cultural heavenly nature of the church, they failed to sensitively, boldly, lovingly proclaim the story of God's grace in Jesus Christ and proclaim the worth of each individual in the eyes of God. Instead of inviting the unloved from every tribe and tongue and people to the worldwide family of God so they too could experience the transforming worship of Christ, they threw up hateful websites, joined anti-government demonstration, railed against wokism, and participated in shutting down our capital city using convoys of trucks.

They also sought to crush their opponents, aggressively attacking even fellow Christians who did not buy into their particular right-wing political agenda, who did not support their aggressive anti-everythingism: anti-government, anti-vaccination, anti-climate change, anti-Islam... Living in their on-line echo chambers, they refused to trust any authority but their own. They too fostered tribalism and factionalism in their desire to aggressively turn the clock back to their own perceived utopian era, a time when Christian values purportedly permeated public discourse. They seemed not to realize that that era, such as it was, was the culmination of the great spiritual revivals of the 18th and 19th centuries, and that without similar revivals the past is past. They moved to political activism instead of Christlike forgiveness. They rejected not the poisons of atavistic resentment and narrow nationalism, nor lived detached from the fundamental values of this world as citizens of the eternal city. Instead of humbly acknowledging human frailty and sinfulness, including their own, they focused on the sins of others. Instead of offering redemption they too sought to harm and humiliate.

There were elements of this in our main supporting church. These, together with divergent views on the appropriate response to Covid shutdowns, eventually led to a very painful split. I listened to both sides but could not reconcile the narratives. In the spirit of Jesus' injunction to Peter to "feed my sheep" (John 21:17), I wrote the same email to both parties: if they needed help, I was available. One party responded, so I preached for them regularly.

Conservative evangelicalism habitually throws up golden-tongued, arrogant leaders. In a sub-culture where "the preached word" is of primary importance, the eloquent control-freak with a degree in theology can quickly rise to lord it over others. The pastor of the small church we attended proved to be such a one. Bruised and grieving, Anna and I eventually left that community of wounded saints.

"We are ecclesiastical refugees," I responded to the director of integration of a large church nearby. West Highland Baptist became our refuge during those ugly times, a haven of sound teaching and sanity in a crazy world, a place where the transformative power of the gospel draws people from every tribe and nation for worship and spiritual growth. Anna serves at the Welcome Desk and helps at a weekly women's Bible study, I am on the missions committee and do some teaching, and son Owen is the associate pastor of discipleship. It is beautiful, and we are happy.

69

A Crown of Thorns

"They gave our Master a crown of thorns.
Why do we hope for a crown of roses?"

Martin Luther

■ ■ ■

I TAUGHT FOR a missionary training organization, became adjunct professor at a Toronto seminary and regularly crossed the herring pond to teach at Cornerstone. I attempted to integrate into Canadian life by absorbing Conrad Black's history of Canada and going backpacking with the kids. A friend and I travelled around Northern British Columbia and the Yukon, as far as Dawson City, where a cousin introduced us to the gold mines, his church and the Dempster Highway to the Arctic circle. But I was restless. One day I wondered aloud if the Lord might lead us back into ministry among Arabs in the Middle East. Anna raised her eyebrows and looked askance but refrained from commenting. I started watching Al-Jazeera to resurrect my moribund Arabic.

One afternoon an American we'd known in Turkey stepped through our door. His agency had just recruited a Syrian living in Calgary, he said, but didn't know what to do with him. Would I touch base with this individual?

Mouner pastored the Baptist Church in Aleppo before it was reduced to rubble during the civil war. His congregation scattered and he and his family landed in Alberta. However his heart was back in Syria where the Lord was drawing both Kurds and Arabs to himself. He felt he was missing out, left watching from the sidelines. Soon Mouner and I were brainstorming how we might provide theological education for Muslims coming to faith in Christ in the Arabic speaking Middle East.

A synergy developed between us. I found him to be a man of wisdom, faith and courage, and with numerous contacts in the Middle East, while my experience with theological training in the region offered a model we might implement. Soon Training Leaders International's European and Canadian directors got involved. We had nothing but hazy ideas but, believing things would gel, kept talking.

> "Peter and three others are brainstorming ways of providing theological training to the Syrian Kurdish church. Pray for great wisdom and stay tuned..."[391]

We met in person for the first time on a Greek island to pray, brainstorm and hash out issues pertaining to inter-mission cooperation, curriculum development, accreditation and how to deliver a program in person in a volatile part of an unstable region. I was tasked with developing a study program which covered our non-negotiables (lots of Bible plus classic evangelical theology). The name we chose was Crown Theological Training (CTT). The Arabic word we selected for crown is that used for Christ's crown of thorns, appropriate, we felt, for those suffering much for their faith.

> "This week we signed an official agreement with TCM. Yay! This is a big step forward! Together with them we can grant an accredited MA in Theological Studies."[392]

TCM was the same seminary in Austria with which I had helped negotiate an agreement for the Hasat program in Turkey over a decade earlier. Hasat's good reputation and my familiar face engendered a measure of trust in the viability of this new program in Arabic. "The Lord prepared the way!"[393]

We held a launch meeting to increase our prayer backing for we were certain Satan would contest the initiative. Sure enough, each of us was attacked in turn. Mouner, who'd experienced excruciating back pain during our meetings in

---

[391] PL December 31, 2020.
[392] PL May 3, 2022.
[393] Ibid.

Greece, was diagnosed with multiple myeloma. He needed back surgery, stem cell transplant, chemo—the full whammo. Athens-based Joost nearly lost his home to wildfires. Henry had a motorcycle accident; the bike was totalled, he walked away unscathed. Then I began to experience severe back pain.

In spite of the pain and Mouner's struggle with cancer we headed for Turkey, on the hunt for newly forming Arab and Kurdish churches. That trip underscored the challenges we faced. Trust is in very short supply in the Middle East, meaning it would take time to earn the right to be heard. Though some of those leading refugee churches were godly men seeking to serve their little flocks as best they could, others were shysters on the payroll of Christian agencies long on compassion but short on discernment. Furthermore, Kurds and Arabs are culturally very different; getting them to study and serve together seemed impossible, and no one we met was eligible to enter our accredited MA program. Most had not completed high school, some had not finished grade school. We wondered if we'd pitched our program at the wrong level.

Upon our return to Canada the family doctor insisted I see a specialist.

> "Immanuel (God with us) is the wonderful truth we celebrate especially at Christmas, but this year His very real presence brings us extra comfort. Peter has been diagnosed with aggressive prostate cancer. The doctor suspects that it has already spread and is the cause of his ongoing lower back pain, but we await the results of bone and CT scans. We are at peace, resting in the promises of Scripture and reaping the benefits of a robust theology."[394]

The scans revealed that my cancer had reached Stage 4, having spread extensively throughout the skeleton; the oncologist drily described my bones as drywall into which someone had punched holes. I was in great pain, swallowed opioids like smarties and lost a lot of weight. When the initial

---

[394] PL December 20, 2022.

prognosis of a maximum of five more years of life was halved, and the pain increased even more, we suspected an element of spiritual warfare. Phil. 1:21-24 took on new meaning: *"For me to live is Christ, and to die is gain. If I am to live in the flesh, that means fruitful labor for me. Yet which I shall choose I cannot tell... My desire is to depart and be with Christ, for that is far better... But to remain in the flesh is more necessary on your account."*

We asked our church's elders to anoint me with oil and pray over me, as per James 5:14. They showed up on January 16, 2023, looking a tad uncomfortable with the assignment—they are Baptists after all, not charismatics. Pastor John anointed my forehead with kitchen olive oil and each prayed, each according to his faith. That evening we experienced a *bona fide* miracle: though not healed, my pain disappeared overnight. We also dared trust the Lord for at least five more years of life. The oncologist, doing his bit, prescribed three aggressive courses of treatment which cost me my beloved beard. Numerous visits, cards, emails, freezer meals and, above all, a tsunami of prayers on our behalf also helped lift our spirits.

Satisfying as it was to have so many people care for us, some were right-wing evangelicals, anti-vaxxers suspicious of any authority but their own, dear people who live in their own echo-chambers wherefrom they liberally dispense the insights gained there: "You're not submitting to chemo are you. That's just the pharmaceutical companies exploiting us." "I know a doctor in the States who developed a diet which conquers cancer. I'll put you on to him." "We have a type of tea in my country which kills all cancer. I'll have my family send some." Beastly stuff! "Black Garlic will cure anything except death". "Taurine will not only kill your cancer, it will reverse aging." "Ivermectin. You've got to take that. It'll cure you." I looked it up. It's used primarily to kill intestinal worms. During the pandemic it was also falsely touted as curing Covid 19. "Chaga mushrooms from northern Birch trees."

Of course I received gratis advice from non-Christians as well. A neighbour assured me that weed cooked in a rice cooker will kill the cancer. We don't have a rice cooker, I responded plaintively, and he said he'd bring his right over. Thanks, that's very kind, I replied, but I'll stick to my current treatment.

Turning a deaf ear to my numerous quacksalver friends, I hearkened to a single authoritative voice: that of the oncologist. I trust him and obey him to the exclusion of all others. Blood tests showed that his cocktail of treatments was suppressing the cancer, though I struggled with fatigue, "brain fog" and insomnia. I experienced neither pain nor nausea through the chemo infusions. I suddenly exhibited a voracious appetite and put on 15 kg.

On June 1, 2023, I had my final chemo infusion. I left the hospital reeling, feeling like a boxer who'd been floored once too often. A mere ten days later we were back. Anna had caught her foot on her bag strap when stepping out of the car, landed hard and fractured her pelvis. She spent the next five painful weeks in a hospital bed and then had to relearn how to walk. 2023 was a challenging year but "the Lord's grace and strength have proved sufficient for each new day, and He has showered us with a multitude of kindnesses through his people."[395]

In the meantime Mouner, still fighting his battle with cancer, taught our first unaccredited seminars to Syrian refugee churches in Turkey. The CTT had launched, albeit only at the non-formal level. Then a violent earthquake struck Turkey, and the cities of Gaziantep and Antakya where we had just launched were badly damaged, and we had to cancel. We had to cancel the June seminars as well because Mouner had been diagnosed with colon cancer on top of his multiple myeloma.

> "Through two years of preparation and challenges the leadership team remained convinced that the CTT was the Lord's initiative. However, he clearly wanted to reduce us to utter dependence on him so that he alone would be glorified. In fact Peter came to thank God for the cancer: he is normally a 'can-do, let's-make-this-

---

[395] PL August 3, 2023.

happen' kind of guy but, drained of energy, was left utterly dependent on the Lord."[396]

---

[396] PL October 9, 2023.

70

Arabia[397]

"With respect to every great work of God,
first it is impossible, then it is difficult, and then it is done."

Hudson Taylor

...

WE RECEIVED A Macedonian-like call to teach the accredited M.A. in a country completely off our radar. They were five Arab professionals—the very number for which we'd prayed—who ran an underground church on the Arabian peninsula.

> "We are delighted, though not surprised!... Pray Satan will not be able to prevent us from going ahead. His opposition has been relentless—but God is sovereign! Pray for stamina for Peter and Mouner, also a cancer patient... Pray for a good connect.... Pray that this be the beginning of a process which will turn these five into church leaders in a context which is very difficult for Christians.... Pray for protection from authorities in a country fiercely opposed to the gospel... Pray!"[398]

We purchased tickets, obtained visas, booked a hotel, packed our bags and set off for, well, we weren't sure. Travelling separately, Mouner and I planned to meet in the hotel lobby.

I was the only Anglo aboard the shabby Boeing, and all night dusky travelers hiked up and down to the bathrooms or prayed ostentatiously in the aisles. I eyed an unhappy-looking daughter watching her bullet-headed hajji father going through the ritual. Why, I wondered, are in-your-face religious types—irrespective of persuasion—the most unattractive of mankind?

---

[397] Exact place left undisclosed for security reasons.
[398] PL October 9, 2023.

A nasal call to prayer reverberated jarringly in Dubai's mammoth, hyper-materialistic airport. All adverts—whether of whisky, watches or perfumes—featured white women. Men in cheap suits pointed droves of Indians to planes departing for various cities on that sub-continent. A bus took me to a frowzy hotel.

Dubai reminded me of futuristic cities on pictures I'd seen as a youngster: sterile, no history, as attractive as an upscale shopping mall. The darker one's skin, it seemed, the less one's job satisfaction. I slept fitfully, breakfasted, and returned to the airport. An old single-aisled Airbus filled with gregarious men in traditional garb cheerfully shoving oversized luggage into overhead bins or under seats, women covered head to toe gesticulated imperiously, a rag-tag mixture of Pakistanis and Bangladeshis and a dapper Englishman sporting a tan vest found their seats. A bejeweled woman had commandeered my extra leg-room seat by the emergency exit, but a hirsute steward experienced in these matters ushered the protesting female to her assigned place. A canned prayer followed emergency instruction and we were aloft. We overflew sand, lots of it. A peaky woman behind me had a hacking cough, a kid wailed loudly. We landed. I was fingerprinted, then made my way to an airport bathroom. There were lots of stalls but only a single urinal; those washing hands, feet and faces wore ankle-length jalabiyas with no middle front openings—an eventuality unforeseen by the prophet. I made for the crowd of imploring taxi drivers and dickered for a ride to the hotel. There I signed in, showered, ate and sank into deep slumbers. Jet lag caught up at 3 AM so I read Tolkien and watched Arabic TV.

I expected to meet Mouner after breakfast but there was no sign of him, nor any record of his arrival. A text message pinged in: the hotel had canceled his booking and he hadn't found a place to lay his head until the early hours. He was exhausted and would appear when he could.

It was mid-morning in winter, and already 36 degrees (97 F) —too hot for a cancer patient to stroll about—but I needed local currency. Dodging various Chinese marques while crossing a highway, I legged it to a shopping mall and found an ATM which accepted my card. It was the longest walk I'd managed for some time. I felt almost healthy.

A bleary-eyed Mouner eventually showed up. Happily, someone checked out and the establishment gave him a room. Then one of the students pulled up. Hearty greetings before he ushered us to his car and blasted off to bob and weave at breakneck speed down that highway. Frazzled but physically intact we arrived at a complex on a busy side-street: marble staircase, slap-dash construction, wiggle-jiggle elevator up several floors to a roomy apartment. The others drifted in soon afterwards, and we spent the rest of that day hanging loose. They shared their hopes and aspirations, and after supper took us on a hair-raising ride to a distant villa where every week some 40 people meet to sing, worship and listen to the preached word. Mouner preached that day, I would do so the following Friday. I was bone-tired but too filled with adrenaline to fall asleep when, after another late-night, heart-stopping drive, someone dropped us off at the hotel.

I woke early, showered, made a cup of tea, and spent some time with God. I struggled to concentrate but started a simple, helpful ritual: pace-pray as I'm wont to do, read Psalm 138, but stop after "*I bow down towards your holy temple and give thanks to your name for your steadfast love and faithfulness, for you have exalted above all things your name and your word.*" At that point I knelt at the foot of the bed and prayed the Lord's Prayer, applying each phrase to myself and Mouner. Then I crawled onto the chair and slowly read through the rest of the Psalm.

I fell into a good routine. Breakfasts were leisurely affairs in which I downed an omelet, bread, cheese, olives and orange juice and then, sipping coffee, sat back to take in my fellow transients. A group of Saudis in their 30s talk quietly, heads close together. Black clad women lift their veils for every bite. Two Yemenis, or were they Omanis, focused on their phones. An overweight, overbearing Arab — the heavily bearded religious type concerned only with their own needs and accomplishments — reaches across the table while declaiming some truism to two veiled women. Then, arms flailing, he commandeers the flunkies, harried men in black slacks and white shirts two sizes too small who scurry about collecting plates, replenishing food trays and refilling urns. A Chinese Shao Lin fighter look-alike—down to the rocking gait, baggy trousers and pony tail, plunks down at the table next to mine, his companion a thin yellow woman with an infectious smile and ready laugh. They seem fond of each other. An older woman sporting woolly slippers joins them. His mother-in-law? Shao Lin fighters must have mothers-in-law too. They are in great spirits. There are whiney English accents, male and female, arguing behind me. Two Americans hogging the space before the coffee machine are solving some abstruse engineering problem. A Japanese lady in stunning kimono, silk obi and high heels steps daintily from table to fruit bowl. After that I kept seeing geishas everywhere; there were at least 6 or 7 of them, along with a support crew. Unlike the Americans, they are quiet and demure. A dapper Black sporting a snazzy, too-tight sports jacket strides around as if he were monied. But monied people wear freshly polished, real leather shoes. Monied people wouldn't stay at that hotel—it catered to the middle classes. It's what made the place interesting.

When Mouner appeared we planned for the day and dreamt of the future: two guys wondering how long they had to live thinking big and long-term. On weekends—Fridays and Saturdays—we taught all day, and midweek all evening. We complemented each other well. Teaching sessions engendered endless discussions which continued late into the night, invaluable hours of bonding and catching glimpses of the issues the students were dealing with. One morning one of the guys enthusiastically taught us a song he had just learnt: the Arabic version of "What a friend we have in Jesus". The freshness of their faith and their eagerness to learn was a great blessing.

One evening we trooped to someone else's apartment for Lord's Supper, and I found the breaking of bread with this hard-pressed little flock profoundly moving. That event broke up at 11:30 PM, at which point a witty fellow decided to take us for a tour of the city. The gent kept up a running commentary as he wove through traffic, me with butt-cheeks pinched nervously together. My Arabic, which had held up pretty well till then, started failing me. Late another evening 10 or 11 people showed up for a prayer meeting during which I offered my first prayer in Arabic since 1985. I had great liberty preaching on the Lord's prayer in that underground villa church the following Friday.

Indulging my passion for exploring, I poked around the old city: tall, picturesque palms lined the waterfront, casting patches of intermittent shadows somewhere out at sea, leaving pedestrians frying under the naked sun. Pungent odors reminded one that the place had once been a hard-scrabble fishing village. I hiked to the nearest mall. The sun now beat straight down and I was knackered when I stumbled through those glass doors into coolness. Several glasses of iced tea and chicken from a spit restored the spirits. I purchased Agatha Christie's *Murder on the Nile* to beef up my Arabic and flagged a cab back to the hotel.

All we'd prayed for, believed God for, came together. For those eager-to-learn men the CTT was "a dream come true". Among long-standing missionaries to the region there was a consensus that it was on the cusp of a long prayed-for spiritual breakthrough.

On our last evening the guys took us to a delightful restaurant. Then I was homeward bound, praising God for the tangible sense of being carried along by a wave of prayers from his people. While I was gone Anna was able to park her walker and stroll about unassisted.

> "We praise him (God) because in spite of relentless opposition, Satan was not able to prevent us from going ahead. Mouner's and my health held up and we complemented each other well... We had no run-in with authorities."[399]

---

[399] PL November 16, 2023.

The Bucket List

"Death is not the end of your bucket list. It's the beginning."

John Piper

. . .

OWEN AND I WERE sipping coffee in a café. "Dad," he asked, "what would you like to see done before you die?" I rattled a number of things off my fingers: "I'd like to see Rita married and have a child, you in ministry, the Crown Theological Training program stabilized and the memoir in print."

Various hopefuls had sat on our red leather couch expressing an interest in our beautiful daughter but each proved too parochial or too wimpish or too non-Christian or was too intimidated or too-whatever. Seeing her married and with child seemed a sure-fire way to push my death far into the future. As for Owen himself, he had only just resigned as assistant professor of Philosophy to pursue an M.Div. in Alberta. The idea of seeing him in full-time ministry also seemed a long way off.

We'd promised the cohort in Arabia three courses per year, so Mouner and I headed over there for a second time. That stint was more than I could handle. Though I remained pain-free, at times I felt weak as a kitten, and concentrating for longer periods became problematic. During our last evening I shared that we would in all probability not see each other again in this life. The tears flowed freely; I felt like the apostle Paul saying farewell to the Ephesian elders.

Then things began to move with remarkable rapidity. Rita met her match in Ruben. They married within the year and eleven months later cradled wee Ian Peter. Owen joined the pastoral staff of our church, and my old Hasat colleague George joined the CTT leadership team. Since then another well-qualified man also signed up, and a capable Arab theologian is working with Mouner. The CTT is stable and in gifted, godly hands, and this memoir is nearing completion. All the things on that bucket list became realities.

My friend David—the same David who candidated for WEC with me a lifetime ago—and I often share a park bench. I'll bust out my pipe, stuff it with a nice aromatic and we talk theology, politics and books we're reading. Every so often we meet with a group of Christian writers to critique each other's scribbles. I audit on-line courses on music, literature and history and, of course, we serve our church within the framework of our capacities. I also do some cooking: omelets, stir fries, one pot meals.

Our apartment overlooks a park. We watch the children play and the trees change with the seasons: the Redbuds flower magenta-pink and the Hawthorns white in the spring, and every autumn the oak, maple, hickory and crab apple trees turn yellow, gold and red. The red-winged blackbirds, blue-jays, sparrows and the rarer cardinals flit about, and a Cooper's hawk built its nest high up a chestnut tree. Sometimes rabbits frolic on the edge of the forest, stopping suddenly to scratch an ear with a hind leg. In the evenings we watch the cerulean sky turn into long bars of ruby and orange.

Anna walks more slowly now, and with a stoop. Though the arthritis and bone degeneration take their toll, she faithfully does her exercises. The twinkle in her eye remains, as does the ready smile. Her heart, lungs and mind function as well as ever. Between us we speak our own patois, a mishmash of various languages. I love her as much as ever I did.

The miracle of no pain ended after two years and eight months. The cancer is aggressively resurgent, and I now thank God for painkillers. We purchased burial plots in the country cemetery where my parents and other family members are interred, and made arrangements with a funeral home.

Owen, Rita, Ruben and wee Ian live nearby and visit regularly. We enjoy hearing what the world looks like from their perspective, and how they navigate the issues their generation of Christians face. Those conversations enable us to intercede intelligently on their behalf.

Every Christian must run their own unique race within the rules laid down by the Triune One, and within that framework endure purging trials and overcome sanctifying hurdles. Is it all difficulty and no joy? Far from it! Having, for the most part, stayed the course, we marvel how the gospel covered our many sins, mistakes and failures—most of which I did not relate as these are now forgotten even by Almighty God. Our hearts are warmed whenever former students touch base to thank us for hanging in there with them, or for teaching them the fundamentals of the Christian faith, or for encouraging them in word and deed to give their all to him who gave his all for them. They are now salt and light to their generation.

Serving God has been a great and satisfying privilege, an adventure with eternal implications animated by a flickering trust in the Trustworthy One's unfailing covenantal promises.

The patiently ticking grandfather's clock chimes Westminster Quarters. *Tempus Fugit*. When God calls me home I will depart a satisfied, happy old man. I look forward to exchanging this ailing body for a perfected version, and will be thrilled to see my saviour face to face.

www.ingramcontent.com/pod-product-compliance
Lightning Source LLC
Chambersburg PA
CBHW051936090426
42741CB00008B/1174